Playhouses AND Privilege

Playhouses AND Privilege

The Architecture of Elite Childhood

Abigail A. Van Slyck

UNIVERSITY OF MINNESOTA PRESS
MINNEAPOLIS • LONDON

Every effort was made to obtain permission to reproduce material in this book. If any proper acknowledgment has not been included here, we encourage copyright holders to notify the publisher.

An earlier version of chapter 3 was published by the University of California Press as "The Spatial Practices of Privilege," *Journal of the Society of Architectural Historians* 70, no. 2 (June 2011): 210–39. A portion of chapter 5 was previously published in a different form as "On Playhouses, Parenting, and Publicity," *PLATFORM* (July 25, 2019), https://www.platformspace.net/, CC BY-NC-ND 4.0.

Frontispiece: Interior of the children's house, Sinnissippi Farm, the Frank O. Lowden and Florence Pullman Lowden estate, in Oregon, Illinois. Pond and Pond, architects, 1909. Pond & Pond Collection, Ryerson and Burnham Art and Architecture Archives, Art Institute of Chicago. Digital file #200101.090805-49.

Copyright 2024 by the Regents of the University of Minnesota

All rights reserved. No part of this publication may be reproduced, stored in a retrieval system, utilized for purposes of training artificial intelligence technologies, or transmitted, in any form or by any means, electronic, mechanical, photocopying, recording, or otherwise, without the prior written permission of the publisher.

Published by the University of Minnesota Press
111 Third Avenue South, Suite 290
Minneapolis, MN 55401–2520
http://www.upress.umn.edu

ISBN 978-1-5179-1695-4 (hc)
ISBN 978-1-5179-1696-1 (pb)

LC record available at https://lccn.loc.gov/2024041110

Printed in the United States of America on acid-free paper

The University of Minnesota is an equal-opportunity educator and employer.

30 29 28 27 26 25 24   10 9 8 7 6 5 4 3 2 1

Dedicated
to the memory of Spiro Kostof and Paul Groth,
and to all my other teachers,
especially John Pinto, Helen Searing, Susan Van Dyne,
and, above all, Dell Upton

Contents

List of Children's Cottages and Playhouses   ix

Introduction *Dynastic Ambitions and the Architecture of Childhood*   1

1. Raising Royals in an Age of Sentiment
   The Family of Victoria and Albert at Osborne   19

2. A Pastoral Paradise for Young Royals
   Osborne's Swiss Cottage   65

3. Making American Aristocrats in the Gilded Age Children's Cottage   117

4. A Conundrum for Elite Parents
   Prioritizing Play in the Early Twentieth Century   159

5. Practicing Domestic Virtue
   Gender Politics and the 1920s Playhouse   203

6. Objects of Middle-Class Desire
   Playhouses in the Leisure Economy   253

7. For Movie Stars and Princesses
   The 1930s Celebrity Playhouse   283

Acknowledgments   313

Notes   319

Index   371

List of Children's Cottages and Playhouses

Grouped by the decade in which the cottage or playhouse was built, entries are listed alphabetically by family surname or, in the case of reigning monarchs, by the name of the royal house. Each listing includes the name of the estate or the street address of the house; the town or city in which it is located; and the names of the parents of the children who used the cottage or playhouse. If the cottage or playhouse was known by another name, that name is given in parentheses after the name of the estate. Unless otherwise indicated, the locations are in the United States.

1850s

Hanover
Osborne (Swiss Cottage)
Isle of Wight, U.K.
Queen Victoria, Prince Albert

1880s

Glessner
The Rocks
Bethlehem, New Hampshire
John Glessner, Frances Glessner

Orange-Nassau
Het Loo Palace
Apeldoorn, Netherlands
Wilhelm III and Emma, Queen of the Netherlands

SEARS
1815 Prairie Avenue
Chicago, Illinois
Joseph Sears, Helen Barry Sears

SLOANE
Elm Court (Cosy Cot)
Lenox, Massachusetts
William D. Sloane, Emily Thorn Vanderbilt Sloane

VANDERBILT
The Breakers
Newport, Rhode Island
Cornelius Vanderbilt II, Alice Claypoole Gwynne Vanderbilt

VANDERBILT
Idle Hour
Oakdale, Long Island
William K. Vanderbilt, Alva Smith Vanderbilt

1890s

FRICK
Clayton
Pittsburgh, Pennsylvania
Henry Clay Frick, Adelaide Frick

ORANGE-NASSAU
Soestdijk Palace
Utrecht Province, Netherlands
Queen Emma, Queen Regent of the Netherlands

1900s

BURTON
Albro House
Cedarhurst, Long Island
Robert L. Burton, Florence Southwick Burton

DOWS
Foxhollow Farm (Fallsburgh)
Rhinebeck, New York
Tracy Dows, Alice Olin Dows

FIELD
Highlawn [first playhouse]
Lenox, Massachusetts
William B. Osgood Field, Lila Vanderbilt Sloane Field

HESSE-DARMSTADT
Wolfsgarten
Darmstadt, Germany
Ernest Ludwig and Victoria Melita, Grand Duchess of Hesse-Darmstadt

LOWDEN
Sinnissippi Farm (Hopi House)
Oregon, Illinois
Frank O. Lowden, Florence Pullman Lowden

WHITNEY
Greentree
Manhasset, Long Island
Payne Whitney, Helen Hay Whitney

1910s

COE
Coe Hall
Oyster Bay, New York
William R. Coe, Mai Huttleston Rogers Coe

FIELD
Highlawn [second playhouse]
Lenox, Massachusetts
William B. Osgood Field, Lila Vanderbilt Sloane Field

PELL
Fort Ticonderoga (Y-D [Yes-Do] House)
Ticonderoga, New York
Stephen Pell, Sarah Pell

PHIPPS
Westbury House
Old Westbury, Long Island
John Shaffer Phipps, Margarita Phipps

PRATT
The Manor House
Glen Cove, Long Island
John Teele Pratt, Ruth Sears Baker Pratt

ROGERS
Black Point / Villa del Mar
Southampton, Long Island
Henry Huddleston Rogers Jr., Mary Benjamin Rogers

1920s

DODGE
Meadow Brook Hall (since 1929, Knole Cottage; before 1929, Hilltop Lodge)
Rochester, Michigan
Alfred Wilson, Matilda Dodge Wilson

LLOYD
Greenacres
Beverly Hills, California
Harold Lloyd, Mildred Davis Lloyd

ZIEGFELD
Burkeley Crest
Hastings-on-Hudson, New York
Florenz Ziegfeld, Billie Burke

1930s

FORD
Gaukler Pointe
Grosse Pointe, Michigan
Edsel Ford, Eleanor Clay Ford

HUTTON
Hillwood (Deen-Wee)
Roslyn, Long Island
E. F. Hutton, Marjorie Merriweather Post

TEMPLE
227 North Rockingham Avenue
Brentwood, California
George Temple, Gertrude Temple

YORK
Royal Lodge (Y Bwthyn Bach)
Windsor Great Park, U.K.
HRH Duke of York (later King George VI), HRH Duchess of York
(later Queen Elizabeth)

Figure I.1. Princess Elizabeth of York, standing in the garden of Y Bwthyn Bach to Gwellt (Welsh for The Little Thatched Cottage), Royal Lodge, Windsor Great Park. The Duke and Duchess of York used this image, by an unknown photographer, as their Christmas card in 1933. Morgan Willmott, architect, 1931–32. RCIN 2808546. Royal Collection Trust / Copyright His Majesty King Charles III 2023.

Introduction

Dynastic Ambitions and the Architecture of Childhood

This book examines children's cottages built primarily for the use of elite youngsters in the Anglo-American world from the middle of the nineteenth century until just before World War II. Perhaps the most famous of these is the small thatched house given to Princess Elizabeth of York on her sixth birthday in 1932, purportedly by the people of Wales (Figure I.1). As recently as 2012, it was featured in *The Diamond Queen*, a three-part series produced by the BBC in honor of Queen Elizabeth's sixtieth year on the British throne. In that broadcast, her granddaughter Princess Beatrice characterized it as "the most glamorous Wendy house ever," using a British term that equates a child's playhouse with the house built around young Wendy Darling in *Peter Pan*.[1] Beyond the royal family and their guests, few people had crossed its threshold since it arrived at Royal Lodge in Windsor, although Y Bwthyn Bach To Gwellt (Welsh for The Little Thatched Cottage) had often been in the public eye during the preceding eighty years. In 1931 and 1932, newspapers on both sides of the Atlantic had reported on this demonstration of Welsh loyalty when the house was put on public display in Birmingham, Cardiff, and London, before being installed at Royal Lodge. If anything, reporters freighted it with even greater significance in 1936 and 1937, around the time of Edward VIII's abdication. In the United Kingdom, it was offered as reassuring evidence that the new heir presumptive shared the values of the British public, embracing conventional gender roles and enjoying the tasks involved in keeping a tidy house. In contrast, the *New York Times* characterized it as "the particular symbol of [Elizabeth's] sovereignty," noting that "no other child has anything like it."[2]

The *New York Times*, however, was wrong. Although never a widespread phenomenon, several important examples of such cottages were built on both sides of the Atlantic in the preceding eighty years. In the 1920s, other children (including heiresses to American automobile fortunes and the daughter of at least one Hollywood movie star) were the proud owners of habitable miniature houses very much like Y Bwthyn Bach. Earlier in the twentieth century, it had not been uncommon for American social elites to build full-size playhouses on the grounds of their country estates. Sometimes architect-designed, always plumbed and electrified, these playhouses, for their part, were the direct descendants of the Gilded Age children's cottages built by the adult grandchildren of Commodore Cornelius Vanderbilt in the 1880s. In turn, these Vanderbilt cottages were inspired, at least partly, by the Swiss Cottage that Queen Victoria and Prince Albert had built for the use of their offspring in 1853–54 on the grounds of Osborne, their estate on the Isle of Wight. In short, although the phenomenon was relatively short lived and never exactly commonplace, children's cottages constitute an identifiable, if heretofore largely unrecognized, building type.

A central argument of this book is that architecture (understood as the building's shell, as well as its fittings and furniture) played a significant role in the interconnected processes of family and class reproduction among social elites. For one thing, it helped frame and support carefully crafted performances of upper-class identity for users of all ages. For another, it was integral to the ineffable process by which elite children learned to internalize upper-class codes of conduct, making some behaviors seem inevitable, while rendering others unthinkable. Youngsters would learn from watching their elders, of course, but ultimately they acted the way they did because the material world they inhabited made it seem instinctive for them to do so. It was a process that allowed them to elide learned behaviors and inherent superiority, thus feeding their own sense of themselves as innately suited to their privileges. Indeed, architecture is particularly well suited to making particular preferences and practices seem natural and authoritative, an ability that, in Pierre Bourdieu's reckoning, is key to allowing the dominant class to maintain control over others.[3]

Seen within this interpretive frame, children's cottages were also key tools for preserving the social position of upper-class youngsters, which was "in part a policing process," according to sociologist Nicola Beisel, as parents endeavored "to keep children from learning practices that [would] undermine [their] future success."[4] Cottages allowed parents to suggest where, how, and with whom their offspring would spend their days, limiting their opportunities to form undesirable social connections. Cottages were also sites where children could practice behaviors they would use later in life, especially offering hospitality to their peers, as well as directing the labor of adults employed by their families. Sometimes fitted out with call buttons and service entrances, cottages tended to minimize the presence of these employees, simultaneously cloaking and naturalizing the workings of class privilege. At the same time, they removed youngsters who had not yet mastered the full repertoire of upper-class behaviors from the elegant rooms inhabited by their elders, preserving the refinement of the all-important social spaces in the main house.

Children's cottages served upper-class parents in other ways as well. Queen Victoria and Prince Albert, for instance, deployed the Swiss Cottage at Osborne in their efforts to fashion the monarch's maternal public persona. American social elites followed suit, especially after 1900, when playhouses (as cottages became known) were increasingly important as material evidence of their commitment to play, an activity to which the new science of child study ascribed serious developmental importance. Initially, the audience for these demonstrations of parental care was other social elites, especially houseguests who had the opportunity to see the children's bedrooms on the upper floors of the main house and to explore the grounds. Increasingly, however, upper-class men and women also realized the broader publicity potential of the playhouse and some even harnessed the power of news syndication to secure national coverage of their parental endeavors. To the extent that those news features encouraged stars of the stage and screen to build luxurious playhouses for their offspring, they inadvertently launched a process that transformed the function and meaning of the children's cottage. What had once been an important tool for family and class reproduction among social elites was, by the 1930s, an object of desire for millions of ordinary families. This book, then, traces both the rise and the fall of the children's cottage as an instrument of upper-class culture.

Characterizing the class status of the families that built these cottages and playhouses poses some challenges. In the case of the British royal family, this is easy enough, as royalty is a clearly defined category. The situation is less clear in the North American context, where class as defined strictly by birth does not exist, but distinctions of wealth, power, and social standing—often related to birth—mean a great deal. Indeed, according to literary scholar Mary Suzanne Schriber, because American society was "rhetorically classless," it countenanced a degree of class mobility that made Americans "sharply conscious of class and anxious to scale the ladder of class status."[5] Scholars have grappled with this American version of class in a number of ways. Focused on "the consolidation of a self-conscious upper class" in the second half of the nineteenth century, Sven Beckert makes a case for using the term *bourgeoisie* to describe "a particular kind of elite whose power, in its most fundamental sense, derived from the ownership of capital rather that birthright, status or kinship," despite the fact that the word itself was not frequently employed by the people he studies.[6] For his part, Frederic Cople Jaher asks whether there is "a comprehensive ruling class that acts in unity," and so finds it useful to make distinctions between two groups who wield hegemony—"the upper class" and "the aristocracy"—noting that "upper class status can be achieved by personal effort," while aristocracy is strictly a matter of birth.[7] In contrast, Clifton Hood examines the values embraced by different groups of elites, with attention to how those values diverged in the post–World War II era. Thus, the key difference for him is between those who have a distinctive way of life, are self-conscious in their possession of prestigious goods, and are bound together by family and friendship—those he calls the "upper class"—and "economic elites," a group composed of economic decision-makers and the bankers, brokers, and lawyers who support them.[8] In short, the terminology used to discuss class status in the United States tends to vary with the particular focus of a given scholar's analysis.

My approach to this issue is to employ a range of metaphors, both to acknowledge that Americans tend to speak of wealth and power in metaphorical terms and to recognize that those metaphors change over time. Thus, I use the phrase *American aristocrats* for the 1880s and 1890s, when the wealthy mimicked the spatial and material practices of British aristocratic culture and when social commentators deployed the term to express their disdain for those who—despite living in the American republic—pursued social exclusivity. In contrast, I refer to their descendants in the early twentieth century as social elites, both to signal a change in their self-perception while also making room for newcomers like Henry Ford and the widow of John Dodge. Although undeniably rich and powerful, these so-called auto barons enjoyed more tenuous claims to aristocratic pretensions, in large part because the cultural capital they brought to the table was different—heavy on goods they could procure, light on knowledge of high culture. In contrast to both groups are the celebrities who dominate the last two chapters of the book—a capacious group that includes movie stars (who were often called Hollywood royalty), stage producers, and others (including real estate magnates) who made a living by selling leisure. By the end of the book, the benefits of this open-ended approach should become apparent, as it makes possible a serious consideration of the similarities and differences between playhouses built in the 1930s for Princess Elizabeth of York and Shirley Temple, suggesting that celebrity culture served to blur the social distinctions that otherwise separated the two girls.

The lack of scholarly attention to children's cottages seems strange at first glance, given that they meet many of the criteria long used, albeit sometimes tacitly, to determine which buildings are worthy of study. Commissioned by wealthy and powerful men and women who provided the substantial financial resources required to erect them, many of these small buildings were also the work of professional architects, who were highly motivated to impress their clients and often devoted great care and creativity to their designs. Nonetheless, most of these buildings have been ignored by historians, who rarely mention them in otherwise carefully considered analyses of the country houses that graced elite estates. The exception, of course, are the royal cottages, as the appetite for information about every aspect of the British royal family seems to be insatiable. As *The Diamond Queen* demonstrates, however, even in these instances, children's cottages tend to be treated as marvelous traces of extraordinary childhoods, as objects of wonder that have nothing to tell us about their historical moment or about important—that is, adult—matters.

In many ways, this reading of children's cottages as ahistorical remnants of an idealized childhood is a testament to their carefully considered designs. Often featuring archaic forms, frequently constructed of preindustrial materials, and sometimes rendered at a reduced scale, these cottages were self-consciously childlike, all the better to sequester their young users from the cares of the adult world. In that sense, they are manifestations of "the good childhood," the term Marta Gutman and Ning de Coninck-Smith (an architectural historian and a historian of childhood, respectively) have used to encapsulate several interrelated beliefs that continue to hold sway in many parts of the world: that children are fundamentally different from adults; that childhood should be protected, nurtured, and playful; that a child's education should be centered on mental, emotional, and physical development; and that clothes, toys, and even child-sized furniture—what they call collectively "the stuff of childhood"—are essential to translate this ideal of childhood into lived experience.[9] To be sure, a family's ability to provide their offspring with a "good childhood" has always been entirely dependent on financial resources, and many families have had neither the wherewithal to forgo their children's labor nor the means to dedicate whole rooms to their use, let alone to procure high chairs, baby carriages and strollers, small eating utensils, sailor suits, dolls, dollhouses, rocking horses, building blocks, board games, picture books, and the like. As a result, children have come to serve as important markers of class status. Indeed, in the nineteenth century, families in the emerging middle class distinguished themselves from their working-class contemporaries by organizing their lives around their properly dressed children who were relieved of productive labor and required instead to take on what American studies scholar Karen Sánchez-Eppler has characterized as "emotional work," specifically "requiring and expressing the family's idealized capacity for love and joy."[10] Ever more insulated from adults in spatial and material terms, the middle-class child was increasingly inseparable from adults' perceptions of themselves.

Elite children, too, were important markers of class status, and their parents were well positioned to bestow upon them an even wider range of goods, as well as goods of a better quality. Nonetheless, it is a mistake to assume that wealthy parents shared precisely the same goals as their middle-class counterparts or to imagine that greater financial resources made it easier for them to raise their children. This is not to imply that they loved their children less or were less committed to preparing their offspring to become successful adults. Rather, it is to acknowledge that family reproduction (that is, reproducing economic and social privileges from one generation to the next) intersects with class reproduction. Thus, being a successful adult meant something different in upper-class circles, where maintaining and enhancing the reputation and social standing of the family were primary concerns. To be sure, abundant financial resources were crucial to family reproduction among social elites. Yet, as Beisel has argued, securing a family's legitimacy was never merely an economic process.[11] Children needed to learn the attitudes and behaviors and to have access to the goods (what Bourdieu called "cultural capital") that would allow them access to exclusive social activities, which in turn provided them with opportunities to amass the social capital they could then translate into legitimacy or prestige (Bourdieu's "symbolic capital").[12] Especially for the newly rich, as Beisel has pointed out, "the premier signal of social acceptance was the marriage of one's children into high-status families—in effect, to families with older fortunes."[13] In this milieu, upper-class children were integral to the realization of their families' dynastic ambitions.

At the same time, the dynamic process of class formation—of which parenting was an important part—varied historically, as the chapters that follow will make clear. By virtue of her regal status, Queen Victoria would seem to stand somewhat apart from this drive to amass symbolic capital. Nonetheless, she and her consort, Prince Albert, were keenly attentive to anything that might diminish their elevated status. At the same time, for all her wealth and power, the monarch had a complicated relationship with money. In order to avoid parliamentary oversight, she financed the construction of Osborne from the Privy Purse. Nonetheless, she and Albert were careful with the budget, in part because they were eager to make common cause with the queen's middle-class subjects, but perhaps also in part because her land-based wealth—as large as it was—grew at a relatively stately pace.

In contrast, American millionaires of the Gilded Age were much more likely to spend lavishly. In part, this may have been because they enjoyed direct control of the industrial concerns that generated wealth at an increasingly rapid pace. A notable example is railroad magnate William Henry Vanderbilt; the eldest son of Commodore Vanderbilt, he doubled his $100 million inheritance in just nine years, providing his adult children with the financial capital they then used to buy their way into New York Society.[14] Preparing their own children to move in those circles and ensuring that they made marriages advantageous to the family—either to a wealthy American or, better yet, a European aristocrat—were among the highest priorities of the Commodore's adult grandchildren.

For their part, the next generation (those who reached adulthood at the turn of the twentieth century) were eager to demonstrate that they had an appropriate relationship with money, using their resources in ways they hoped would provide evidence of both their moderation and their dedication to their children. Their efforts, however, were also arguably an attempt to forestall social reforms (such as the institution of an income tax) that would erode their capital. Equally indicative of their commitments to maintaining their class status was their steadfast adherence to social practices—including child-rearing methods—that would have been familiar to their parents: employing staff to oversee their children's daily routines, sending their offspring to private schools and universities, and encouraging them to recreate with others of their class on private estates or at exclusive clubs.

By the 1910s and 1920s, the relationship between wealth and status was further complicated by the emergence of new forms of capital that resulted when mass production and mass media were harnessed to reach a mass audience. Whether they produced automobiles (as did Henry Ford and John Dodge), mounted Broadway revues (as did Florenz Ziegfeld), or produced and starred in silent films (as did Harold Lloyd), these entrepreneurs moved rapidly from the modest circumstances in which they had been raised to positions in which they directed great fortunes. Eager to demonstrate their success in material terms, they nonetheless responded to their new situations in different ways. Some of those whose wealth derived from the auto industry took their cues from upper-class society in New York, a city to which they were connected by flows of capital. Ford, however, was always something of an outlier. Envisioning himself as the founder of a powerful industrial dynasty, he saw the lifestyles pursued by those with inherited wealth as antithetical to the cultivation of entrepreneurial vigor.[15]

Hollywood stars, on the other hand, were less concerned with establishing and nurturing dynasties in the same sense and took it upon themselves to create completely new tropes for living well. In large part because a flair for enjoying themselves was important to their public personas, they adopted lifestyles that put a particular emphasis on informality and that centered on forms of recreation that could be experienced in company, all in the mild climate of California. Their estates often featured swimming pools, tennis courts, and sometimes golf courses, as well. Ostensibly private oases, these settings were also designed to be seen by members of the adoring public, primarily on the pages of fan magazines, where photographs of the stars' homes were offered as visual evidence that their owners were happy-go-lucky and fun-loving. In this context, children were not expected to secure the family's long-term stability. Instead, they were photogenic components of the public relations campaigns that helped sell the movie tickets that ultimately financed their parents' glamorous lifestyles.

It is important to recognize that the reproduction of class privilege—the process at the center of this book—was highly racialized. Systemic racism facilitated the consolidation of wealth in white hands while simultaneously limiting the access of non-whites to the institutions that enabled the ready conversion of financial assets into social and symbolic capital. At the same time, a potent element of this class privilege was that it allowed wealthy whites to take the racial component of their privilege for granted. As a result, racial attitudes were not always explicitly expressed in the architectures of upper-class childhood, despite the fact that they were always there. This study includes a number of episodes in which the workings of race are particularly evident: at Osborne, where racial hierarchies are made evident in the differences between the treatment of the cultural production of Europeans (works categorized as art and used to adorn the main house) and the cultural production of Britain's colonial holdings (objects categorized as artifacts and displayed along with specimens of natural history for educational purposes in the Swiss Cottage Museum); at American country houses of the early twentieth century, where the desire for aesthetic reform resulted in the construction of Georgian revival piles that evoked eighteenth-century plantations—architectural forms that were inseparable from the exercise of white privilege; at the playhouse erected at the Edsel and Eleanor Ford estate, where Clara Ford's gift to her granddaughter reinscribed increasingly reactionary gender norms informed by her husband, Henry's, politics, including his widely publicized anti-Semitism; and at the New York World's Fair of 1939, where a replica of Shirley Temple's playhouse was photographed exclusively with white visitors. Although this book is not primarily about racial dynamics, it is important to acknowledge that tacit assumptions about race impacted the built environment, even as the material world helped shape those unspoken attitudes.

A transnational study, *Playhouses and Privilege: The Architecture of Elite Childhood* acknowledges the web of economic and cultural connections that bound Europe and the United States together in a single complex unit, while also highlighting the particularly close relationship between England and Anglo North America, where, since the middle of the eighteenth century, wealthy colonists had modeled many of their social, cultural, and material practices on those of the British aristocracy, the better to distinguish themselves from their less well-to-do neighbors.[16] Within this expanded geographical scope, this study depends upon a close examination of each house and its grounds as a system of interdependent spaces that guided the movements of its many inhabitants and shaped the interactions among them—establishing the basic framework of what I call the site's social choreography. Fittings and furniture can be read as the stage settings and props that supported these social performances, while two- and three-dimensional representations of the family provide additional insights into the scripts that adults hoped their offspring would help them enact.

Yet, there are challenges to finding this material evidence. In the United States, many elite country estates were swept away in the postwar period to make way for middle-class suburban development. While the main houses were often well documented, inside and out, the children's cottages were not subject to the same interest or scrutiny, or at least not consistently. Rather than simply bemoan the dearth of period images, however, this study acknowledges that scarcity as a piece of historical evidence that merits attention. The converse is also true. When a description or an image of a particular children's cottage was published, it is worth asking not just why but also why at that particular moment and—critically—for what audience. Indeed, these are key considerations when examining the role these structures played in shaping the public perception of the parents who brought them into being.

Even children's cottages that are known, either because they are still standing or because they were photographed during their heyday, have not always left robust traces within the archive, although what constitutes "robust" is relative. In contrast to middle-class and working-class youngsters, upper-class children were more apt to keep diaries and write letters; their parents were more likely to preserve those writings; and, under the rubric of "family papers," these youthful writings were more liable to find their ways into archival collections, where they have been preserved, organized, and listed in finding aids, right alongside the documentary relics of their elders. In this sense, it is remarkable to have access to the diary of a fifteen-year-old Gertrude Vanderbilt; the letters a young Helen Clay Frick wrote to her father, steel tycoon Henry Clay Frick; or the correspondence that passed between siblings in the Field family—great-great-grandchildren of Commodore Vanderbilt. All offer tantalizing glimpses into the experiences of the privileged youngsters who used these cottages.

At the same time, the archive—at least as conventionally imagined—leaves large gaps. To compensate for these holes in the written record, this study also turns to evidence that is not often used in architectural history. An intricately carved Swiss desk purchased by Queen Victoria at the Great Exhibition just as she and Prince Albert were actively contemplating the choice of a future husband for their ten-year-old daughter, Vicky, suggests that they intended the Swiss Cottage at Osborne to have particular resonance for the young Princess Royal. A half-completed baby book signals the extent to which an elite mother was aware of middle-class practices that put children at the very center of their parents' lives in both spatial and temporal terms, even as it also sheds light on how difficult it was for her—despite her greater financial resources—to follow suit. An autograph book pressed into service as the guest book for the miniature playhouse of the heiress to the Dodge Brothers Motor Company fortune reveals the presence of over one hundred adult guests at one afternoon event, while simultaneously exposing the absence of the young "hostess." Poems and illustrations from children's books; family photograph albums; a royal Christmas card; mass-produced dollhouses and paper dolls—most of these objects provide an indication of the parental preoccupations that prompted the building of children's cottages, while some of them also help gauge the public understanding of these small structures.

Attentiveness to language is also important to understanding what these buildings meant to their users. The fact that nineteenth-century social elites called these buildings "cottages" is particularly significant. For centuries, the term referred to the simple dwellings of the rural peasantry, buildings that often seemed unsanitary to nineteenth-century housing reformers. Yet, as architectural historian John Archer notes, the term acquired a wide range of meanings in the eighteenth and nineteenth centuries, including a close association with "the presumed innocence and simplicity of a 'primitive' life, passed in harmony with nature."[17] In this sense, the cottage was understood as an appropriate model for middle- and upper-middle-class houses, offering bourgeois householders access to what they imagined as "the bucolic, uncomplicated existence of agricultural laborers."[18] As a result, in the late nineteenth century, a cottage was not necessarily a small building; the term could be applied to any dwelling that embraced informality and a connection to the countryside. Hence, American millionaires called their Newport mansions cottages not in a show of false modesty but rather to signal that they valued these houses for their proximity to nature. By the late nineteenth century, the term *cottage* took on special resonance for spaces devoted to children, as evolutionary theory suggested every child (at least every white child) "recapitulated" the evolution of the human race from primitivism, through barbarism, to civilization. In this highly racialized view of human development, cottages were considered ideal settings for youngsters who were understood to be closer to the primitive past than they were to the state of civilization Anglo-Saxon adults had achieved.[19]

By the twentieth century, the term *cottage* had all but disappeared in favor of the word *playhouse* (sometimes rendered as "play house" or "play-house"). The change in nomenclature is related to the new importance of play in developmental theory, a phenomenon explored in greater depth in chapter 4. Worth noting here is the fact that the term *play* (once used to mean an enjoyable activity pursued by someone of any age) became particularly associated with children in the twentieth century, so much so that many commentators characterize any pleasurable activity a child undertakes as "play." Nonetheless, it is productive to distinguish between the different kinds of activities playhouses were designed to encourage. Some, for instance, provided spaces where children could amuse themselves in a variety of ways—reading, doing puzzles, playing with toys and games, even cooking—without pretending they were anyone but who they were. Other playhouses, however, were predicated on the world of make-believe, requiring the youngster to pretend she was a grown woman and the mother to her dolls—in short, an adult with full responsibility for maintaining her miniature home. Especially popular in the 1920s and 1930s, these playhouses were provided exclusively for girls and reveal the extent to which children's play—often conceptualized as natural, innate, and timeless—was touched by the gender politics at work in the supposedly separate realm of adults.

Being attentive to the room names used by architects and their clients is also particularly important, especially in the United States, where social elites were engaged in an ongoing process of reimagining domestic space, discarding established room types and inventing new ones. Equally important, some room names—notably the nursery—took on new meanings during the period under consideration. While I take up these issues at some length in the text, labeling building plans posed a challenge. For the plans of the main houses, I have used one-, two-, and three-letter designations that I hope will be (or will become) intuitive for readers: for example, DR for dining room, Bal for ballroom, Bil for billiard room, Bre for breakfast room, Bou for boudoir, and BR for bedroom. At the same time, the key for each building provides the room names supplied by the architect, both capturing idiosyncratic room types (such as the Vanderbilts' watercolor room) and also acknowledging that different terms were sometimes used to describe similar room types; bedrooms, for instance, were often called chambers. When a plan includes more than one room of a given type, I have also included numbers to allow readers to see the distance between bedrooms occupied by parents and those designated for their children, for instance, or to distinguish between the sitting room of the Prince of Wales and that of his sisters. When the original room names are unknown (a fairly common occurrence in children's cottages and playhouses), I have used the letters of the alphabet on the plans, so that readers will be able to identify which room is under discussion in the text.

Another challenge in discussing these cottages and playhouses centers on questions of size and scale, terms that are often conflated. Size refers to the absolute dimensions of an object, and cottages and playhouses considered in this study display some variation in size. The largest building is the Swiss Cottage at Osborne, a two-story building with a footprint of approximately 48 by 23 feet. In contrast, Fanny Glessner's log house on the grounds of the Rocks, her family's summer house in Bethlehem, New Hampshire, was a single-story building that covered less than 200 square feet. Nonetheless in the context of their respective properties, both buildings (and the others discussed in the chapters that follow) can be considered small in size.

The scale of these buildings varies dramatically. Only a small subset of twentieth-century playhouses was built on a small scale—that is, with their proportions consistently reduced in relation to a full-size house. Even within this group, most were designed to allow adults to stand erect within them. In a sense, these playhouses stood in a liminal position in terms of their scale, at once small-scale versions of full-size houses and also large-scale versions of miniature dollhouses. Yet, a much more common pattern involved the provision of some child-sized furniture and fittings in spaces that otherwise readily accommodated adults as well, as most of these cottages and playhouses were designed to support a range of intergenerational interactions. Nonetheless, in the twentieth century, the association with youngsters and small-scale objects had become so strong that the presence of any small-scale object was sometimes sufficient to convince observers they were in a child-sized building, whether or not the structure itself was built to a consistently reduced scale. In order to preserve meaningful distinctions in scale, I will reserve the adjective *miniature* to characterize structures built on a consistently reduced scale, while using the noun *playhouse* for habitable buildings and *dollhouse* for house-shaped objects too tiny even for a child to occupy.

A central aim of this book is to put to rest the misperception that the architecture of childhood is solely about children. Childhood is a stage of life conceptualized by adults, who are also responsible for making decisions about the spatial arrangements that give shape to young lives, whether at home, at school, or in the many other child-centered settings that emerged in the twentieth century. Although often articulated in terms of the needs of the child, these decisions are inseparable from parental concerns and anxieties: about the well-being of their offspring; about their own abilities as parents; and about how their own successes or failures in that role will impact their esteem in the eyes of other adults. Equally important, the architecture of childhood intersects with spaces used by adults and has a direct impact on those spaces, determining, for instance, the degree to which they would remain unaffected by the palpable energy of the young. To be sure, children have agency of their own and often exercise it by declining to perform the script their elders attempt to write into the built environment. Ultimately, however, the architecture of childhood is the product of adult action, with consequences for the lives of young and old alike.

Chapters 1 and 2 present Osborne, Queen Victoria's maritime villa on the Isle of Wight. Unlike Buckingham Palace or Windsor Castle, official residences built and repeatedly reworked by Victoria's royal predecessors, Osborne was built from scratch, designed largely by Prince Albert and paid for by Victoria's private wealth. Thus, it is an ideal site at which to investigate how these royal parents used architectural space to support their child-rearing responsibilities, something they took very seriously, given the adult roles they anticipated for their offspring. At the same time, the children played a more immediate role in Victoria's self-presentation as a thoroughly domesticated woman, whose commitment to marriage and motherhood served to reassure her subjects that she would not use her "unnatural" position as queen regnant to challenge the patriarchal foundations of British culture. Ensconced in a nursery suite in the floor above their parents' rooms in the Italianate-style Pavilion, the younger children were central to their mother's public persona. Once they left the nursery, however, the royal offspring were provided with suites of rooms, carefully arranged to support and underscore their social positions—not just in relation to the aristocratic men and women who attended their mother and to other adults employed to educate and serve them, but also in relation to the line of succession, in which birth order and gender played defining roles. Because these living spaces were fundamentally at odds with the self-consciously domestic architecture of the Pavilion, they were located instead in a separate building, the so-called main wing, where they were arrayed along double-loaded corridors in an arrangement akin to early office buildings. At least in part because of this institutional layout, the suites originally designed for the elder children were obliterated when that part of the site was converted into a convalescent home after Victoria's death in 1901. By bringing attention to the upper floors of the main wing, chapter 1 highlights an important, but largely unrecognized, facet of royal life at Osborne.

Chapter 2 focuses on another set of children's spaces at Osborne, namely, a children's precinct located about a half mile from the main house. Its centerpiece is the Swiss Cottage, a two-story building constructed between 1853 and 1854 to provide kitchen facilities for the use of the royal children (on the first floor), as well as a room on the second floor where they (and sometimes their parents) could take simple meals and another chamber where they could display the natural history specimens their father encouraged them to collect. Inspired in part by a comparable building on the grounds of Rosenau, the country house where Albert had spent much of his boyhood, the Swiss Cottage at Osborne also belongs to a home-grown tradition. Indeed, many British aristocrats had signaled their appreciation for the work of Jean-Jacques Rousseau by building so-called Swiss Cottages on their estates, structures that could serve as the focal point of Picturesque vignettes, while also providing viewing platforms from which to enjoy vistas into the landscape. Like those buildings, the Swiss Cottage at Osborne was understood to offer its high-born users a respite from the pressures of court life and the chance to enjoy what was romanticized as the idyllic life of rural peasants. While there is evidence that Victoria and Albert's offspring used their own Swiss Cottage in this way, the building and its contents suggest it was also deeply connected with royal concerns: ensuring the Princess Royal entered into a marriage that would serve Britain's foreign policy interests; instilling in all of the children a sense of innate British superiority over its imperial holdings; and providing opportunities for the youngsters to practice interpersonal skills required of them at court.

The next three chapters feature cottages and playhouses built by American social elites between 1885 and 1930. Chapter 3 deals with the introduction to the United States of the children's cottage as a building type, an episode in which three of Commodore Vanderbilt's adult grandchildren played a central role: William Kissam Vanderbilt at Idle Hour in Oakdale, on Long Island; Emily Thorne Vanderbilt Sloane at Elm Court in Lenox, Massachusetts; and Cornelius Vanderbilt II at the

Breakers in Newport, Rhode Island. This last building is the only one that exists in its original form and is the example analyzed most closely. In essence, it served as a vestigial parlor—a room type that had no place in elite houses devoted to adult sociability and the accumulation of social and symbolic capital. The cottage thus allowed the family to enact (albeit somewhat sporadically) nuclear family togetherness, while also giving parents control over the friendships of their offspring. At the same time, the cottage allowed the children to experience independent control over domestic staff in a space that framed housework, especially cooking, as a pleasant task upper-class children would outgrow.

Chapter 4 considers the broader adoption of the building type in the early twentieth century in light of new concerns, both the widespread recognition of the importance of children's play as it was articulated by the new discipline of child study, as well as growing anxieties among social elites about flaunting their great wealth. The first set of concerns resulted in a reorganization of the nursery suite, which had once been tucked away, out of sight, on an upper floor. In the early twentieth century, upper-class children no longer slept together in a night nursery but instead were provided with individual bedrooms. Although these rooms tended to be adjacent to those of a nurse who continued to supervise the youngsters, this suite of bedrooms was given a central location that made it more visible to houseguests. The functions of the day nursery were likewise brought down from the upper reaches of the house and made visible to visitors. At times, these functions were subdivided into more specialized rooms within the house, notably a playroom (often near a children's entrance) and a children's dining room. At others, freestanding playhouses (as children's cottages were now called) kept the functions of the day nursery together, but separated them entirely from the main house, which was still devoted to adult sociability. Set in the garden, the playhouse offered visible evidence of parental care, while keeping the children well out of earshot. The second set of concerns prompted social elites to eschew the aesthetic preferences of their parents' generation, rejecting the styles of eighteenth-century France and adopting instead Colonial Revival styles or, less frequently, forms associated with the Arts and Crafts movement. When applied to children's playhouses, the result was a contradiction in terms: luxury objects of conspicuous simplicity.

Chapter 5 takes up the question of how these twentieth-century playhouses were used. Thanks to a handful of family letters and rare period photographs, it is clear playhouses were used by boys and girls to enact homely virtues, at least until about 1920. Cooking was the favorite activity and one that stood elites in good stead as they pursued endeavors, such as camping and higher education, that were increasingly taken up as a part of upper-class life. After 1920, the Red Scare politicized the domestic sphere, and especially household labor, prompting a new approach to elite playhouses, in which gender was the most salient factor. Log cabins, once built for girls as well as boys, became closely associated with fostering upper-class masculinity, one in which boys were free to choose from a range of leisure-time activities. In contrast, playhouses for female children took the form of complete middle-class houses, albeit on a consistently reduced scale. Bestowed on an individual girl, each of these structures provided a narrow playscript for its owner, one in which she was to pretend that she was the mistress of a house that required her perpetual attention. Given that these heiresses would never be required to wash a dish or sweep a floor as adults, these playhouses were never direct preparation for their future lives, although they were sometimes framed that way. Ultimately, it was less important that these girls be able to engage in housework than it was that they be seen to care about it. Indeed, these reduced-scale playhouses helped communicate the impression that these girls and their parents embraced patriarchy, sometimes even providing cover, as it were, for upper-class mothers who opted to step well outside the domestic sphere.

The last two chapters consider the demise of the playhouse as a tool of elite culture. Chapter 6 reviews sumptuous playhouses built by parents who were willing to spend lavishly on their children, but who were not particularly concerned with long-term dynastic stability. In other words, rather than pursuing a long-term campaign to amass social and symbolic capital, their motivation was to maximize their financial capital in the short run. Beginning in the early twentieth century, adults whose livelihoods were enmeshed in the commercialization of leisure found that reduced-scale playhouses made good business sense. For a real estate developer such as Robert Burton, a splendid playhouse could reassure upper-class customers that he understood how they lived and the range of spaces they would require. For those involved in mass entertainment, impressive playhouses helped attract favorable press coverage, which in turn helped sell tickets. In the process, playhouses were transformed into objects of desire for middle-class consumers, who increasingly fueled a market for mass-produced play sheds in a range of forms and materials. As these modest playhouses became more widely available, costly playhouses lost much of their luster in the eyes of social elites.

Chapter 7 looks closely at two playhouses from the 1930s: Y Bwthyn Bach, the two-story thatched-roof cottage presented to Princess Elizabeth of York, and a one-story glass block playhouse given to Shirley Temple. Despite their dramatically different forms, the two playhouses were remarkably similar in origin and intent. Neither was a parental undertaking, emanating instead from the actions of commercial interests that sought to leverage the celebrity of an adorable little girl in order to call attention to a particular segment of the building industry. At the same time, these two playhouses ultimately came to serve very different roles in the lives of their young owners. Following the example of American social elites, the Duke and

Duchess of York readily embraced Y Bwthyn Bach—a luxury object of conspicuous simplicity—to present themselves to the British people as loving parents committed to raising modest, home-loving, daughters. In contrast, Shirley Temple's playhouse was of little benefit to the young star's parents and was used instead by other adult decision-makers to support endeavors wholly unconnected to Shirley and her family. Officials at the Owens-Illinois Glass Company hoped the playhouse erected in the Temples' backyard would garner free advertising for their new Insulux glass blocks, while the president of the New York Infirmary for Women and Children (cognizant of a comparable use of Y Bwthyn Bach) anticipated raising funds for a new hospital by displaying a replica of Shirley's playhouse at the New York World's Fair of 1939. In part because of the state of the global economy, the replica playhouse failed to generate a surplus that could be deployed for charitable purposes. It did, however, play a role in severing the long-standing connection between extravagant playhouses and elite culture.

In the end, this is not a book about playhouses per se, but rather about the emergence and the eventual decline of a particular social practice on the part of upper-class parents, namely, using children's cottages and playhouses to help instill in their offspring a certain set of class-inflected attitudes and behaviors. This is not to say that other playhouses, whether mass produced or homemade, don't have rich stories to tell.[20] Rather, it is to focus attention on the spaces of elite childhood and on architecture's role in the reproduction of class privilege. Seen in this light, the small buildings at the heart of this study were integral to the effective functioning of the large estates on which they stood: removing youngsters from the main house, which could then be devoted to adult sociability; supporting the youngsters as they worked to master their own performances of elite identity; and, perhaps most important, providing a physical setting in which the offspring of wealthy and powerful families could experience their privileges as natural and inevitable. In all these ways, then, children's cottages were never just about children, and playhouses were always more than simply places to play.

Figure 1.1. West front of Osborne, Isle of Wight. Thomas Cubitt, architect, 1846–51. André Adolphe-Eugène Disdéri, photographer, 1867. *The Osborne Album: Thirty-three Photographic Views of the Queen's Marine Residence at Osborne* (London and Paris: [André Adolphe-Eugène] Disdéri, 1867), 26.

CHAPTER ONE

Raising Royals in an Age of Sentiment

The Family of Victoria and Albert at Osborne

*I*n 1867, Queen Victoria allowed a French photographer access to Osborne, her maritime villa on the Isle of Wight. The site was particularly dear to the widowed monarch, as her beloved consort, Prince Albert, had played a major role in the design of the house and its surrounding parkland. The images published in *The Osborne Album* speak volumes about the royal couple, as Albert had taken a particular interest in the new medium of photography and had been quick to see its potential for helping to craft Victoria's public persona.[1] These photographs also signal the importance of architecture in this publicity endeavor, especially the so-called Pavilion which was given center stage in the image of Osborne's west front (Figure 1.1). With its asymmetrical massing, its campanile-like tower rising above a sheltering porte-cochère, and its round-arched windows, the Pavilion is a cousin of the modest Italianate villas that had appeared in pattern books published on both sides of the Atlantic since the 1830s. In that sense, it gestures toward the royal couple's appreciation of a particular—albeit transnational—mode of domesticity, one in which a single-family house nestled in a natural setting was understood to protect its inhabitants from the demands of urban life and offer an ideal situation for rearing children.

At the same time, this photograph reveals realities that conflicted with that domestic ideal, namely, that the royal household (including the noblemen and -women who attended the monarch) required types of accommodation the Pavilion could not provide. Hence, the presence of a second building, one that is both more dignified than the Pavilion in formal terms, but also significantly shorter than its statuesque companion. If the Pavilion was an Italianate villa writ large, the adjacent building (which has no name and is only known by its component parts: main wing, household wing, and the Grand Corridor) was essentially a small-scale palace. In this sense, Osborne was a building at odds with itself.[2]

This complex project had its inception in 1843, when Victoria and Albert began to search for a house of their own. What they wanted was a cozy, *gemütlich* dwelling where they and their offspring could enjoy both access to healthful sea breezes as well as a degree of privacy not readily available at their other residences. At the suggestion of Prime Minister Robert Peel, they turned their attention to the Isle of Wight, just off England's south coast and familiar to Victoria from two visits to Norris Castle in the 1830s. Soon they settled on the Osborne estate, which they leased for a year before purchasing it in 1845.[3] Initially, the royal couple imagined retaining the existing house (a structure that had been remodeled in the 1770s), although the queen admitted that they would need to make "some few alterations and additions for the children."[4] Before long, they determined that the old house was too small for their needs and engaged Thomas Cubitt to undertake the construction of a new house. A master builder responsible for developing large parts of Belgravia, Bloomsbury, and Pimlico, Cubitt worked closely with Albert to transform the estate, which soon also included the adjacent Barton Manor, a site Albert later used as a model farm. Victoria continued to purchase land around Osborne, so that the estate eventually covered some two thousand acres.[5]

In its location at a distance from London and its setting in a vast park where the only other structures were sparsely scattered outbuildings, Osborne was a country house. Characterized by architectural historian Mark Girouard as "power houses," such structures had been a key feature of British aristocratic culture for centuries, helping their owners consolidate or, in some cases, amass power. Osborne, however, played a somewhat different role in Victoria's life than did the country estates inhabited by her aristocratic lords. As art historians Kate Retford, Gill Perry, and Jordan Vibert have pointed out, aristocratic country houses were family seats, "spaces that nurtured dynasties, handed down over generations."[6] There, the family portrait collection was displayed, not merely because a large country house had more space than the family's (often leased) townhouse, but also because the country house (typically owned outright) was "expressive of permanence, status, and inheritance," and thus "lay at the heart of an elite family's identity."[7] For Victoria, the reverse was true. The residences she had inherited (although they were owned by the state) and those most closely associated with her dynastic predecessors were Buckingham Palace and Windsor Castle, located in or near London. These were the large and stately buildings where the family portrait collection was displayed and that expressed the queen's inherited status and the permanence of her family line. In contrast, Osborne offered Victoria a way to distance herself from her unpopular Hanoverian uncles who had, among other failings, squandered public monies on lavish residences. Indeed, she and Albert explicitly rejected the Royal Pavilion at Brighton, the extravagant Orientalist concoction built for the Prince Regent in the 1810s. Never planned to house a young family and anything but cozy, the Royal Pavilion was situated in an increasingly popular seaside resort town, which meant it no longer offered its royal inhabitants the privacy they desired. In 1846, Victoria agreed to sell that residence to help offset the cost of additions to Buckingham Palace, where she also reused some of the Pavilion's exotic furnishings.[8]

Rather than using Osborne as a setting in which to display portraits of the queen's antecedents, Victoria and Albert filled their country house with images of their descendants; among them were Franz Xaver Winterhalter's oil painting *The Royal Family in 1846* in the dining room and Mary Thornycroft's nine marble portrait statues of their children in the drawing room.[9] Given their tendency to look forward in this way, Victoria and Albert may well have imagined that they were establishing a new family seat, a house that would pass on to their eldest son and through him to generations beyond.[10] As a young mother, the queen could not have anticipated that her heir would thwart that plan so soon after her death by giving the estate to the nation in 1902.

Whatever its differences may have been from conventional aristocratic country houses, Osborne was often in the public eye during Victoria's lifetime, when it was strategically offered as proof of the monarch's dedication to a mode of domestic life focused on her husband and children. Its renown was such that it also became the touchstone for a transnational surge in country-house construction that extended from the middle decades of the nineteenth century into the early twentieth century. Indeed, on both sides of the Atlantic, those with substantial (albeit often recently acquired) wealth often built country houses to demonstrate their readiness to operate in the highest social circles. Thanks to Victoria's position at the apex of the Anglo-American social hierarchy, many of her contemporaries looked to emulate at least some of her domestic arrangements, including those in which her children played an important part.

THE IMPORTANCE OF ROYAL CHILDREN

Children, of course, are axiomatically central to any monarchy, as they are the primary method for guaranteeing a smooth succession and ensuring dynastic stability. Victoria, who came to the British throne in 1837 only because her dissolute uncles had failed to produce legitimate male heirs, was acutely aware of this fact and took her duty to reproduce seriously. In early 1840, she married her first cousin, Albert of Saxe-Coburg and Gotha, and by the end of the year had given birth to a girl, Victoria, the Princess Royal, known in the family initially as Pussy and later as Vicky. The next year, the queen gave birth to a male heir, Albert Edward (the Prince of Wales, known as Bertie), who was followed by Alice in 1843, Alfred (Affie) in 1844,

Helena (Lenchen) in 1846, Louise in 1848, Arthur in 1850, Leopold in 1853, and Beatrice (Baby) in 1857. Such "long families"—historian Leonore Davidoff's term for large sibling groups in which elder children become parents while their own brothers and sisters are still infants or toddlers—were not uncommon in nineteenth-century Britain.[11] Within a royal family, all the children could be expected to play a role on the world stage, if not as monarch, then in military careers (for younger sons) or (for the girls) via marriages into other royal courts, alliances that—it was hoped—would help secure peace in Europe. In this context, bearing and raising children was a political act.[12]

Both Victoria and Albert were extremely attentive to their parental responsibilities and, in many ways, embraced a sentimental view of childhood that, according to historian Philippe Ariès, had blossomed in the newly privatized domestic sphere of the eighteenth century.[13] For one thing, they devoted a great deal of attention to the health and education of their children, so much so that Pussy's temporary failure to thrive in infancy triggered perhaps the biggest crisis of their early married life. For another, they gave many of their children nicknames, something Ariès identified as a means of emphasizing "by a sort of hermetic language the solidarity of parents and children and the distance separating them [that is, the modern nuclear family unit] from other people."[14] They devoted time and attention to celebrating their children's birthdays and thus acknowledged each child's unique place in the life of the family. And while Victoria is known for disliking pregnancy and for comparing newborn infants to frogs, she and Albert also spent hours in the nursery, especially when their four eldest children were small. The young queen's diaries and sketchbooks are replete with her own drawings and watercolors of her young children as they were bathed by their nurses, played with toys at child-sized tables, sat in small chairs, or hugged one of the dogs—all the while dressed in the distinctive clothing that marked them as children (Figure 1.2). As these images make clear, the royal couple embraced the ideal of "the good childhood" and the plethora of material goods on which it depended.[15]

Yet Victoria and Albert were also unlike other modern parents in important ways. For one, their family life was never completely private, conducted as it was in the presence of an extended household—both noble ladies-in-waiting and equerries, as well as more humble servants. Equally important, Victoria and Albert came to understand the importance of giving the British people access to their family via tender depictions of their children in a wide range of media. They were not the first to do so; art historian Simon Schama has argued that George III inaugurated the practice of presenting himself, his queen, and their offspring not as a dynastic gathering but as a modern family (in Ariès's sense of that phrase).[16] While there was nothing inevitable about this transition from dynastic to domestic depictions of the royal

FIGURE 1.2. The Princess Royal and the Prince of Wales in the nursery, using a child-sized table and chair, surrounded by toys. Etching by Prince Albert, after a drawing by Queen Victoria, dated 8 January 1843. RCIN 816188. Royal Collection Trust / copyright 2023 His Majesty King Charles III.

family, Schama also suggested that there was no going back: "Once the means of mass production and distribution of such images was available, allegiance (or at least the sentimental bond forged between monarch and subjects) depended on a steady flow of appealing images."[17] Schama is right to highlight the role of sentimentality in sustaining modern monarchs, as it all but required that those appealing images would include charming royal children.

Victoria and Albert were also unlike other parents in that they could never allow their own sentimentality to trump dynastic concerns. They expected their children, above all else, to sustain the institution of the monarchy. This expectation was most visible (at least to middle-class people who could only comprehend marrying for love) when the children reached their maturity and were required to put family duty before personal preference, entering into marriages arranged for the good of the dynasty. Indeed, Schama had just this practice in mind when he argued that "nineteenth-century royal families were, in all their essentials, the very opposite of the image that they projected."[18] Schama's implication—that families can either prioritize dynastic interests or embrace sentimental attachments, but not both—deserves further examination. Arguably, Victoria and Albert sought to partake of both these ideals.

The spaces for the royal offspring on the Osborne estate speak to this aspiration, highlighting the extent to which the royal couple embraced a widely shared ideal of a good childhood, while also revealing the degree to which royal concerns and preoccupations impacted Victoria and Albert's pursuit of that ideal. Architecture played a crucial role in supporting what may have felt like conflicting versions of royal childhood. It created children's spaces that were distinct both in location and design from those inhabited by adults. It also provided spatial proximity between parents and children (at least those still in nursery), supported parental efforts to keep the youngsters safe and healthy, and facilitated child-specific activities. At the same time, architecture helped the royal children present themselves in ways that would convince the world—themselves included—that it was right, even natural, for them to occupy privileged places at the top of a strict social hierarchy. Seamless performances of royal privilege may well be more important to maintaining the institution of the monarchy than arranged marriages; certainly, the fact that the quotidian practices of royal privilege are rarely identified as antithetical to middle-class values suggests that Victoria and Albert succeeded at making the monarchy seem somehow inevitable. Their children—and the architecture of royal childhood—were central to this endeavor.

MONARCH AND MOTHER

Victoria and Albert were especially conscious of the challenges of raising royals. After all, Victoria's grandfather, George III, had been beloved by the British people during much of his reign at least in part because he was devoted to his wife and large family. Not only did he and Queen Charlotte beget fifteen children, thirteen of whom lived to adulthood, but, as art historian Kate Retford has pointed out, they were also "widely perceived as indistinguishable from the ideal of domestic virtue promoted in contemporary literature."[19] Victoria certainly learned much from George's example. Yet, from the perspective of the 1840s, he had also made missteps as a father, failing to instill in his sons, particularly, a sense of duty to the House of Hanover and to the British nation. Selfish, pleasure-seeking reprobates all, the seven sons who survived to adulthood had by 1817 produced only one legitimate heir among them; the four unmarried sons only rushed to marry acceptable princesses and produce legitimate children when George IV's only daughter died in childbirth and they saw an opportunity to father the next monarch and thus receive an increase in their parliamentary allowances.[20]

Faced with decisions about raising their own children, Victoria and Albert sought the counsel of Baron Christian Friedrich von Stockmar, their close and trusted advisor, who may have added to their anxieties by highlighting "the magnitude of the parental responsibility of Sovereigns to their Children," given that "the prosperity and happiness of a Nation depends upon the personal Character of its Sovereign." The very "welfare of England" was at stake.[21] This difficult task was further complicated by the fact that Victoria's role as queen regnant gave her rights—over her person, over property, and over the raising of her children—that no other married woman in Britain enjoyed. To be sure, many thinkers held that women inevitably played an important role in the education of their children, especially when they were young; at the end of the eighteenth century, Mary Wollstonecraft had argued for the reform of female education at least in part so women could fulfill that duty effectively.[22] Yet, Albert (whose experience in becoming the consort of a queen had already sensitized him to what he perceived as the many assaults on his manhood) and Victoria (who was anxious on her husband's account) were both inclined to accept Stockmar's insistence that her position as queen regnant had put both of them in an "unnatural" position, one that could lead "to the subversion of the natural order of things and of the paternal authority, as established by divine and human laws."[23] Only by entrusting Albert with decisions about the education of the children could the royal couple safeguard the gendered hierarchy at the heart of British family relations.

Victoria's situation, however, also had a more public dimension. For centuries, a strong strain of British political discourse held that the king was to the nation as the father was to the family. In *Patriarcha: or the Natural Power of Kings* (published in 1680), Robert Filmer had asserted that monarchs were the direct successors of Adam, who had derived his right to rule from his role as the father of humanity, and that it was "by Right of Father-hood" that Adam's successors were endowed with "Royal Authority over their Children"—that is, their people.[24] Motherhood did not always carry the same regal resonance. To be sure, Elizabeth I had presented herself as the mother of her people and succeeded in using that symbolic maternity as a source of political power.[25] When Anne had attempted to follow a similar path in the early eighteenth century, she was disappointed, at least in part because the strategy inevitably called attention to her own failures as a mother; unlike the Virgin Queen, she had been pregnant seventeen times and yet came to the throne childless. Even more important, however, was the fact that the very meaning of motherhood was in flux in Anne's time. As literary scholar Toni Bowers has pointed out, her reign coincided with a chorus of voices (particularly in conduct manuals and sermons) that increasingly insisted that "maternal authority could only be legitimate—indeed, could only be imagined—in the context of isolated, private households, not as a constitutive presence in public affairs."[26] By the time Victoria came to the throne, these views were firmly entrenched: respectable wives and mothers were expected to limit their interests to the domestic sphere and to shun any active role in the public realm. In this context, a female monarch seemed to be a contradiction in terms. "On the one hand," literary scholar Margaret Homans has noted, "being a queen may grant improper power to a woman; on the other, a proper woman may be too weak to be monarch even of a parliamentary democracy."[27] In nineteenth-century Britain, female rule created an inherently anxious situation for the queen's subjects.

Victoria's response, according to Homans, was to forge a public persona that emphasized her role as a pliant wife. Working together, she and Albert sought to "disseminate a complex picture of royalty's superordinary domesticity, to publicize the monarchy as middle-class and its female identity as unthreateningly subjugated and yet somehow still reassuringly sovereign."[28] In Homans's formulation, this strategy was not just a matter of consolidating Victoria's popularity; it was also an acknowledgement that "the characteristics required of the monarch of a nineteenth-century parliamentary democracy were those also required of middle-class wives," namely, remaining aloof from party politics, spending her family's (and, in the case of the queen, her nation's) wealth carefully, and serving as a public representation of her family's and her nation's values.[29] Homans has further argued that by giving away power over herself, Victoria gained influence over her subjects, influence that she used to help Britain see itself as a middle-class nation and thus to become both powerful and prosperous. Ultimately, in this line of thinking, by presenting herself as a domesticated woman, Victoria succeeded in "completing Britain's transition to parliamentary democracy and symbolic monarchy," during a time when many other European monarchies disappeared.[30]

At the same time, Victoria and Albert understood that the queen's public persona as fully domesticated woman depended to a great degree on her status as a mother, a role that would also ultimately have a broader impact on the future of Europe.[31] Indeed, images of the royal children were particularly important to Victoria's self-presentation; putting her private virtues as a fond mother on public display would resonate not only with the queen's middle-class subjects, but also with multiple audiences from different social strata. At the same time, a focus on the royal children—and especially the spaces built for their use—also reveals the very real limitations of Victoria's aspirations to present herself as essentially a middle-class woman. After all, both she and her entire family were embedded in court society, where rank mattered and where (as sociologist Norbert Elias has argued) the continuation of the "House" superseded the hopes and dreams of any one member of the family.[32]

REPRESENTATIONS OF THE ROYAL CHILDREN

From the earliest years of their marriage, Victoria and Albert commissioned a plethora of images of their children, both for their private use (participating in what art historian Freya Gowrley has characterized as "the commercialization of affection") and for broader consumption.[33] Often representations of their children moved fluidly between these two realms. Consider the nine portrait sculptures produced by Mary Thornycroft, most with an allegorical component: the seasons for the four eldest children (Figure 1.3); Lenchen and Louise as "Peace" and "Prosperity," respectively; Arthur and Leopold as a hunter and a fisher boy, respectively; and Beatrice in a nautilus shell.[34] Intended for Osborne, where they were (and still are) displayed in the drawing room, the marble versions of the statues were commissioned by Albert and presented to Victoria as birthday or Christmas gifts between 1845 and 1858. Despite the intimate circumstances surrounding the creation of these tender images, the royal couple ensured that they were also in the public eye, not only (in the case of the first four) at the Great Exhibition, but also in bronze and plaster versions that Victoria herself commissioned for display at other royal residences, as well in reduced versions in parian by Minton and Copeland, which may have been available more widely.[35] Engravings of the statues were also published in periodicals, which ensured that they were well known.

Franz Xaver Winterhalter's 1846 painting of the Prince of Wales in a sailor suit was also an intimate object that entered the public realm. The sailor suit itself was Victoria's idea; as a surprise for Albert, she asked the tailor who outfitted the crew of the Royal Yacht to make it for her four-year-old heir.[36] (Perhaps she knew she was maintaining a family tradition, as eighty years earlier another Prince of Wales [later George IV] was dressed as a sailor and danced a hornpipe for his parents on his fourth birthday.)[37] Albert was so delighted that he commissioned the oil painting and presented it to Victoria as a Christmas gift. By the next spring the painting was displayed at St. James's Palace as part of an exhibition that attracted over one hundred thousand visitors during a two-month period.[38] Afterward, the image became widely available, both as an engraving and in a variety of figurines; Minton's was made of parian, monochrome, and finely modeled in imitation of marble, while the Staffordshire Pottery issued a polychrome version in glazed earthenware (Figure 1.4).[39] In some ways, Victoria was following another practice established in the reign of her grandfather George III, when Johan Zoffany's 1770 portrait of the king, Queen Charlotte, and their six eldest children was both engraved and reproduced by the Derby Porcelain Works in biscuit porcelain. These exquisitely detailed castings are perhaps more akin to the bronzes that Victoria commissioned—expensive copies intended for elite audiences; the set currently held in the Royal

Collection is thought to have originally belonged to Princess Sophia, the twelfth child of George III and Charlotte.[40] In this context, the issuing of relatively inexpensive parian and earthenware versions in Victoria's time seems to set a new precedent. Certainly, the many versions of the Winterhalter image helped bolster the popularity of the sailor suit for young boys, especially after 1857, when the naval ratings' uniform was redesigned to follow the pattern worn on the royal yacht.[41] The episode confirms that the royal family had a special relationship to the material culture of modern childhood. In this case, Victoria both followed the widespread practice of dressing her offspring in what were understood to be children's clothes while also introducing new forms into that repertoire.

If these images of the royal children in the garb of working men and women helped frame public understandings of them—and by extension, their parents—as modest, natural, and innocent, others highlighted the central part they played in their parents' dynastic ambitions. Take, for instance, another work by Winterhalter, *The Royal Family in 1846* (Figure 1.5). Commissioned by the royal couple for the dining room at Osborne (the landscape of which is evoked in the background), the large oil painting was first displayed at the well-attended 1847 exhibition at St. James's Palace and later made widely available in engraved form.[42] Although less grandiose than the full-length pendant portraits of Victoria and Albert in Garter robes that Winterhalter completed in 1843, the 1846 image shows a distinctly regal queen and consort. She is wearing an evening dress and an emerald-and-diamond diadem designed by Albert, while he is in court dress. Both wear the ribbon and star of the Garter, signaling their membership in Britain's oldest and most senior order of chivalry. In addition to wearing the Garter itself, Albert also wears the Badge of the Golden Fleece, the first foreign order he received after his marriage, and one that would have come to Victoria, had she been male.[43] The painting makes other references to Albert's proximity to the crown, notably by showing the couple seated on what can easily be mistaken for a throne-like settee. In fact, they sit on imposing matching armchairs that were part of a suite of fifty-six pieces made for George IV's private apartments at Windsor Castle, where the portrait sittings took place. Albert's figure, however, is positioned so that his torso and right hand mask the gap between the two chairs, contributing to the impression that he and the queen share the seat of power. At one

FIGURE 1.3. *Victoria, Princess Royal, as "Summer,"* in situ in drawing room at Osborne, Isle of Wight. One of a set of sculptures of the four eldest children of Victoria and Albert as the Four Seasons, this marble original and its companion pieces were displayed at the Great Exhibition of 1851, where they were identified with rural occupations—in this case, a gleaner. Copies were made in parian and in bronze. Mary Thornycroft, sculptor, 1846. Photograph by the author.

level, Victoria is the central figure; near the center of the canvas, her diadem is outlined by a patch of blue sky. Yet, she is also framed—bracketed and contained—by two of the painting's three male figures, her heir and her husband, who look toward one another. (The third male figure is two-year-old Prince Alfred, not yet out of skirts.) What is more, Albert's dominance is signaled by the fact that his head is higher than Victoria's and that his is the only face presented in full profile, reminiscent of the regal visage on coins and medals. In an important sense, Winterhalter achieved what Victoria had been unable to accomplish: he presented Albert (albeit uncrowned) as Victoria's king consort, a title that Victoria had tried and failed to have Parliament bestow upon her husband at the time of their marriage.[44] It is little wonder that she deemed this work "a 'chef d'oeuvre'" and declared herself "enchanted with it."[45]

At the same time, Winterhalter was representing not only the royal couple but also their children, inevitably revealing the ways age and gender shaped the family as a unit. At one level, this was nothing new. As Kate Retford has noted, from at least the mid-sixteenth century on, "The family group was usually pictorially categorised according to age and sex," with mothers, daughters, and sometimes unbreeched sons on one side of the canvas and fathers on the other, along with any older sons.[46] Not surprisingly, heirs typically received special attention in such family portraits, being shown in close proximity to their fathers, sharing their interests and sometimes assuming similar postures. Adjusting these visual tropes to the specificities of this royal family, Winterhalter painted the queen with her arm around the shoulders of her young heir, who in turn leans into her full skirt, his hand on her lap. Perhaps to reduce the emasculating tenor of such a representation, the elder son meets his father's stern gaze, even as the red of his Russian blouse echoes the red of the ribbon around Albert's neck. Likewise, in gesturing toward his elder son, Albert's right hand almost touches the queen's left hand, which is close to Bertie's; this trio of hands signals, perhaps, that both queen and consort will play a role in preparing their son to succeed his mother and to steer the ship of state. While unbreeched sons were often depicted close to their sisters, young Affie shares the side of the canvas dominated by his mother and brother, to whom he gestures with a chubby hand. In this way, the composition serves to remind viewers that Victoria had produced both an heir and a spare, thus ensuring that the succession would not revert to her dissolute and unpopular Hanoverian uncles.

FIGURE 1.4. Parian figure of the Prince of Wales in a sailor suit, after a painting by Franz Xaver Winterhalter from 1846. Minton, circa 1846. Less expensive versions of the figure were produced in earthenware, while the painting was also reproduced as an engraving. Courtesy of Drove House Antiques.

Figure 1.5. Franz Xaver Winterhalter, *The Royal Family in 1846*, 1846. RCIN 405413. Royal Collection Trust / copyright 2023 His Majesty King Charles III.

The painting is also notable for the treatment of the family's three eldest daughters, who in contrast to their standing brothers, remain seated, gathered docilely at Albert's feet. Just as Victoria's physical proximity to Bertie indicates that he is destined to take her place, Albert's physical proximity to his daughters portends that they are likely to share his fate: marriage to one of the small number of European royals and life as a consort in a foreign court. In Albert's view, this was more than just a fact of royal life; he saw it as an opportunity to influence the political landscape of Europe. His first priority was a unified Germany, and he eventually came to believe that a dynastic alliance would be an effective mechanism for encouraging the establishment of a constitutional monarchy in Prussia—the strongest of the German states and so the most likely center for this new Germany. Certainly, by 1851, he and Victoria were actively pursuing this plan, inviting the Crown Prince of Prussia and his family to visit the Great Exhibition and thus creating an opportunity to bring together the ten-year-old Princess Royal and nineteen-year-old Fritz, son of the Crown Prince. On a return visit four years later, Fritz proposed and the young couple married in early 1858, two months after Vicky's seventeen birthday.[47] While it is not clear to what extent the royal couple had in mind a specific match for Vicky when Winterhalter was completing his large family portrait in 1846, it seems prescient that he presents the Princess Royal (who turned six during the months the painting was in progress) as a prematurely maternal figure who gazes down fondly at her baby sister Helena. The only member of the family to engage the viewer's eye, Helena in turn uses the power of her gaze to draw the viewer's attention to the tender scene.[48]

Victoria's delight with Winterhalter's "chef d'oeuvre" suggests that the royal couple relished the opportunity it afforded them to proclaim their success in meeting the goals Stockmar had set for them four years earlier. Here, it seemed, was proof that theirs was a well-ordered family unit with patriarchy firmly in place and contented, well-behaved children, ripe with the promise of bringing happiness and prosperity to the nation. Yet, the reality was more complicated, as the painting was inevitably an expression of their aspirations as parents, rather than a simple reflection of their achievement. If idealized children could be contained within, and their significance largely controlled by, such two-dimensional images, actual children—living, breathing beings with ideas and aspirations of their own—evaded easy containment and control. Raising real children, as Albert certainly realized, was inherently a spatial problem.

CHILDREN'S SPACES IN ROYAL REGULATIONS

Albert's concern with the spatial dimension of child-rearing is evident in a series of "regulations" that the methodical prince used both as a tool to hammer out agreements with the sovereign about their approach to managing the upbringing of their offspring and also as a means of presenting a united front to the staff entrusted with carrying out the wishes of the royal parents. Drafted by Albert in December 1840, just weeks after Vicky's birth in November, the first of these provided written instructions for the nursery's management. A revised version was signed by both Victoria and Albert in 1841—presumably early in that year, given the similarities between the two texts and the fact that the revision names both Vicky's wet nurse (Mrs. Ratsey, a sailmaker's wife from Cowes on the Isle of Wight) and her monthly nurse.[49] In most cases, the role of the monthly nurse was to attend the birth and care for both mother and newborn for a number of weeks afterward. Victoria, however, had her own monthly nurse, Mrs. Lilly, who attended all nine of her confinements.[50] Together, the documents reveal the size of the nursery staff; the degree to which the nursery was already a site of conflict between Albert and Victoria's former governess, Baroness Lehzen; and the extent to which the prince understood the space of the nursery as a proxy for his own presence.

At the head of the nursery staff was the superintendent, Mrs. Southey, whose "quiet, simple and pleasing" appearance impressed the queen when they first met in February 1841.[51] Soon, however, it became clear that she was ill suited to the role outlined for her in the 1840–41 regulation, which gave the superintendent great authority over the management of the nursery, specifying that "the persons attached to it are to obey her in every respect." That staff included the wet nurse; the nurse, a Mrs. Roberts; the nursery maid, Charlotte Whiting; and an unnamed housemaid. Connected with the nursery on a temporary basis, the monthly nurse stood somewhat outside the nursery pecking order, as the superintendent was instructed "not to interfere with the management of the Child's person as long as the monthly nurse Mrs. Pegley is charged with it."[52]

If the monthly nurse was given a certain amount of latitude in her work, the wet nurse was not. Indeed, Albert's first version of the nursery regulation instructed the superintendent "to watch especially the wetnurse," suggesting that he shared widely held anxieties about the practice of hiring a stranger to breastfeed an infant born into an elite family. Worries about moral contagion were particularly acute in situations where the wet nurse was an unmarried woman, who may have had few other options for making a living in the months after giving birth herself. Victoria and Albert were able to insist on hiring only married women to feed their children, but there were still concerns that the milk of lower-status women might harm the constitutions of babies born to parents of a higher class. In addition to "standard concerns about a wet nurse's diet and drinking habits," literary scholar Melisa Klimaszewski has noted that middle-class and aristocratic mothers were also cautioned that "ostensibly healthy nurses could transmit negative moral, mental, physical, and emotional traits to infants through their nearly magical breast milk."[53] Although Albert's instruction "to watch especially the wetnurse" was not included in the revised regulation of 1841, the final document did command that "the Wetnurse is always to get up, when she nurses the child."[54] While biographers have interpreted this directive as an attempt to ensure that the wet nurse stood in order to acknowledge the rank of the royal infant at her breast, it may have also addressed more widespread concerns.[55] As stereotypes of the drunken wet nurse took hold, so too did worries that a recumbent nurse might "overlay," and so suffocate, the infant in her care.[56] Alternatively, the directive can be read as ensuring that the wet nurse did not cradle the child in her lap while nursing, thus mitigating the possibility that she might replace the birth mother in the child's affections.[57]

While the regulation that Victoria and Albert signed in 1841 entrusted the superintendent with complete authority over the regular nursery staff, it also called upon her "to conform herself to the wishes of the Queen & Prince & not to attend or listen to the directions given to her by *anybody* else, but the Queen & Prince in *person*, to whom she alone is responsible" (emphasis in the original).[58] This last instruction seems to have been an early attempt on Albert's part to circumscribe the influence of Lehzen, who still served as Victoria's closest confidante and someone of whom Albert's biographers agree he was fiercely jealous.[59] Eventually, Victoria agreed to make changes in the nursery staff and sent Lehzen away with a generous pension.[60] From April 1842 on, the Lady Superintendents of the royal nursery were aristocratic widows, first Lady Sarah Lyttelton (from 1842 to 1851) followed by Lady Caroline Barrington (from 1851 until Princess Beatrice left the schoolroom in 1865; although she retained the title of Lady Superintendent, Lady Barrington essentially served as Princess Beatrice's lady's maid from 1865 until her own death ten years later).[61]

Woven throughout the regulation of 1840–41 are references to the use of space:

> She [the superintendent] is expected whenever the Child leaves the room to go with it. Not to show the Child to anybody whomsoever without the Queen's or Prince's leave or to take the child out except with their permission. The Child is never to be left alone. . . . For seeing Persons, she [the superintendent] has a room downstairs, as nobody is allowed to visit the nursery. When leaving the room she is to entrust the Child to the care of the Nurse.[62]

These tight restrictions on the use of space speak to the concerns of the royal parents, who sought to foreclose any possibility of their infant daughter's either accidentally injuring herself or being harmed by an intruder. When Vicky was just a few weeks old, the press reported that a seventeen-year-old boy (a tailor's son by the name of Jones) had managed to make his way into the heart of Buckingham Palace, where he claims to have sat upon the throne and "heard the Princess Royal squall."[63] Although Jones does not seem to have meant any harm to the royal baby, the royal couple may have also already started receiving written threats against the child; certainly, by February 1842, after Bertie's birth, Albert had installed what Lady Lyttleton described to her daughter as an complicated system of "intricate turns and locks and guardrooms," to control access to the children's apartments. "The most important key," she noted, "is never out of Prince Albert's own keeping."[64] At the same time, the royal parents seemed intent on protecting the infant princess from the merely curious, who might share their impressions of the queen's offspring with the wider world. Although the royal couple would certainly make images of Vicky and her future siblings publicly available, they preferred to manage that process themselves. In short, faced with their own royal duties, Victoria and especially Albert sought to use space as a means of exerting a level of control they were not able to impose in person.

In January 1847, weeks after Vicky turned six and Bertie reached the age of five, Victoria and Albert signed yet another joint memo in which they outlined a long-term plan for the education of their children (who at that point numbered five), dividing them into age-based classes. From the age of one month until they were five or six years old, children would be in the first class and cared for in the nursery. The "chief objects here" were to be "their physical development, the actual rearing up, [and] the training to obedience." Although they were understood to be "too little for *real* instruction," they were expected to learn their figures and counting and to receive instruction in speaking English, French, and German.[65]

At age five or six, the children were to enter the second class. While they would continue to sleep in the nursery, they would begin to receive instruction in arithmetic, geography, history, and English grammar from the governess, Miss Sarah Anne Hildyard, who started her duties in early 1847 and continued in the role until 1865, when Beatrice left the nursery.[66] Even with these new studies, children in the second class were expected to devote an hour a day each to French and German, under the tutelage of their French and German governesses.[67] The memorandum also specified that upon entering the second class, the Princess Royal would have a maid to herself.

Upon entry into the third class, the paths of male and female children would begin to diverge. Not only did Victoria and Albert envision Bertie entering the third class earlier (that is, at age six or seven), they also imagined that this would be the moment at which his education would be directed by a male tutor and that he would begin to be attended by a valet. In contrast, they envisioned the Princess Royal entering the third class in her ninth or tenth year. Although she would continue to have "masters for various sciences and arts," they underlined the fact that "the acquirement of good manners is one of the main objects of this class." Thus, at this point, she would receive "a Lady Governess, who will be able to go into society with her & may stay with her till she marries."[68] The fourth class was reserved for male children, who at age of twelve or thirteen—at least according to the memo—would require "a person to introduce him into life & the world," in short, a governor.[69]

The gendered character of this educational schema would have been familiar to British elites, who ensured that daughters and sons were educated differently. In their study of masculinity among the landed gentry in the eighteenth and nineteenth centuries, historians Henry French and Mark Rothery have noted that fathers, particularly, sought "to ensure that their sons were weaned from dependence upon female care and attention," and saw their departure from the nursery as a definite stage of development.[70] While sons of gentry families commonly left home for boarding school by age eight or nine, girls were typically educated at home, remaining dependent on their families. Lenore Davidoff has suggested that education was "meaningless" to the future life of an elite girl, who was destined only for the role she would play in the "status theatre" of the marriage market. Thus, she argued, "from the time the little girl entered the school room at about the age of five until she 'came out' at seventeen or eighteen, there was nothing to mark her progress in the way of promotions, certificates or even variation in dress."[71] To be sure, Victoria and Albert did not consider the education of their daughters meaningless and were particularly attentive to the instruction of the intellectually gifted Vicky. Nonetheless, they shared with Victoria's subjects a sense that education played different roles for their male and female offspring, enough so that they deemed just three classes sufficient for the girls, whose ultimate destination was the polite sphere of "society," while their boys had access to a fourth class, which constituted their entry into a wider realm—"the world."

Other aspects of the education Albert and Victoria imagined in 1847 would have seemed less familiar to the queen's landed subjects, among them the attempt to determine in advance the age at which their children would move from one class to another. Although such age grading had been introduced in Prussia in the late eighteenth century, and would eventually become commonplace in Great Britain with the introduction of a national system of education, in the 1860s British public schools included a wide age range in each form or division.[72] As a result, nineteenth-century gentry families accepted the idea that children matured at different speeds and sometimes found it difficult to decide exactly when a given boy was ready to leave home for boarding school.[73] In the end, Victoria and Albert foud it impossible to stick to the age ranges they had determined for each of the classes. Instead, they made important decisions—such as when one of their sons would come under the control of a governor—based on the aptitudes and interests of the individual boy. Bertie, for instance, was seventeen when he received his first governor, Colonel Robert Bruce, in 1858, while his brother, Affie, was twelve when Lieutenant John Cowell was appointed his governor in order to help the boy prepare for the Royal Navy.[74]

Equally innovative was the content of the education outlined in the 1847 memorandum, which emphasized proficiency in French and German and specified instruction in arithmetic, geography, history, and English grammar for children in the second class. The memo is vague about the content of lessons in the third class, perhaps because the eldest children would not reach this stage in their education for some years. By the time Henry Birch was employed in 1849 as Bertie's first male tutor, Albert had devised a rigorous schedule that structured the Prince of Wales's day from the time he got up at 7:00 a.m. to soon after 8:00 p.m., when he went to bed. While Birch reported that he varied what he taught at any given moment of the day "according to the state in which he finds the Prince" (who was a notoriously recalcitrant pupil), he covered religious instruction, arithmetic, spelling, writing from dictation, reading, geography, history, maps, and elementary readings in botany, natural history, and Latin grammar; Bertie had other teachers for German and French. In addition, the Master of the Queen's Music provided piano lessons for half an hour four times a week, while watercolorist William Leighton Leitch came in twice a week to teach the Prince of Wales to paint.[75] Strikingly modern, this curriculum was distinctly different from the classical education elite boys received in these same years, as they learned to read and write ancient Greek as well as Latin.[76]

Perhaps the most important difference between the education the royal parents planned for their sons and that experienced by the male offspring of Victoria's elite subjects was its context, that is, where it would take place and the role of other boys. The 1847 memo makes it clear that Bertie would be educated at home (that is, at Buckingham Palace, Windsor Castle, Osborne, and eventually at Balmoral) under the direction of a private tutor, as had been the practice for at least a century. As boys in the 1740s, the future George III and his brother Edward had received private tutelage at Kew. In the late 1760s, George III's own elder sons, the future George IV and Frederick (later the Duke of York and Albany) were also educated at Kew, where they lived with their own household, including their governor and tutors.[77] In contrast, the sons of elite families commonly left home for boarding school at age eight or nine, sometimes spending a few years in a small prep school or at a private school in the home of a tutor before continuing on to Eton, Winchester, or another of Britain's "public schools." As French and Rothery have argued, the primary goal of these educational experiences was to prepare boys for adult masculinity, defined as the "autonomous exercise of authority" and particularly important for the landed elite precisely because "their position as the 'natural rulers' of the country depended on the demonstration of their fitness to rule, which emphasized gendered qualities of personal autonomy, independent judgment, and self-command."[78] At public schools, this imperative resulted in a heavy reliance on "boy government"; a master's purview was limited to his classroom, while everywhere else senior boys were empowered to dominate their juniors, a system that could result in verbal, physical, and sexual abuse.[79] The reform of public schools was debated between the 1830s and 1860s and famously enacted under Thomas Arnold at Rugby in the 1830s and 1840s. Nonetheless, boy government remained a fixture, its supporters arguing that it was integral to "the great glory of the English public school—the free development of character, its social expansiveness, in short its *liberty*."[80] Arguably, an educational experience that prepared boys to control themselves so that they would be fit to command others in their adult years would have been particularly important for Victoria's sons and especially her heir. The private education to which Bertie was subjected certainly failed in this regard. The Prince of Wales often lost control of himself, flinging things about, kicking away his stool, grimacing, calling his tutor names, and even striking him with a stick.[81] He was also educated largely in isolation. Affie shared his lessons for a short time, in hopes that the second son would serve as a role model for his older brother, but when Affie began to follow Bertie's lead, the experiment was abandoned. Eventually, Bertie attended Oxford, although he was not allowed to live with other students.

Given the royal couple's commitment to educating their children at home, Albert was attentive to the architectural settings in which the new system would play out. Regarding the first class, for instance, the 1847 memo explicitly stated that it "is in a state which will require no alteration. The Locality is well adapted." The timing of the memo makes it clear that the locality they had in mind was Buckingham Palace and the nursery wing that had been reworked by architect Edward Blore, acting under Albert's direction, in 1844 (Figure 1.6). Some of these changes focused on increasing room sizes. In the service end of the nursery wing, the nursery kitchen (G) and the room next to it (F), for instance, were enlarged by allowing them to encroach on the corridor. At the other end of the wing, Albert had Blore remove a wall that had once divided one of the day nurseries (A on the plan) into two smaller rooms. This change may have been motivated by a desire to enhance the nursery's natural lighting and air circulation, as each of the original rooms had only a single window; although the room was located on the building's public face directly above the

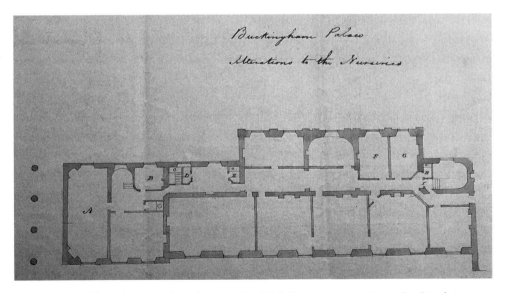

FIGURE 1.6. Plan, showing alterations to the third-floor nursery suite at Buckingham Palace. According to a note on the drawing, these changes were "seen & approved by Prince Albert July 6th 1844." Edward Blore, architect, 1844. RCIN 918132. Royal Collection Trust / copyright 2023 His Majesty King Charles III.

Queen's luncheon room, John Nash's neoclassical design called for a sculptural frieze that superseded any fenestration at the attic level. The balance of the changes were focused on enhancing nursery hygiene: laying on hot water in the bath (B), adding a closet for dirty clothes (D), adding a water closet (E), relocating the entrance to an existing water closet (H), placing a coal box in the nursery kitchen (G), and making existing skylights operable. Albert ordered no changes to the nursery bedroom (the largest room in the nursery wing) or to the nursery dining room (the rectangular room on the other side of the corridor and located adjacent to the curved stair).

As for the second class, the 1847 memo specified that the governess Miss Hildyard was to have two rooms, "a bedroom to herself & a room adjoining for the School room." Indeed, there was some urgency in deciding on the spatial container for this class, as the memo also specified that "the Princess Royal and the Prince of Wales are to enter this class & the new System is to begin on our return to town at the end of February."[82] A month later, in February 1847, Blore's plans for enlarging the nurseries at Windsor Castle were accepted. According to these plans, a room that had most recently served as Albert's sitting room was converted into the schoolroom, while Albert's former dressing room became Miss Hildyard's bedroom.[83] At Buckingham Palace, rooms adjacent to the queen's audience room were used as a schoolroom and the governess's room at some point during Victoria's reign, although the only evidence of this scheme is a plan generated toward the end of her life. Nonetheless, the widowed queen was notoriously loath to change any arrangement Albert had put into place; the same plan, for instance, retained the Prince Consort's dressing room, some forty years after his death. Given that the schoolroom and governess's room are adjoining, as specified in the memo, this may be the arrangement put in place in the late 1840s.

In contrast, the memo was silent on the spatial implications of the third class and the fourth class, which were, after all, still abstractions in January 1847. Far from losing interest in the spaces that would help mold his children as they approached their maturities, Albert maintained an acute interest in the issue. Indeed, within months of signing the memo, Albert would begin to oversee the design and construction of the so-called main wing at Osborne, a project that was underway until 1851.[84] By 1850, he had also established a children's precinct at Osborne, where in 1853 work would begin on a Swiss Cottage designated for the use of his offspring.[85] In short, Albert's endeavors at Osborne from 1847 on can be understood as an attempt to give shape to the needs of the older children, as they entered the third class and their educations were more explicitly determined by gender and rank. At the same time, the children's spaces he created highlight the dual character of Osborne—in part a country house arranged for relatively intimate domesticity, in part a royal palace supporting the functions of court society.

OSBORNE AS A COUNTRY HOUSE

Albert took the lead role in the design of the new Osborne. Indeed, the decision to employ a builder, rather than an architect, was controversial at the time and may well have been motivated by a desire on the part of the Prince Consort to play a central role in the design process. Thomas Cubitt brought other strengths to the project. His experience in developing large swaths of terraced housing meant that he had in place an extensive integrated organization that allowed him to coordinate every aspect of the large and complicated project. Except for the fancy painting in the state rooms, his crews took on all the work. They built roads, moved earth, constructed the building's purportedly fireproof shell, installed the plumbing and heating systems, fitted out the kitchens, and applied a wide range of finishes, calibrated to the importance of any given room. With few exceptions (among them the chandeliers and Minton tiles), Cubitt provided everything, from the hot-water system to the doormats. He even opened a brickworks about three miles from the site, although other materials (including the iron girders used to support the brick arches that formed the floors) came either from London or farther afield. This integration facilitated the prompt completion of every stage of the project and kept the costs within Cubitt's estimates, a consideration of no little import to the royal couple, who were paying for the house out of the privy purse.[86]

Cubitt was also known for the stylistic consistency of his output, so much so that engaging his services suggests Albert had already settled on the Italianate mode for Osborne, a choice often traced to the fact that the coastline of the Isle of Wight reminded the Prince Consort of the Bay of Naples and more recently interpreted as an attempt to emulate the formal qualities of any number of country houses designed for the Prussian royal family by Karl Friedrich Schinkel and his pupil Ludwig Persius.[87] Certainly, the use of this formal vocabulary allowed Osborne to communicate on a variety of levels to a range of audiences, a quality that may well have enhanced its appeal. During his travels in Europe in the 1830s, Albert had absorbed Picturesque theory and embraced the Italianate mode as an effective means of cladding an asymmetrical composition in the language of classicism, one he associated with English Palladianism and the Whig aristocracy.[88] Indeed, architect Charles Barry had already started using the Italianate in the 1830s for the Whig Reform Club (1837–41), as well as for aristocratic country houses, notably Trentham Hall (1834–42) in Staffordshire, for the 2nd Duke of Sutherland (the duchess was one of Victoria's ladies-in-waiting), and Walton House (1835–39) in Surrey, for the 5th Earl of Tankerville. Equally important, books such John Claudius Loudon's 1833 *Encyclopedia of Cottage, Farm and Villa Architecture* had brought the mode to the attention of middle-class Britons, while Andrew Jackson Downing's publications, among them

The Architecture of Country Houses (1850), did the same for many genteel Americans. As architectural historian Rosemary Yallop has noted, the Italianate comprised two "parallel strands"—one palatial (popularized by Barry and evident at the main house at Osborne, especially on the garden façade) and the other rustic (often associated with John Nash and used by Cubitt at some of Osborne's outbuildings).[89] Thus, the Italianate was simultaneously Picturesque, and therefore redolent of informality for elite and middle-class audiences, but also capable of communicating, in Yallop's words, "hierarchy of function and status."[90] This multivalence served the needs of the royal couple admirably.

As completed in 1851, Osborne consisted of two distinct buildings sitting in juxtaposition to one another without cohering into a unified whole (see Figure 1.1). Largely completed by September 1846, the Pavilion was self-consciously domestic in design and originally contained most—but not all—of the spaces used by the royal family when Victoria and Albert's children were young. In contrast, the adjacent U-shaped building was designed primarily—but not exclusively—to accommodate court functions: a council chamber and audience room on the first floor of the main wing (the leg of the U closest to the Pavilion) and accommodations for Victoria's ladies-in-waiting, equerries, and their own maids and valets in the household wing (the leg of the U farthest from the Pavilion). The main and household wings are connected by the Grand Corridor, which forms the bottom of the U and faces the entry courtyard. The whole is distinctly nondomestic in form, at least in nineteenth-century terms. Lower and broader than the Pavilion, these wings present a reserved and disciplined façade to the carriage circle; from this vista, nothing breaks the skyline or interrupts the regular rhythm established by two levels of arcades, an arrangement that ultimately harks back to Italian palazzi of the early modern era, but that was used in the eighteenth and nineteenth centuries for structures associated with bureaucratic order.[91]

Osborne's lack of coherence has sometimes been seen as a design flaw resulting from Cubitt's want of professional architectural credentials.[92] Mark Girouard, for instance, opined that "the professional ease with which Barry would combine symmetrical parts into an irregular whole is noticeably lacking at Osborne."[93] At the same time, he also suggested that Osborne's spatial organization was ultimately derived from Barry's design for Trentham Hall, where a compact family pavilion was attached to the side of an expansive main block containing the principal entertaining rooms. As Girouard notes, the benefit of the arrangement was that it allowed the activities of the house to shrink down into the family pavilion when the Sutherlands were not hosting a large house party. If the footprints of the two estates are superficially similar, however, the houses functioned quite differently. At Osborne, for instance, the Pavilion is arguably the main block, as the house's principal entertaining rooms (dining room, drawing room, and billiard room) are located there on the first floor. Equally important, it was never possible for the activities of the house to shrink into the Pavilion, in large part because most of the people who used the household wing were not houseguests, who would come and go. Instead, they were members of the queen's household, a stable presence in Victoria's residence at Osborne. Ultimately, it may be more productive to acknowledge that the country house of a reigning monarch was destined to be a one-off—in this case, a complex set of spaces that both emphasized the intimacy of the nuclear family (so important to Victoria's presentation of self), while also supporting the rigid social hierarchies that structured and defined royal life. The spaces of childhood are especially informative about the difficulties involved in balancing these competing priorities. In particular, the architecture of the main wing points to challenges the royal children posed to the queen's public persona as they approached their maturity and highlights the extent to which architecture helped mitigate their potentially disruptive presence.

THE SPATIAL ORGANIZATION OF THE PAVILION

On the inside, many aspects of the Pavilion's spatial arrangements were akin to those in country houses being built or remodeled by Victoria's monied subjects and by their American counterparts, including wealthy industrialists whose fortunes enabled them to buy estates and enjoy the prestige that accompanied such purchases. Chief among them was the strict separation of rooms for entertaining (on the first floor) from those more private spaces (on the upper floors) devoted to the family's use, with attendant service spaces in place on all levels (Figures 1.7 and 1.8). As Girouard has noted, from about 1770 on, the state bedrooms that had once claimed prime real estate on the first floor had either disappeared, as the concept of state waned, or moved upstairs, as "people began to feel that upstairs bedrooms were part of the order of things."[94] This shift allowed the first floor to be given over to entertaining rooms, which at Osborne included a dining room, drawing room, and billiard room. Separate billiard rooms became increasingly commonplace in English and American country houses in the nineteenth century, and on both sides of the Atlantic they were increasingly located at the heart of a distinctly male preserve that often included some combination of other rooms used by the male owner: a study, a business room, and a smoking room.[95] At Osborne, where Victoria was inevitably the center of attention, there was no such masculine zone; indeed, the billiard room opened onto the drawing room, a space Victorians on both sides of the Atlantic understood as distinctly feminine.[96] Nonetheless, the billiard room was positioned around the corner from the drawing room in an arrangement that allowed the gentlemen to skirt

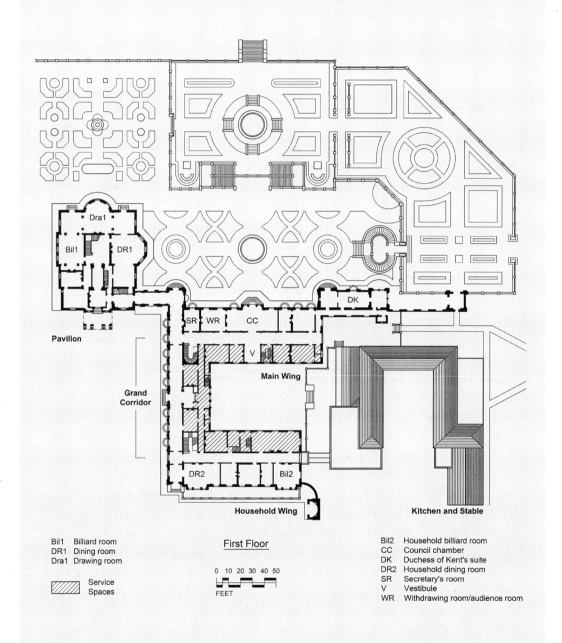

FIGURE 1.7. First-floor plan, Osborne, Isle of Wight. Thomas Cubitt, architect, 1846–51. Drawing by Daniel De Sousa.

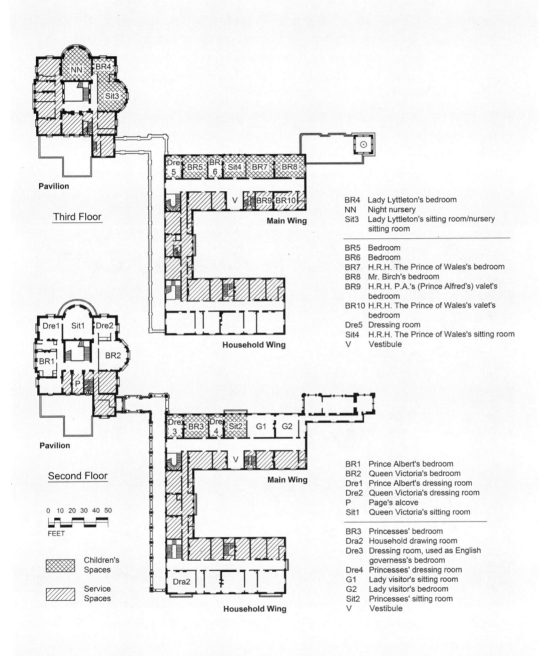

FIGURE 1.8. Second- and third-floor plans, Osborne, Isle of Wight. Thomas Cubitt, architect, 1846–51. Drawing by Daniel De Sousa.

the protocol that required them to stand in the queen's presence, unless given permission to sit.[97] This nod toward informality also touched the design of all three entertaining rooms, each of which was subdivided by flat arches, supported by piers in the dining room and by freestanding columns in the drawing and billiard rooms (Figure 1.9). The result was a series of nearly square spaces that moderated the axial organization of each room and could accommodate the kind of informal gatherings that had been introduced toward the end of the eighteenth century, when society abandoned the "circle" (and the accompanying expectation that everyone present would socialize together) in favor of social events that allowed smaller groups of people to do different things at the same time.[98]

Other aspects of the Pavilion's first-floor arrangements would have seemed outmoded by 1846, especially the presence of three entertaining rooms, organized in a

FIGURE 1.9. Drawing room in the Pavilion at Osborne, Isle of Wight, showing Mary Thornycroft's marble portraits *Prince Alfred as "Autumn,"* 1846 (to left of window), and *Princess Beatrice in the Nautilus Shell*, 1858 (on table in the window bay). Thomas Cubitt, architect, 1846–51. André Adolphe-Eugène Disdéri, photographer, 1867. *The Osborne Album: Thirty-three Photographic Views of the Queen's Marine Residence at Osborne* (London and Paris: [André Adolphe-Eugène] Disdéri, 1867), 14.

single circuit around a central stair. Similar arrangements had been commonplace in the second half of the eighteenth century, accommodating elegant balls in which dancing, card games, and supper would take place in separate rooms, all of which communicated with the stair hall. By Victoria's youth, however, house parties had replaced balls as the favored mode of sociability in English country houses. Where once elite adults had spent their days in individual suites reserved for their use, by the early nineteenth century, guests were expected to spend their time in common rooms on the first floor, where the breakfast room served as a morning sitting room and the library was the main informal living room.[99] In fact, Osborne had neither breakfast room nor library, suggesting that Victoria and Albert did not envision Osborne as a setting for this mode of entertaining. Indeed, some members of the household had their own sitting rooms and there were both a drawing room and a dining room in the household wing for the use of ladies-in-waiting and equerries, while overnight visitors—often European royals—were provided with suites of their own in the main wing, as was Victoria's mother, the Duchess of Kent. In short, the dignity of the royal family and their regal guests required spatial arrangements that might well have seemed somewhat old-fashioned and stiff to the inhabitants of country houses where the architecture itself nurtured informality.

If aspects of the Pavilion's first-floor arrangements differed from those favored by Victoria's subjects, its upper floors followed the tendency to create family quarters that supported spousal and family intimacy. To be sure, the original design continued an older pattern in which husband and wife were provided with separate apartments, each of which included a dressing room, bathroom, and bedroom. In practice, however, Albert's bedroom, adjacent to his bathroom, was not often used for its original purpose and in the 1870s was converted into a schoolroom for Beatrice's children.[100] Equally telling, both dressing rooms communicated with Victoria's sitting room, where the couple worked side by side at matching desks.

Even more significant was the proximity of the younger children to their parents. Conventionally, children's rooms had been an afterthought in elite British houses, with nurseries often wedged into leftover spaces in the attic, as indeed they had been at Buckingham Palace. Thus, Victoria experienced Claremont (a house she and Albert borrowed from their uncle Leopold) as a revelation. On one visit in 1843, just before the birth of her third child, the young queen wrote in her diary: "All this is so pleasant here, at Claremont, where the Nursery is so close to our room, whereas alas! at Buckingham Palace, it is literally a mile off, so that we cannot run in & out as we would like."[101] Indeed, during that stay at Claremont, Victoria recorded frequent visits to the nursery, which she described as "such a delightful large room." There, she noted, "both little things [that is, Vicky and Bertie] were playing about so happily, & Albert & I helped them to arrange their bricks, building up a tower for them."[102] One of the great benefits of building Osborne from scratch, then, was the opportunity it afforded to provide a similarly delightful nursery situated directly above the parental apartments, an arrangement that was becoming commonplace by midcentury.[103] As in the houses of Victoria's monied subjects (and increasingly of their American counterparts as well), the nursery at Osborne was a suite of rooms used to corral the daily activities of young children, ensuring they did not disrupt their parents' routines.[104] When the family first moved into the Pavilion, the queen noted in her diary that "the Children's quarters" included "nurseries, school room, governesses room, &c." As was common practice in middle-class and aristocratic houses, the younger children slept all together in the nursery bedroom, just above their mother's sitting room (Figure 1.10). Although Osborne did not provide a private stairway to connect the nursery and Victoria's dressing room, as did some nineteenth-century country houses, the queen, nonetheless, declared the arrangements "convenient, spacious & well carried out." In her view, "M[r] Cubitt has done it admirably."[105]

FIGURE 1.10. Nursery bedroom in the Pavilion at Osborne, Isle of Wight. English Heritage has re-created this room based on a photograph taken in 1873, when the nursery was used by Queen Victoria's grandchildren. Thomas Cubitt, architect, 1846–51. Photograph by the author.

Parental visits to the nursery tapered off as the family grew and as Albert took on a greater public role. Nonetheless, the royal children remained an important part of their parents' lives, often spending at least a small part of each day with the royal couple. In this, they followed the practice of Victoria's grandparents: the clock on the wall in Zoffany's portrait of Queen Charlotte with her two eldest sons from 1764 gives the hour as 2:30, the time each day that the princes were brought in to see their mother.[106] Although Victoria and Albert did not plan their own schedules around their children's activities on a daily or weekly basis (as was becoming the norm for middle-class families), they did make a special point of celebrating each child's birthday as a family. Whether they were at Osborne, Windsor Castle, or Buckingham Palace, the day began in the same way: the royal couple arranged the birthday gifts on a table in the breakfast room and then fetched the child from the nursery or schoolroom. The family—often including the Duchess of Kent—breakfasted together, while gifts were opened, and then walked out as a group.[107] The children also featured largely in their parents' birthday and anniversary celebrations—not just as the subjects of the works of art that Victoria and Albert gave each other, but also in a range of special performances. When the children were very young, the royal couple treated their offspring as charming playthings, dressing them up in specially prepared costumes. In 1844, for instance, Albert had Vicky and Bertie dress as peasants of Gotha as a surprise for Victoria's twenty-fifth birthday, while on the couple's anniversary in 1846, two-and-a-half-year-old Affie was dressed as Henry VIII. (Again, the parallels with George III and Charlotte are striking; in the Zoffany portrait mentioned earlier, the princes are in fancy dress, the future George IV impersonating Telemachus and his brother, Frederick, clad as a Turk.)[108] As the children grew, their contributions to these celebrations were more substantial: reciting poetry, playing musical instruments, and performing plays. On the couple's wedding anniversary in 1852, Victoria had the six eldest children perform a fragment from Racine's *Athalie*—in French—as a surprise for their father. The next year, it was a "very pretty little German Children's piece," and the year after, a series of *tableaux vivants* of the four seasons.[109]

In many respects, then, the Pavilion functioned like other nineteenth-century country houses on both sides of the Atlantic. To be sure, the first-floor entertaining rooms had been adjusted to the needs of a royal household, as the informality embraced in other domiciles had its limits in the presence of a queen regnant. Nonetheless, the house nurtured spousal and family intimacy by creating a private family zone on the building's upper floors. A nursery suite—designed for the purpose and located in proximity to the parental apartments—facilitated regular interaction between parents and children. Inside and out, the Pavilion celebrated Victoria's maternal role and announced the importance of children and family life to the queen and her consort.

And it worked. When the new structure was described in *The Builder* in 1848, the anonymous author "was most anxious not to present even the appearance of an attempt to invade a privacy to which the illustrious owners have a right to claim," and thus limited the discussion of interior arrangements to the entertaining rooms on the ground floor of the Pavilion. Yet, even this limited examination prompted the writer to opine that "we shall be deceived if Osborne do[es] not become hallowed in the eyes of Englishmen as the seat of such quiet virtues, affectionate solicitudes, and intellectual enjoyments, as are not usually the characteristic of the occupants of thrones."[110] In short, the Pavilion served as material evidence that Victoria was an appropriately domesticated woman and thus a commendable queen.

INSIDE THE MAIN AND HOUSEHOLD WINGS

Osborne, however, was more than the Pavilion, and Victoria was more than a wife and mother. However much she may have wanted to understand and experience Osborne as a retreat from her regal responsibilities, the person of the sovereign inevitably defined the locus of the court; as queen regnant, she could not escape court life entirely. Indeed, the U-shaped building containing the main and household wings accommodated the functions of court and reinforced the hierarchies that were inseparable from its effective operation. In its size, spatial organization, room functions, and human inhabitants, it contrasted sharply with the Pavilion. At the same time, it also offered an important complement to the Pavilion, freeing up the Italianate villa to serve—to the extent that it did—as the *gemütlich* family home Victoria imagined when she wrote of "poor dear, modest unpretentious Osborne."[111]

State visitors approached the house from one of two routes. Those arriving by land—if royal—gained access to the estate via The Arch and continued along a tree-lined drive called The Avenue (indicated by a solid line in Figure 1.11). Those arriving by water alit at the Osborne Pier and were conveyed via carriage on the Pier Road that skirted the estate's informal Park (indicated by a dashed line) and converged with The Avenue not far from the heavily planted Mount, a landscape feature that temporarily obscured the house from view. Thus, both routes presented the house as a revelation, a stately pile dramatically breaking the horizon line. In contrast, those of lesser rank entered through the Prince of Wales Entrance and followed a secondary road (indicated by a dotted line) that provided easy access to the kitchen wing and stable in the estate's service area; this road also communicated with the carriage ring in front of the house, but it ran alongside the household wing, undercutting the drama of the approach afforded from The Avenue.

State visitors alit from their carriages not under the Pavilion's porte-cochère, but in front of a door in the middle of the U-shaped building's restrained façade.

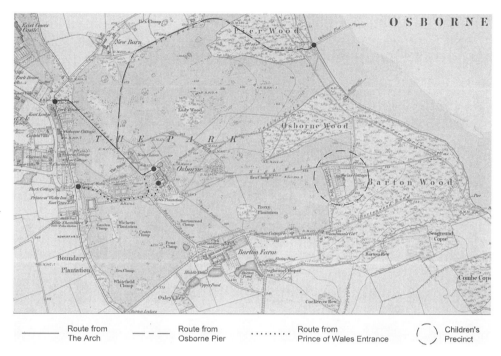

FIGURE 1.11. Osborne estate, Isle of Wight, as surveyed in 1863. The solid line marks The Avenue, running from The Arch to the house; the dashed line follows the drive from the Osborne Pier; and the dotted line indicates the route from the so-called Prince of Wales Entrance. The dashed circle marks the location of the children's precinct. Ordnance Survey Map of Hampshire and Isle of Wight, published in 1866, sheet XC, with annotations by Daniel De Sousa. CC-BY. Reprinted with permission of the National Library of Scotland.

Once inside, they immediately encountered a full-size marble statue of Victoria in a shrine-like setting (Figure 1.12). Elevated on a deep shelf above a fireplace, in a situation that evoked the household gods revered by the Romans, and set against a gilded background, it stood in a compass-headed niche within an alcove framed by freestanding classical columns. Sculpted by John Gibson, the original was commissioned in 1844 by Victoria and installed in Buckingham Palace in 1847; the version at Osborne is a replica Victoria presented to Albert on his birthday in August 1849. Both versions show the queen crowned, dressed in classical garb, and holding a laurel wreath and a scroll—in short, in her official role as sovereign, the upholder of law and the bestower of honor.[112] At Osborne, the figure is flanked by bas-relief rondels of "Day" and "Night" personified by female figures, works first modeled by Bertel Thorvaldsen in 1815 and widely reproduced in a range of media throughout the nineteenth century. While Day flies upward embraced by a cherubic Genius of Light,

Night carries two babies, her children, "Sleep" and "Death." Associated with maternity and (in the case of Night) sentimental understandings of death as a gentle sleep, these rondels helped frame the public queen with symbols of the private woman and mother.[113]

If the imagery of the alcove reveals some of the tensions attendant upon Victoria's dual role as sovereign and mother, the larger architectural setting focused exclusively on the queen's official position. Lined with statuary, the Grand Corridor provided an imposing and iconographically rich route to the privy council chamber and its adjacent audience room, the most important and stately rooms on the ground floor (Figure 1.13). These were settings where Victoria conducted state business and hosted less intimate gatherings at which she enacted her official role as sovereign, accommodating what sociologist Norbert Elias called "the characteristic double face" of court society, one in which a social event that provided relaxation, amusement, and conversation was simultaneously "the direct instrument of one's career." In this context, social occasions—even glittering ones—were "experienced as duties."[114]

Perhaps the most unusual aspect of the main wing was that two of its three floors were devoted to the use of the four eldest children, who had left the nursery and entered what the memo of 1847 described as "the third class." In many country houses, the practice was to arrange family spaces along a continuum from youngest to eldest. Children's spaces were often clustered together and (if not located in the attic) set at the juncture between the service wing and the main body of the house. Typically, the nursery suite was situated nearest the rooms of servants responsible for handling the messier aspects of childcare: diaper changing, toilet training, bathing, dressing, and feeding. Although often also situated in the service wing, the schoolroom and other spaces devoted to the use of older children were generally positioned closer to their parents' rooms in the main wing.[115] The arrangement at Osborne inverted that practice. Victoria and Albert kept their youngest children close to them in the Pavilion, while the older children were housed at a greater distance from their parents. Indeed, they inhabited what was in essence a separate building, one in which their royal stature and their place in the hierarchy of Victoria's court could be fully expressed, both socially and spatially.

The spaces devoted to the older children were strictly sorted by gender, with the girls and their dressers on the second floor and the boys, with their tutors and valets,

FIGURE 1.12. *Queen Victoria*, in situ in the Grand Corridor of Osborne, Isle of Wight. The life-size portrait, executed by sculptor John Gibson in 1849, faces the entrance to the main wing. The edges of bas-relief rondels of "Day" and "Night," originally modeled by Bertel Thorvaldsen in 1815, are visible on either side of the arched opening. Photograph by the author.

Figure 1.13. The Grand Corridor, Osborne, Isle of Wight, looking toward the household wing. The niche containing John Gibson's *Queen Victoria* is flanked by the freestanding columns visible on the left. Thomas Cubitt, architect, 1846–51. André Adolphe-Eugène Disdéri, photographer, 1867. *The Osborne Album: Thirty-three Photographic Views of the Queen's Marine Residence at Osborne* (London and Paris: [André Adolphe-Eugène] Disdéri, 1867), 6.

on the third. To be sure, gender segregation was a common practice in nineteenth-century country houses, both in the areas where male and female servants worked and slept, as well as in the accommodations provided for houseguests, which separated visiting bachelors from young ladies.[116] In the main wing at Osborne, the practice also helped spatialize the gendered hierarchy that determined the royal succession by elevating the male heir above his elder sister. The architecture of the main and household wings ensured that dynastic concerns structured the daily routines of the young royals.

The main wing had particular significance for the Prince of Wales, as his suite was designed to signal that he had reached a new stage of life. Indeed, the arrival of Bertie's first male tutor (which the memo of 1847 had associated with the entry of a royal son into the third class) coincided precisely with the prince's being moved to his own rooms in Buckingham Palace. On the day Henry Birch first took up his post as tutor in April 1849, Victoria noted in her diary that "we went after luncheon with the Children upstairs to Bertie's rooms, comprising a sitting room, bedroom & Mr Birch's room. They are in the new part of the building, just beyond the Nursery, & very light & airy."[117] That the family went together to inspect this new arrangement and that the queen mentioned this inspection in her diary both suggest that this move was a watershed moment in the life of the Prince of Wales. What is more, the fact that Birch's room was considered one of "Bertie's rooms" indicates that this suite was understood as the young heir's domain. Its location "just beyond the Nursery" makes it clear that the suite was located on the third floor of the palace's new east wing, well away from the rooms inhabited by the prince's royal parents and directly above what came to be called the Princesses' Corridor, which provided rooms for the royal daughters after they left the nursery.[118]

These spatial arrangements at Buckingham Palace were reproduced in the main wing at Osborne, where Bertie's rooms (and those used by his brother Affie) were located directly above the rooms of the elder princesses and well away from the rooms used by the princes' royal parents. Given that there is no connection between the main wing and the Pavilion at the third floor, the princes were even more isolated from their parents than were their sisters, who had relatively easy access to the royal couple. The princes' rooms were cut off from Osborne's other inhabitants as well; the annex that housed on its first floor the suite used by the Duchess of Kent did not extend to the third floor, while the service area formed an effective barrier between the main and household wings at this level. As at Buckingham Palace, three interconnected rooms were designated as belonging to Bertie; the original plans identified the Prince of Wales's sitting room (at the midpoint of the wing's double-loaded corridor), the Prince of Wales's bedroom, and Birch's bedroom. On the other side of Bertie's sitting room were two bedrooms and a dressing room. Although the occupants of these rooms were not identified on the original plans, Affie presumably used one of the bedrooms, as his valet had a bedroom next to that of Bertie's valet on the other side of the corridor. Other auxiliary functions on the side of the corridor facing the service court included W.C.s and two spare bedrooms.[119]

Although this arrangement provided the prince with some of the distance from parental oversight that other elite boys enjoyed at boarding school, the omnipresence of his tutor meant he did not enjoy the freedom that was understood as central to a public-school education. In important ways, it is akin to the setting in which the elder sons of George III had been educated—in their own household at Kew. At Osborne, this isolated situation borders on the punitive and can be seen as the architectural adjunct to the unrelenting schedule imposed upon the heir to the throne, as Albert used spatial and temporal control over his son in his campaign to force the youngster to meet his own exacting standards. According to biographers, Bertie's resistance to this parental pressure only resulted in more discipline and sterner punishment, including isolation from his siblings, setting into motion an endless loop of filial defiance and parental disapproval.[120]

On the floor below were spaces initially used by the two elder princesses—Vicky and Alice—as well as important guests. At the center of this level, facing the garden, was the princesses' shared sitting room; like that of their brothers it was located at the midpoint of the wing's double-loaded corridor. Given that one photograph of the room was labeled "princesses' sitting room" and an identical image was labeled "princesses' school room," the room may have done double duty, particularly for girls now in the third class, where "one of the chief objects" was not book learning but "the acquirement of good manners" (Figure 1.14). The sitting room was flanked on one side by a sitting room and bedroom reserved for important lady visitors and on the other by a suite for the princesses. Originally, this suite included two dressing rooms of identical size communicating with a shared bedroom. However, by the time the main wing was ready for occupation, the dressing room closest to the Pavilion had been pressed into service as a bedroom for Miss Hildyard, and the princesses found themselves sharing a dressing room, as well as a bedroom. On the other side of the corridor, facing into the service courtyard, were auxiliary spaces: W.C.s, the princesses' dressers' rooms, bathrooms, and the service stairs. The corridor also communicated with the small wing housing on its ground floor the suite of rooms used by the Duchess of Kent.

On each floor, the sitting room of the royal children was marked both inside and out as the most important space. Outside, the sitting rooms of the royal children featured tripartite windows, framed with classical orders. The princesses' window is topped with a triangular pediment, while the princes' window takes the form of a Palladian or Serlian window. The tripartite organization not only sets these windows apart from all the others on this façade, but it also draws attention to the fact that these rooms sit directly above the council room. Without usurping the importance of the royal presence in the Pavilion, this façade uses the privy council to elevate—quite literally—the elder royal children and to highlight their regal status.

Inside, the central location of each room was originally highlighted by a vestibule creating a cross axis that extended through the sitting room, out into the formal garden, and down the Broad Walk to the Solent, the strait separating the Isle of Wight from the mainland (Figure 1.15). Not only did this location weave each sitting room into the larger estate, but it also ensured that the elder royal children enjoyed a vista that reached from sitting room to estate, from estate to the Solent and Portsmouth (visible just beyond), from Portsmouth to the rest of Great Britain. Just as at

FIGURE 1.14. The elder princesses' schoolroom, sometimes referred to as the elder princesses' sitting room, in the main wing at Osborne, Isle of Wight. Thomas Cubitt, architect, 1846–51. Photograph by Jabez Hughes, 1873. RCIN 2103660. Royal Collection Trust / copyright 2023 His Majesty King Charles III.

Louis XIV's Versailles, a limitless vista symbolized the extent of the viewer's regal and, ultimately, imperial authority.[121]

The view of the Solent is particularly noteworthy. Characterized by naval historian Andrew Lambert as "the parade ground of the British Empire," the Solent had been central to the display and celebration of England's naval power at least since the eighteenth century, when George III reviewed the fleet at Spithead in 1773.[122] Osborne's proximity to the Solent had been a feature of the estate that particularly appealed to the royal couple, who acknowledged its military importance by commissioning distinguished Scottish artist William Dyce to create a fresco titled *Neptune Resigning the Empire of the Seas to Britannia* (Figure 1.16). Measuring over sixteen feet wide in order to fill the wall at the head of the grand stair hall in the Pavilion,

FIGURE 1.15. View from the princesses' schoolroom in the main wing at Osborne, Isle of Wight. The axial vista extends across the upper terrace, down the Broad Walk, and toward the Solent, the strait between the Isle of Wight and mainland Great Britain. Photograph by the author.

this large and prominently located work confirms that Victoria and Albert reveled in England's naval glories and encouraged their guests to do the same, even it if meant compromising the *gemütlich* character of the Pavilion.[123]

If the internal organization of the main wing expressed the gendered hierarchies that structured the relationships among the royal children, the main wing also functioned in tandem with the household wing to underscore the ultimately unbridgeable distance between the aristocratic men and women of the queen's household and the royals they served (see Figures 1.7 and 1.8). Not only were their quarters distant from the royal presence in the Pavilion, but subtle architectural differences also marked the household wing as distinct from and lesser than the main wing, with its state rooms and accommodations for the elder royal children. To be sure, both wings shared a similar spatial logic, with double-loaded corridors giving access both to the more important rooms (those facing out toward the estate's grounds) and also to the less important spaces (those facing into the service courtyard). Both wings were also designed with separate stairs in the service zone facing the courtyard and a service passageway parallel to the Grand Corridor in order to minimize the presence of the maids and valets who served nobles and royals alike. The dignity of the members of the suite was further expressed by the provision of dressing rooms adjacent to their bedrooms. In contrast, their own attendants had no dressing rooms, just smaller bedrooms overlooking the service courtyard.

FIGURE 1.16. Main stair hall of the Pavilion at Osborne, with *Neptune Resigning the Empire of the Seas to Britannia*, an allegorical fresco painted by William Dyce in 1847. Photograph by the author.

For all these similarities, the main and household wings displayed differences that would have been meaningful to those whose ability to succeed at court depended on their ability to read their environment for every nuance of social hierarchy. For one thing, the service areas functioned as a barrier between the two wings, requiring the queen's noble attendants to use either the Grand Corridor on the ground floor or the arcade on the floor above to move between their accommodations and the main wing. On the third floor, their segregation was absolute, as there was no genteel means of moving directly between the household wing and the Prince of Wales's rooms. They would have also noticed that the corridor in the household wing was shorter and narrower than that in the main wing, that its plastered ceilings were less ornate, and that its broad principal staircase was a simpler, rectilinear version of the curved principal staircase that helped signal the royal character of the main wing (Figure 1.17).

Equally important, the main wing was distinguished from the household wing by the presence of spaces labeled "vestibule" on Cubbitt's plans. Although situated on the central axis on each floor of the main wing, they were located in the service zone that overlooked the courtyard and can be read as service adjuncts to the most important room on each level—that is, the council room on the first floor and the sitting rooms of the princes and princesses on the stories above. Despite Cubitt's labels, however, these spaces did not function as conventional vestibules, in that none of them were adjacent to exterior doors. Instead, they were broad, windowed alcoves similar to the pages' alcove situated directly above the main entrance to the Pavilion and, like it, located adjacent to a service stair. In the Pavilion, a page of the back stairs was on duty in the pages' alcove from 8:00 a.m. until the queen retired and was easily beckoned into the royal presence by the call buttons installed in her desk.[124] The so-called vestibule on the ground floor of the main wing undoubtedly served a similar purpose when the queen was in the council chamber. That there were once identical spaces on the floors above suggests that the attendance of pages was one of the social practices introduced into the lives of the elder royal children once they left the nursery. That there are no comparable spaces in the household wing further marks the main wing as distinctly royal space. At the same time, it points to a parental conviction that even young royals merited a level of attendance that was withheld from the adult nobles who were themselves in attendance on their mother.[125]

If members of the queen's suite readily accommodated themselves to the hierarchies that structured life at court, their private correspondence reveals the extent to which they were nonetheless keenly aware of it. In an 1846 letter to her mother, long-serving maid of honor Lady Eleanor Stanley wrote:

> I met the Queen walking in the garden yesterday, without the Prince, but with the two eldest children, one in each hand, Princess Alice following in a sort of go-cart with

FIGURE 1.17. Stairway in the main wing, at Osborne, Isle of Wight. The curve of this stair contrasts with the rectilinear shape of the corresponding stair in the household wing and helps signal the royal character of the main wing. Thomas Cubitt, architect, 1846–51. Photograph by the author.

Mdlle. Gruner [the German governess], besides three footmen, one to draw the cart, one to carry cloaks, &c., and one with scraps of bread for the swans and ducks. I never saw a more imposing group by way of a quiet family party.[126]

Her concluding comment in particular conveys something of the dissonance she experienced between Victoria's self-presentation and the realities of the queen's privileged existence. Whereas Lady Stanley was describing a scene at Buckingham Palace, Lady Lyttelton wrote from Osborne about the "Patches of children, each attended by their scarlet footmen, shining in the distance."[127] Even at the family's maritime villa, liveried footmen were in constant attendance on the royal children.

Notably, Victoria only mentioned in her diary the presence of footmen when they acted in an exceptional manner, as when an unnamed footman had the presence of mind to pour water over fifteen-year-old Vicky when her sleeve caught fire while she was attempting to seal a letter.[128] In the normal course of events, footmen merited no mention whatsoever. On the day described by Lady Stanley, for instance, the queen wrote only: "After luncheon, Albert went to his Commissions.—Thorburn has begun a miniature of Affie, whom he much admires. I walked with the 3 other[s]."[129] Such an omission confirms Norbert Elias's assertion that footmen and other types of servants were so socially distant from the queen that their constant spatial proximity was rendered invisible to her. Thus, despite Victoria's failure to mention them, footmen were an ever-present fixture of royal life. Indeed, their presence helped create a bubble of royal space that could travel with the queen and her children everywhere they went, including Osborne's children's precinct.

THE PARADOX OF ROYAL CHILDREN

The architecture of Osborne points to the multiple and paradoxical roles the royal children played in the lives of their parents. On one hand, Victoria and Albert were keen to interact with their offspring and arranged the Pavilion to facilitate their access to the nursery. At the same time, the royal couple were also well aware that their children were central to the public persona Victoria (with Albert's help) had crafted so carefully. Not only were the youngsters visible assurance that she understood her duty as a queen to secure the succession, but they also were living proof that she embraced her responsibility as a woman: to marry, to bear her husband's children, to submit to his will about their education and rearing—in short, to uphold patriarchy. Only by presenting herself as a devoted wife and mother could Victoria defuse the concerns raised by the unnatural specter of a queen regnant.

Yet, as the royal children matured, they needed to be prepared to fulfill their parents' dynastic ambitions in other ways. For one thing, they had to grow accustomed to their regal status, something that was expressed in social terms that also ultimately had to be expressed spatially as well. Attended by tutors, governors, governesses, valets, maids, and footmen, they were increasingly at the center of social configurations that bore no resemblance to a nuclear family. Equally important, their relationships with one another were increasingly shaped by the hierarchies of court life, which placed all the children above the noble adults who waited upon the monarch and located all save Bertie below their eldest brother who would one day also become their sovereign.

Ultimately, then, the Pavilion could not contain the elder children, as their presence would disrupt the *tableau vivant* of intimate family life their parents worked so hard to stage there, threating to expose its fragility. For the Pavilion to maintain its effectiveness as a celebration of Victoria's maternal role, the elder children needed to be elsewhere. Initially, Albert's strategy was to design separate accommodations for them in the main wing, a setting where the hierarchies of court life could be recognized and maintained. Yet, even before that wing was finished, he devised another, complementary, strategy, creating a setting where his offspring could temporarily sidestep court hierarchies altogether and indulge the daydream that theirs was a good and happy childhood—playful, natural, carefree, and innocent. Such a fantasy required a fantastic backdrop, a kind of alternate reality that materialized about a half mile from the Pavilion in the form of the Swiss Cottage.

FIGURE 2.1. *The Swiss Cottage, Osborne House.* Acquired by Queen Victoria in 1856, this watercolor sketch shows the Swiss Cottage before the construction of the Swiss Cottage Museum. The garden plots maintained by the royal offspring are visible in the foreground. William Leighton Leitch, 1855. RCIN 919867. Royal Collection Trust / copyright 2023 His Majesty King Charles III.

CHAPTER TWO

A Pastoral Paradise for Young Royals

Osborne's Swiss Cottage

In September 1856, Queen Victoria acquired a painting from William Leighton Leitch, a favorite artist who also often provided her and her children with instruction in the art of watercolor (Figure 2.1).[1] At first glance, the painting might be mistaken for a scene in Switzerland; any number of British tourists had returned from a sojourn in the Alps with similar images of Swiss chalets. Yet, the structure Leitch depicted clung not to the side of an Alpine crag but stood instead on a gently sloping site on the grounds of the Osborne estate, about a half mile from the queen's maritime villa. Known as the Swiss Cottage and completed in May 1854, the structure had been built for the use of the royal children, who since 1850 had been tending the planting beds visible in the foreground of the image. Indeed, the young male figure depicted in the painting's midground is undoubtedly one of the royal princes (probably Bertie or Affie), shown working alongside a gardener, presumably Thomas Warne, who lived on the first floor of the Swiss Cottage with his wife, Louisa, and his mother-in-law. This pair, in turn, is observed by female figures (probably ladies-in-waiting), while the group to the left may include a princess or two, perhaps accompanied by a governess. In contrast, the dark-clad figure to the right of the cottage may be Mrs. Warne, who served as the building's caretaker. All in all, the scene is one of well-ordered serenity and ease. The cottage is well maintained. The planting beds abound with bright flowers and flourishing vegetables, which obligingly remain within their neat grassy boundaries. Even the figural groups in the background are visually corralled within arched trellises. The sun shines on everyone, regardless of rank.

Leitch's image was destined for one of the View Albums that Victoria and Albert worked together to assemble. Reviewed when the two were alone or with members of their family, these personal volumes illustrated places and events especially significant to the royal couple.[2] The significance of the Swiss Cottage was spelled out a few years later in William White's *History, Gazetteer, and Directory of Hampshire and the Isle of Wight*. At the Swiss Cottage

> the younger members of the royal family spend much of their time, and are permitted to throw off some of the restraint of royalty, and to amuse and improve themselves by collecting, arranging, and classifying the various objects of natural history and curiosity which they can procure. They each have a set of garden tools and a plot of ground, and enter into a generous rivalry with each other in the study and practice of horticulture. The cottage contains a beautiful kitchen and dairy, in which the young princesses are instructed in domestic economy.[3]

The importance of the Swiss Cottage, then, hinged on the freedom it purportedly offered the royal offspring, as well as the opportunities it afforded for them to engage in homely skills while interacting with one another as siblings, independent of their place in the line of succession. The sunny, relaxed scene Leitch captured—nay, crafted—was calculated to appeal to the regal couple, who seem to have judged their success as parents (at least in part) by their ability to give their children (at least from time to time) the kind of carefree existence widely understood as central to a good childhood.

At the same time, the Swiss Cottage served to reinforce the exalted status of the royal children. Indeed, its humble architecture evoked the distinctly elite practice of cottage building that had emerged in the eighteenth century to provide classically educated British adults with places of arcadian retreat in the service of intellectual exercise. Aristocrats built many such cottages from the 1760s on, although the type took on special resonance for royals, who were understood to require respite from the pressures of court life. One of the earliest examples was Queen Charlotte's Cottage, built in the 1770s and still standing in the gardens at Kew.[4] A subcategory of the type was the Swiss cottage, many of which graced aristocratic and royal estates from about 1790 on, with the fad petering out about 1830. Albert put his own stamp on the practice, both by designating the Swiss Cottage at Osborne as a children's space and also by amplifying the educational purpose of the site. That cottage also bears the imprint of the prince's interest in the design of "improved cottages" for agricultural laborers, an interest evident in the workingmen's cottages built by the Society for Improving the Condition of the Labouring Classes in conjunction with the Great Exhibition of 1851. In an important sense, that exhibition nourished ideas and launched projects—dynastic, educational, and philanthropic—that became deeply intertwined at the Swiss Cottage.

BUILDING THE CHILDREN'S PRECINCT

In 1850, even before the main wing of Osborne had been completed, Albert began work on the children's precinct, reached by the tree-lined High Walk but otherwise invisible from the main house (see Figure 1.11). The first component was a children's garden, followed in 1853–54 by the Swiss Cottage, which became the centerpiece of the precinct. The subsequent decade saw the addition of a miniature earthen fortress called Victoria Fort, created in 1856; the similarly small-scale brick-built Albert Barracks, constructed in 1860; and a freestanding museum built along the lines of a Swiss cottage in 1862 (Figure 2.2). There was also a small menagerie, which by 1860 included a gazelle house. Not too far away is the Osborne beach, where the children learned to swim and enjoyed collecting shells and digging in the sand.[5]

In the children's garden, each of the royal offspring was provided with an individual plot where they were encouraged to grow fruit and vegetables using child-sized wheelbarrows and other gardening tools. According to architectural historian

FIGURE 2.2. Exterior of the Swiss Cottage Museum, Osborne House, Isle of Wight. The Swiss Cottage included a museum room when it was first built, but the children's collection of natural history specimens and artifacts from many parts of the British Empire quickly outgrew that space. Prince Albert began planning this freestanding museum building before his death in 1861. Architect unknown, completed 1862. Photograph by the author.

Hermione Hobhouse, the wheelbarrows were crafted by members of Thomas Cubitt's construction crew.[6] Given his own interest in horticulture, Albert may have anticipated that his children would share his joy in cultivating plants. Yet, the garden also served dynastic interests by allowing the royal children to pursue agricultural interests that had long been understood as an indication of the capacity to rule. Albert may well have had in mind the example of George III, who was known for exercising his own interest in farming at Kew, where he also encouraged his elder sons to grow a small patch of wheat; reportedly, they processed the wheat into flour and baked a loaf of bread for the royal table.[7] In a similar vein, Albert encouraged his children to understand the place of their modest crops in larger systems of exchange and food production. The story is often told that he embraced the opportunity to introduce the children to the economic realities of agricultural labor by paying them the going rate for their produce.[8] At the same time, the Swiss Cottage that was soon constructed adjacent to the garden provided the children with a kitchen, where—like their regal great-uncles before them and like elite American children to come after them—they could transform their fruits and vegetables into simple dishes that were often shared with their parents in a second-floor room fitted out with a family-sized dining table. Here sentiment and dynasty went hand in hand.

Construction on the Swiss Cottage began in May 1853 with a ceremony described by Victoria in her diary:

> In the afternoon . . . we went with all the 7 Children to their garden, where they laid the 1rst stone of a Swiss Cottage, built for them there, each putting on some mortar & striking the stone with a small hammer. Arthur was great fun. Bertie read aloud the inscription of the date, with all the signatures, written at full length on a piece of parchment. This was deposited in a bottle, which was put into a hole in the stone work. The Children were greatly excited & delighted.[9]

Three weeks later, she wrote that "the Children's Swiss Cottage is progressing nicely. The masonry was done in part by the Boys & Affie worked as hard & steadily as a regular labourer."[10] Like the garden, then, the building of the Swiss Cottage provided the royal sons with the opportunity to experience manual labor and to demonstrate their industriousness. At the same time, the laying of its foundation stone gave the young Prince of Wales the chance to practice the kind of ceremonial public speaking he would be called upon to do in later life.

The process of building the Swiss Cottage between the laying of its stone foundation and its formal presentation to the children on the queen's birthday in May 1854 is somewhat murky. In 1867, Doyne C. Bell, a member of the royal household, claimed that it was built "in exact imitation of a Swiss Châlet" and that "the furniture, ornament, and decorations for it, were expressly imported from Switzerland."[11] After that, the story that the cottage had been prefabricated in Switzerland and shipped to Osborne was repeated so often that it was accepted as fact by many twentieth-century commentators.[12] To be sure, the building appeared authentically Swiss to British eyes; originally rocks were placed on the roof, following a practice that in the 1820s architect Peter Frederick Robinson had asserted was common in Switzerland for preventing the wind from lifting shallow roofs.[13] In fact, this apparently authentic national Swiss style was a foreign invention of the late eighteenth and early nineteenth centuries. According to architectural researcher Daniel Stockhammer, Robinson and other foreign architects made drawings of vernacular buildings during their travels in Switzerland, capturing some of the wide range of regional and local traditions that characterized Swiss architecture. Once home, they reworked their drawings to reflect their own imagined version of a unified national style. With the advent of mass tourism, these images helped determine what foreign visitors expected to see, which in turn prompted the Swiss to construct buildings in this purportedly national style invented abroad.[14] Adding to the supposedly foreign character of the Swiss Cottage at Osborne was a frieze carved with proverbs and quotations from the Psalms, rendered in German (Figure 2.3). Exhorting the building's users to perseverance, hard work, patience, and faith in God, the carvings point to the values that the royal parents, Albert in particular, sought to instill in their children. The effect enchanted Victoria who wrote in her diary that the Swiss Cottage "looks so real that one would fancy oneself suddenly transported to another country."[15]

As plausible as its foreign manufacture may have seemed in the nineteenth century, a materials analysis completed in 1990 revealed that the wood is North American, while an 1856 plan makes it clear that the dimensions were in imperial measure—facts that undermine any assertion of the structure's Continental origin.[16] Perhaps with the exception of the casement windows with their circular glazing patterns (which were rare in England and may have been imported), the building could well have been designed and built in England, given that British architects had been designing so-called Swiss cottages for decades and also disseminating their designs via pattern books. Indeed, a plate from Robinson's *Rural Architecture, or a Series of Designs for Ornamental Cottages* of 1823 could have suggested some of the features incorporated into the Swiss Cottage at Osborne: not just the roof rocks, but also the shallow pitch of the roof, walls of horizontal timbers shaped to produce pronounced shadow lines, and external stairs (Figure 2.4).

On its ground floor, the Swiss Cottage provided living accommodation for the housekeeper, as well as the kitchen facilities where the royal children learned to make simple meals (Figure 2.5). Two of the three kitchen rooms were photographed early and their contents inventoried after Victoria's death.[17] The larger of the two rooms

FIGURE 2.3. Exterior of the Swiss Cottage, Osborne, Isle of Wight. The plaque in the gable gives the construction date in Roman numerals (MDCCCLIV), while the frieze just below the roof brackets is carved with proverbs and quotations from the Psalms in German. Architect unknown, 1853–54. Photograph by the author.

FIGURE 2.4. Design for a Swiss cottage by Peter Frederick Robinson, a British architect who helped invent an ersatz national style that was eventually introduced into the Swiss landscape to meet the expectations of foreign tourists. P. F. Robinson, *Rural Architecture, or a Series of Designs for Ornamental Cottages* (London: Rodwell and Martin, 1823), design no. VIII, Plate 32.

was the kitchen proper, fitted out with a coal-fired range, manufactured by J. Mathys, a Brussels-based ironmonger who had displayed his wares at the Great Exhibition of 1851 (Figure 2.6). With its double oven, the range had an innovative design, which has led to the speculation that this device or a version of it had been part of that display. At about three-quarters the size of a normal range, it was ideal for the use of children. (Although some commentators assert that the Swiss Cottage is a miniature building in which everything is child-sized, this is only true of the range and the children's garden tools. In every other way, the Swiss Cottage is a full-sized building.) The room next to the kitchen was most likely the scullery, with a sink for washing up and cupboards to store serving pieces. The third room seems to have been a larder that probably was also used from time to time for dairying activities, such as butter-making.[18]

The entirety of the upper level was devoted to the use of the royal family, which meant that it was inventoried in 1904 and that it remained largely untouched afterward. Reached by exterior stairs, the main entrance on the building's north side led

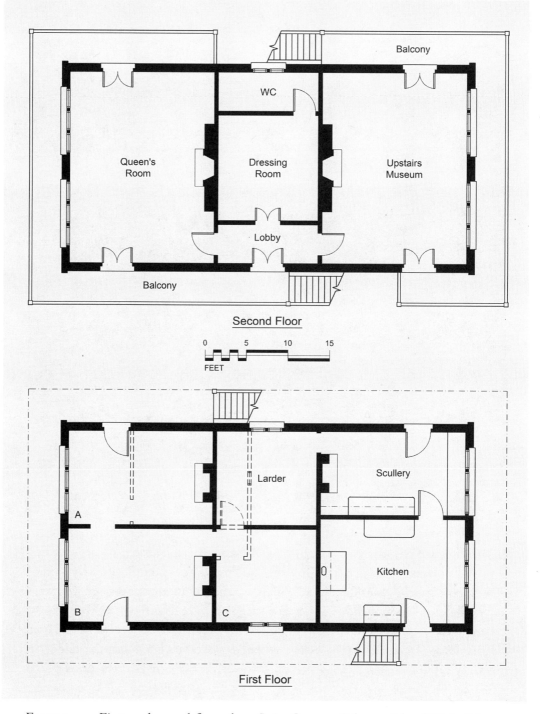

FIGURE 2.5. First- and second-floor plans, Swiss Cottage, Osborne, Isle of Wight. The dotted lines show walls added in 1856. Room A was subdivided to provide a bedroom for the mother of Mrs. Warne, the caretaker. A lobby was created in Room C (originally the building's only bedroom) to protect the privacy of its inhabitants, an addition necessitated by the introduction of a water closet into one end of the larder. Architect unknown, 1853–54. Drawing by Daniel De Sousa.

FIGURE 2.6. Kitchen in the Swiss Cottage, Osborne, Isle of Wight. On the back wall is a coal-fired range that is slightly smaller than conventional fixtures, while on the right is a set of charcoal chafing stoves. Architect unknown, 1853–54. André Adolphe-Eugène Disdéri, photographer, 1867. *The Osborne Album: Thirty-three Photographic Views of the Queen's Marine Residence at Osborne* (London and Paris: [André Adolphe-Eugène] Disdéri, 1867), 25.

into a small lobby that communicated with three rooms: in the center, a dressing room (with a water closet), which was flanked on either side by rooms identified in the 1904 inventory as the Queen's Room and the upstairs museum. The Queen's Room was furnished with a dining table, made by a local Newport firm of American birch (Figure 2.7).[19] Provided with eight leaves, the table could accommodate the royal children, who took many of their meals there, as well as larger groups, as when the youngsters shared tea with their parents and other guests. A second door leads into this room directly from the exterior balcony on the building's north side, facilitating the delivery of foodstuffs from the kitchen on the floor below. On the other side of the dressing room was the upstairs museum, which could also be reached from an exterior stair on the building's south side. Fitted out with wall-hung cabinets to receive the natural history specimens the Prince Consort encouraged the children to collect, this museum room speaks to the overtly pedagogical purpose at the heart of the children's precinct, even as it is also related to a longer history of elite retreats.

THE SWISS COTTAGE AS A ROYAL RETREAT

In building the Swiss Cottage, Albert may have had in mind the *Schweizerei* his father, Ernest I, had had built around 1820 on the grounds of Rosenau, the summer residence outside Coburg, where he and his brother Ernest (later Ernest II) spent much of their youth. Indeed, on their visit to Coburg in 1845, Victoria and Albert visited a later *Schweizerei* that Ernest II had built in 1840.[20] Victoria's diary entries convey her delight in the building, while also revealing that it accommodated a very different range of functions than those that would eventually be incorporated into the Swiss Cottage at Osborne. "A charming place, where Ernest & [his wife] Alexandrine are now living," it was in Victoria's words, "a regular Swiss Cottage, with pretty little rooms, one enters by an outside wooden staircase, & they are immediately above where the cows & bulls are kept."[21] The *Schweizerei* was also included in a series of watercolors that Victoria and Albert commissioned to remember the trip and to recall a site that the queen associated with the Prince Consort's supposedly happy childhood.[22] In fact, Albert's early life was tinged with great sadness, especially after his mother abandoned her loveless marriage, leaving her young sons (just five and six years old at the time of her departure) in the care of a father who showed little interest in them.[23] While some commentators have interpreted the Swiss Cottage and its museum in light of Albert's desire to replicate his youth, it may be more accurate to interpret them as attempts to redeem it as well. In contrast to the paternal disinterest that characterized his childhood, Albert sought to be a very different kind of father to his children—one who would spend time with them, teaching them to swim, hunting butterflies together, or tasting their culinary efforts.

Yet, to explain the children's precinct and especially the Swiss Cottage solely in terms of Albert's biography is to miss the building's larger historical context and the range of meanings it evoked. Indeed, in its function, the building is closely related to eighteenth-century cottages inspired by the pastoral poetry of Virgil and Horace, works that celebrated the virtuous nobility of simple rural life. Built on the grounds of country estates, these rustic structures were imagined by their elite owners as arcadian retreats from the bustle of the city, from the formality of the county house itself, and—for royals—from the cares of court life.[24] One of the earliest was Queen Charlotte's Cottage on the grounds of Richmond Lodge (near its somewhat fluid border with the royal estate at Kew), where George III's consort could take tea with

FIGURE 2.7. Queen's Room in the Swiss Cottage, Osborne House, Isle of Wight. Although contemporaries claimed that the Swiss Cottage and its furnishings had been imported from Switzerland, the dining set in this room was produced on the Isle of Wight of American birch. Architect unknown, 1853–54. Photograph by the author.

close friends and family, pursue her interest in botany, and "escape from the constant scrutiny to which she was subject at court" (Figure 2.8).[25] Begun in 1771, this cottage was initially a one-story brick building adjacent to the so-called New Menagerie, which by the 1790s housed water buffalo, kangaroos, meerkats, dingoes, and other exotic animals. Sometime before 1788, the cottage had gained a timber-framed second story, seventeenth-century window frames, and a thatched roof of reed and rye straw—all in the service of what Susanne Groom and Lee Prosser have described as "a carefully contrived rustication."[26] Like other elite cottages of the eighteenth century, the building's rustic exterior contrasted sharply with its refined interiors, which were governed by the principles of decorum, that is, the use of furnishings calibrated to the occupant's rank and wealth.[27] In its enlarged iteration, the cottage had two main rooms for the use of the queen and her family: a first-floor dining room, known as the Print Room because it was decorated with prints of "elegance and humour" (many of them after Hogarth) pasted directly to the walls, as was the fashion of the day; and, on the second floor, the Picnic Room, with windows overlooking the gardens.[28]

FIGURE 2.8. Exterior of Queen Charlotte's Cottage, Kew. Architect unknown, begun in 1771. The second story and thatched roof were added before 1788. Photograph by Peter Broster. Licensed under CC BY 2.0. https://commons.wikimedia.org/wiki/File:Queen_Charlotte%27s_Cottage_Kew_Gardens_(6761105457).jpg.

The cottage in this expanded form may have had particular resonance for Charlotte, who by 1783 had given birth to fifteen children. Indeed, the introduction of timber framing and thatch took place during the years Thomas Gainsborough produced five cottage door scenes, images that associated humble cottages with nursing mothers and their many well-fed children. As art historian Ann Bermingham has pointed out, the images are imbued with "the Freudian notion of the *Heimlich*, that is to say, the home-like with all its connotations of shelter, comfort, intimacy, safety, quiet content, and the inevitable association of these qualities with the maternal body."[29] More than just a retreat from court, this cottage may have also served as a celebration of Charlotte's maternal success. Given that she often used this cottage and another she had built on the Frogmore estate at Windsor with her unmarried daughters, Charlotte may have valued these buildings as places that could help instill her own maternal feelings in the next generation.

Charlotte's third daughter took a particular interest in the site. In 1804–5, Princess Elizabeth (then in her midthirties) oversaw improvements to the cottage, evidently as a surprise for her father on the anniversary of his coronation. In addition to commissioning new furniture and fittings (including a trompe l'oeil painting of a trellis entwined with flowers on the coved ceiling of the Picnic Room), she may have contributed her own handicraft, in the form of painted velvet chair cushions. Princess Elizabeth's renovations also improved the kitchen facilities (once completely separate from the polite area of the cottage), so that the royal family could use them to take breakfast and tea and occasionally to dine there as well.[30]

Queen Charlotte's Cottage was a distinctly adult space and a feminized one as well, and in those ways quite different from the Swiss Cottage at Osborne. Nonetheless, it helped establish patterns of royal life that were incorporated into the later site. Both buildings offered places for royals to escape from the pressures of court, deemed necessary even on the grounds of the summer residences that were themselves understood as retreats. Both were associated with gardens and menageries, although the menagerie at Osborne was never as extensive as that at Kew. Even so, Victoria clearly associated the Swiss Cottage with exotic animals; when she was gifted a Chihuahua in 1856, she could only describe it as "something like a very diminutive Italian grey hound" and promptly sent it down to the Swiss Cottage, where Mrs. Warne was charged with its care.[31] Both cottages were informal places where the royal family could take tea or other light meals together, surrounded by evidence of royal accomplishments, both curatorial (in the Print Room at Richmond or the museum at Osborne) and manual (in the velvet cushions likely painted by Elizabeth or the garden plots and simple foodstuffs produced by Vicky and her siblings). Finally, despite their different architectural forms, both sites evoked rural simplicity as the ideal backdrop for this respite from the formalities of court life.

The Swiss Cottage at Osborne (as well as the original *Schweizerei* at Rosenau) can also be understood in light of a fad for Swiss garden cottages that flourished both on the Continent and in Great Britain from about 1790 until 1830, thanks in large part to the mania for the writings of Jean-Jacques Rousseau.[32] Especially popular was *Julie, ou la Nouvelle Héloïse* (1761), which built on a then-recent literary trend to present Switzerland as a rural Arcadia, its mountains protecting its rural inhabitants from the corruption of contemporary civilization.[33] Rousseau's contribution was to suggest that the Alpine setting could also redeem cultured elites. Indeed, in the eyes of Julie's former lover, her secluded orchard—her so-called Elysium—was both the product of and also setting for the exercise of her virtue as a faithful wife and dedicated mother. British tourists flocked to Switzerland, often seeking out the places mentioned in the novel. Indeed in 1816, Lord Byron wrote that he had "traversed all Rousseau's ground with the *Héloïse* before me," his travels confirming "all that I have ever heard or imagined of a pastoral existence [. . .] pure and unmixed—solitary, savage, and patriarchal: the effect I cannot describe."[34]

If some of these British tourists brought back prints of Swiss landscapes to fuel their ongoing pastoral reveries, others incorporated "savage" Alpine gardens into the Picturesque gardens on their aristocratic estates and ornamented them with Swiss cottages.[35] This was an extension of the eighteenth-century practice of composing Picturesque gardens as a series of vignettes, each of which featured a garden folly in a different (and often exotic) architectural vocabulary, the better to trigger a range of associations in the minds of viewers. Among those who built such Swiss cottages were the Duke and Duchess of Bedford, who in the early nineteenth century hired architect Jeffry Wyatt (later Wyatville) and landscape gardener Humphrey Repton to design the house, grounds, and outbuildings at Endsleigh, their Devon estate. Every aspect of Endsleigh's design was touched by the Picturesque. Even the main house was a large and sprawling *cottage orné*, very different in character from the Palladian pile at Woburn Abbey, the family seat.[36] Among the fantasy outbuildings was a Swiss cottage, which originally stood "in a sort of Alpine garden" overlooking the river Tamar.[37] Completed by about 1816, the Swiss cottage was designed as a two-and-a-half-story timber structure, with a thatched roof and unpeeled logs applied to the exterior walls in vertical, horizontal, and diagonal patterns, evidently to evoke vernacular Swiss building techniques. The building's supposedly Swiss character was enhanced by a two-story gallery wrapping around three sides. The cottage included living accommodation for a laborer at ground level and on the top floor under the gabled roof. On the story in between and reached by exterior stairs were rooms "furnished *a la Suisse* with wooden chairs and platters, horn spoons etc.," which the Bedfords used for picnics and shooting parties.[38] Although the Bedfords had twelve children and provided them with a children's cottage (attached to the main house by a passage and rustic colonnade) and their own garden, the Swiss cottage was distinctly a site for adult leisure. Indeed, the artist Edwin Landseer made a watercolor of Endsleigh as seen from the Swiss cottage, suggesting that it played a role in the long love affair that he conducted with the Duchess of Bedford.[39]

Wyatt was associated with a number of other Swiss cottages built in the 1810s and 1820s, some on aristocratic estates (such as Bulstrode Park, owned by the Duke of Somerset), others on estates of the landed gentry (such at Langold Park in Yorkshire and at Calverton Manor in Bath, owned respectively by Henry Gally Knight and William Selby Lowndes, both MPs), and one sometimes referred to as a Swiss cottage at Virginia Water at Windsor for George IV.[40] Another built sometime between 1809 and 1818 for the Earl of Essex at Cassiobury in Hertfordshire has been attributed to him as well. Like that at Endsleigh, the Cassiobury Swiss cottage was a two-and-a-half-story timber structure with external stairs leading to the upper level of a two-story gallery that wrapped around all four sides of the building (Figure 2.9). Although the tile roof proposed for the Cassiobury cottage was different from the thatched roof at the Endsleigh cottage, both buildings were clad with unpeeled logs to call to mind Swiss building practices. And like the cottage at Endsleigh, that at Cassiobury housed one of the earl's domestics on the ground floor, while accommodating picnics and parties for the earl and his guests on the upper floor, in a practice that recalls Queen Charlotte's Cottage. By the early 1840s, tourists could apply for permission to take refreshments in the gallery and may have been allowed in the "visitor's room" that had been attached to the main cottage. "Carefully furnished, so as to give the idea of the domestic hearths of the brave and free mountaineers of the Alps," this room also served as a cabinet of curiosities; according to the *Penny Magazine*, it contained Bolivar's boots, a Ceylonese umbrella made from a single leaf of a talipot tree, and the head of a Maori chief who had led an unsuccessful night attack on a merchant ship out of Liverpool plying its trade in New Zealand.[41] In short, Swiss cottages remained adult retreats.

By the 1820s, the Swiss cottage phenomenon was spreading beyond royal and aristocratic circles, thanks in part to the work of Robinson, one of the most prolific authors of architecture books in the nineteenth century.[42] His first book, *Rural Architecture, or a Series of Designs for Ornamental Cottages*, appeared in 1823 and helped solidify and advertise his specialty in Swiss cottages (see Figure 2.4). Robinson's designs are characterized by low-pitched roofs and walls made of stacked logs, which made it possible to cantilever the galleries and do away with the rather spindly posts of Wyatt's designs. Robinson designed a Swiss cottage for at least one aristocrat: Lord Ongley, at the Old Warden estate in Bedfordshire.[43] He also designed for clients further down the social scale, such as Welsh copper magnate John Henry Vivian at Singleton Park in Swansea. (This Swiss cottage included a plaque with its date of

FIGURE 2.9. View of the Swiss cottage, Cassiobury Park, Hertfordshire. Attributed to Sir Jeffry Wyatt (later Wyatville), circa 1830. The "visitor's room" is the one-story wing on the left. John Britton, *The History and Description with Graphic Illustrations of Cassiobury Park, Hertfordshire: The Seat of the Earl of Essex* (London: John Britton, 1837), Plate XV.

completion and on another part of the building an inscription in German, both features incorporated into the Swiss Cottage at Osborne twenty-five years later.)[44] By 1832, he had also designed a Swiss cottage at the Colosseum in Regent's Park, a commercial amusement. Considered "the *bijou* of the whole" by a commentator for *The Mirror*, it was fitted out "in imitation of the fanciful interior of the dwellings of the Swiss mountaineers," an illusion "not a little enhanced by the prospect from the windows, consisting of terrific rocks and caverns, among which a cascade is to fall from an immense height into a lake, which is to spread immediately beneath the windows."[45] Now anyone with a shilling to spare could experience the terrifying landscape and cozy domesticity of Switzerland.

By the 1830s, ersatz Swiss cottages were so commonplace that a young John Ruskin (writing under the pseudonym Kata Phusin) condemned them in the pages of *The Architectural Magazine*. To be sure, he admired the real thing, extolling it as "the loveliest piece of architecture I had ever had the felicity of contemplating.... Its power was the power of association; its beauty, that of firmness and humility." He continued:

> How different is this from what modern architects erect when they attempt to produce what is, by courtesy, called a Swiss cottage. The modern building known in

Britain by that name has very long chimneys.... Its gable roof slopes at an acute angle, and terminates in an interesting and romantic manner, at each extremity, in a tooth pick.[46]

Although Ruskin's critique was directed at middle-class houses, he might have been describing Wyatt's aristocratic retreats with spiky finials attached to their gable ends.

The phenomenon of building Swiss cottages on the grounds of elite estates slowed down after about 1830. Nonetheless, a fifth edition of Robinson's *Rural Architecture*, replete with its Swiss designs, was published in 1850, just three years before work began on the Swiss Cottage at Osborne.[47] As late as 1865, the actor Charles Fechter, a friend and admirer of Charles Dickens, presented the novelist with a prefabricated version; its ninety-four pieces arrived in fifty-eight boxes. Erected initially at Gad's Hill, in Hingham, Kent, the small cottage (with just one room on each of its two stories), served as Dickens's writing hut until his death in 1870. Given the timing of its arrival, this Swiss chalet may be at least in part responsible for giving credence to the narrative that began circulating in 1867 that the Swiss Cottage at Osborne was prefabricated in Europe.[48]

Victoria and Albert certainly knew of royal and aristocratic Swiss cottages before they visited the *Schweizerei* at Rosenau. As a girl, Victoria had visited Virginia Water in Windsor Great Park and probably saw the Swiss cottage there. She and Albert stopped at several others, including the one at Cassiobury, when they visited the Dowager Queen Adelaide there in 1846. They were even familiar with the Swiss cottage at the Colosseum, which they visited with their children in May 1845. Enchanted by its "Swiss scenes with waterfalls, & views of Mont Blanc," Victoria wrote in her diary that "the whole thing was most entertaining & wonderfully arranged, indeed some of it was quite like magic."[49]

SWISS COTTAGE AS AN ORNAMENTAL DAIRY

Victoria made one other reference in her diary to a Swiss cottage that she encountered on an aristocratic estate, when she visited Lord and Lady Breadalbane at Taymouth Castle in Scotland in 1842 (Figure 2.10). On a rainy September morning, Lord Breadalbane and Albert set out for a day's shooting, while Victoria took a walk with the Duchess of Norfolk, one of the ladies of the bedchamber. In her diary, she wrote that they followed "a path which overlooks the beautiful Tay which is so clear & ripples along over the stones, the high hills forming such a beautiful background. We went up to the Dairy, which is a sort of Swiss Cottage, built of quartz, & so clean & nice. From the top, there is a very pretty view of Loch Tay. Had a glass of fine cold milk at the Dairy, & then returned as we came."[50]

FIGURE 2.10. Exterior of the Dairy, Taymouth Castle, Perth and Kinross, Scotland. Queen Victoria referred to this building as "a sort of Swiss Cottage" when she visited in 1842. William Atkinson, architect, 1830–31. Postcard from the collection of thefollyflaneuse.com.

The entry is notable for a number of reasons. For one thing, it suggests that the building the ladies visited was, in fact, an ornamental dairy, a building type that art historian Meredith Martin argues "enabled the crown and nobility to project an image of Arcadian peace and prosperity and to profess an enduring devotion to the land, while also playing with new forms of courtly refinement, leisure and display."[51] The earliest example in France dates from 1560, when Catherine de' Medici, serving as regent for her minor son, built an ornamental dairy (called a pleasure dairy in France) near Fontainebleau, a building Martin sees as "proclaiming the fertility and benevolence of its patron."[52] French queens and royal mistresses continued to build pleasure dairies throughout the ancien régime. Madame de Pompadour built five between 1748 and 1756 and promoted drinking milk for health, while thirty years later Marie Antoinette added them to her Hameau, in what became the most famous and indeed notorious appropriation of the pastoral by French royalty.[53]

English queens embraced ornamental dairies as early as the 1690s, when Queen Mary II built one of the earliest examples at Hampton Court.[54] As in France, the type was increasingly popular in the last two-thirds of the eighteenth century, when the vogue for breast-feeding was at its height, thanks in part to Rousseau's campaign to encourage the practice among elite women, who then sought to associate themselves with milk. In that century, George II's Queen Caroline and George III's Queen Charlotte both built ornamental dairies at Richmond Gardens near Kew and at Frogmore in Windsor Home Park, respectively. Although aristocratic women also built ornamental dairies, Martin posits that they were particularly resonant with royal women who may have seen them as helping to "signify their ability to provide for England and ensure its continued health and prosperity."[55] Victoria and Albert certainly knew the dairy at Frogmore. Indeed, Albert oversaw the replacement of Queen Charlotte's ornamental dairy, which had become derelict by the 1850s. Although elaborately decorated, his 1858 building was not an ornamental dairy intended for female leisure, but rather its later and distinctly masculine counterpart: a model dairy designed to showcase the most up-to-date dairying methods.[56]

Erected in 1830–31 to the designs of William Atkinson, a pupil of James Wyatt, the Taymouth dairy was a relatively new building when Victoria visited, but its architectural forms and use confirm that it was an ornamental dairy.[57] To be sure, its quartz walls that glittered in the sun were unusual, but the contrast between its rustic exterior and refined interior was a defining feature of the type. At Taymouth, the temple-front motif around the door was supported by unpeeled tree trunks, a reference to the primitive hut at the center of so much eighteenth-century architectural theory in England, as well as in France, and which had informed the design of many an architect-designed cottage retreat.[58] In contrast, the decorous interior sported tessellated marble floors and carved plaster ceilings. The dairy may well have been fitted out with white marble tables and shelves, which were typically used in ornamental dairies to keep the building and its contents cool and to project an image of purity. Certainly, the published memorial of the monarch's visit described the "delightfully cool temperature" of the rooms. As was common for the type, the Taymouth dairy consisted of multiple rooms, so that the labor of dairying (carried out by dairymaids) was kept separate from the spaces in which elite women sampled milk and other dairy products and from those devoted to the display of exquisite porcelain versions of common dairying implements produced by Wedgwood and others. At Taymouth, "Many of the vessels [were] of fine raised china . . . [and] were placed on a shelf running around the apartment." Victoria herself "assayed the operation of making butter, by turning the wooden handle of a beautiful little china churn."[59] As Martin points out, dairies provided an outlet for conspicuous consumption, while also giving the practice a sheen of moral goodness, especially for the women who often commissioned dairies and who were certainly their principal users.[60] As was the case with Victoria's visit to Taymouth, other elite women were the primary audience for their message of purity, fecundity, and domestic responsibility. So taken was the queen with the site that she took Albert to see it on the morning of their departure and together they climbed to the second-floor balcony to appreciate the view. According to the published account, "The Prince entered fully into all Her Majesty's admiration of it"—presumably, that is, the vista, but perhaps the building as well.[61]

Victoria's report of her visit to the dairy at Taymouth is also noteworthy for revealing that, at least in her mind, there was not a bright line between ornamental dairies and the Swiss cottages that dotted aristocratic estates.[62] As architectural historian Sue Wilson points out, as early as the sixteenth century commentators had begun associating the dairy products of the Alps with good health, thanks to the belief that Swiss cattle had greater resistance to disease.[63] This slippage, made apparent in Victoria's diary, opens the possibility that she and Albert envisioned the Swiss Cottage at Osborne as akin to an ornamental dairy, an association borne out by the presence of dairying equipment in the collection of cooking materials inventoried in 1904 and by the fact that after her marriage Vicky was familiar enough with the process to set up her own dairy in Prussia; indeed, she felt expert enough to critique the dairying technique of the woman employed to manage it.[64] Published descriptions of the Swiss Cottage (including that in William White's *History, Gazetteer, and Directory of Hampshire and the Isle of Wight*) often claimed that it contained both a kitchen and a dairy. Given that the larder had tiled walls and a drain in the floor, this room may have served as a dairy from time to time.

Imagining the Swiss Cottage as a sort of ornamental dairy would have appealed to the royal couple on several levels. They were, after all, keen to distance themselves from the example of Victoria's Hanoverian uncles; their own rejection of the Royal Pavilion at Brighton as their seaside retreat sent a clear signal that they were fundamentally different from George IV, who had devoted so much of his time and energy to the pursuit of pleasure in luxurious surroundings. If anything, Albert augmented the contrast with Brighton by developing a model farm at Barton on the Osborne estate, efforts that attracted admiring commentary. White's *History, Gazetteer, and Directory of Hampshire and the Isle of Wight* assured readers that Barton "displays a perfect system of farming," thanks to "the fostering care of the Prince Consort, who personally takes great interest in its management." Noting that under the stewardship of the royal couple "this naturally sterile estate has ... been brought into the highest state of fertility," the author played on an established trope that equated the ability to farm with the ability to rule, an observation that certainly pleased the royal couple.[65]

In this context, Victoria and Albert might well have been drawn to the meanings evoked by an ornamental dairy, a building type that was understood to encourage elites to undertake their responsibilities as landholders, while at the same time confirming that they merited their lofty status. Not only did the Swiss Cottage provide a site where the younger royals could practice the homely activities understood to engender reform among the ruling classes, but it also made these activities manifest, even if the children were not there at the time. Royal and noble visitors familiar with ornamental dairies could be expected to interpret the Swiss Cottage as an indication that Victoria and Albert's children were being prepared to embrace the responsibilities of their royal birth, whether as the sovereign at home or as a regal consort abroad.

In this context, it is worth noting that Victoria made it a regular practice to escort royal visitors to the Swiss Cottage, as she did in September 1854, when she showed the cottage to Pedro V, the young king of Portugal, and his brother Luis. On this occasion, the queen amplified the symbolism of the Swiss Cottage by taking the royal brothers on an extensive tour of Barton, including the laborers' cottages (a particular interest of Albert), "the cleanliness of which pleased Pedro very much."[66] In August 1857, she accompanied Napoleon III on a walk to the sea, returning by way of the Swiss Cottage. Two days later, she drove the same route with Empress Eugénie; at the Swiss Cottage, Victoria noted in her diary, "we got out & showed her all over it," suggesting that the queen expected female visitors to take a particular interest in the site.[67] A few days later, Victoria and her fourteen-year-old daughter, Alice, walked with Sophie of Württemberg, Queen of the Netherlands, to the Swiss Cottage, "driving back through the woods."[68] The summer of 1861 saw three sets of royal visitors: Prince Augustus of Saxe-Coburg and Gotha (first cousin to both Victoria and Albert), who visited Osborne with his wife, Clémentine, Princess of Orleans, and their daughters, Clotilde and Amélie; Archduke Maximilian (who became the emperor of Mexico in 1864) and his wife, "dear Charlotte," another first cousin to both Victoria and Albert; and King Oscar I of Sweden and his son Prince Oscar.[69] Victoria made sure all saw the Swiss Cottage.

A further indication that Victoria and Albert may have imagined the Swiss Cottage as akin to an ornamental dairy can be found in Victoria's tendency to associate the site with her eldest daughter. Martin notes that such dairies were often presented to women shortly after marriage and posits that they functioned something like an engagement portrait. These portraits typically showed well-born women pursuing productive activities in a pastoral setting; in 1770, for instance, Joshua Reynolds depicted Mrs. Pelham, First Baroness of Yarborough, in a cotton frock, feeding chickens. Never a simple reflection of reality, such paintings served to remind an aristocratic woman of her responsibility for nurturing her husband's estate and also to reward her by celebrating her in that role.[70] In a similar vein, ornamental dairies could help socialize elite women to their domestic roles, while at the same time distancing them from the actual labor involved (that was done by others) and surrounding them with luxury goods that further confirmed their elevated status. To be sure, the Swiss Cottage is different from ornamental dairies in that it was built for all the children and used by the boys as well as the girls. The timing of the Swiss Cottage suggests that the royal parents intended it to have special resonance for the Princess Royal.

THE PRINCESS ROYAL AND THE GREAT EXHIBITION OF 1851

The construction of the Swiss Cottage is firmly dated to 1853, yet Victoria and Albert seem to have started contemplating the project in 1851. In that year, Victoria's half sister, Princess Feodora of Hohenlohe-Langenburg, wrote to say that she had had a Swiss cottage built for her children in the garden of the Villa Friesenberg in Baden-Baden.[71] In 1851 Albert also visited Shrubland, the Suffolk estate of Sir William Middleton, where he saw a Swiss cottage built sometime before 1840, a building decorated with German quotations akin to those later incorporated into the design of the Swiss Cottage at Osborne.[72] More important is the fact that 1851 was also the year of the Great Exhibition, arguably Albert's greatest legacy. Not only was it the first international exhibition, but it also produced profits sufficient to help establish a host of cultural institutions in South Kensington—an area often referred to as Albertopolis. While its primary focus was the display of industrially manufactured goods, the exhibition also provided the royal couple with opportunities to make a public show of themselves as devoted parents, ones who provided their children with the right kind of childhood (that is, carefree and innocent), all while confirming their royal status.

A case in point is a boxwood cradle Victoria had commissioned for her sixth child, Louise, who was born in March 1848 (Figure 2.11). Carved by renowned woodcarver William Gibbs Rogers, it was delivered to Victoria in spring 1850 at Osborne, where the queen showed it off to her dinner guests and recorded in her diary that "everyone [was] full of admiration." She herself declared it "a 'chef d'oeuvre'—finer than anything of the kind, either antique or modern." She was particularly pleased that it was "full of emblems of the Houses of Gt. Britain & Saxe Coburg"—a reminder that the small inhabitant of the cradle had weighty dynastic connections.[73] Less than a year later, Victoria visited "our beautiful cradle" in the Fine Arts Court at the Exhibition.[74] Lest visitors miss the opportunity to see the royal cradle, a colored lithograph was included in official guidebooks and other publications associated with the exhibition. Secretary of the Exhibition Matthew Digby Wyatt declared it "one of the most pleasing revivals of the Cinque-cento style of wood-carving which has yet been executed in England."[75]

Also on display at the Great Exhibition were Thornycroft's portrait statues of the four eldest children, although the official catalogue disregarded the allegorical content, identifying the children not as the seasons, but connecting them instead to rustic

FIGURE 2.11. Cradle commissioned by Queen Victoria for Princess Louise. Carved with emblems from the Royal Houses of England and Saxe-Coburg, the cradle was displayed at the Great Exhibition of 1851 and images of it often appeared in related publications. William Gibbs Rogers, wood-carver, 1850. M. Digby Wyatt, *The Industrial Arts of the Nineteenth Century: A Series of Illustrations of the Choicest Specimens Produced by Every Nation, at the Great Exhibition of Works of Industry, 1851* (London: Day and Son, 1851–53), volume 2, Plate CXXX.

occupations: a shepherd (in the case of the Prince of Wales) and a gleaner (in the case of the Princess Royal; see Figure 1.3).[76] For classically educated Britons, the presentation of the heir as a shepherd would have seemed particularly apt; as architectural historian Daniel Maudlin notes, the shepherd was "an enviable figure of simple wants given to peaceful reflection," so much so that the poet John Dryden asserted that "for the first thousand years of the world . . . the Founders of the most renown'd Monarchies in the World, were Shepherds."[77] Given Albert's close involvement with the exhibition, this part of the catalogue text undoubtedly received careful scrutiny. Indeed, the association of the royal children with peasant life may well have been suggested by their father, who may have already been envisioning a cottage where they could practice homely tasks without undermining their regal status.

That the royal couple may have been envisioning a Swiss cottage as the ideal setting for their children to enact such a pastoral idyll is suggested by one of the queen's purchases at the Great Exhibition: a desk that was part of the Swiss display and that eventually found a home in the Swiss Cottage (Figure 2.12). Manufactured by Michel L. Wetli of Berne, it was described in the *Official and Illustrated Catalogue*:

Lady's mechanical escritoire, of white wood, constructed in such a manner as to enable the person to write either in a sitting or standing posture. It comprises seventeen drawers, all of which are locked with the same key. The lower part, used for writing in a sitting posture, is provided with a peculiar kind of mechanism, so that by pulling the drawer the upper part of it disappears to make room for the operation.[78]

Although this kind of mechanical contrivance appealed to the judges, who awarded a Prize Medal for "Cabinets with mechanical action" to a French *secrétaire* with a comparable locking mechanism, the Wetli desk received critical attention—an honourable mention for "Decorative Furniture and Upholstery, including Paper Hangings, Papier Maché, and Japanned Goods"—for its elaborate carvings of "the rustic economy and Alpine life of the inhabitants of Switzerland."[79]

The award is somewhat puzzling, given that the jury charged with judging furniture included strong advocates for design reform. Indeed, they opened their report by noting that "it is important, both for the strength and good effect of furniture, that the principles of sound construction be well carried out, that the construction be evident, and that if carving or other ornament be introduced, it should be by decorating that construction itself, not by overlaying it and disguising it." While they critiqued "unnecessary embellishment" of all kinds, carved furniture came in for particular, if tactful, censure. Although they noted that there were "many magnificent examples" of carved furniture, they also pointed out that "utility and purpose have in some degree been forgotten."[80] Perhaps the queen's association with the Wetli desk prompted them to look more favorably upon it than they might have otherwise. Indeed, the desk was regularly pictured in the exhibition's official publications, suggesting that the royal intention to purchase it was known even before the exhibition opened. While these publications did not mention the desk's new owner, the queen's purchase seems to have been widely known. *The World's Fair; or Children's Prize Gift Book of the Great Exhibition of 1851* praised it as "a beautiful writing table for ladies, which is one of the most splendid things in the exhibition." After describing the mechanism and carvings, the anonymous author concluded, "it is a writing table which the greatest lady in England might use."[81]

In its carvings, the desk evoked not just the joys of peasant life but specifically the delights of Swiss peasant life. Indeed, the desk's topmost register highlights activities associated with the canton of Berne: a lively scene of men hunting chamois (an activity mentioned as particularly Swiss in the *Children's Prize Gift Book*) is flanked on one side by a single male figure engaged in *Steinstossen* (a centuries-old Swiss stone-throwing contest) and on the other by two male figures engaged in *Schwingen* (a style of folk wrestling that had been revived at the first Alpine shepherd's festival in 1805).[82]

FIGURE 2.12. Carved desk exhibited in the Swiss section of the Great Exhibition of 1851 and purchased by Queen Victoria. Referred to at the time as an *escritoire*, the desk included two writing surfaces (including an architect's slope to be used while standing) and drawers, all hidden within its cabinetry, which could be locked with a key. Michael Leonz Wetli, cabinetmaker, 1851. RCIN 42714. Royal Collection Trust / copyright 2023 His Majesty King Charles III.

The contrasting woods used in the desk's relief carvings contributed to the identification with Switzerland; according to the *Children's Prize Gift Book*, they represented the Swiss national colors of red and white. Indeed, both the description of Swiss peasants elsewhere in that book and the balance of the desk's carvings reflect and reinforce common perceptions of Swiss peasant life as particularly idyllic and admirable. For instance, the text notes that "the people of Switzerland are very remarkable for their industry, contentment and ingenuity. Among the villagers, their chief occupations are the management of dairies, and the breeding of cattle."[83] Images of cattle herding figure prominently on the desk, including in the relief frieze on the desk's front, where the act of leading cows to pasture was ennobled by evocations of the Elgin marbles. Other carvings highlight the family unit, whether returning from town with a heavy-laden wagon in which the mother clasps an infant in a fond embrace, or gathered at their cottage door, where she works at an outdoor pump with her young son nearby, the scene observed by her husband, who sits within a sturdy wooden house (Figure 2.13). The latter image may have inspired the use of circular panes of glass in the windows of the Swiss Cottage. Together, these images seem to confirm the author's assertion that "the women are extremely domestic, delighting in their children; and all the Swiss are remarkable for their passionate love of home.... The inside[s] of the[ir] dwellings are so neat and look so comfortable."[84] In short, the desk purchase suggests both that the royal couple embraced this common understanding of Swiss peasant life and also that they understood a Swiss cottage as a setting where all of their offspring could experience the "industry, contentment and ingenuity" that characterized Bernese peasants.

The royal couple may have intended the desk and the Swiss Cottage it inspired to have particular resonance for Vicky, whose marriage prospects they were already actively contemplating in 1851. The Great Exhibition was not only the excuse to invite William, heir presumptive to the throne of Prussia, and his family to England so that Victoria and Albert could determine if his son, Frederick William (Fritz), might be a suitable match for the Princess Royal; it was also the setting, it is often said, where the intellectually precocious ten-year-old girl made a lasting impression on nineteen-year-old Fritz, taking him on a tour of the exhibits and explaining many of their contents.[85] The desk's depictions of the contented domesticity of Swiss peasant women may have seemed an ideal way to help Vicky embrace her future role as wife and mother. Even if she would never draw water from a well, the desk framed marriage and motherhood as the only secure paths to female contentment.

The Swiss Cottage would eventually take this message a step further, both in encouraging the Princess Royal to practice the homely domestic tasks at which Swiss women were understood to excel and also in creating a setting in which she could be seen to practice these skills. The visibility of the Swiss Cottage was an important

FIGURE 2.13. Detail of the carved desk exhibited in the Swiss section of the Great Exhibition of 1851, showing a family scene in front of a Swiss cottage. The circular motif in the upper part of the window may have inspired the circular windows at the Swiss Cottage at Osborne. Michael Leonz Wetli, cabinetmaker, 1851. RCIN 42714. Royal Collection Trust / copyright 2023 His Majesty King Charles III.

part of its function, framing the children for important visitors and, through news coverage, for the nation at large. To be sure, the Swiss Cottage would play this role for all of Victoria's children, male and female. Yet, the project's timing—initially imagined in 1851, when Vicky was first introduced to Fritz, and completed in 1853, a year before the young couple became engaged—suggests that it was built with Vicky in mind. Indeed, in keeping with Martin's interpretation of ornamental dairies, the Swiss Cottage can be understood as a three-dimensional engagement portrait of the Princess Royal.[86]

In this context, it is also telling that the desk was an *escritoire*, or what the French called a *secrétaire*. The latter word had originally referred to a person, someone employed to write letters for a master. When applied to a piece of furniture, the particular form of which was invented in the eighteenth century, the term *secrétaire* signified "a fundamental change in the act of writing."[87] According to furniture historian Dena Goodman, such desks "signaled a new authorial need for a personal surface on which to write, as private persons shifted from dictating their letters to a confidential secretary to penning them themselves."[88] Yet, if the distinction between composing and copying had lost its currency in the eighteenth century, the division between personal and professional writing took on greater importance and resulted in two kinds of desks. Professional writing, associated almost exclusively with elite men, took place on a *bureau* or *bureau plat,* a large flat desk designed to accommodate more than one person, as bureaucrats and other men of affairs continued to employ secretaries in a business setting and needed a desk over which they and their secretaries could confer with clients. The *bureau plat* was characterized by an expansive writing surface, mounted with leather. Both that surface and the presence of drawers below it were highly visible, announcing the function of the desk and the public importance of the writing that took place there. In contrast, *secrétaires* were intended for the private writing, especially the private epistolary writing, of both elite men and women. Designed to protect the privacy of the letter writer, the *secrétaire* did not announce its function as a desk, but instead kept the writing surface and drawers hidden within and secured by a lock. As the Swiss desk and other *secrétaires* displayed at the Great Exhibition demonstrated, this emphasis on privacy was still a concern in the nineteenth century; indeed, the mechanical ingenuity of their elaborate locking mechanisms was usually a matter of comment. Goodman notes that "*secrétaires* were always identified as personal furniture."[89] Each *secrétaire* had one owner, the person who held the key to its lock.

To whom did the Swiss desk belong? Despite the allusion in the *Children's Prize Gift Book* to its being fit for "the greatest lady in England," it was certainly never intended for Victoria's own use. All of her desks took the form of a *bureau plat,* an indication that she understood its connotation as a place for professional writing and chose to ignore the masculine associations of the type. Indeed, as a reigning monarch, she may have well made no distinction between her personal and her professional writing; arguably, her personal letters had national and even international import. Even when she spent time at the Swiss Cottage, she used a small *bureau plat.*

Yet, the desk's identification as "a ladies' escritoire" confirms that it was intended for female use. The very term *escritoire* (which in French refers not to a desk, but to a container for writing utensils) seems to have had a gendered connotation in the British context, where letter writing was also understood as a skill that respectable women needed to master. A version of the word (*escrutoire*) appeared in *The Young Lady's Book: A Manual of Elegant Recreations, Exercises, and Pursuits,* published in 1829, as the title of a chapter devoted to the finer points of letter writing.[90] A version of the book from 1859 had a more intellectually ambitious subtitle (*A Manual of Elegant Recreations, Arts, Sciences, and Accomplishments; Edited by Distinguished Professors*), but its chapter on letter writing (its title now rendered as "The Escritoire") remained largely unchanged. It noted the importance of letter writing for women, noting the "various . . . occasions on which ladies are called upon to exercise their skill in the art of epistolary composition; this, generally speaking, is the only style of writing of which they will find it inconvenient to be ignorant."[91] The anonymous author reassured readers that "a correspondence between two persons is, simply, a conversation reduced to writing," one in which the goal should be "ease and simplicity, an even flow of unlabored diction, and artless arrangement of obvious sentiments."[92] Yet, the chapter also detailed the many fronts on which these communications would be judged, suggesting that producing letters of artless and unlabored simplicity required careful attention to handwriting, grammar, word choice, clarity, concision, paper quality, and above all, the ability to adapt one's tone and even to adjust the length of the letter to the status of the recipient and to the nature of the news being communicated. Every aspect of the letter should "be governed by the relative situations in life, as to age, rank, character, &c., of the parties addressed and addressing. . . . We should never forget what we are, and what the person is whom we are addressing."[93] Lest the young lady fail to give her full attention to the complicated task before her, the author reminded her that the stakes were high: "bear in mind that our letters are, in every respect, representatives of our own persons—that they may be said to speak for us; and that an estimate of our character and manners is frequently formed from the style and language of our epistles."[94] In short, letter writing—even the private correspondence of sheltered young ladies—was understood to be a challenging form of communication that called upon a range of skills, the mastery of which required study, attention, and practice.

If letter writing was understood to be a part of every respectable woman's life, it would be central to the future Victoria and Albert envisioned for Vicky. As consort in the Prussian court, she would need to rely upon letters as her primary means of staying connected to her family, and particularly to her parents, who expected so much of her union. Early in the marriage, Victoria wrote often and expected Vicky to write several times a week, demanding detailed accounts of every aspect of her routine—what she ate and drank, how much time she spent out of doors, her menstrual periods, what she wore on particular occasions, the layout of the palace, the temperature of her rooms—as well as information on the behavior, demeanor, and activities of the Prussian royal family.[95] Although Albert eventually interceded, encouraging Victoria to moderate her expectations, the correspondence between mother and daughter was regular (Victoria wrote twice a week, Vicky almost as often) and—after forty years—voluminous. Roger Fulford, who edited the correspondence for publication in five volumes issued between 1964 and 1981, estimates that there are more than 300,000 words in Victoria's letters alone.[96] Albert's correspondence with Vicky was less frequent, but at least as demanding, albeit in a different sense. In their weekly exchange of letters, Albert encouraged Vicky to read the English and German newspapers dutifully and to pen reports on developments in Europe. Shortly after her marriage, for instance, he praised her "report on the situation in France [as] *very well* thought out" (emphasis original).[97] Given the centrality of letter writing to Vicky's effectiveness as a conduit of information—both personal and political—with her parents, one can imagine them encouraging her to hone her epistolary skills by entrusting her with the key to a richly embellished *escritoire*.

Finally, that the Swiss Cottage had been built with their eldest daughter in mind is borne out by Victoria's diary entries, which repeatedly assert Vicky's close connection to the site, without making similar claims about any of the other children. On the day in May 1857 that the queen made the declaration of Vicky's upcoming nuptials to the privy council, she was in a pensive frame of mind, noting that it "seemed quite a dream to me, so like but yesterday, that she was born." After the council meeting, she and Albert went for a drive, making their way to the Swiss Cottage, where they "found Vicky," who drove back to the house with her mother.[98] In mid-December of the same year, just six weeks before the wedding, Victoria wrote about Vicky's attachment to the Swiss Cottage on three consecutive days. On the first day, she noted that her eldest daughter was "terribly sad at taking leave of dear Osborne, her beloved Swiss Cottage & all the scenes of her happy childhood."[99] The next day, she recorded that Vicky "went to bid farewell to her dear Swiss Cottage which quite upset her."[100] On the third day, Victoria and Albert "walked out with the 4 eldest children, going to the Swiss Cottage, where Vicky will keep her garden, which please[d] her very much."[101] In order to mark her connection to the site, Vicky planted a tree there. On her own birthday in May 1860, the Queen wrote that she "thought much of dear Vicky & missed her," before consoling herself with "the sight of her works of which we are so proud [two bas-reliefs she had created and sent to her mother as a birthday gift], her kind letter & telegram, *all* [of which] seemed to bring her to us, as if she were there."[102] After breakfast, the family went out walking and Victoria planted a tree at the cottage. Symbolically, these two trees brought mother and daughter together at a place with special meaning for them both.

THE EDUCATIONAL CHARACTER OF THE CHILDREN'S PRECINCT

If the Swiss Cottage was meant to have special resonance for Vicky, it was never intended exclusively for her use. Indeed, all the royal offspring used the children's precinct extensively. Outside, they tended their garden plots with miniature tools, staged battles at their miniature fortress, and (in the case of Affie) messed about with air pumps and steam engines out in the summer house, where their tools were stored.[103] Inside they prepared and consumed simple meals and arranged objects for display in the museum. While the children seem to have savored these activities as a break from the formal education offered by their governesses and tutors even while at Osborne, their father was attentive to the ways their enjoyment of the Osborne estate could supplement the lessons imparted in the schoolroom.

While there are some similarities between this approach and those of Swiss pedagogue Johann Heinrich Pestalozzi and his German student Friedrich Froebel, Albert remained aloof of the nascent kindergarten movement; his large private library contained works by neither of those educators. Perhaps, the Prince Consort shared Prussian concerns that kindergartens were socialist institutions calculated to raise children as atheists.[104] Still reeling from the revolutions of 1848, Prussia had moved in 1851 to prohibit all kindergartens. Certainly, none of Froebel's gifts were on display at the Great Exhibition, as they would be at the Centennial Exposition in Philadelphia in 1876, where Frank Lloyd Wright's mother is said to have first encountered them. (At least part of the explanation is timing; the American toy company, Milton Bradley, only started mass-producing Froebel's blocks in 1869.)[105] Whatever Albert's reservations may have been in the 1850s, twenty years later, Vicky came to embrace the kindergarten as an institution of social uplift. In the 1870s and 1880s, as Crown Princess of Prussia, she was an active supporter of the Pestalozzi-Froebel House (a kindergarten and training program for kindergarten teachers) and a School for the Domestic Arts (a cooking school), both in Berlin.[106]

Albert used the children's precinct at Osborne to encourage his offspring to take up activities he had pursued in his youth. Chief among these were natural history excursions on which they collected rocks and plants from the estate grounds or hunted butterflies. The educational aspect of these activities was enhanced in the museum room on the second floor of the Swiss Cottage. There the children were responsible for grappling with the challenges of arranging their specimens into some kind of order, just as their father and uncle Ernest had in their own youthful museum in Coburg.[107] At the same time, Albert's educational approach also had the imprimatur of science, or at least pseudoscience. In 1852, he had engaged Scottish phrenologist George Combe to examine the four eldest children. In his written report, Combe noted that all four were "characterized by a development of the organs of Self-esteem, Love of Approbation, Firmness and conscientiousness (differing slightly from each other in the degrees of development of particular organs) greatly beyond the general English brain." The upshot, he argued, is that "all unnecessary severity, all reproofs which exceed the accusations of their own consciences and all exactions of performance which go beyond their powers of accomplishment, will be felt as injustice and injury, and lead to resentment and bitter recollection, as of unkindness." Combe counseled Albert to treat his children with "the kindest feeling"; any "wrong always expounded and condemned, but the erring culprit gently dealt with." Equally telling, for the development of the children's precinct, was his suggestion that the children would benefit from object lessons to supplement their formal learning.[108]

If the children's museum encouraged the royal children to spend time out of doors, evidence suggests that its displays were not limited solely to the specimens they collected on-site. Even before the Swiss Cottage was completed, the children had been presented with other kinds of objects that eventually ended up in the museum. One example is a free-standing display of cotton threads, yarns, and woven fabrics that (according to its label) had been presented to the Prince of Wales by Sir Thomas Bazley, a Manchester-based cotton manufacturer, in November 1851. Given both the timing of the gift (some five weeks after the Great Exhibition closed) and also the fact that Bazley had served as one of the exhibition's commissioners, the Great Exhibition seems to have served as one conduit for displays to make their way to the museum at the Swiss Cottage. Soon, the children's collection boasted a range of objects: natural specimens from exotic locations; cultural artifacts, some of them dating from antiquity, some produced more recently in distant corners of the British Empire; and a handful of industrially produced goods. With the exception of large-scale machinery, the collection, at least superficially, included a range of objects comparable to those displayed at the Great Exhibition.

The children's collections grew so quickly that at the time of his death in 1861, Albert was planning a free-standing museum for the children's precinct. Completed in 1862, it also took the form of a Swiss cottage, albeit a one-story version (see Figure 2.2). Although it is a small wooden building decorated with overtly quaint ornamentation, the Swiss Cottage Museum owes something to the practices of display introduced at the Great Exhibition, practices that also informed the design of South Kensington Museum (later renamed the Victoria and Albert Museum), which officially opened in 1857. Like the Crystal Palace, it was axially organized around a tall central nave-like space, with its structure exposed and an entrance at each end (Figure 2.14). As at the Crystal Palace, the displays helped define the alcoves, three on each side of the nave, that increased the building's vertical display surfaces. Provided with ample fenestration, the building was also like the Crystal Palace in bringing in natural light from all sides and notably from on high, thanks to windows set above the entrances on each of the building's gable ends.

Perhaps Albert anticipated that his children would receive the same impressions from their collection that he had hoped spectators would take from the Great Exhibition: first, "deep thankfulness to the Almighty for the blessings which He has bestowed upon us already here below"; and second, "the conviction that they [that is, God's blessings] can only be realized in proportion to the help which we are prepared to render each other; therefore, only by peace, love, and ready assistance, not

FIGURE 2.14. Interior of the Swiss Cottage Museum, Osborne, Isle of Wight. The arrangement of artifacts seen here dates from 1916 and is the work of Sir Guy Laking, the first keeper of the London Museum. Architect unknown, completed 1862. Photograph by the author.

only between individuals, but between the nations of the earth." Indeed, in the same widely reprinted speech, he celebrated "the unity of mankind" as "that great end to which, indeed, all history points." At the same time, Albert's vision for that unity was entirely compatible with British imperialism—both dependent on what he called "the peculiar characteristics of different nations" and also perfect harmony with "the great principle of division of labor." In this sense, he may have understood the museum as more than just an adjunct to schoolroom lessons in geography or botany; he may have seen it as offering a deeper message about Britain's understanding of itself as a benevolent power firmly ensconced at the top of an international hierarchy of peaceful nations.[109]

There were striking differences between the Great Exhibition and the Swiss Cottage Museum, especially in the ways the collections were formed. Explicitly seeking universal coverage, the organizers of the Great Exhibition had invited foreign nations to select, submit, and sometimes arrange the objects that would represent them to the world. In contrast, the Swiss Cottage Museum collection was the result of an approach that was at once less systematic and at the same time more firmly connected to the racial hierarchies that structured the British Empire. Indeed, some of the museum's contents were gifts presented to the children by adults to whom they were close and whose travels were linked to Britain's imperial project in ways that may have seemed inevitable to the younger royals. Lady Charlotte Canning, a former Lady of the Bedchamber, sent the children a collection of centipedes, tarantulas, scorpions, praying mantises, and stick insects from India, where she became the first vicereine.[110] Others were cultural objects the children bought or were given in their travels in either an ambassadorial capacity or (in the case of Alfred and Arthur) in connection with military service. When the Prince of Wales traveled to Canada in 1860, he was presented with a number of objects made by the Mi'kmaq people.[111] Still other objects were tributes to their sovereign mother, such as a *kaitaka* (a chiefly cloak made of flax) presented by Maori chief Hirini Pakia during his visit to Osborne in 1863.[112] Still other components of the display were military trophies, such as a Zulu spear taken by the Thirteenth Light Infantry at the Battle of Kambula during the Anglo-Zulu War in 1879.[113] Finally, there were taxidermied birds and animals that had been killed by members of the royal family; a snow wolf (purported to be the last wolf in Belgium) had been shot by the Belgian king Leopold, uncle to both Victoria and Albert, and served to highlight royal mastery over the more threatening elements of the natural world.[114] In its wide-ranging exhibitions, the Swiss Cottage Museum underlined the empire's racial logic by equating cultural artifacts produced by non-whites with the natural world or with antiquity; in contrast, contemporary artifacts created by Anglo-Saxons and Europeans were considered *objets d'arts* and displayed in the main house.

The Swiss Cottage Museum also differed from the Great Exhibition in terms of its audience. Open to the public (albeit for a fee), the Great Exhibition had, in Tony Bennett's formulation, rendered the crowd visible to itself as "a voluntarily self-regulating citizenry" understood to be in common cause with the powerful. In the process, the Great Exhibition helped constitute its myriad visitors into "the public."[115] In contrast, the Swiss Cottage Museum was a completely private space and one in which the royal children were not just spectators, that is, passive consumers of knowledge. Instead, they played an active curatorial role and thus played a part in knowledge production. In this sense, the museum functioned like an early modern cabinet of curiosities, sites where elite adults assembled their own collections in overtly artistic arrangements, creating eye-catching displays and reveling in the unusual, the exotic, and even the grotesque, qualities they also celebrated in menageries. Situated close to Osborne's small menagerie, the Swiss Cottage Museum had its share of grotesque objects, some of which seem to have made their way to the collection via other royal menageries. One such was a taxidermied five-legged deer, the "beloved companion of H.R.H. Princess Beatrice, Windsor Great Park," according to its handwritten label.[116] As the children curated their collection, they learned that their actions—not those of the people who made the cultural artifacts—brought order and meaning to what seemed to white British eyes like the inchoate output of the uncivilized corners of the empire. Not only did the museum allow the royal children to enjoy settings and engage in activities usually reserved for elite adults, it did so in ways that naturalized a sense of cultural superiority in which race was such a salient factor that its importance often went unremarked.

Very little is known about how the royal children ordered this growing collection, as the current arrangement dates from 1916, when Sir Guy Laking, then keeper of the London Museum, was engaged to prepare the Swiss Cottage for public visitation and to reorganize the display at the Swiss Cottage Museum, which had been open to the public since 1904.[117] Nonetheless, adult visitors were generally impressed with what they saw. In May 1863, Affie served as guide to the prominent geologist Charles Lyell, who wrote about the experience to his wife: "I have been . . . this morning over Prince Alfred's museum, and find that there is less disorder than I thought. Some rubbish to be thrown away of course, but most of it is very fairly grouped."[118] Lyell's experience also points to the fact that the Swiss Cottage Museum provided the young royals with opportunities to practice the conversational skills they were expected to master at an early age. Even as youngsters, the royal children were expected to *cercler*, that is, "to enter a room and move around it, speaking to each of the assembled company." According to her biographer, Princess Louise understood that the goal of the endeavor was for her "to make each one feel at ease and believe that she liked them and was interested in meeting them." Far from an inherent talent, this mode of conversation was a skill that had to be practiced. Louise refined her ability to *cercler* "with her sisters and assorted chairs strategically placed around the schoolroom."[119] Given that royal youngsters were most often in the company of adults, they needed to be able to converse with men and women many years their senior. The Swiss Cottage Museum was perhaps the perfect place to practice this skill—a private setting where the young royals had both a proprietary interest in their surroundings, as well as myriad opportunities for pointing out objects of particular interest and to field polite questions in return. Just as the laying of the foundation stone at the Swiss Cottage had provided Bertie with a chance to practice his public speaking skills, the museum gave all the siblings the opportunity to hone the equally important ability to speak one-on-one with their mother's subjects.

FAMILY TOGETHERNESS AT THE SWISS COTTAGE

As much as the royal children enjoyed arranging the museum, cooking seems to have been the central activity in the children's precinct, as it would be at elite children's cottages and playhouses for decades to come. The kitchen and scullery were lavishly equipped with goods supplied by the same firms that outfitted the royal kitchens. The youngsters had ready access to a pancake pan, wafering irons, baking sheets, pastry jaggers, and what food historian Annie Gray has characterized as "a veritable profusion of pastry cutters."[120] Although there was also a gridiron for grilling meat, its pristine condition suggests that it was rarely used. According to Gray, "The most used items all suggest that the bulk of the children's culinary experiments were concerned with the kinds of dishes that made up a Victorian tea or light lunch or supper—pastries, cakes, omelettes, fritters, custards, puddings, and biscuits."[121] Victoria's diary confirms that the children often had their supper at the Swiss Cottage, while she and Albert (and occasionally her mother and her ladies-in-waiting) sometimes enjoyed a tea prepared by the children. Although newspaper stories often claimed that the Swiss Cottage was where the royal daughters, in particular, learned the rudiments of cooking, Victoria made no such distinctions. Indeed, in July 1860, she reported that she "walked to the Swiss Cottage, where all the children were assembled for a supper of their own cooking."[122] In 1866, she specified the young cooks by name: Beatrice and Leopold "went to cook at the Swiss Cottage[,] always a great treat."[123]

While the royal children often seem to have been able to decide for themselves whether they would go to the Swiss Cottage and what they would do there, family birthdays were the exception. On those days, the cottage became the site for more coordinated enactments of family togetherness. Initially, the site was associated with the celebration of Victoria's birthday on May 24. On that date in 1854, she and Albert officially handed the Swiss Cottage over to the children. The next year, the family all walked together to the cottage, where Victoria planted a tree, the first of many memorial trees planted at the site. By 1856, the association with Victoria's birthday was less strong and the royal couple visited the Swiss Cottage only late in the day on a walk with "the girls" (presumably Vicky and Alice), Fritz, and Albert's brother, Ernest. That the visit was unplanned seems evident from the fact that they "found Mama & all the other children" there. Yet, in Victoria's mind, everything that happened that day was in honor of her birth; when "the Boys" (Bertie and Affie) showed her the little fort they had built under the direction of Affie's tutor, John Cowell, she interpreted it as a birthday surprise for her.[124] Over her next five birthdays, she visited the cottage three times, including in 1860, when the absent Vicky was much on her mind and she planted a tree at the site for a second time.

By 1858, the Swiss Cottage had become more closely associated with the birthdays of the children, who often marked the day by preparing and consuming a meal at the site, sometimes with their parents. On Louise's eleventh birthday in March 1859, Victoria noted that she and Albert "walked & drove, ending up at the Swiss Cottage, where all the Children had been cooking & we had tea with them."[125] Likewise, when Lenchen turned fifteen in May 1861, Victoria and Albert walked with Alice, Lenchen, and Louise to the cottage, "where Baby [that is, Beatrice] & Leopold met us, & we had tea."[126] On other occasions, the royal parents did not join the repast. When Affie turned fourteen in August 1858, they "went with the children to the Swiss Cottage, which was all decked with flags, in honour of the birthday, & they had luncheon there."[127] On Lenchen's thirteenth birthday in May 1859, Victoria and Albert again "went to the Swiss Cottage, where Vicky & all the others cooked."[128] (This entry is also noteworthy for confirming Victoria's sense that Vicky, who was visiting Osborne some five months after the birth of her first child, had a special relationship with the site. The sight of the young mother cooking with her siblings prompted the queen to write: "She is still *quite* the *child*, yet with the knowledge of a married woman." At the cottage, Vicky seemed—to her mother, at least—to inhabit a liminal state, simultaneously child and adult.) Similarly, on Beatrice's fourth birthday in April 1861, they "went to the Swiss Cottage, where we found a supper prepared for all the children."[129]

If the actual performance of family togetherness at the Swiss Cottage was somewhat uneven, it took on a greater consistency in hindsight. Indeed, in the years after Albert's death in December 1861, Victoria regularly recalled these occasions as moments when the family ate all together. In April 1864, the queen was missing her second daughter, Alice (by then the Duchess of Hesse-Darmstadt), on her birthday—"the first she has ever spent away from home." Later in the day, she and Beatrice "went to the Swiss Cottage, where *all* the others joined us for tea, just as dearest Albert would have wished & liked."[130] The suggestion that such birthday celebrations had originated with Albert is borne out by another diary entry later that summer, when the royal family continued the birthday tradition into the next generation by celebrating the fourth birthday of Charlotte, Vicky's second child, with a supper at the cottage. On any such anniversary, Victoria's practice throughout her long widowhood was to recall the last time Albert had been present and to dwell on her loss and grief. In this case, she remembered a time "3 years ago on this *very* day, when there was such a happy tea there, in which dearest Albert joined" and admitted that "such scenes are now especially painful to me."[131] The only thing Victoria held on to more tightly than her grief was her resolve to maintain practices Albert had established. As late as April 1871, on Leopold's eighteenth birthday, she recorded that she "walked down to the sea & back by the Swiss Cottage with my children, picking primroses of which there are quantities in the woods. Took tea at the Swiss Cottage."[132]

Victoria's insistence on maintaining Albert's approach to family birthdays also resulted in new practices, as she also tried to modulate her grief by changing where she was on important holidays and anniversaries. During Albert's life, the royal family had always been at Osborne for Victoria's birthday, but after his death, she made sure she was elsewhere, primarily Balmoral. In contrast, with very few exceptions, Christmas celebrations moved from Windsor Castle to Osborne. The same is true of the royal couple's wedding anniversary on February 10, which had never been celebrated at Osborne during Albert's life. After his death, that date found Victoria at Osborne every year but two between 1862 and 1900.

When, on February 10, 1862, Victoria was for the first time in her life at Osborne on the anniversary of her marriage, it must have seemed appropriate to do what she had done on so many other family occasions: pay a visit to the Swiss Cottage. Yet, rather than take tea with all her children, she and Alice drove to the cottage, where they planted trees. In her diary, she recorded that "the sun shone brightly & I felt *He* was very near us. Drove home round by the sea.—Dreadful as all was still the day was so blessed & precious, having brought me 22 years of such happiness, & I felt a sort of reflection of the past, which nothing can rob me of!"[133] Over the next nine months, she returned again and again to the cottage in the company of family members who planted trees there in Albert's memory: Vicky in late February, Affie in early March, Albert's brother, Ernest, in July, and in November Princess Alexandra of Denmark, who would become Bertie's bride the following March. The practice was revived briefly on her wedding anniversary in 1869, when Victoria, Beatrice, and Leopold walked to the Swiss Cottage, where "the three dear little children (Bertie's three eldest offspring Albert Victor, George, and Louise) met us & they & I each planted a tree."[134] Merging this new commemorative practice with the family's older custom, she returned later in the afternoon with Beatrice, Leopold, and her daughter Louise—those of her own children in residence at Osborne at the time—to take tea at the Swiss Cottage.

Tree planting continued at the Swiss Cottage throughout the 1870s, on several occasions to mark the marriages of her children. In April 1874, Affie and his new bride Marie, Grand Duchess of Russia, each planted a tree at the cottage.[135] Five years later, the newly married Arthur and Princess Louise Margaret of Prussia planted two trees "near Affie and Marie's."[136] For Victoria, these trees and others came to stand for the people who planted them, as is evident from an entry in December 1878, when she visited the Swiss Cottage and "looked at all the trees planted by my children & grandchildren, amongst them dear Alice's and little May's!"—her daughter and granddaughter who had recently died of diphtheria.[137] Even as late as 1888, Victoria continued to visit the cottage—in February of that year traveling by pony chair, while Bertie, Beatrice, and granddaughter Victoria walked, "where we looked at the historical trees."[138] In short, throughout Victoria's long life the Swiss Cottage was associated with reinforcing familial bonds among the members of the queen's immediate family—both among siblings, as well as between parents and children and between grandparents and grandchildren, although the nature of those bonds and the cottage's role in building and maintaining them varied, depending on the age, marital status, and physical proximity of the members of the royal family.

PUBLIC PERCEPTIONS OF THE SWISS COTTAGE

If the Swiss Cottage was the site where such familial togetherness could be enacted, it was also in the public eye, beginning in 1859, when the first published description appeared in White's *History, Gazetteer, and Directory of Hampshire and the Isle of Wight*. Reprinted in somewhat abbreviated form in the *Sheffield & Rotherham Independent* in June 1859, it focused exclusively on the younger royals and their activities; while readers could be expected to understand that the royal parents played a role in providing the cottage and its fittings, they are not mentioned explicitly.

That changed after Albert's death, when the Swiss Cottage became a tool of hagiography, presented as a powerful testament to the Prince Consort's excellence as a father. In his 1863 book, *The Prince Consort's Farms: An Agricultural Memoir*, John Chalmers Morton called out the Swiss Cottage and the gardens of the royal children as "interesting for the proof they give of the practical good sense that has guided the education which the Prince thought necessary for his family." The author was particularly struck by the material character of the site, seeing

> in the orderly arrangement of the tools, each one bearing its owner's name—in the well-tilled plots—even in the arrangements for practice and instruction in the kitchen, as well as in the admirable collections illustrative of various branches of natural

history in the Museum upstairs—proofs of that regard for the systematic, the useful, and the practical which the Prince Consort was known to possess.

According to Morton, the Swiss Cottage served not only an educational purpose but also an affective one: "still more interesting is it to learn . . . that the family bond is strengthened, here as in humbler instances, by every homely, family enjoyment shared in common." His evidence for this assertion was that "the Crown Princess of Prussia still retains her little garden, and produce from it is sent each summer from Osborne to Berlin."[139] Morton's views on the Swiss Cottage reached a wide audience, thanks to a number of newspaper reviews, several of which quoted long passages from his book and all of which mentioned the cottage and produce being sent each summer to Vicky in Berlin. Indeed, this last detail was repeated so often that it became lodged in newspaper accounts of the Swiss Cottage for the next decade, not just in the United Kingdom but also in the United States, where it certainly piqued the interest of American elites.[140]

This message of parental care was reinforced in the text of *The Osborne Album: Thirty-three Photographic Views of the Queen's Maritime Residence at Osborne*, published in 1867. In the written commentary provided by Doyne C. Bell, a member of the royal household and secretary to the committee overseeing the completion of the Albert Memorial, the Swiss Cottage was presented as "an apt illustration . . . of the kind and thoughtful care which the Royal parents have ever evinced towards their children." Albert's imprint was most closely associated with the garden, "where each son or daughter could exercise his or her skill in horticulture, and so thoroughly did the Prince Consort carry out this most sound principle, of teaching by illustration and personal experiment, that rows of shrubs, with their exact nomenclature, are planted in these gardens to illustrate certain classes of botany."[141] Both in associating Albert with the gardens and in interpreting them as evidence of his orderly mind, Bell's presentation of the site is in line with Morton's. If anything, he may have embellished Morton's themes by claiming that Albert used the gardens as a living textbook for teaching the children botany; in contrast, other sources highlight the role of the gardens in introducing the royal children to economic principles. So it is with hagiography, which often conveys more about the author's values than it does about the actions or intentions of the venerated person.

As its title suggests and its subtitle indicates, *The Osborne Album* also included photographs of the estate, taken by André Adolphe-Eugène Disdéri, the French photographer credited with having invented the carte de visite portrait photograph. His photographs of the French imperial family and other celebrities helped establish him as the most fashionable photographer in Paris. By the spring of 1865, he had opened a branch studio in London, where he was undoubtedly eager to follow a similar strategy. Perhaps the Empress Eugénie (of whom Victoria was very fond) recommended Disdéri to the British monarch. However it came to pass, Disdéri was soon making cartes de visite of Victoria and her children and also taking photographs of both Osborne (see Figure 1.1) and Windsor Castle.[142] Victoria already recognized the power of the new medium of photography, as she and Albert had used it (and especially cartes de visite produced by British photographer John Edwin Mayall in 1860 and 1861) as part of the deliberate promulgation of their domestic image.[143] After Albert's death, Victoria continued to use photography to present herself to her people, while also experimenting with ways to keep her husband's memory alive. Many photographs of Victoria or her children included Albert's visage, either in a portrait bust, a portrait painting, or in a miniature incorporated into her jewelry, the technique she used in the photograph circulated during her Jubilee in 1897. Disdéri's images of Osborne—where "everything . . . bears the impress of the Prince Consort's talented mind," according to Bell's commentary—were another way of commemorating Albert through photography.[144]

The Osborne Album broke new ground by giving Victoria's subjects the chance to see aspects of her maritime residence that before they had only been able to imagine from verbal descriptions. The Swiss Cottage was featured in two photographs: one, a panoramic exterior that includes both the two-story cottage proper, with rocks still holding down its shallow roof, as well as the Swiss Cottage Museum, with the gazelle house beyond; and the other, an interior view of the kitchen, centered on its unusual range, dark against the pale tiled walls that reflect the light of the windows behind the photographer (see Figure 2.6). The composition highlights the similarities between the Swiss Cottage kitchen and German *Puppenküchen* or Nuremberg kitchens, as they were often called in English. Enormously popular in the nineteenth century, when Germany was beginning to dominate the European toy market, Nuremberg kitchens were single-room dollhouses with a floor and three walls, but no ceiling. Typically, a kitchen stove was centrally located on the far wall, as in Disdéri's photograph of the Swiss Cottage. As historian James E. Bryan points out, the appeal of Nuremberg kitchens was enhanced by "the sheer superabundance and variety of their miniature cooking paraphernalia," tiny objects that overwhelm the storage capacity of the cupboards and shelves and often cover much of the floor, diminishing the toy's instructional value.[145] To be sure, the floors of the cottage kitchen were kept relatively clear. Yet, like toy kitchens, Disdéri's representation of the kitchen used by the royal offspring offered somewhat exaggerated "displays of material abundance." The open shelves of the dresser on the left make visible the plethora of cooking utensils at the disposal of the royal children, while the lower doors and drawers (some of them left ajar) hint at additional kitchen equipment lurking within. Indeed, the kitchen is so well equipped that several tools have no designated place and instead stand rather untidily in the room's back corners.

A business-savvy photographer, Disdéri sold several of his Osborne photographs as stereograph cards; purchased individually, they brought images of the queen's residence to a much broader market than the deluxe *Osborne Album*. Among these stereograph cards is an image of the Swiss Cottage scullery not included in the album (Figure 2.15). The photographer took a similar approach to representing the kitchen and the scullery. In each case, he stood near the south corner of the room and aligned the camera so that the door in the northwest wall of each room was just outside the left edge of the photograph. Given the slightly different placement of those doors, the image of the scullery focuses on the northwest and northeast walls and includes a tantalizing peek into the no longer extant larder beyond. Like the image of the kitchen, the focus is on material abundance; not only is every surface covered but pitchers hang from the shelves, blocking easy access to the impressive row of matching plates that disappear into the distance.

Disdéri's photograph of the scullery may not recall Nuremberg kitchens quite as forcefully as did his image of the Swiss Cottage kitchen. Nonetheless, it suggested the presence of children by the inclusion of two toys: a doll stove in the corner under the hanging clock and a model grocer's shop on the only free-standing piece

FIGURE 2.15. Scullery in the Swiss Cottage, Osborne, Isle of Wight. The photograph offers a glimpse of the third room of the kitchen suite. Probably a larder, the room was converted to other uses in the early twentieth century. Architect unknown, 1853–54. Stereograph by André Adolphe-Eugène Disdéri, circa 1867. Digital image courtesy of Getty's Open Content Program.

of furniture in the room. Larger than the stoves in Nuremberg kitchens and often fueled with alcohol, the former was a popular toy for allowing older children to heat food. The latter, with a sign that reads "Spratt, Grocer to Her Majesty" still stands in the cottage and gave the children practice in keeping accounts that Albert checked for accuracy.[146] Perhaps Disdéri's photographs, with their multiple evocations of toys, inadvertently fueled the oft-repeated description of the Swiss Cottage as kid-size in every detail. At the same time, they undoubtedly served to help Victoria's subjects imagine her offspring enjoying a carefree childhood, free from "the restraint of royalty," as the *History, Gazetteer, and Directory of Hampshire and the Isle of Wight* asserted in 1859.

Even twenty and thirty years later, the Swiss Cottage was mentioned in the press as material evidence that Victoria and Albert had been exemplary parents, ones who had raised modest, capable, and, above all, happy children. In 1879, an Indiana newspaper celebrated the cottage as a site where "the Queen taught her girls that there is nothing degrading in knowing how to cook, and that it is every woman's duty to be able to manage her own household."[147] Six years later, a review of Alice's biography (published after her death in 1878), associated the Swiss Cottage with encouraging "a certain independence on self" among the royal children, allowing each "to choose its own occupation and to enjoy perfect liberty."[148] The queen's jubilee in 1887 prompted additional interest in her children, including an article that quoted a letter Alice had written to her mother in which she reported that whenever she and Vicky were together, "We both always say to one another that no children ever were so happy, so spoilt with all the comforts and enjoyments that children could wish for, as we were." As evidence, the article goes on to describe the "delightful Swiss cottage" and its "real cooking stove, kitchen utensils, china-closet, small brooms and brushes, to be plied by busy housewives."[149] To be sure, the assumption that only the princesses learned to cook says more about the gender expectations of the late nineteenth century than it does about the royal offspring's actual use of the children's precinct. For commentators in the 1890s, who could not imagine boys learning to cook, Bertie and Affie were more closely associated with the tool shed, which they were said to have built. According to the one article, the shed revealed that the young princes "were no mean adepts at carpentering, the boarding of the sides being substantially put together and the gables of the roof mortised in true form."[150] Certainly, the story implied, a boy who could build so sturdy a structure would grow into a man who could keep Britain equally strong.

The point is not that these stories were accurate; they often contain a good deal of misinformation. They do confirm that the children's precinct, and especially the Swiss Cottage, played a key role in framing Victoria's offspring as the products of a happy childhood and as adults who (at least in the views expressed in anonymous news stories) were well prepared to carry out their regal duties. Many of the queen's subjects, it seems, accepted the premise that sentiment and dynasty were not necessarily at odds. Indeed, the Swiss Cottage seemed to offer them something more: assurance that sentiment could in fact serve dynastic ends.

THROWING OFF THE RESTRAINT OF ROYALTY

In Disdéri's photograph of the Swiss Cottage kitchen, the collection of long-handled tools in the corner on the left may have served to highlight the material abundance of the site; there was simply too much equipment for the cottage's storage cupboards. They also, perhaps inadvertently, served another purpose, pointing toward the two call bells, set high on the northwest wall. Especially in light of the claim that the Swiss Cottage was a site for carefree relaxation, the existence of these call bells is a useful reminder that the Swiss Cottage was also a place of work for a range of adults whose duties included attendance on the royal children.

Chief among the adults who worked at the cottage was its caretaker, Louise Warne, who lived on the first floor with her husband, Thomas, who worked as a gardener on the estate, and her aged mother. When the royal children were small, Mrs. Warne, presumably, helped them learn to cook and made their meals when they were not inclined to do for themselves. Like other members of the household staff, she only merited a mention in Victoria's diary when she did something unusual; in Mrs. Warne's case, it occurred in May 1856, when she took charge of the Chihuahua the queen had received as a gift.[151] Otherwise, the caretaker's constant presence did not receive comment. Only after Mrs. Warne's unexpected death in 1881 did Victoria reflect in her diary about "that good excellent Mrs. Warne," recalling that "she had been at the Swiss Cottage, ever since it was built in 55" and that "all our children were so fond of her."[152] In another entry, Victoria recalled that the children had called her "Warnie," suggesting that they interacted with her in somewhat the same way they did their nurses and governesses, whom they also gave pet names.[153] The Superintendent of the Nursery, Lady Lyttelton, was "Laddle," the English governess Sarah Anne Hildyard "Tilla," and the French governess Madame Rollande "Rollet." Retrospectively, Victoria framed the cottage as Mrs. Warne's domain, writing in her diary that "one cannot think of the place without her."[154] In a similar vein, she noted after a visit in December 1881 that she found "all, just the same in the little well known room where good Mrs. Warne, always used to welcome us with her kind smile."[155] The material reality of the site reveals that Mrs. Warne was not the queen's welcoming hostess but her well-behaved servant, ever prepared to respond to the tinkling of call bells in the kitchen.

Relatively little is known about spaces set aside for the Warnes' use, as their rooms were neither photographed during Victoria's lifetime nor inventoried (as was the rest of the Swiss Cottage) after the queen's death. The only firmly dated documentary evidence is a plan from 1856, which has sometimes been interpreted as a record of the building's original arrangement but is better understood, I argue, as a tool for communicating changes introduced within a few years of the structure's completion. Chief among these changes were the installation of a small W.C., and the introduction of a second, windowless, bedroom, presumably for the use of Mrs. Warne's mother, Jane Farley. Described in the 1851 census as "a pauper and former laundress," the older woman lived with the Warnes throughout their marriage.[156] Designed before the Warnes had been employed as caretakers, the original layout, I believe, consisted of two entirely separate L-shaped apartments, each composed of just three rooms. One contained the kitchen, scullery, and larder for the use of the royal children, and the other included one bedroom and two other rooms for the caretakers (see Figure 2.5).

This conjecture is supported by Albert's activities in other realms and particularly his involvement with the full-scale model houses that the Society for Improving the Condition of the Labouring Classes had built as part of the Great Exhibition. As president of the Society, Albert had a strong interest in the design of worker housing and supported, both politically and financially, the construction of the two-story building (with two family flats on each floor) at the Cavalry Barracks in Hyde Park. According to contemporary estimates, these model houses attracted some 250,000 visitors; they certainly earned the Prince Consort a Council Medal (the highest honor bestowed at the Exhibition) in the area of Civil Engineering, Architecture and Building Contrivances, despite the fact that they were designed by the Society's honorary architect Henry Roberts.[157]

The model houses were designed specifically for families of "manufacturing and mechanical operatives" who lived in urban settings. Nonetheless, they exemplify design principles understood to be more generally applicable. Chief among these was the protection of the family's privacy. Visitors were required to negotiate both an open-air gallery and an interior lobby in order to reach the living room, which itself served as a buffer between visitors and family sleeping spaces (Figure 2.16). Another important principle was the provision of three bedrooms, so that parents slept apart from their children, who were in turn separated by gender—"so essential to morality and decency." The location of the children's bedrooms was carefully considered to afford "the exercise of parental watchfulness, without the unwholesome crowding of the living room, by its use as a sleeping apartment." Physical health was as important as moral well-being, with each bedroom fitted out with "a window into the open air." The multipurpose living room with its cooking range was the largest room in

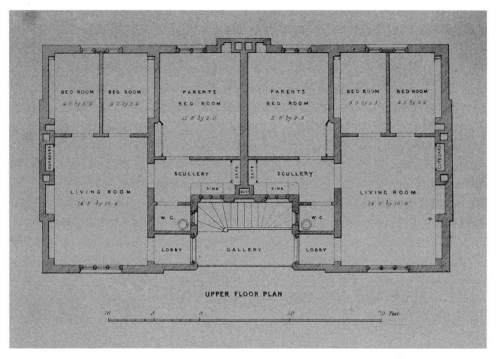

FIGURE 2.16. Plan of upper floor of the model house for families constructed under the aegis of the Society for Improving the Condition of the Labouring Classes for the Great Exhibition of 1851, with the financial support of Prince Albert. Henry Roberts, architect, 1851. Henry Roberts, *The Model Houses for Families, Built in Connexion with the Great Exhibition of 1851* (London: Society for Improving the Condition of the Labouring Classes, 1851), n.p.

the house and communicated with a separate scullery. Fitted out with a sink, coal bin, dust shaft, and ventilated meat safe, this small room also served to buffer the parents' bedroom from the bustle of the living room, "particularly in the case of sickness."[158] Across the scullery from the parents' bedroom was a W.C., complete with Staffordshire glazed basin, fed from a cistern on the roof. There was also attention given to how abutting units met, with the parents' bedrooms providing a sound buffer between the children's bedrooms and the neighboring apartment. In short, both within each dwelling and between dwellings, visual and acoustical privacy was understood to be essential to decent housing.

Given these principles, Albert is highly unlikely to have countenanced a design for the Swiss Cottage that included a windowless bedroom in the caretakers' quarters. Indeed, just one room could have served this purpose; only room C had "a window to the open air" that was so important to bedroom design, but not an exterior door that would have compromised marital privacy. Accommodating an aged mother on the premises was unexpected, but evidently not unacceptable. It did require compromises to the purity of the original design: the creation of a second (windowless) bedroom and the subdivision of the royal larder to create a W.C. internal to the house.[159]

While it may not be possible to demonstrate beyond all doubt that the Swiss Cottage was originally designed with only a single bedroom, it certainly did not have three—Albert's prerequisite for housing a family with children in decency. Thus, the layout of the caretakers' quarters indicates that the royal couple did not imagine that they would ever employ a caretaker with children. (After the Warnes died in 1881, they were replaced by another couple without children in their household, George and Julia Stone.) Indeed, the very presence of non-elite youngsters would have compromised the smooth functioning of the children's precinct, where normal social hierarchies (those that required youngsters to defer to their elders) were upturned. In the children's precinct, as in the main house at Osborne, the royal children deferred only to their parents and other royal visitors and could—and did—expect due deference from any other adult they encountered.

To be sure, the presence of other adults rarely merited comment in the queen's diaries. The evidence of Lady Stanley's letters confirms that even when quite young the children were always attended, whether by one or more of their governesses, a footman for each child, or some combination thereof. Indeed, being in the company of those of lesser rank was the sine qua non of royal existence, for both the queen and her children. While the Swiss Cottage was not fitted out with alcoves for footmen and pages that marked both the Pavilion and the main wing as royal spaces, it is possible to imagine these liveried figures standing on the balcony, poised to respond to a royal command from the rooms within. Even more than any architectural trappings, the presence of these attendants marked the Swiss Cottage as royal space.

This fact of royal life—the omnipresence of members of the royal suite—provides important context for contemporary assertions that the Swiss Cottage allowed the offspring of Victoria and Albert to "throw off the restraint of royalty." To be sure, the royal children may well have experienced the site in this way. Especially in comparison to the strictly hierarchical children's spaces in the Pavilion and the main wing, the cottage allowed the children relatively unstructured access to their siblings. At the same time, it also allowed them to undertake homely activities that seemed distinctly nonroyal to their contemporaries and that—according to those who observed them firsthand—brought the children great joy. Even before the children's precinct was established, Lady Stanley wrote that at Osborne "the children dine and tea in the garden, and run about to their heart's content, and yesterday evening they . . . washed a basketful of potatoes, and shelled a ditto of peas, which they are to cook for themselves to-day if they are good. Did you ever hear of such happy children?"[160]

While Lady Stanley came to find life at Osborne "of the quietest and most monotonous description," she also admitted to her father that "the children have so much more space and freedom to amuse themselves here than anywhere else."[161] In short, the royal children seem to have experienced Osborne generally and the Swiss Cottage in particular as a welcome change from the formalities of court life.

At the same time, the children were surrounded by adults who were never allowed to escape the demands of court etiquette. Mrs. Warne, footmen, governesses, even the noblewomen in waiting to the queen—all were bound to show due deference to the royal offspring, no matter how young they might be. In anything, the fact that the children could opt to ignore court etiquette while the adults who attended them could not only served to reinforce the youngsters' exalted status. In this sense, the Swiss Cottage served the interests of the royal children in two ways: providing them some relief from the formalities of court life, while simultaneously confirming the seemingly inalienable privileges of royal birth.

RAISING ROYALS AT THE SWISS COTTAGE

In this sense, the Swiss Cottage and the main house represent different, albeit complimentary, parental strategies for coping with the friction between sentimental attachments and dynastic interests. At the main house, these forces were held in tension, made manifest architecturally in the narrow corridor that both separated and connected the Pavilion and the main wing—the former supporting a version of family life that foregrounded sentiment, the latter sustaining the dynastic importance of the elder children. In contrast, the cottage was an attempt to give sentiment free rein by banishing dynastic interests altogether. This strategy was so at odds with the realities of royal life that it could only be attempted in its own distinct zone, made doubly remote by its distance from the main house and by the purportedly Swiss character of its buildings.

Nonetheless, there were limits to this strategy, as dynastic considerations were never entirely forgotten. If the somewhat exotic character of the children's precinct gave the youngsters a sense that they were escaping the constraints of royal life, it also helped disguise the fact that—even at this distance from Buckingham Palace and Windsor Castle—their social contacts remained tightly controlled by their parents. They interacted primarily with one another; with their grandmother and other members of their extended family; and with other European royals, who visited Osborne at their parents' invitation and were also often distantly related. There was never a chance they would encounter nonroyal children or form social connections that might lead to marriages of which their parents did not approve. If anything, the Swiss Cottage was calculated to highlight the virtues Vicky would bring to her future role as a royal consort in the Prussian court. To be sure, the cottage and its adjacent museum provided a pretext for the royal children to interact with some of their mother's more prominent subjects (such as geologist Charles Lyell). Yet, again, these visitors were vetted by the royal parents, and, even more telling, their encounters with young royals inverted conventional relationships between children and adults; as Lyell's letter suggests, the museum allowed a young prince to assume the role of a knowledgeable guide to an erudite man many years his senior. Finally, the children's interactions with those who attended their family—whether aristocratic ladies-in-waiting, the Warnes, or any number of unnamed footmen—reveal the extent to which the Swiss Cottage was embedded in court hierarchies. Even in a setting purportedly free from the formalities of court, nonroyal adults were required to treat the royal offspring with deference. However much Victoria and Albert may have wanted to give their children a "normal" childhood, the needs of the Crown also meant that these royal parents had to prepare their offspring for future roles that would be anything but ordinary.

When Victoria died in her bed at Osborne in 1901, the estate became the personal property of her heir, Bertie, by then Edward VII, who promptly gave it to the nation. The Pavilion served as the centerpiece of a site devoted to the late queen's memory. From 1904, the public was allowed to visit the Durbar Wing, the ground floor of the Pavilion, its terraced gardens, and the Swiss Cottage Museum; the Swiss Cottage proper was opened in 1916.[162] Although Victoria and Albert's apartments on the upper floor of the Pavilion were preserved as a shrine of sorts, accessible only to members of Victoria's family until 1955, early visitors were encouraged to look back at the house from the High Walk, to contemplate

> an object of national interest ... the room with the bay window on the first [in American usage, second] floor of the Pavilion Wing ... [where] Queen Victoria died. It may be readily recognized by the drawn blinds—a mute reminder of that day of universal mourning, the 22nd of January 1901.[163]

In contrast, the main and household wings were pressed into service as the Edward VII Convalescent Home for Officers serving in His Majesty's Forces, which opened in April 1904 and by October 1919 had cared for "no fewer than 7885 Officers," according to a 1919 Osborne guidebook.[164] The upper floors of the main wing, which had once provided accommodation for the elder princes and princesses and their attendants, were used for patient bedrooms, a ward kitchen, a sterilizing room, and a telephone exchange. The attendant renovations were substantial, obscuring many of the finishes, fittings, and furnishings that had been integral to expressing court hierarchies. In short, the parts of the estate that resonated most powerfully with Victoria's self-presentation as a domesticated wife and mother took center stage, while the interiors of those parts of the original house that were more closely associated with the formality of court life were all but obliterated.

In this context, it was perhaps particularly easy for visitors to accept the idea that the Swiss Cottage was simply a place for the royal children to enjoy a "normal," carefree childhood. Its role in preparing Vicky for her future as a royal consort in a foreign court was not in evidence. While the Swiss *escritoire* was on view, the guidebooks did not mention it, drawing the visitor's attention instead to the small *bureau plat* used by the late queen.[165] Perhaps, by 1916, the less said about Albert's vision of a unified Germany, closely allied with Britain, the better. Nor does the cottage conjure for visitors an image of the range of adults who attended the royal children involved there in their homely pursuits. Without a sense of Mrs. Warne, the ladies-in-waiting, the all-but-invisible footmen, it would be difficult indeed to understand the extent to which court etiquette remained in place, even at the Swiss Cottage.

Well before that date the cottage had made its mark in other ways. In 1902, for instance, Victoria's grandson, Grand Duke Ernest Ludwig of Hesse-Darmstadt, commissioned the Viennese architect Joseph Maria Olbrich to design a playhouse for the use of his six-year-old daughter. Although its miniature form and quaint architecture have more in common with somewhat later twentieth-century playhouses, the project, which still stands at Wolfsgarten in Darmstadt, may well have been inspired at least in part by the Grand Duke's childhood visits to Osborne.[166]

More direct descendants of the Swiss Cottage date from the last decades of the nineteenth century. In 1881, King Wilhelm III of the Netherlands built a chalet on the grounds of Het Loo Palace, in Apeldoorn, as a first birthday present for his daughter, Princess Wilhelmina; a kitchen and a boudoir were added in 1888–89. Soon after the ten-year-old Wilhelmina ascended the throne in 1890, her mother had another chalet built for her use on the grounds of the Soestdijk Palace, near Baarn in the province of Utrecht.[167] In 1897 it was mentioned in a glowing profile of the young queen, offered as evidence that the young monarch had received "practical instruction in the art of dairy farming, cooking, and general housekeeping, all acquired in the true childish fashion, under the guise of play."[168] Like the Swiss Cottage at Osborne, these chalets were understood to support the young queen's carefree childhood while simultaneously confirming her ability to rule.

Yet not just other European royals looked to the example set at Osborne. During the last thirty years of Victoria's long reign, a new class of superwealthy American industrialists adopted dynastic ambitions of their own. Enhancing the family's reputation was a social process, to be sure, but also one with substantial spatial implications. New forms of domestic space supported their efforts to amass social and symbolic capital. Children were integral to this endeavor, prompting some parents to hold out hopes that they might bring a title into the family by marrying a daughter to a dignified, if impecunious, nobleman. Although securing a royal husband was out of the question, they could certainly imitate some of the domestic arrangements Victoria and Albert had put into place for themselves and for the children on whom their all-important dynastic aspirations rested.

FIGURE 3.1. Children's cottage commissioned by Alice and Cornelius Vanderbilt II for the grounds of the Breakers, in Newport, Rhode Island. Peabody and Stearns, architects, 1886. Courtesy of Division of Rare and Manuscript Collections, Cornell University Library.

CHAPTER THREE

Making American Aristocrats in the Gilded Age Children's Cottage

In July 1886, the *Newport [Rhode Island] Mercury* reported that "Cornelius Vanderbilt ... had built at his Ochre Point residence a Toy house for the pleasure of his children." The story made no comment on the architectural features of this one-story, two-room cottage: not the whimsical figures supporting the roof of its porch, its bay windows, its half-timbered gables, nor the brick chimney rising high above its low roof line (Figure 3.1). The cryptic note included only three other facts: the architects were Peabody and Stearns of Boston; the builder was a Mr. McNeil, also of Boston; and the cost was $5,000.[1]

Astute *Mercury* readers would have known that Vanderbilt was the grandson of another Cornelius Vanderbilt (known as Commodore Vanderbilt), whose steamship lines had laid the groundwork for a family fortune subsequent generations increased by investing in railroads. They may have also been aware that the Commodore's son and heir, William Henry Vanderbilt, had died the previous December, leaving an estate reportedly worth some $200 million ($6.4 billion in 2024 dollars).[2] The greater part of the family's wealth was concentrated in the hands of his two eldest sons: Cornelius (the person mentioned in the *Mercury* and often identified as Cornelius II), who succeeded his father as chairman of the board of the New York Central Railroad, and William Kissam Vanderbilt. Nonetheless, sizable bequests to William Henry Vanderbilt's other six children consolidated their place among America's multimillionaires, a small, but highly visible group whose lives—particularly outside the boardroom—were a topic of great public interest.[3]

Many *Mercury* readers would have also known that Vanderbilt's Ochre Point residence was the Breakers, a rambling Queen Anne–style house designed by Peabody and Stearns for tobacco heir Pierre Lorillard (Figure 3.2). Completed in 1878, Lorillard's Breakers was just one of the many sizable summer "cottages" constructed by New

117

Figure 3.2. Exterior of the first Breakers, Newport, Rhode Island. Designed for Pierre Lorillard, the house was purchased by Alice and Cornelius Vanderbilt II in 1885. Peabody and Stearns, architects, 1877–78. Courtesy of Redwood Library and Athenaeum, Newport, Rhode Island.

York millionaires bent on transforming Newport, once a bustling eighteenth-century seaport city, into the chief venue for their summer social season.[4] Although it lasted just two months, the Newport season allowed New York's elites to escape the heat of the city, while maintaining the rigorous schedule of lavish entertainments integral to securing and protecting one's position within an exclusive social circle.[5] Cornelius II purchased the Breakers in 1885 and set about making changes that would allow his wife, Alice Claypoole Gwynne Vanderbilt, to entertain on a grand scale. (House and hostess became so closely identified that Mrs. Vanderbilt came to be known locally as "Alice of the Breakers.")[6] By the end of 1886, the Vanderbilts had engaged Peabody and Stearns to update the interior finishes of the main house and to construct an expansive new dining room.[7]

Before commencing that work, however, the Vanderbilts' first undertaking at the Breakers was the construction of the so-called Toy house for their growing brood: sons William Henry (born 1870 and known as Bill), Cornelius III (born 1873 and known as Neily), Alfred Gwynne (born 1877), and Reginald Claypoole (born 1880), and daughters Gertrude (born 1875; later, as Gertrude Vanderbilt Whitney, the founder of the Whitney Museum of American Art) and Gladys Moore (born 1886).[8] If the timing of the project suggests its importance to the Vanderbilts, so too did their choice of architects. By 1886 Peabody and Stearns were emerging as Boston's preeminent architects, well known for large houses in seacoast locations.[9] Equally telling was the structure's cost. At a time when a full-scale middle-class house and its lot could be had for $3,000, spending $5,000 to build a two-room structure for the use of one's children, on land one already owned, was unprecedented, at least in the United States.[10]

Yet, even the most perceptive *Mercury* readers were unlikely to have recognized the wider import of that so-called Toy house. Nothing about the snippet of news revealed that the building was a distant relation of the Swiss Cottage at Osborne, which had been designed to serve a remarkably similar set of functions. Nor was there any indication that two of Cornelius's siblings were responsible for building comparable structures on their country estates, presumably around the same time. Finally, no one could have foreseen in 1886 that these Vanderbilt outbuildings would play a foundational role in convincing other American elites that the reproduction of a family's class standing—the safeguarding of a family's social privilege—depended on creating a new range of children's spaces, both inside the house and out on the grounds.

Of the three children's cottages built by these Vanderbilt siblings, only the one commissioned by Cornelius II at the Breakers in Newport can be positively dated to 1886 and firmly attributed to an architect. Nonetheless, the others seem to have been built around the same time. In 1885, the same year Cornelius purchased the Breakers, his sister Emily Thorn Vanderbilt Sloane and her husband, William Douglas Sloane, started Elm Court, their estate in Lenox, Massachusetts, and like her brother, hired Peabody and Stearns to undertake the design.[11] Certainly, the Sloanes would have known of their architects' work on the Breakers children's cottage (as it came to be called), whether or not they employed the firm on their own "Cosy Cot." Although no longer extant, the building is visible on a 1905 Sanborn map, which indicates that it was a one-story structure with a porch incorporated into its simple rectangular footprint. In that sense, it was both comparable to the Breakers' children's cottage, but also somewhat less architecturally ambitious.

The third Vanderbilt property with at least one children's cottage was Idle Hour, the Long Island estate built for William K. Vanderbilt and his first wife, Alva Vanderbilt. Designed by Richard Morris Hunt, the main house had been completed in 1879 but then enlarged in 1883 and again between 1887 and 1889. At some point during the 1880s, these Vanderbilt parents added two outbuildings often used by their children, Consuelo (born 1877), William (born 1878 and known as Willie), and Harold (born 1884 and known as Mike).[12] One was the so-called teahouse (sometime rendered as "T" house), used by Consuelo for clambakes and picnics.[13] It is worth noting that the Breakers children's cottage was initially referred to as a teahouse as well, suggesting that the adult brothers (or perhaps their spouses) saw parallels between the two buildings. The name also suggests the children's cottage as a building type was so new that there was not yet an established nomenclature to describe it. In addition to the teahouse, Consuelo's memoirs indicate that she was also given "an old bowling alley" as her playhouse. This building stood much closer to the main house, in a location that accords with her recollections that she and her brother "would stroll home by the river in the cool of the evening."[14]

Arguably, all three Vanderbilt structures occupy a pivotal position in the history of the children's cottage as a building type. Yet, the cottage at the Breakers is the only one to survive in anything close to its original form and the only one to leave at least a modest trace in the archive. Thus, it offers the best opportunity for understanding how this generation of American elites used domestic architecture, and especially those spaces destined for the use their offspring, to serve their dynastic ambitions.

ARCHITECTURE, CHILDHOOD, AND PRIVILEGE

During the first decade of Vanderbilt ownership, the Breakers underwent a dramatic transformation. After a fire destroyed the main house in 1892, the couple entrusted its rebuilding to Richard Morris Hunt, who had designed (or was in the process of designing) at least four other houses for Cornelius II's brothers.[15] By the time of young Gertrude's coming-out ball in 1895, the gardens had been redesigned, the stables and greenhouses removed, and in place of the picturesque wooden house stood a stately, symmetrical limestone pile that evoked the palazzi of Renaissance Genoa (Figure 3.3).[16]

This later Breakers has been well documented in the history of architecture, where its design is recognized as playing a key role in the success of the lavish entertainments with which Cornelius II and Alice Vanderbilt made a place for themselves in society.[17] In contrast, the children's cottage has been assiduously ignored, perhaps because a small-scale, intentionally charming building purportedly designed for play does not appear to be a serious work of architecture. Certainly, it has been treated as distinct from the main house and unrelated to the adult activities and concerns manifest there.[18]

Yet, the children's cottage is integral to an understanding of the Breakers, insomuch as adulthood and childhood (like gender, race, class, and other social constructs) are constituted in relationship to one another. Indeed, children played an important role in the articulation of upper-class identity, albeit in ways that were quite distinct from

FIGURE 3.3. Exterior of the second Breakers, Newport, Rhode Island. This house was designed for Alice and Cornelius Vanderbilt II after the first Breakers was destroyed by fire. Richard Morris Hunt, architect, 1892–95. Courtesy of Redwood Library and Athenaeum, Newport, Rhode Island.

the British royal family. In contrast to Victoria and Albert, who deployed their children to highlight the values they shared with the queen's middle-class subjects, the Vanderbilts and other newly rich Americans were apprehensive about their social status and anxious to distinguish themselves from the middle class. Thus, they chose not to pursue the sentimental ideal of childhood favored among the bourgeoisie, although they had the financial resources to do so with vigor. Rather than organize their lives around the daily routines of their children, they focused on translating economic capital into cultural and social capital, the latter defined by Pierre Bourdieu as resources "linked to possession of a durable network of more or less institutionalized relationships of mutual acquaintance and recognition."[19] For these parvenus, the acquisition of social capital was perhaps the more elusive achievement, and these American aristocrats (as they liked to think of themselves) poured their wealth, time, and energy into the "unceasing effort of sociability" that Bourdieu has identified as central to the process in which social "recognition is endlessly affirmed and reaffirmed."[20] Although typically characterized as leisure, hosting and attending balls, tea parties, and other entertainments constituted a form of labor, especially for the women who acted as hostesses, but also for the men who often played large roles in commissioning the elegantly appointed houses—a major form of cultural capital—that served as the settings for these gala entertainments. In this sense, the acquisition of cultural capital and the maintenance of social capital were mutually supporting efforts.

In these social circles, children were explicitly excluded from adult sociability but implicitly central to their parents' drive for social status. Although Thorstein Veblen singled out the leisured woman as a public announcement of her husband's material wealth (for one thing, her restrictive clothing made it impossible for her to engage in "all vulgarly productive employment"), his formulation of conspicuous consumption applies equally to clean, well-dressed, leisured children.[21] In other respects, however, children were both more important and more threatening than their mothers to the family's social status, as they possessed untapped potential for establishing social connections, even as their own social inclinations were unpredictable and difficult to control. A daughter might marry a European aristocrat and thus bring her family a treasured form of symbolic capital they could not attain in other ways. Yet, it was equally possible for a child to befriend someone who would expose the family to distasteful and socially damaging connections.[22] Thus, at a time when middle-class offspring were becoming emotionally priceless to their families, the children of American aristocrats were valuable to their parents in a more concrete sense—dynastic resources that needed to be husbanded (in both senses of that word) in order to establish, maintain, and enhance their family's place in the upper echelons of society.

For American aristocrats enhancing class status was a complicated process that had a spatial component (creating new kinds of architectural spaces), as well as a generational one (managing the social interactions of their children in distinctly gendered ways). Space was integral to the project of using children to enhance privilege, while children were essential to using space to accomplish that goal. Yet, the relationships among space, class, gender, and generation were sometimes contradictory and not always easy to discern and interpret. Like their wealthy peers, the Vanderbilts tended to emulate the social and spatial practices of the British aristocracy, looking to a social milieu in which dynastic ambitions were understood to trump individual happiness. Yet, they were also enmeshed in a cultural moment in which the nuclear family was normative and the meaning of childhood had been transformed. They may not have embraced middle-class modes of family life, but they did not remain completely untouched by the cultural attitudes that buttressed them.

The children's cottage at the Breakers speaks directly to these contradictions. In its form and content, it evoked middle-class domesticity, but it did so in the service of an upper-class identity that sought to distinguish itself from the middle class. Ostensibly a site of play, it was also a place of work, both for the Vanderbilts' servants as well as for the Vanderbilt offspring, whose activities in the cottage were integral to preserving their value as potential conduits of social and symbolic capital. Modeled on an almshouse and devoted to the homely skills of cooking and sewing, the building made claims to humbleness that were refuted by its size and expense and by spatial arrangements that supported the Vanderbilt children and their parents in seamless performances of their privileged status.[23]

DOMESTIC SPACE AND ELITE IDENTITY

The importance of using domestic space to consolidate class status is suggested by the extended building campaign undertaken by the Vanderbilt family in the last quarter of the nineteenth century. This included Vanderbilt Row on New York's Fifth Avenue, as well as a number of country houses, notably the Breakers and Biltmore (1892–95), the Asheville, North Carolina, estate of George Vanderbilt, another brother of Cornelius II.[24] This family building campaign is regularly interpreted as the product of intense sibling rivalry, and certainly Cornelius II and William K. Vanderbilt saw themselves in competition to succeed their father as head of the family and its business affairs, while Alice Vanderbilt was deeply disapproving of her sister-in-law Alva.[25] But the constant rounds of building, expanding, and rebuilding suggests that the Vanderbilts—individually and collectively—were also involved in an effort to create new types of domestic containers in which they could build and maintain their place in society, while managing an unprecedented degree of public scrutiny. This struggle was less with their siblings (who faced the same challenges) and more with their own abilities to imagine these spaces and to articulate their needs to architects and other designers.[26]

This tension was exacerbated by the fact that there were few ostentatious houses to use as points of reference, even in New York, which had emerged after the Civil War as the social capital of the nation. As Wayne Craven has pointed out, New York elites of the previous generation—so-called Knickerbockers—favored brick and brownstone row houses that could be quite grand, but that shared key characteristics with their middle-class neighbors.[27] With the emergence of new social practices, particularly lavish private entertainments, the Vanderbilts and other Gilded Age millionaires found their domestic routines in flux. Increasingly they needed new types of rooms (ballrooms, picture galleries, and large dining rooms), while their need for some traditional room types—notably the parlor—evaporated.[28] The houses that emerged in response to these changes were not merely lavish in the extreme (although that is perhaps their most visible characteristic); they were also remarkably complex spatial models of human relationships, places that supported the performance of a range of social identities that were constantly constructed in relationship to one another.

The Vanderbilts' New York houses reveal the gradual emergence of new kinds of domestic space. Commodore Vanderbilt built his first house in Manhattan in 1845 at 10 Washington Place at Fourth Street. An ample four-story building with simple Federal details designed by Trench & Snook, it was a middle-class row house writ large, with a double parlor on one side of the entry hall and a reception hall and dining room on the other.[29] The Commodore's son, William H. Vanderbilt, followed suit in 1867, when he built a house on the southeast corner of Fifth Avenue and Fortieth Street. As shown in *Going to the Opera*, a family portrait painted by Seymour Guy in 1873, the room types and spatial arrangements of the house, with its double parlor, were familiar from 10 Washington Place and countless middle-class domiciles (Figure 3.4). The family's wealth was made manifest only in the size of the parlor and its human and material contents: the presence of servants, the sumptuous opera gowns of the family's grown daughters, the interior's fashionable décor, its up-to-date lighting technology, and the beginnings of what would become William H.'s vast art collection. Yet, despite these signs of the family's wealth, the apparatus of middle-class domesticity remained in place.

By about 1880, the Vanderbilts began moving in new directions. Not only did they relocate ten blocks north on Fifth Avenue (initiating a new neighborhood of elite housing), but the houses they built on Vanderbilt Row between 1877 and 1882 also departed from the domestic conventions of the Knickerbocker elite and the upper middle class in their materials, size, elaboration, and, eventually, in their room types and spatial arrangements as well.[30] Both William H.'s house (a portion of the triple palace he built to house himself and two married daughters, including Emily Sloane of Elm Court) and William K.'s French chateau (designed by Richard Morris Hunt) included parlors on their main floors. Yet, William H.'s Japanese parlor, exotically decorated to showcase its owner's growing porcelain collection, was a far cry from the room depicted in *Going to the Opera*.[31] These parlors were dwarfed and outnumbered by a new array of gala entertaining rooms (in addition to the enduring dining room): a drawing room, library, and 48-by-32-foot picture gallery in the father's house, and a library, breakfast room, billiard room, and salon (almost a third larger than the parlor) in the son's chateau. At West Fifty-Seventh Street, Cornelius II commissioned George B. Post to design a house in the early French Renaissance style (Figure 3.5). There he did without a parlor entirely, at least after this new house was expanded in 1892–94. In its final iteration, the house included, on the ground floor, separate reception rooms for ladies and gentlemen; on the first floor, a library, breakfast room, small salon, large salon, and three double-height spaces: ballroom, smoking room, and dining room. The fifth floor accommodated a bowling alley.

Unlike middle-class houses in which the parlor gathered the family, the new generation of Vanderbilt houses featured room types that segregated their inhabitants

Making American Aristocrats

FIGURE 3.4. Seymour Guy, *Going to the Opera*, 1873. A portrait of the family of William Henry Vanderbilt and Maria Louisa Vanderbilt, set in the parlor of their house at Fifth Avenue and Fortieth Street, New York City: Cornelius Vanderbilt II (of the Breakers) stands at the far right, next to his seated wife, Alice Vanderbilt. Emily Thorn Vanderbilt Sloane (of Elm Court) stands nearby, holding the hand of her husband, William Douglas Sloane, who is seated next to Alice. William K. Vanderbilt (of Idle Hour) stands in the background in the center of the composition. He had not yet married Alva Smith, who was not included in the group portrait. Reprinted with permission from The Biltmore Company, Asheville, North Carolina.

for much of the day by sex, age, and class. The billiard room, the smoking room, the library, and the dining room were understood as male spaces, while the drawing room and breakfast room accommodated the social activities of women. Accompanied by increasingly complex arrangements for disguising the presence of a large number and variety of service spaces (as well as their human operatives), this multiplication of entertaining spaces facilitated a degree of spatial separation between men and women and between gentry and servants that architectural historian Annmarie Adams has pointed out was "a significant indication of class."[32]

Figure 3.5. Exterior of Cornelius Vanderbilt II house, northwest corner of Fifth Avenue at West Fifty-Seventh Street, New York City, before it was expanded in 1892–94. George B. Post, architect, 1879–82. Courtesy of Division of Rare and Manuscript Collections, Cornell University Library.

THE DEMISE OF THE PARLOR

While the emergence of these new room types is meaningful, the disappearance of the parlor is also significant for an understanding of class-based differences in parent–child relationships. For middle-class Americans, the parlor was the most important room in the house. To be sure, it was understood as the setting in which the family's cultural refinement was on display and in some households was reserved for receiving guests and other formal occasions. However, it was also closely associated with emotional intimacy within the nuclear family, a social entity gaining in importance even as it was shrinking in size.[33] Consider, for instance, *Family Devotion*, an idealized scene of a middle-class parlor published by Currier and Ives in 1871 (Figure 3.6). In it, youthful parents and their three young children gather around a parlor table and its small circle of light. Seated in their chairs, father and mother frame the scene, defining the space inhabited by the children. While mother and children turn their attention to the father, who is pictured in profile reading aloud from the Bible, the

FIGURE 3.6. *Family Devotion: Ask, and it shall be given you; seek and ye shall find, Matt. VII.7.* Currier and Ives, 1871. Popular Graphic Arts Collection, Prints and Photographs Division, Library of Congress, cph 3b50177.

frontal presentation of the mother and her physical contact with the two younger children highlight her importance to the family structure. The children may be read either as passive recipients of their parents' religious instruction or as the wellspring of the moral sentiment that pervades the scene. As Karen Sánchez-Eppler argues, nineteenth-century temperance literature was full of tender young moral agents whose submissiveness and innocence were responsible for the redemption of their fathers.[34] In either case, the parlor here is both the incubator for and the outward expression of close relationships between parents and children. Indeed, the title has a double meaning; as these family members use the parlor as a setting for religious devotion, they also enhance their devotion to one another as a family.

Contrast that scene with Guy's 1873 representation of the Vanderbilts in the parlor they would abandon by the end of the decade (see Figure 3.4). At one level, *Going to the Opera* suggests that William H. and his wife, Maria Louisa, imagined the parlor in ways that their middle-class contemporaries would have recognized—as a venue for the display of the family's cultural sophistication and as a site where parents and children could acknowledge and celebrate the familial bonds uniting them. Yet, the scene is hardly a celebration of close emotional ties between youthful parents and their small children. In 1873, William H. and Maria Louisa Vanderbilt had been married thirty-two years and had eight surviving children, four sons and four daughters, ranging in age from twelve to thirty.[35] Three of these children were married and by the end of the year would have produced four offspring of their own. These married children stand in the right foreground of the canvas; their spouses sit near them or stand in the middle ground beyond. They almost dominate the scene, except that the sharp gazes of the two married daughters return the viewer's attention to their dignified father, who sits in perfect profile in the left foreground, pocket watch in hand. Their mother is a secondary figure in the middle ground beyond; rather than framing the action with her husband, she herself is framed by her two youngest sons. Bracketed by the figures of William H. and his eldest son Cornelius II (who ignores his father), *Going to the Opera* presents a distinctly patriarchal version of family structure, even as it hints at the tensions involved in transmitting patriarchal authority from one generation to the next. Family unity is represented here as a matter of dynastic continuity. Emotional closeness may have existed among various individuals, but it was not the glue expected to bind the family together. The Vanderbilts had little use for a room type closely associated with fostering the tender emotions that united middle-class parents and their offspring, and it is little wonder that parlors soon disappeared from the plans of their houses.

The next generation went even further than William H. in treating their offspring as resources whose marriages were integral to the failure or success of dynastic ambitions. This was notoriously true for William K.'s daughter, Consuelo, who was forced by her mother, Alva, to marry Charles Spencer-Churchill, 9th Duke of Marlborough, in 1895, despite the fact that the eighteen-year-old girl was in love with a rich young American man to whom she considered herself engaged. Although loveless, the marriage was for some years a success in dynastic terms in that it produced two male heirs and provided Marlborough with the funds to maintain Blenheim Palace, his ancestral home.[36] In her turn, Alva (who divorced William K. the year her daughter married) achieved an entrée into a form of aristocracy the United States could not offer her.[37] Scandalized by Alva's behavior, the rest of the family did not attend Consuelo's wedding. Yet, their actions reveal similar aspirations and a comparable willingness to discount emotional happiness as a factor in approving their children's choices in marriage partners. Cornelius II and Alice, for instance, refused to speak to their son Neily when in 1896 he successfully resisted patriarchal authority and married Grace Graham Wilson, whom the senior Vanderbilts considered an adventuress.[38] Like Alva, Alice (widowed in 1899) also had the pleasure of seeing a daughter married to a European aristocrat, when in 1908, her youngest child, Gladys, wed the Hungarian Count László Széchényi.

The Vanderbilts' desire to connect themselves to European aristocrats highlights their fraught relationship with mainstream culture. To be sure, this ambition was widely shared among American multimillionaires eager to secure for themselves a social status money could not buy. At the same time, public opinion held that that was precisely what they had done.[39] The Vanderbilts were not totally immune to the judgment of their middle-class contemporaries and encouraged press coverage that assured readers they were "fitting [their children] for life as well as any mother or father could do." An 1890 story in the *Ladies' Home Journal* praised the Vanderbilts for establishing a regular routine for their offspring: "never permit[ting] their children to remain up late at night," ensuring that breakfast was "an unpretentious meal," and filling their days with study, punctuated by frequent airings in the park. What is more, these wise parents did not allow any display of "elaborate dress." According to the anonymous author, "If you were to see these children on the street, you would not for a moment suspect that they were other than children of parents in ordinary circumstances." The story may have overstated the ordinariness of the existence of the young Vanderbilts; even the author had to acknowledge that they "have their own ponies, dog-carts, and boats, and they go to dancing-school and swimming-school, [and] are taught to fence and box, [and] ride horseback."[40] Despite these expenditures, the Vanderbilts shared with their bourgeois critics the desire to do all they could to help their offspring thrive, both in their youth and as adults. Indeed, like their middle-class contemporaries, they continued to live as nuclear families and to understand childhood as a distinct phase of life. The differences arose primarily in the preparation they gave their children to accept their social privilege as a matter of course.

CHILDREN'S SPACES IN AN ELITE NEW YORK CITY HOUSE

The Vanderbilts' domestic arrangements speak to the challenges they faced as parents. If they had little need for parlors, they did require nurseries like those in middle-class houses, rooms that protected adult areas of the house from the sights, sounds, and smells of infants.[41] Unlike their middle-class contemporaries, the Vanderbilts and other American aristocrats also built a wider range of children's rooms to complete the spatial segregation that organized the rest of the house; to give material expression to distinctions among children, by age, gender, and rank (as determined by birth order); and to provide settings in which children could prepare for their adult roles.

The types and functions of various children's spaces were explained in detail by British architect Robert Kerr in *The Gentleman's House, or How to Plan English Residences, from the Parsonage to the Palace.* Despite its nationalistic title and the vignette of Osborne that graced its title page, this 1864 book was influential on both sides of the Atlantic, where it was the bible of the spatially segregated, parlorless planning embraced by the Vanderbilts and their ilk.[42] The author's tendency to illustrate these spatial principles with plans of manor houses may well have increased the book's popularity among wealthy Americans who modeled their behavior on the social practices of British aristocrats and often harbored aspirations of joining their ranks, if only through marriage.

Kerr identified the treatment of children's spaces as one of the chief distinctions of class. In houses above "a certain mark," he noted, "the completeness of the withdrawal [of children] will be the chief object."[43] The precise location of this withdrawal depended on both the age and gender of the child. Infants and younger children of both sexes were cared for in a nursery under the supervision of a nurse. In its most complete form, the nursery was an extensive suite of rooms: a day nursery, a night nursery (preferably with a bathroom attached), a nursery scullery (expected "in every case of pretension"), and, "in superior houses," a nurse's room as well. Arranged like "a cheerful Sitting-room," the day nursery needed to be large enough to accommodate the play of the children of the house, their friends, and the children of their parents' guests. Fitted with beds for several children and the nurse, the night nursery would ideally have "a cheerful morning aspect . . . and a comfortable fireside for seasons of illness." Kerr noted that "the most usual position for the Nurseries in a good house is at that point where the Family Sleeping-rooms and the Servants' rooms meet at the Back Staircase, and on the First [in American usage, second] Floor."[44] In the plans Kerr used in the second and third editions of his book to illustrate what he considered ideal arrangements, the nursery suite was on the servants' side of the back stairs, suggesting that the nursery was closely associated with the abject—preverbal infants, soiled bibs, and dirty diapers (Figure 3.7).[45]

Older children of both sexes slept in their own bedrooms but were expected to spend their waking hours in the schoolroom, where their daily routines were overseen by a tutor (for boys) or a governess (for girls). Like the nursery, the fully equipped schoolroom was a suite of spaces: the schoolroom itself (a combination study/dayroom for the pupils and sitting room for the governess), a bedroom for the governess (preferably close to the bedrooms of the young ladies), a separate entrance lobby, and a washroom with water closet. Unlike the nursery, the schoolroom (housing as it did children old enough to control their bodily functions) could be placed in proximity to the family bedrooms. Boys, according to Kerr, could be expected to leave the schoolroom before their sisters in order to attend boarding school. Girls, presumably, would spend their days in the schoolroom until they were old enough to join the adults in other parts of the house.[46]

The built evidence suggests that Cornelius II and Alice Vanderbilt were aware of the principles of spatial segregation described by Kerr, although they adapted them

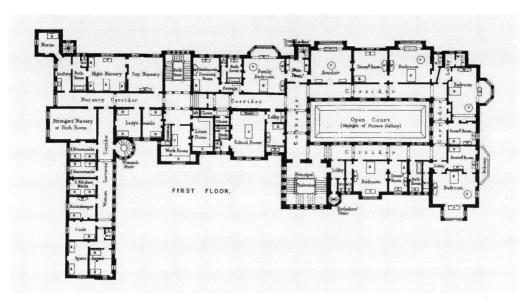

FIGURE 3.7. Second-floor plan of Bear Wood, Berkshire. The extensive nursery suite is in the upper left portion of plan, separated from the parental sleeping quarters by the back stair. Robert Kerr, architect, 1865–74. Robert Kerr, *The Gentleman's House, or How to Plan English Residences, from the Parsonage to the Palace*, second edition (London: John Murray, 1865), plate 36.

somewhat to their particular needs. In the first iteration of their New York house on Fifth Avenue at Fifty-Seventh Street, the relatively constricted site meant that the spatial segregation of children was achieved vertically, with most of the building's third floor dedicated to their use, well away from the ground floor rooms devoted to adult sociability.[47] The third floor featured the key room types Kerr recommended for the care and maintenance of elite youngsters: a schoolroom at one end of the hallway and, at the other, day and night nurseries opening onto a subsidiary corridor that helped insulate them from the main hall (Figure 3.8). A spiral stair led down from the night nursery to a large chamber in the second-floor bedroom suite shared by the senior Vanderbilts, giving the parents relatively easy access to their small children.[48]

In 1894, some eight years after the construction of the children's cottage at the Breakers, the Vanderbilts expanded their New York house and renovated many of its existing rooms (Figure 3.9). In large part, these changes were motivated by the desire for an expanded range of spaces for gala entertainment (notably a vast first-floor ballroom) and by the aspiration to keep pace with changing tastes (shifting from the Aesthetic movement interiors initially designed under the leadership of John La Farge to Louis XIV and Louis XV interiors, many of which were created in Paris by Jules Allard et Fils).[49] Yet, in meticulous drawings that show the entire building

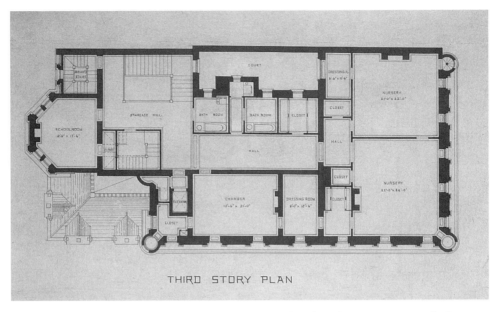

FIGURE 3.8. Third-floor plan of the Cornelius Vanderbilt II house in New York City, before the 1892–94 expansion. The smaller of the two nurseries (identified in later plans as the night nursery) communicated via a circular stair with the bedroom suite of the senior Vanderbilts on the floor below. George B. Post, architect, 1879–82. Collection of The New-York Historical Society.

and all its human inhabitants, architect George B. Post made it clear that he and his clients understood the house not solely as a set of gala rooms that fulfilled its destiny during fancy-dress balls, but as a carefully designed container for an intricate social system that functioned around the clock, day after day, and of which children were integral parts.

The expanded house continued to facilitate the withdrawal of children from the main part of the house, while allowing for the different treatment of sons and daughters of different ages. The third-floor nursery suite was largely unchanged, although alterations on the floor below meant that it connected with a dressing room (rather than a chamber) in the parental suite. As they left the nursery, female children were kept closer to their parents, perhaps because their presence was considered less disruptive to adult routines or because they were considered in greater need of parental oversight. In contrast, spaces for male children were kept at some remove (a pattern familiar from Osborne), allowing boys greater scope for independent action, while keeping them out of earshot. In both realms—and in contrast to middle-class practice—the eldest son and elder daughter were provided with rooms that helped each of them prepare for the adult activities they would soon be expected to perform.

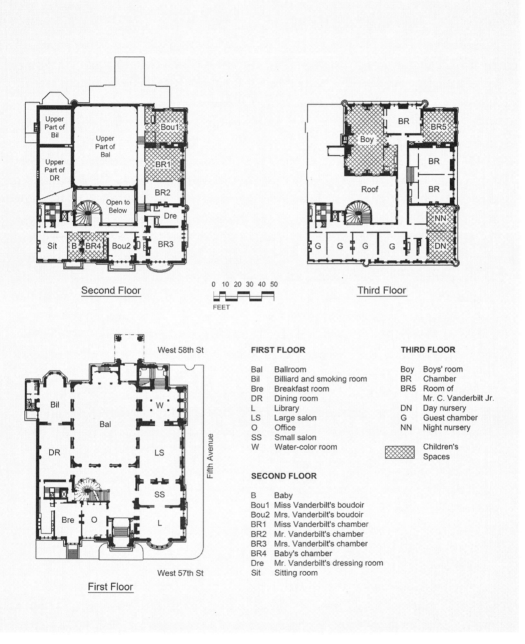

FIGURE 3.9. First-, second- and third-floor plans of the Cornelius Vanderbilt II house in New York City, as expanded. The Vanderbilts kept their daughters' rooms close to their own on the second floor, while their sons enjoyed greater freedom from parental supervision on the third floor. George B. Post, architect, 1879–82, 1892–94. Drawing by Daniel De Sousa.

Gertrude, for instance, who was quickly approaching her coming-out in society, was provided with accommodation on the second floor that paralleled her mother's: a chamber, a connecting boudoir, and a private bath.[50] The curtains hanging in the doorways between boudoir and bath acted "as both screen and frame" and, according to architectural historian Laura Jenkins, allowed the bathroom to serve competing aims, namely, "to preserve a body that was untainted sexually and morally, and to initiate one that could elicit desire and invite admiration on a physical level."[51] For a debutante to fulfill her ultimate purpose—making a brilliant marriage—achieving both objectives was essential.

On the third floor, her brother Neily was provided with a private chamber, albeit sans private bath.[52] Although Neily's chamber was only the size of Gertrude's boudoir (located directly below it), he and his brothers also enjoyed the use of a new room type: the "boys' room." The significance of this room is signaled by both its size and its location. Situated directly above the all-important double-height ballroom, it was one of the largest rooms in the house. Covering an area larger than the grand dining room on the first floor, it was also taller than any other room on the third floor. This height difference was made possible by the introduction of a light court between the boys' room and the guest rooms that faced West Fifty-Seventh Street. In addition to providing fenestration on three sides of the room, this arrangement served to set the room apart from the rest of the house, providing the Vanderbilt sons with a degree of spatial autonomy very different from that of their sisters. Indeed, in Post's presentation sections, the room has the appearance of a free-standing pavilion, an impression that was enhanced by the tall pyramidal roof that sits atop the boys' room and the adjacent guest chamber (Figure 3.10). From the exterior, this roof made the boys' room a commanding presence on the West Fifty-Eighth Street façade (Figure 3.11). Inside, the room was dominated by a massive fireplace whose over-life-size caryatids (designed by Augustus Saint-Gaudens and representing Pax and Amor) supported a mosaic overmantel by John La Farge (Figure 3.12).[53] The entire ensemble had once graced the original entrance hall of the house, while the room's carved ceiling panels of mythological figures (also by Saint-Gaudens) were recycled from the older dining room. Furnished as it was with a pool table, sofas, and chairs, the boys' room accommodated at least some of the activities that older men pursued in the Moorish billiard and smoking room. That it shared the scale and finish of first-floor gala rooms suggests that the boys' room was intended as a place where Vanderbilt sons could entertain their friends, while also practicing elite modes of male sociability they would soon encounter in the world of adults.[54]

These new mansions of the Gilded Age were much more than a constellation of gala rooms for new modes of entertaining. Equally important were a wide variety of family spaces, many of them devoted to the use of children. In addition to preserving

FIGURE 3.10. Detail of a longitudinal section through the Cornelius Vanderbilt II house, after it was expanded. On the left is the original house with its front door facing West Fifty-Seventh Street. On the right is the new addition, which included large, ornate, double-height spaces housing the ballroom on the first floor and the boys' room above it. George B. Post, architect, 1879–82, 1892–94. George B. Post Collection, PR 053, New-York Historical Society, 100323d.

the gala rooms for adult sociability, the children's spaces helped youngsters, especially those approaching adulthood, practice and perfect the performance of elite identity.

CHILDREN'S SPACES AT THE FIRST BREAKERS

The importance of children's spaces to the effective operation of an elite household is particularly clear in the changes Cornelius II and Alice Vanderbilt made at the Breakers. Commanding a dramatic ocean-front site on Ochre Point, the main house was something of a hybrid. With its Queen Anne details, irregular footprint, and lively silhouette, the exterior of the Breakers incorporated forms that (thanks in large part to the writings of John Ruskin) had become requisite expressions of cozy domesticity for any family that aspired to gentility (see Figure 3.2). In that sense, except for its great size, the Breakers has a great deal in common with upper-middle-class houses. The plan, however, boasted many of the room types and spatial arrangements familiar

FIGURE 3.11. Exterior of the Cornelius Vanderbilt II house, after it was expanded, showing the new ceremonial entrance, with its porte-cochère, facing West Fifty-Eighth Street. The broad pyramidal roof marks the location of the boys' room and an adjacent guest room on the third floor. George B. Post, architect, 1879–82, 1892–94. Library of Congress, Prints and Photographs Division, Detroit Publishing Company Collection, LC-DIG-det-4a08584.

from British country houses and necessary to sustain the house parties and lavish balls at the center of the Newport summer social season (Figure 3.13). Like the houses on Vanderbilt Row in New York, the first Breakers lacked a parlor, the symbolic and physical core of any middle-class domicile. A prominent fireplace—the other symbol of family togetherness—was located in the capacious entrance hall near the stairs, an arrangement also apparent in other Newport cottages of the 1870s and 1880s, notably the William Watts Sherman house (designed by H. H. Richardson and completed in 1875) and the Isaac Bell house (designed in 1881–83 by McKim, Mead & White). At the Breakers, however, this stair hall was an immense space that did double duty as a ballroom. On one side of the hall were a morning room, drawing room, and library—essentially the distaff side of the house. On the other side were rooms associated with men: the billiard room and the dining room (the site for the

Figure 3.12. Boys' room in the Cornelius Vanderbilt II house, after it was expanded. During the expansion, the mantlepiece featuring caryatids sculpted by Augustus Saint-Gaudens was relocated from the first-floor entrance hall to the third-floor boys' room. The mantelpiece is now in the collection of the Metropolitan Museum of Art. George B. Post, 1892–94. Collection of The New-York Historical Society.

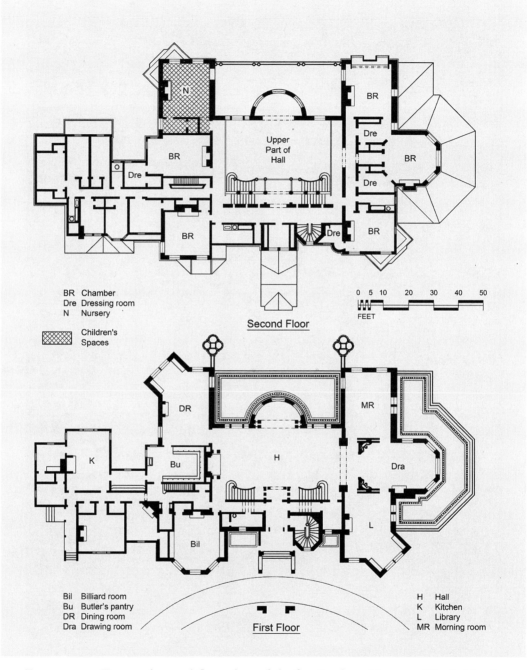

FIGURE 3.13. First- and second-floor plans of the first Breakers, Newport, Rhode Island. The nursery is located near the service wing, on the opposite side of the house from the interconnecting bedrooms presumably used by the children's parents. Peabody and Stearns, architects, 1877–78. Drawing by Erin Okabe-Jawdat; revised by Daniel De Sousa.

male ritual of after-dinner port and cigars). The first Breakers also provided essential service spaces, including a spacious butler's pantry fitted out with cabinets (for the storage of china, crystal, and silver in vast quantities) and countertops (for the transformation of dishes prepared in the enormous kitchen into highly wrought sculptural concoctions deemed appropriate for the dining room).

The elite character of the first Breakers was also evident on the second floor, notably in the provision of five spacious sleeping chambers, all of a similar size, two of which (those located above the morning room and the drawing room) were linked by a communicating dressing room—an arrangement that provided separate bedrooms for husband and wife. The second floor also provided a nursery, located (as Kerr recommended) well out of sight of ground-floor rooms devoted to entertaining and in a liminal space closer to the back hall and servants' rooms than to the parents' chambers. Yet, Lorillard's Breakers did not include the full range of children's spaces enumerated by Kerr and in evidence in the first iteration of the Vanderbilts' New York house, despite the fact that in 1878 Pierre and Emily Lorillard had four children ranging in age from five to twenty.[55] Perhaps because it was built for use only during two months each summer, the original Breakers included no school room—the room type that served as a catchall space for children who had outgrown the nursery.

To correct this deficiency, even before the Vanderbilts set out to expand the gala rooms of their Newport estate, they added the children's cottage. While no extant written documents record the Vanderbilts' decision to undertake this project, an analysis of the building's siting, exterior design, interior arrangements, and social use reveals that the cottage was an integral component of the larger estate—part of the complex spatial system that Cornelius II and Alice Vanderbilt created to provide a stage on which to perform their own sense of themselves as American aristocrats, to prepare their children to maneuver successfully in this exclusive social milieu, and to manage parent-child relationships complicated by great wealth.

LOCATING THE CHILDREN'S COTTAGE

One of the first steps in the process of constructing the cottage was to identify a site for it on the grounds of the estate, a picturesque garden originally designed for Lorillard in 1877 by Ernest Bowditch, a Boston-based landscape architect. Bowditch maintained an active interest in the site into the 1880s; in the years bracketing the construction of the cottage, he designed landscapes for Vinland (the adjacent estate owned by Lorillard's cousin, Catherine Lorillard Wolfe) and Wakehurst, which stood across Ochre Point Avenue from Vinland. Bowditch envisioned the Breakers and Vinland as "foils for each other"—conceptually, at least, one contiguous landscape whose serpentine paths were intended to enhance the natural appearance of what was, in fact, a highly contrived layout.[56]

Circulation was considered with care and helped orchestrate cross-class interactions between the Vanderbilts and their guests on one hand, and the men and women who lived and worked at the Breakers as servants on the other (Figure 3.14). A gatehouse at the center of the Ochre Point Avenue side of the property marked the main entrance where an oval driveway led to the main house before continuing on to the carriage house and stable (marked in plan with an X). Narrower drives and footpaths formed two secondary, and sometimes overlapping, circulation systems. One connected the oval drive with service outbuildings concentrated in the northwest corner of the site.[57] The other system—for use by family and guests—emanated from the main house and made a leisurely circuit around the balance of the estate. Plantings reinforced the different characters of the two systems. Lush vegetation along the service paths and drives shielded the house from public view and helped disguise the existence of outbuildings (Figure 3.15), while low floral borders and a broad expanse of lawn provided the family and their guests with an unimpeded view of the ocean.

The children's cottage was situated between these two circulation systems. Sitting on the edge of the property's service-oriented quadrant, it was similar to the stable and greenhouses in that it was not accessed directly from the oval drive and remained only partially visible from the drive and from the ocean. Yet, its porch and main door faced away from the service buildings, addressing a family footpath that connected

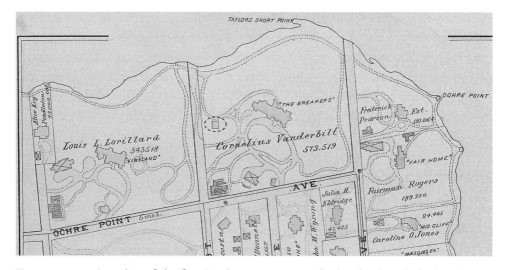

FIGURE 3.14. Site plan of the first Breakers, Newport, Rhode Island. A dashed oval marks the location of the children's cottage, which was added to the site in 1886. L. J. Richards & Co., *Atlas of the City of Newport, Rhode Island* (1893), plate B. Courtesy of Redwood Library and Athenaeum, Newport, Rhode Island.

Figure 3.15. The first Breakers, seen from Ochre Point Avenue, Newport, Rhode Island. The lush plantings all but hide the house from view. Peabody and Stearns, 1877–78. Courtesy of Redwood Library and Athenaeum, Newport, Rhode Island.

the house to the sea. In many ways, the situation of the cottage on the estate grounds was akin to the location of the nursery inside the house. Plantings reinforced the distinct character of the cottage zone. Hollyhocks, associated with "old-fashioned" cottage gardens, dominated the rear planting beds, while a garden of individual plants on the south side of the house (perhaps a kitchen garden) contrasted sharply with the dense flower beds that lined walks and surrounded the main house.

After the first Breakers burned in 1892, the cottage remained unchanged. The landscape, however, underwent a dramatic transformation, as Ernest Bowditch (now working with his brother James) reworked the site to parallel Hunt's radical changes to the architectural character of the house (Figure 3.16). The new design highlighted the differences between the formal drive—now broad, straight, and arranged to make two crisp turns in front of the house before continuing out to the side street— and the secondary circulation system, which retained its narrow, curving paths. Significantly, the stables and greenhouses were removed entirely from the environs of the house; their replacements were built some four blocks away.[58] Also gone were the

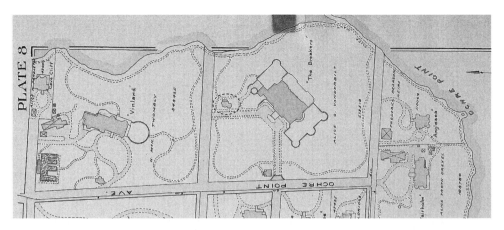

FIGURE 3.16. Site plan of the second Breakers, Newport, Rhode Island, completed in 1895 to the designs of Richard Morris Hunt. A dashed oval marks the location of the children's cottage. L. J. Richards & Co., *Atlas of the City of Newport and the Town of Middletown and Portsmouth, Rhode Island* (1907), plate 8. Courtesy of Redwood Library and Athenaeum, Newport, Rhode Island.

close web of curving paths and dense plantings that had once characterized the northwest quadrant of the property. The gently curving footpath that connected the house to the ocean was extended to circumscribe the entire site, thus vastly expanding the amount of outdoor space devoted to the family's leisure, which included lavish garden parties.

The new Breakers was predicated on a different attitude toward the visibility of the house. Rather than shielding it from public view on the Ochre Point Avenue side, the landscape plan and entrance gates designed by Hunt offered passersby a carefully framed view of the house's main façade and its porte-cochère. Standing just off the driveway that extended from the house to Sheppard Avenue, the rear elevation of the cottage became newly visible from the public street (see Figure 3.3); eventually, this view was also framed by an imposing gate. At a time when play was becoming culturally valuable as evidence of a good and happy childhood, this new configuration served as proof the Vanderbilt children played. Given the avalanche of negative public commentary directed toward another branch of the Vanderbilt family at the time of Consuelo's marriage in 1895, Cornelius II and Alice may have been particularly eager to make a public demonstration that they were caring parents.[59] Simultaneously, the cottage also came to serve—at least visually—as a pendant to the gatehouse, a foreground feature whose small size, modest scale, and dark colors offered a sharp contrast with the monumental limestone palazzo and thus enhanced its grandeur. In short, the children's cottage played multiple roles at the Breakers, only one of which was accommodating the needs and desires of children.

DESIGNING THE CHILDREN'S COTTAGE

Even before these changes of the 1890s, the cottage was not simply a miniature version of the main house, although the same architects designed both buildings in the Queen Anne style. In both, front-facing gables identified the location of rooms devoted to socializing, while the service spaces were housed in side wings distinguished by lower roofs and simpler silhouettes. Yet, the architectural vocabulary of the cottage differed in important ways from that used at the main house. Designed just after the United States celebrated its centenary in 1876—an event that fueled the fire of the emerging Colonial Revival in art and architecture—the main house reveals Robert Swain Peabody's interest in the architectural forms of Colonial America and particularly the classical details of stately Georgian houses.[60]

In contrast, the children's cottage, as initially built, was untouched by Colonial Revival sensibilities. Instead of elements drawn from the American past, the cottage features an eclectic mix of motifs—a blind-arched chimney, half-timbered gables, both bow and bay windows, and a squatly proportioned front door—popular in British versions of the Queen Anne style. In fact, the exterior details of the cottage were inspired by a group of almshouses designed by British architects Ernest George and Harold Peto (Figure 3.17).[61] Built in 1879 in Guildford, England, on land given by William Hillier, 4th Earl of Onslow, the Hillier Charities provided housing for twelve poor widows. A plan, elevation, and perspective view had been published in the *Building News and Engineering Journal* in 1879, but it seems more likely that Peabody became familiar with the almshouses via the *British Architect*, which published perspective views and details of five porch figures in December 1885, just as he and his firm were beginning their second phase of work at the Breakers.[62]

Cryptic notes in Peabody's travel diaries provide glimpses of the interaction between the architect and his clients in the initial stages of the project. Cornelius II and Alice Vanderbilt met with Peabody on 7 January 1886, when the architect traveled to Newport with his initial designs for what he called the "tea house" and secured his clients' approval. By the end of the month, the architect traveled to New York to bring Mr. Vanderbilt construction estimates. Peabody noted that these estimates were "too high," the one indication that Vanderbilt did set limits on the amount he would spend on his children. Including the notation to "arrange to have tea house smaller or wood," Peabody's diaries also reveal that the initial scheme did not call for the wooden building ultimately constructed, suggesting that he may have originally envisioned something even closer to the brick almshouses in Guildford.[63]

No other correspondence between the architect and his clients survives to illuminate the choice of almshouses as a model for a cottage for the children of the richest man in America.[64] As an architecture of caring, the almshouses may have seemed appropriate for a building to be used by dependent offspring. Peabody may also have

FIGURE 3.17. Hillier's almshouses, Guildford, England, 1879, as published in *British Architect* 24 (18 December 1885). The figural posts on the far left and the far right evidently served as models for two of the porch figures at the Breakers' children's cottage. Ernest George and Peto, architects, 1879.

been attracted to these almshouses precisely because they were humble cottages of English origin. By the last quarter of the nineteenth century, architectural theorists had idealized the cottage—the rural dwelling of the peasantry—as an appropriate model for small houses in many settings. To the extent European and American architects also associated the cottage with England (something Amy Ogata has demonstrated was the case by the 1890s), they turned for inspiration to British architectural publications and particularly to the domestic projects of Richard Norman Shaw, Ernest George and Harold Peto, and, somewhat later, C. R. Ashbee, among others.[65] A set of connected cottages arranged around three sides of a rectangular lawn, the Hillier almshouses displayed in happy combination many of the type's key visual tropes: small size, modest scale, sheltering roofs with eaves that extend below eye level, half-timbering, prominent chimneys, deep porches, bay windows, and materials left in their natural state (or stained to suggest that state).[66]

Peabody was also evidently attracted to the almshouses' iconographic program— or what he may have imagined that program to be, as the meaning of the buildings' porch figures was explained neither in *British Architect* nor in *Building News*.[67] Of the four figures supporting the porch roof, the two male figures are directly based on sketches from *British Architect*. In Newport, they stand on either side of the porch steps and are understood to represent Music and Gluttony (Figure 3.18a). While Music is paired with a female figure identified as Drama, Gluttony's female partner is Vanity.[68] All four figures are more charming than grotesque; in comparison to their British counterparts, Music and Gluttony are shorter, squatter, clean-shaven, and perhaps intentionally more childlike (Figure 3.18b). They nonetheless seem to offer the young Vanderbilts a stern admonition about the fine line between cultural pursuits and self-indulgence.

The decorative panel in the main gable of the cottage is an even more direct exhortation to clean living. In it, two pastoral youths torment the tongue of a horned satyr, either to banish obscene speech from the cottage or to punish him for violating the decorum of the place. Given that Commodore Vanderbilt was widely known for his profanity, this may have been a way for his refined and upright grandson and namesake to distinguish himself from the coarse man who founded the

a

b

FIGURE 3.18. (a) Porch figure said to represent Music at the children's cottage on the grounds of the Breakers, Newport, Rhode Island. The figure is more youthful than its counterpart at the Hillier's almshouses. Peabody and Stearns, architects, 1886. (b) Porch figure formerly part of Hillier's almshouses, Guildford, England. Ernest George and Peto, architects, 1879. Photographs by author.

family fortune.[69] These details are akin to the iconography of Italian Renaissance villas whose owners, perhaps like the Vanderbilts, worried about their propensity for hedonism and disguised it with allegories of restraint and sin punished.[70] The architectural form of the new Breakers would soon confirm that the Vanderbilts came to see their Newport house as a site akin to an Italian Renaissance villa.

The interior of the cottage was hardly a setting designed for hedonistic pleasures. The main room was dominated by a broad fireplace with a built-in stone bench similar to the cozy hearths that graced the pages of picture books by Walter Crane, Kate Greenaway, and others.[71] This fireplace and the room's irregular footprint suggest the architect conceived of this space as a parlor (Figures 3.19 and 3.20). Fitted out with a circular table, it conjures up the parlor that was notably absent from the main house in the Breakers, but that continued to be celebrated in sentimental prints, like *Family Devotion*, as the architectural manifestation of the intimate family

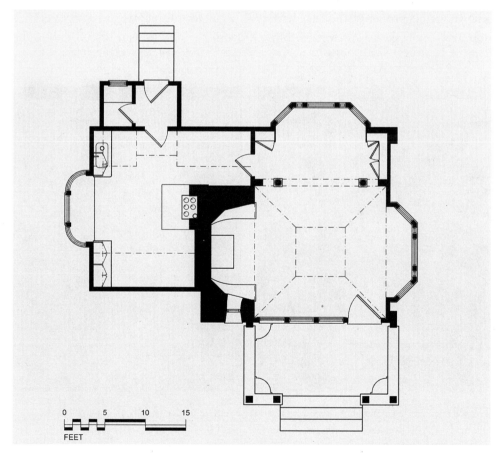

FIGURE 3.19. Plan of the children's cottage on the grounds of the Breakers, Newport, Rhode Island. Peabody and Stearns, architects, 1886. Drawing by Daniel De Sousa.

Making American Aristocrats   147

FIGURE 3.20. Main room of the children's cottage on the grounds of the Breakers, Newport, Rhode Island. The canted ceiling in the main part of the room creates a vertical axis that enhances the importance of the circular parlor table. Peabody and Stearns, architects, 1886. Photograph by the author.

circle. Toward the back of the room, two columns and a change in flooring pattern helped distinguish the parlor proper from the alcove beyond. Flanked with storage cupboards and offering discrete access to the kitchen, the alcove seems to have been designed to play the role of the dining room.

The kitchen was fully functional. Sharing the chimney stack that served the parlor fireplace was a working range—not a toy, but a modest-sized fixture manufactured by Richardson & Boynton Company of New York (Figure 3.21). Called the Provident, the model was advertised in the company's 1886 catalog as "first-class in all respects" and touted as "the best and cheapest range sold." Although the stove in the cottage was built in, the Provident also came in a portable model, which the catalog recommended "for French flats, apartment houses, or for use by small families."[72] On the opposite wall, overlooking the garden, was a bow window, flanked on one side by built-in cabinetry and on the other by a fully plumbed sink.

The cottage's external characteristics suggest some of the internal conflicts with which the senior Vanderbilts grappled when creating suitable spaces for their children.

FIGURE 3.21. Kitchen of the children's cottage on the grounds of the Breakers, Newport, Rhode Island. Designed for use in apartments, the range is small but not miniature. Peabody and Stearns, architects, 1886. Photograph by the author.

They were certainly aware of the sentimental view of childhood embraced with fervor by their middle-class contemporaries. Having themselves served as Sunday school teachers in young adulthood, they may well have also been familiar with the temperance literature in which innocent children were depicted as powerful moral agents. To the extent the domestic hearth was the mise-en-scène for the moral triumphs of these fictional children, a cottage that evoked middle-class domesticity in its exterior forms, interior arrangements, and full-size fittings may have seemed the ideal setting for the full flowering of the moral compass within each of their flesh-and-blood offspring. Yet, their drive for social status also prompted Cornelius II and Alice to reject the parlor as the physical and emotional center of their own daily routines. Thus, the location of the cottage—at some remove from the main house—allowed them to choose when (and if) to cross its threshold and thus to distance themselves from its middle-class connotations.

USING THE CHILDREN'S COTTAGE

If the cottage served as visible evidence that the Vanderbilt children played, it also suggested the content of that play, which often centered on domestic labor. In a diary she kept in the summer of 1890, fifteen-year-old Gertrude mentioned the cottage as the locus of sewing lessons. She also recorded the events of one August day when rain prevented her (and perhaps her siblings) from visiting the family's nearby farm.[73] "Instead," she wrote,

> we cooked our own dinner in the cottage. I had sent word to Sybil [Sybil Sherman, daughter of William Watts Sherman] to come, but did not mention that we were going to cook, so she appeared in a silk dress. I immediately marched her over to the house and made her put on one of my white dresses. It was very amusing and with a good deal of Martha's help we cooked a most delicious lunch.[74]

Presumably, Martha was thirty-six-year-old Martha Falow, who was employed by the Vanderbilts as a servant.[75]

This episode speaks to the range of roles the cottage played in the lives of the Vanderbilt children. At one level, it was a seasonal variation of the schoolroom in the family's New York house—a place where the Vanderbilt children could spend their days (always accompanied by a governess and often in the company of friends) well away from the rooms devoted to adult sociability. As the later expansion of the New York house suggests, creating physical distance was an important—even essential—consideration when the senior Vanderbilts commissioned entertaining rooms; indeed, as these rooms became increasingly elegant, the children's spaces became increasingly distant. In Newport, the sequencing of the projects undertaken by Cornelius II and Alice suggests that they saw the construction of a free-standing children's cottage as a necessary prelude to the changes they envisioned for the ground-floor entertaining rooms in the main house—renovations they undertook only after the cottage was under way. These entertaining rooms were already very large, but the Vanderbilts felt compelled to enlarge the dining room to an enormous size; at 40 by 70 feet, it was reportedly the largest dining room in Newport. Their renovations also changed the relationships among ground-floor rooms, organizing the drawing room, hall, and dining room along a single axis and aligning the doors of these rooms so that the Vanderbilts and their guests could take in the entire space from a single vantage point. Children, it seems, would have marred this carefully arranged vista.

Other aspects of the Vanderbilt renovations confirm the extent to which the main house was designed primarily for adult use. As well as adding the dining room, they also called upon Peabody and Stearns to update the interior decoration in several other ground-floor rooms. This work was carefully documented in a series of professionally produced photographs (Figure 3.22).[76] The images reveal furnishings and fittings inspired by seventeenth- and eighteenth-century French designs, a fashion increasingly favored by American elites, who, in the words of Laura Jenkins, understood "'eighteenth-century French' as a metonym for good taste and gracious comportment."[77] Indeed, the Vanderbilts and other elites adopted not just the stylistic vocabulary of French furnishings but also their arrangement. Large pieces of furniture lined the perimeter of the room, echoing its materials and forms, while smaller, lighter furnishings could be rearranged for a variety of social activities. As furniture historian Mimi Hellman has argued, these eighteenth-century French objects were integral to "the apparently effortless fabrication of elite identity itself" in that they served both as backdrop and stage props for public performances in which "the cultivated body . . . produced the appearance of leisured, sociable ease." From Hellman's point of view, this mode of civilized leisure was work, a form of labor in which it was essential to disguise the effort involved.[78] To join the ranks of the civilized, elite

FIGURE 3.22. Drawing room of the first Breakers, Newport, Rhode Island. The décor and furnishings of this room were updated by Peabody and Stearns soon after the house was purchased by Alice and Cornelius Vanderbilt II. Peabody and Stearns, architects, circa 1887. Courtesy of Redwood Library and Athenaeum, Newport, Rhode Island.

children needed to learn how to perform in such settings, but until they did, this stage was no place for them.

Why encourage young Vanderbilts to play at domestic labor? In some ways, their activities were akin to the play of middle-class children whose pretend work was often enhanced by toys that were miniature versions of tools their parents used. At the children's cottage, however, Gertrude did not pretend with the aid of toys. She and Sybil actually cooked an edible meal on a real range, albeit with the help of Martha, who may have provided the expertise and muscle involved in starting and maintaining the fire. In short, the content of their play might have been familiar to their middle-class contemporaries, but their mode of play was quite different.

It may be that this participation in domestic labor was intended to train Gertrude and her siblings for a future in which they would be called upon to direct servants in households of their own. Yet, working in the trenches to prepare a simple luncheon had little to do with the labor actually undertaken by a society hostess, who typically functioned more like a military general. Her command center was her exquisitely decorated boudoir, where she constructed guest lists, determined menus, and issued orders to a chef and other high-ranking functionaries, who communicated those orders down the chain of command to an army of servants, also hierarchically organized and laboring out of sight in an extensive suite of workspaces. Indeed, at the Breakers the cottage's small kitchen—with its apartment-sized range—bore no relationship to the bustling, technologically advanced facility in the main house, which was equipped like a hotel kitchen.[79]

In this case, playing at domestic labor may have had less to do with preparing the Vanderbilt children for their future roles than with insulating their present selves from the refinements of society, much as the Swiss Cottage had offered Victoria and Albert's royal offspring a respite from the formalities of court life. Both settings were informed by the Enlightenment belief that children were closer to nature and more attuned to the simplicity of peasant life than their parents, an idea that had prompted eighteenth-century British painters such as Joshua Reynolds and Johann Zoffany to depict aristocratic children playacting at rural labor.[80] In the last quarter of the nineteenth century, these ideas were particularly valued, given the widespread glorification of the rustic that nurtured the Colonial Revival and Arts and Crafts movements. Both peasants and children were understood to be dependent, humble, innocent, somewhat simpleminded, eager to work with their hands, and happily ignorant of the ways of the modern world. From this derived the wide popularity of Greenaway's books, the first of which, *Under the Window*, was published in 1879; in them, children—in distinctive dress based on early nineteenth-century fashions—inhabited a pastoral world in which adults played only a minimal role.[81] Thus, well before psychologist G. Stanley Hall had posited that child development was a literal recapitulation of human evolution and that young children should not be forced to adopt the trappings of civilization before their time, upper- and upper-middle-class parents sought to provide their children with settings where they could dig in the garden and make simple meals.[82]

While there is no evidence that young Gertrude cultivated vegetables, her luncheon party with Sybil Sherman falls squarely within the range of pursuits the royal children had enjoyed at the Swiss Cottage. The same can be said of the activities Gertrude's first cousins pursued at their playhouse at Idle Hour on Long Island, where they did have a vegetable garden to tend, although Consuelo Vanderbilt admitted in her published memoirs that they were "bad gardeners"; her impatient brother Willie "would pull up the potatoes long before they were ripe." In Consuelo's recollections, going to the playhouse was a special treat, as "good behavior found its reward in the pleasure of cooking our supper in the playhouse." These meals were supervised by the German governess whose taste for sauerkraut the children did not share. Nonetheless, the Vanderbilt heiress recalled that she and her brother were "utterly happy" to cook their own meal and to wash the dishes afterward.[83] Other reports note that Consuelo made preserves and cooked, while Willie did carpentry and waited at table. Their mother recalled that she and her friends "often went there for afternoon tea. It was prepared by the children and was most excellent."[84]

Referred to as a "tea house" in Peabody's early notes and on a photograph preserved in the collections of the Newport Historical Society, the Breakers cottage may have served as a setting for comparable events. Certainly, its situation—facing the path that linked the main house to the ocean—is suggestive. The senior Vanderbilts and their guests were bound to stroll right past the front steps of the cottage and could easily venture in. The expense lavished on the cottage and the level of detail that resulted from this expenditure suggest that the senior Vanderbilts anticipated displaying the cottage to their guests. Adults were an important audience, both for the admonitions of the iconographic program on the building's exterior and for the performances of domesticity that took place inside.

When Gertrude's mother (and perhaps her friends) took tea with the children in the cottage, the building became the symbolic parlor of the Breakers, a space not solely for the use of youngsters, but one where adults and their children could reenact the bonds of intimacy that seemed out of place in the main house. In this sense, the cottage accommodated play in two distinct senses of the word. For Gertrude and her siblings, it was a place to play—in the sense of taking part in a lighthearted game; they *played* at the domestic skills that would have only a small place in their future lives. For Gertrude's mother, it was a place to play in a different sense; she *played* the part of a doting mother in a sentimental performance of family togetherness that had only a small place in her existence as "Alice of the Breakers."

These activities, however, did nothing to threaten their privileged status. In contrast to a real middle-class house where the acquisition of domestic skills was a sign of a girl's maturity, the cottage framed domestic labor as a sign of dependency, the purview of children and servants. By providing a space where she could watch her dependents practice homely skills without exposing her to the heavy labor taking place a few hundred yards away in the main house, the cottage allowed Alice to enjoy the fiction that her leisured state was effortless. At the same time, the mother's presence in the cottage could reassure the daughter that she—Gertrude—would outgrow her dependent status, even if Martha would not.

If the Vanderbilt children were only playing at domestic labor in the cottage, they were also performing work in a different sense—as potential conduits of social and symbolic capital. The fact that memoirs mention few children other than Vanderbilts using the cottage suggests that one important function of this little building was to give Vanderbilt adults some measure of control over their children's friendships.[85] Given that the younger generation's ill-chosen alliances could make the entire family vulnerable, this was no small matter, and Vanderbilt family lore is filled with conflict between parents and children over the appropriateness of the youngsters' friends. Alice protested Gertrude's friendship with Esther Hunt, daughter of the family architect, even before both parents broke with Neily when he married Grace Wilson.[86]

Wealthy parents might feel their offspring required even greater management during their adolescence than when they were small children. This was especially true of daughters, for whom the transition to adulthood—at least socially speaking—took place in a single evening when they "came out" in society. For Gertrude this took place in 1895, when she was twenty. Before that time, it was hard to know exactly where she belonged during the balls her parents hosted. During one such event in August 1890, she was relegated to the gallery above the entrance in the first Breakers. There, seated with "Fräulein" (her governess) and Elsa (the nurse for her younger siblings), she was well removed from the event and encountered only five people who came up to the gallery to speak with her briefly. Nonetheless, she had an excellent view of the courting rituals being played out below her and later recorded in her diary her fascination with "who the men talked most to, and whether the girls liked some better than others, if they showed it."[87] In short, the gallery was not altogether successful in keeping Gertrude insulated from society. While nurseries might keep younger middle-class children out of sight until they were old enough to join adult sociability in the parlor, families of great wealth required a wider range of spaces in which to manage the social interactions of older adolescents.

The cottage also shaped the interaction between the Vanderbilt children and the class of users represented at Gertrude's luncheon party by Martha: the servants who were integral to the smooth operation of high society. At a basic level, the cottage provided a venue in which Gertrude and her siblings interacted directly with servants over domestic matters—something Leonore Davidoff and her coauthors have argued was essential in helping middle- and upper-class children learn about their own place in the world. In their speech, dress, carriage, and behavior, servants were Others against whom elites defined themselves.[88]

Even more significant were the spatial practices embedded in the cottage and in the cultural landscape of the Breakers, practices that helped to naturalize patterns of deference that characterized the interactions between adult servants and their young mistresses and masters. For Gertrude and her siblings, the cottage was a site for the exercise of authority. Ironically, perhaps this included the prerogative *not* to use the cottage on a given day, if they decided instead to undertake an outing to the farm. If they opted to use the cottage, they determined not only the agenda for the day (like cooking lunch) but also who else would be involved and even what they would wear. For Gertrude and her friend Sybil Sherman (who had the authority to decline Gertrude's invitation and even her loan of a white dress), playing at cooking tasks in the cottage was a lark, something they found "very amusing."

For the adult servants who worked alongside the children at these domestic chores, the cottage was a site that required both heavier labor and deference to a child. Unlike Sybil Sherman, Martha Falow could not decline to participate in Gertrude's luncheon. Indeed, she and other uniformed servants could be summoned to the cottage at any moment via call buttons located in the dining alcove and in the kitchen. (In each location, one button was labeled "Butler" and another "2nd story.") Once beckoned by their young masters, servants presumably entered the cottage through the back door, which led past a water closet and into the kitchen through a disguised door that matched the kitchen paneling. The spatial system of the Breakers limited the movement of servants by setting them on predetermined paths as they passed from the kitchen door of the main house to the rear door of the children's cottage. The physical arrangement of the cottage—especially its rear entrance—effaced the presence of servants and denied their centrality to the activities that took place there. In contrast, when Gertrude played at domestic tasks, the cottage guaranteed her greater freedom of movement than these adults, who were employed to perform household labor.

The cottage stood at the intersection of two distinct but mutually defining spatial practices in which gender and generation played key roles. Tightly choreographed and carefully costumed, the spatial practices of deference required self-conscious action on the part of servants. In contrast, the spatial practices of privilege allowed elites—including elite children—much greater scope for individual action. Not only did they exercise greater choice in their attire, they also were free to follow a greater variety of paths through their immediate environment. The choreography suggested by the material world was less insistent and thus less evident—even to those who performed it. While servants would have been acutely aware of the spatial practices of deference they were required to perform, Gertrude and her siblings may have taken for granted the spatial practices of privilege they enacted. The cultural landscape they inhabited was arranged to support and sustain their performances of self, making those performances look and feel entirely natural.

RETHINKING THE CHILDREN'S COTTAGE

It is impossible to dismiss the Breakers' cottage as an architectural confection, a site for the supposedly carefree activities associated with children's play. The physical qualities of the cottage were the result of calculated choices by adults engaged in the serious work of inculcating their children into their dynastic responsibilities, an endeavor that sometimes brought them into conflict with the wider culture of which they were a part—a culture that celebrated a sentimental ideal of the close-knit nuclear family. In a sense, Cornelius and Alice Vanderbilt found themselves in a situation comparable to that of Victoria and Albert, who also faced the challenge of reconciling sentiment and dynasty. Yet, thanks in large part to her royal lineage, Victoria could embrace a public persona that highlighted her sentimental attachment to her husband and children without undermining her own exalted status. In contrast, the Vanderbilts had only recently maneuvered their way into New York Society and were all too aware that staying there required constant vigilance. As happy as they may have been to have their middle-class contemporaries read about their excellent parenting in the pages of the *Ladies' Home Journal,* they needed to do all they could to guarantee that their children were prepared to maintain and enhance the symbolic capital of the Vanderbilt name, ideally, for generations to come. In short, their ambitions for their children were distinctly dynastic.

New kinds of domestic space were integral to this process, but so was the process of carefully managing their offspring. Standing at the nexus of these concerns, the cottage played several roles: helping to keep children at some distance from a house devoted almost entirely to formal entertaining; prolonging childhood for these youngsters who would not join the world of adult sociability until they were almost twenty; insulating adolescents from problematic social connections; and maintaining spatial arrangements that reinforced class privilege.

This last feature is particularly important for the larger project of understanding the relationship between architecture and its role in reproducing class privilege among elite children like Gertrude Vanderbilt and her siblings. It was not simply that adults employed as servants were required to respond when summoned, no matter the youthfulness of the finger pressing the call button. The built environment was also arranged to channel their movements to paths that minimized their visibility, cloaking their role in ensuring the success of the Vanderbilts' social endeavors—whether lavish entertainments in the main house or simple lunches prepared and consumed in the cottage. This built environment also granted Vanderbilts and their guests—young and old—a freedom of movement that was denied to the adults employed as their servants. Curving paths encouraged them to meander through the site, allowing them to develop a kind of muscle memory of leisured existence. They did not need to think self-consciously about exercising their social privileges; they would simply act naturally—that is, in the way their environment suggested—and they would find that others naturally treated them with deference.

A Gilded Age children's cottage, then, should be understood as an integral component in a network of spaces that supported a family's performance of elite social status. Its small size belied its importance to the process of amassing social capital, even as its value in that process outweighed the costs involved in its design and construction. Despite the fact that the new century ushered in new ideas about the nature of childhood, the next generation of American aristocrats continued to build small outbuildings devoted to the use of their offspring. Reconceived as playhouses, these often charming little structures nonetheless continued to serve as powerful tools of elite culture.

FIGURE 4.1. Garden façade of Highlawn, the W. B. Osgood Field and Lila Vanderbilt Sloane Field estate, in Lenox, Massachusetts. The first playhouse is at far right. Delano and Aldrich, architects, 1908–9. William B. Osgood Field Estate records: [High Lawn Estate], 1908–29, box 3, folder 22, Drawings and Archives, Avery Architectural and Fine Arts Library, Columbia University.

CHAPTER FOUR

A Conundrum for Elite Parents

Prioritizing Play in the Early Twentieth Century

In 1910, an unnamed photographer took a picture at Highlawn, the country estate in Lenox, Massachusetts, that had been completed just the year before for William B. Osgood Field and Lila Vanderbilt Sloane Field (Figure 4.1). At first glance, the photograph seems to offer a conventional portrait of a grand house. Presented frontally almost as though it were an architect's elevation, the house itself sits at the very center of the composition, which is neatly bifurcated by a pathway that underscores both the formality of the landscape as well as the symmetry of the Georgian Revival pile. Visible on the far right edge of the image is one of the two single-story outbuildings attached to the house by low curving walls that work together to define a forecourt and enhance the formal approach to the front door. The arrangement is reminiscent of Mount Airy, an eighteenth-century plantation house in Richmond County, Virginia, and suggests that the appeal of the Colonial Revival lay, at least for some, in its ability to speak a language of racialized privilege.[1]

A closer examination reveals that the 1910 photograph, while balanced, is not quite symmetrical. When viewers seek out a second outbuilding on the left edge of the composition, they find instead a large tree, which helps disguise the absence of the expected architectural feature. In fact, the presence of the second outbuilding is registered in the photograph, albeit just to the left of its twin, its roof and chimney barely visible above the wall of the forecourt. The image, in fact, shows not Highlawn's entrance façade, but the side of the house facing the flower garden. The lane that divides the composition in two and that invites the viewer to step into the frame is not the main drive, but a garden path. The outbuilding on the right edge of the image is not the laundry (which is on the right as visitors approach the house's main entrance), but a structure identified by the architects sometimes as the playroom and sometimes as the children's playhouse.

The only human figure in the photograph is a small boy, presumably the Fields' eldest child, six-year-old William Osgood Field, a great-great-grandson of Commodore Vanderbilt. Sporting a broad-brimmed hat and dressed in short pants and a white tunic, a typical outfit for upper- and middle-class boys who had not yet started school, the youngster does not seem to have wandered into the camera's field of view by mistake. Like the house, he presents himself to the camera square on. Indeed, standing with his feet apart, arms at his sides, looking straight at the camera, he strikes a confident, if not quite masterful, pose. While the photograph appears to be a snapshot, the composition of the image—with the boy in the midground, just left of the center line that runs through both photograph and the house—melds the heir and the estate into a compelling amalgam, a double portrait that installs Osgood (as he was known) in a long pictorial tradition in which elite children were portrayed with the family's country house in the background, exerting a powerful visual and symbolic draw.

The playhouse is central to the 1910 photograph in that it is the compositional feature that allows viewers to orient themselves within a somewhat disorienting image. In this way, the photographer—however inadvertently—signaled the importance of this small building to the site and to the family. Architecturally, it worked in concert with the laundry and the main house in a carefully orchestrated presentation of the estate. Functionally, it provided Osgood (and his siblings) with a place to play, an activity that was increasingly understood as integral to the health of the individual youngster, the nation, and the human race. Representationally, it melded form and function to support a seamless performance of elite identity in which childhood played a newly important role. It is not that the provision of a small building devoted to the children's use was a new phenomenon. In her own youth, Osgood's mother had used Cosy Cot, the cottage her parents had had built at nearby Elm Court. Yet, the prominent location of a building explicitly called a playhouse points to a new set of parental concerns, chief among them accommodating children's play and doing so in ways that would be visible to members of the Fields' social circle.

This concern with play was hardly exclusive to elite families like the Fields. At the turn of the twentieth century, American adults of all classes were devoting more—and more serious—thought to children's play than ever before. To be sure, Friedrich Froebel's educational theories had inspired the establishment of kindergartens as early as 1860, sites where play with geometrical toys (Froebel called them "gifts") was the cornerstone of a new child-centered pedagogy. Yet, in the 1880s and 1890s, a mode of evolutionary thinking yoked to white supremacy had raised the stakes to a new level. A key figure was psychologist G. Stanley Hall, who is recognized as the founder of the new field of child study and who also promulgated the theory that each child recapitulated the evolution of the human race, from savagery through barbarism to civilization. Implicitly, this formulation applied only to Anglo-Saxon children, as Hall and his contemporaries believed that only white races were capable of reaching the evolutionary apex of civilization. In their view, other races had stalled in either a savage or barbarous state. Explicitly, this concept had important implications for play, as it transformed children from blank slates into beings hardwired with instincts—including play instincts—inherited through countless generations. Thwarting those instincts not only threatened to derail the healthy development of the individual, but doing so also had far greater consequences, including for the physical and moral health of the United States. Hall believed that by denying their sons the opportunity for boisterous play, doting middle-class mothers were turning boys into "sissies," a trend that put the nation's military preparedness at risk. He was equally concerned with creative play, convinced that it was central to leveraging "all the vital imaginative power of the race."[2] Indeed, parents who were inattentive to their children's play risked disrupting evolution itself, a process Anglo-Saxon Protestants believed would bring about the perfection of the most civilized—that is, white—races. Persuaded by the Lamarckian theory that organisms could inherit acquired traits, they believed their actions could impact the pace and even the direction of human evolution. As historian Gail Bederman has argued, they embraced their role in promoting human evolution with a millennialist zeal once reserved for serving as instruments of God's plan to vanquish evil.[3] Play had become serious business.

In this context, many elite parents built playhouses for their offspring, although it is impossible to know the exact number. Playhouses, like other service outbuildings, were rarely mentioned when elite estates were published in professional architectural journals or other periodicals that commented on the settings in which elites pursued their lives. As grand estates were pulled down and subdivided in the 1930s and 1940s, many unpublished playhouses undoubtedly went with them. While this chapter and the next touch on over a dozen playhouses built by American elites between 1897 and 1930, there were certainly more.

The playhouses at the center of these chapters are those that have left the most robust physical, visual, or archival evidence.[4] At the same time, they suggest that the playhouse phenomenon grew via personal connections; elites were aware that their peers were building playhouses and followed suit. Three of the playhouses in this chapter have Vanderbilt connections: a Colonial Revival playhouse at Greentree in Manhasset, on Long Island, commissioned by Gertrude Vanderbilt's brother-in-law, Payne Whitney and his wife, Helen Hay Whitney, in about 1905; and two commissioned by Lila Vanderbilt Sloane Field (Gertrude Vanderbilt's first cousin) and her husband for the grounds of Highlawn: the one-room Georgian playhouse in the forecourt (mentioned at the opening of this chapter) and a multiroom version erected in 1916.[5] Another three were built on Long Island by families with connections to

Standard Oil. Two of these were built by the adult children of Henry Huttleston Rogers, whom the *New York Times* dubbed "the master mind of Standard Oil": a tile-roofed stucco playhouse at Black Point, the Southampton estate of his son Henry H. Rogers Jr.; and the stucco playhouse with an eyebrow roof (in reality a converted garden shed) at Planting Fields, the Oyster Bay estate of his daughter Mary (Mai) Huttleston Rogers Coe and her husband W. R. Coe.[6] The third was designed for the offspring of John Teele Pratt and his wife, Ruth Sears Baker Pratt, at the Manor House in Glen Cove; Pratt was son of oil tycoon Charles Pratt and himself an executive with Standard Oil Company.[7] Two others have connections to business associates of Andrew Carnegie: the gambrel-roofed playhouse built in 1897 at Clayton, the Pittsburgh estate built by Carnegie's lieutenant, Henry Clay Frick, and his wife, Adelaide Frick; and the thatched playhouse at Westbury House, in Old Westbury, New York, on Long Island, built in about 1916, and commissioned by Margarita "Ditta" Grace Phipps and her husband, John "Jay" Shaffer Phipps, son of Henry Phipps, a partner in the Carnegie Steel Company.[8] Other well-documented playhouses include one at Foxhollow Farm, in Rhinebeck, New York, commissioned by Tracy Dows and Alice Olin Dows in 1908, and another—sporting forms associated with the Arts and Crafts movement—at Sinnissippi Farm, in Oregon, Illinois, commissioned in 1909 by Frank O. Lowden (who became governor of the state in 1916) and his wife, Florence Pullman Lowden, heiress to the Pullman Palace Car Company fortune.[9]

These elite playhouses—most of them architect-designed outbuildings commissioned by adults of wealth and status—shed important light on this moment. Indeed, they both reveal the extent to which elites participated in what amounted to a cult of the playing child, while also suggesting that their participation was limited by the realities of their lives, in which the accumulation and maintenance of social capital continued to depend on modes of adult sociability in which young children had no place. With the aid of their architects, men and women of wealth and status used architecture to address this conundrum of elite parenting, teasing apart activities that had once been taken place in multipurpose day and night nurseries and housing them in a new range of purpose-built spaces, both within the country house and across the estate landscape. In this process, play activities that had once taken place in the day nursery were ejected from the main house and given architectural expression in the freestanding playhouse. Clothed in conspicuously humble forms, these playhouses seemed appropriately childlike at a time when child study experts theorized that elite children were developmentally closer to peasants than they were to their own parents. At the same time, in commissioning conspicuously humble playhouses, these parents rejected the aesthetics of affluence their own parents had embraced in order to demonstrate that they and their children had the right relationship to wealth and that they deserved their riches. In short, architectural innovations introduced in the early decades of the twentieth century ultimately sought to preserve the status quo, both in insulating adult areas of country estates from children's play and in forestalling social critiques that may have destabilized the social hierarchies that kept these families in positions of privilege.

THE CULT OF THE PLAYING CHILD IN THE MIDDLE-CLASS HOME

At the turn of the century, children's play was the subject of a growing body of expert advice. Mounting persuasive arguments bolstered by scientific authority, child psychologists helped position play at the very core of a "normal" childhood, so much so that by 1930 it was a truism to assert (as did the delegates at the White House Conference on Child Health and Protection convened by President Herbert Hoover) that play was "every child's right."[10] At the turn of the century, the challenges to healthy play seemed particularly dire for the children of the urban poor, who had nowhere to play except sidewalks and streets, the dangers of which loomed large in the public imagination.[11] A wide range of entities established organized playgrounds, fitted out with sturdy gymnastic equipment, where adult play leaders could guide the active play of immigrant children.[12] Yet, middle-class children were also understood to be at risk, in part because their access to small amounts of cash meant that they could frequent penny arcades, nickelodeons, amusement parks, and the like—commercially available amusements that threatened to undermine purposive play and, in the words of historian Lisa Jacobson, seemed to represent "a corruption of children's playtime and a perversion of play itself."[13] The result was what historian Howard P. Chudacoff has characterized as an "invasion of children's play culture," as well-meaning middle-class parents sought to ensure that their offspring were "engaging in healthy games and playing with proper toys in protected places."[14] Among the American middle classes, channeling children's play instincts was understood as an important parental duty.

Unlike poor families whose children used publicly accessible playgrounds, middle-class parents accommodated children's play in the private, domestic sphere. Indeed, advice literature encouraged middle-class parents to put playing children at the center of their lives, both temporally and spatially. Early twentieth-century garden magazines were one source of such advice, suggesting various ways of incorporating play equipment into the garden in ways that would not disrupt the picturesque aesthetic that brought social capital to middle-class families: allowing a grape arbor to double as a playhouse, using a garden pergola as a "sand house," or hanging swings from garden trellises.[15] In the same years, manufacturers of precut houses recognized a market opportunity and began including play structures among their offerings. In 1907, the National Construction Company of Buffalo, New York, offered a one-room, 6-foot-by-9-foot version that featured a front porch, a window with diamond panes, and some decorative shingles—all to evoke domestic architecture. Nonetheless, the building was essentially a garden shed, built with single-wall construction and sporting a canvas roof. Indeed, the manufacturer noted that it could "also be used as a Bath or Tool House."[16] About the same time, Mershon & Morley Company of Saginaw, Michigan, used the very same image in their catalog, albeit with the addition of a decorative ridge board. Their catalog copy emphasized opportunities for customization; the porch, for instance, could be extended around two, three, or four sides of the play-shed, while parents who opted to forgo a porch entirely could instead order wooden awnings for the door and window. The Mershon & Morley Company also offered a smaller, cheaper model that measured just 5 feet by 6 feet and that could be erected "by a good smart boy of 12" (Figure 4.2).[17]

By the interwar period, the tension between picturesque aesthetics and active play was eased by corralling children's activities in fenced backyards, spaces that became increasingly available for leisured use as the provision of indoor plumbing obviated

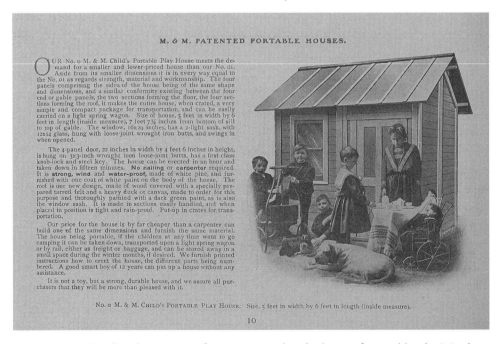

FIGURE 4.2. Catalog description of a one-room play shed manufactured by the Mershon & Morley Company, the sort of simple play structure within the means of many middle-class parents. *M. & M. Portable Houses, Catalog No. 5* (Saginaw, Michigan: Mershon & Morley Co., [1906]), 10.

the need for backyard privies. The market response was robust with manufacturers such as the E. F. Hodgson Company of Boston offering a wide range of play structures: three types of sand houses (the simplest version of which was a sand box with an awning top, while the most elaborate featured a cedar roof and was completely screened) and six play sheds, all of which included a single room and a front porch. The smallest (measuring 6 by 7 feet with a 3-by-6-foot porch) cost $150 in 1916 (just over $4,300 in 2024 dollars), while the largest measured 12 by 12 feet with a 6-by-12-foot porch. When fitted out with a latticed porch and seats, which allowed it to do double duty as a tea pavilion for adults, this large play shed cost $273 (just over $7,800 in 2024 dollars).[18] It is not clear how many middle-class parents bought these play sheds or built similar ones for their children, but swings and sandboxes were certainly common features by the 1930s.[19]

At the same time, popular magazines also encouraged middle-class parents to plan the domestic interior around the needs of the playing child. The ideal was to provide two rooms: a bedroom for sleep and a second room for daytime activities. Typically, this second room was called a playroom, although sometimes the term *workshop* as applied to rooms for the use of boys, who were understood to be inveterate collectors, in need of space for tinkering and particularly deserving of privacy.[20] Fitted out with child-sized furniture, smooth walls painted in cheerful colors, and amply furnished with books and games, the idealized middle-class playroom isolated play in time and space, ensuring the play was appropriately free from the adult world of work and responsibility, while simultaneously reducing household friction by insulating adult spaces from the sights and sounds of unthwarted play.[21]

Experts, however, also recognized that many families would only be able to devote one room to the child's use and suggested ways of accommodating sleep, play, and storage for toys and collections within a single space. These multipurpose rooms were sometimes called the child's room, although the term *nursery* was still in wide use. Indeed, authors often used these terms interchangeably in the same article. This continuity in nomenclature has tended to disguise the fact that middle-class American homes in the early twentieth century no longer had nurseries of the sort that had been common in the second half of the nineteenth century on both sides of the Atlantic, namely, a room or set of rooms overseen by a nurse, who shared living and sleeping space with her charges. In the American context, the middle-class nursery of the nineteenth century had often been a single room, sequestered at the back of the house or in the basement, with the children using unfinished attic space as their shared playroom.[22] In contrast, early twentieth-century experts imagined the middle-class nursery as a single room situated on the same floor as the parental bedroom, where the mother herself could keep an eye on her children. Equally important, it was understood to be "the child's own room," the domain of an individual child who could pursue (with adult guidance) their natural play instincts, independent of any older or younger siblings. In practice, in middle-class houses, the term *nursery* simply came to designate the bedroom-cum-playroom of the youngest child, albeit a room that parents were urged to decorate and furnish with great care.[23]

Increasingly, middle-class parents were encouraged to let their offspring use spaces once considered off-limits to youngsters. Chief among them was the parlor, a room that in the second half of the nineteenth century was chockablock with heavy furniture and fragile bric-a-brac, all aimed at displaying the family's culture and refinement to visitors. This was no place for children, at least unsupervised ones. When youngsters were brought into the parlor, it was often to put them on display in specially designed furniture that constrained their movement: swings, bassinettes, and (in the dining room) high chairs. As historian of material culture Karin Calvert argues, these furnishings of containment and display were as much about "keeping the house safe from the child as the child safe from household injuries."[24] In contrast, early twentieth-century parents were expected to invite children to play in this space, eventually renamed the living room to signal its greater informality and its use by the entire family.[25]

This version of the child-centered home depended on keeping indoor play relatively subdued—clean, quiet, and safe. Children might play alone with toys and games purchased by their parents or with a few carefully selected playmates, also vetted by their parents. Commercially available toys were key to this mode of play, giving parents the opportunity to suggest the nature of their children's play while also allowing children to direct their own play, either by choosing from among their toys or by flipping the script of the toys with which they did play.[26] These toys also encouraged middle-class children to engage in imaginative play, although historian Gary Cross points out that even imaginative play tended to reinforce conventional gender roles. Dolls encouraged girls to pretend they were mothers; toys based on "the latest machines of men" encouraged boys to imagine themselves as machine operators or builders.[27]

One way middle-class parents made their commitment to this mode of family life visible was through the purchase and use of baby books, commercially available ledgers in which parents were prompted to record the activities and developmental milestones of their precious offspring. Typically illustrated with images of clean, white babies, such books celebrated and normalized an approach to family life in which both time and space were organized around children and their needs. In this version of family life, mothers, especially, were expected to plan their days around their infants, ready to catch the first word, witness the first step, and observe the emergence of the first tooth. Recording these "firsts" also allowed mothers to compare their infants to the developmental "norms" promulgated by child study experts and thus given the imprimatur of science. For both parents, the annual calendar revolved around their children's birthdays and (in Christian families) Christmas, occasions that had emerged as important gift-giving opportunities.[28] *Baby's Record*, a memory book first published in 1898, underscored the importance of presents by making "Gifts" (followed by five blank lines) the first prompt on the First Christmas page; "Incidents" was second and allotted just three blank lines. On the First Birthday page, "Gifts" (followed by eight blank lines) was the only prompt, except for the date itself. Anticipating that the book would appeal to middle-class consumers, as well as to those with greater disposal income, the publisher issued several styles: one "nicely bound in cloth" for $1.88; that volume, boxed, for $2.50; another boxed volume with gilded pages for $3.50; and a deluxe version bound in China silk, boxed, with gilded pages, for a whopping $5.00 ($188.00 in 2024 dollars).[29]

As historians of childhood have readily acknowledged, this was a version of domestic life well beyond the reach of the urban poor. Living in small tenement apartments that could not accommodate children's play, these parents—many of them recent immigrants—had no choice but to allow their children to play on sidewalks and streets or in organized playgrounds where adult play leaders offered guidance in the proper use of gymnastic equipment. In truth, even the ability to devote long hours to play was a clear sign of racialized class privilege; while middle-class girls were provided with dolls that allowed them to play at childcare, immigrant girls were often responsible for the actual care of their younger siblings. Likewise, when middle-class boys—especially little ones—indulged in impulsive behavior, their parents saw it as a manifestation of their wondrous innocence and celebrated it as impishness.[30] When immigrant youths failed to control their impulses, they risked being ejected from the organized playground.[31] In short, putting the playing child at the center of their lives was a key mechanism through which native-born middle-class parents established and performed their racialized class identity.[32]

THE CONUNDRUM OF ELITE PARENTING: THE CASE OF HELEN HAY WHITNEY

Elite families certainly had the means to shower their children with gifts and to surround them with the things that were increasingly understood as essential to a good childhood. Indeed, historians of childhood have tacitly assumed that wealthy parents adopted the same child-rearing values embraced by their middle-class contemporaries and simply used their greater means to engage in the associated material practices with gusto. The case of Helen Hay Whitney, an elite woman who revealed much about her attitudes toward children and child-rearing in her published poems and in a baby book devoted to her first-born child, provides an opportunity to test that assumption.

By any measure, Helen Hay Whitney was a woman of both wealth and status. Her mother, Clara Stone Hay, was the heiress to a railroad and banking fortune. Her father was John Hay, who had been secretary to Abraham Lincoln and who had served briefly as U.S. ambassador to the United Kingdom before becoming secretary of state in 1898. Born in 1875, Helen had been presented at the Court of St. James in 1898 and married Payne Whitney in 1902. *Harper's Weekly* found her engagement of sufficient note that her photograph graced its cover in December 1901.[33] Her husband was the son of William Collins Whitney, who had served as secretary of the navy in the 1880s and was included among the Four Hundred, Ward McAllister's list of New York society. When his widowed father remarried in 1896, Payne broke with the older man and further signaled his loyalty to his dead mother (and her brother, his wealthy uncle, Colonel Oliver Hazard Payne) by dropping William, the first name given him at birth, and using only his middle name, which was also his mother's maiden name: Payne. The steadfast nephew would eventually inherit the bulk of his uncle's fortune; at the time of his own death in 1927, Payne Whitney's estate (close to $179 million) was the largest ever appraised in the United States. In the meantime, Colonel Payne commissioned McKim, Mead & White to design a five-story house on Fifth Avenue as a wedding gift for Payne and Helen. His other gifts to mark the happy occasion included a diamond necklace for the bride, a yacht, a private railcar, and fifty thousand dollars in cash. By the time of their marriage, Payne's elder brother, Harry Payne Whitney, was already married to Gertrude Vanderbilt, which may have played a role in the amount of time Payne and Helen devoted to the Newport social season.[34]

At the time of her marriage, Helen Hay had already published three volumes of verses, two of which were written (ostensibly at least) for children: *Beasts and Birds*, published in New York in 1900, and *The Little Boy Book*, published simultaneously in New York and London the same year. As a young mother, she continued to produce books of poetry; those for children included *Verses for Jock and Joan* (1905; Joan and Jock were her young children), *The Punch and Judy Book* (1906), and *The Bed-Time Book*, which appeared in seven editions between 1907 and 1912.

Taken together, Helen Hay Whitney's poems evoke the spaces, activities, material goods, and human actors of elite childhood. The young narrators reveal that their days unfold in nurseries and gardens, and that their families' homes include private libraries (the domain of their fathers) and stables. They go to dancing classes and take piano lessons; their mothers entertain ladies at tea; and their aunts hunt foxes. They wear red morocco leather boots, dancing slippers, and velvet suits; their hats change with the seasons—felt in winter, straw in spring. They have access to a wide variety of playthings. And they take for granted the presence of nurses, gardeners, and coachmen, as well as their adult relations. The genteel character of this world is underscored by the illustrations, provided by Frank Ver Beck, Charlotte Harding, and Jessie Wilcox Smith, all artists associated with the so-called Golden Age of American Illustration. Despite the differences in their styles, all three illustrators presented fresh-faced youngsters, dressed in clean clothes designed specifically for children, and either surrounded by toys, seated in child-sized furniture, or embraced by well-dressed, leisured women (or sometimes by a grandfather). For all their references to elite life, the books were aimed at a middle-class audience. None of the books mentioned above retailed for more than $1.50 and several of them were also well represented in the collections of public libraries as far-flung as Brooklyn, Peoria, and Atlanta.[35] Indeed, the poems would have had a double appeal for middle-class and upper-middle-class parents: validating their belief that *things* could secure their children's well-being and also giving them the pleasure of imagining themselves in such genteel settings.

Whitney's verses are also notable for the frequency with which the narrator is an impish boy—a figure historian Gary Cross argues had particular appeal for middle-class adults. Take, for instance, "The Best of All," in which the young boy admits he is not "so very good— / As good as boys in books! I run around and tear my clothes / And tumble into brooks." He continues:

> I hate to work, and love to play,
> And then, sometimes, I fight.
> O yes, I'm sure I never do
> Exactly what is right.

By the verse's end, it is clear that such behavior is not just tolerated but also accepted as normal by the narrator's loving mother who "sometimes tip-toes to the bed / Without the leastest noise, / And kisses me, and says, 'You're just / The best of little boys.'" The poem does not merely allow for youthful naughtiness among young boys; it celebrates it.[36]

At the same time, Whitney's poems suggest that youthful impishness was more easily tolerated in some spaces than others. Take, for instance, "My Painting," from *Verses for Jock and Joan*. In this verse, a young boy reports on the praise he had received from his father for the (childish) paintings he had executed in his painting book (presumably in the nursery or another space designated for play). Hoping to give his father a birthday surprise, he had subsequently "crept right in the library" and "painted fast" in order to add comparable paintings to the biggest (and, adult readers could assume, most expensive) of his father's books. In his innocence, the impish narrator cannot understand why his father was "not pleased at all."[37] While the poem intimates that the father's displeasure was tempered by his son's youthful naïveté, it also suggests that parents were more likely to relish the inevitable naughtiness of their offspring if it were limited to spaces associated with children and play, rather than allowed to find full expression in spaces inhabited by adults.

At times, the illustrations that accompanied the poems suggested how this generational segregation might be accomplished. In "The Dream," from *The Little Boy Book*, the narrator fanaticizes about throwing his food on the floor, exclaiming

And Oh! what jolly fun it was
To be so rude and rough,
I think I'd do it every day
If I was bad enough![38]

Because the narrator is merely imagining the joys of bad behavior, rather than actually behaving badly, readers are free to enjoy his impishness without condoning youthful misconduct. Ver Beck's illustration of the poem is noteworthy, in that it shows the "rude and rough" protagonist and his ill-used sister at a child-sized table just big enough for two, eating and drinking from small plates and cups (Figure 4.3). The table is set just in front of a window that looks out onto green space. The fact that the window is the width of the table and that its sill sits just above table height suggests that the space is likewise on a reduced scale. Certainly, it is simply furnished. All in all, it evokes children's playhouses and hints that in the early twentieth century they were imagined as places for youngsters to be themselves without disrupting adult space. In short, Helen Whitney's poems evoke an attitude toward innocent and impish children that resonated with middle-class readers, but also gesture toward the difficulties she saw in putting the impish, playing child at the center of domestic life.

If these poems provide a window into how Helen Whitney imagined the relationship between elite parents and their offspring, a copy of *Baby's Record* devoted to Joan's early years offers insights in how this elite woman interacted with her children in practice. The book was presumably a gift from her mother, who mentioned in a letter to Helen in July 1903 that she had seen an advertisement for a "baby's book" in *Babyhood* and that she planned to order one for her other daughter, Alice Hay Wadsworth, who had just given birth to her first child.[39] Perhaps Clara Stone Hay came to realize that it would be awkward to give a baby book only to Alice, as Helen had also become a mother for the first time just a few months earlier. Indeed, some entries in Helen's copy of *Baby's Record* seem to have been added well after the events they record, suggesting that she only received the book in the summer, after some of Joan's "firsts" had already taken place.

The Whitney baby book makes it clear that Helen Whitney and her mother, despite their wealth and status, were a part of their cultural moment. The fact that Clara read *Babyhood* (a periodical established by Dr. Leroy M. Yale, who served as its medical editor) attests to her awareness of and interest in a growing body of expert

A Conundrum for Elite Parents

FIGURE 4.3. Illustration for "The Dream," by Frank Ver Beck, showing children seated at a child-sized table positioned just below a similarly sized window, suggesting that the scene depicts a playhouse. Helen Hay (later Helen Hay Whitney), *The Little Boy Book* (New York: R. H. Russell, 1900), n.p.

advice on child-rearing. Indeed, child-rearing experts of every ilk argued that things played an important role in shaping children, thus lending scientific legitimacy to perpetual parental consumerism—including the purchase of expensive baby books. In buying copies of *Baby's Record* for her daughters, Clara also signaled her appreciation for the version of parenting it encouraged.

Helen Whitney's entries in the baby book confirm that wealthy parents were like their middle-class contemporaries in embracing Christmas and birthdays as opportunities to shower their children with presents. Soon after receiving *Baby's Record*, Helen used the page meant to document the baby's first birthday to record the gifts they bestowed on Joan when she was "½ year old": gold beads, a rattle and bells, and a toy. On Joan's first Christmas, the list of gifts was even longer: four dolls, a mechanical rabbit, other toys too numerous to record individually, and a big cart, among other things. When the baby (finally) turned one, her gifts included toys, a blue silk wrapper, a canary in a cage, and, from her father, a pony and cart.

At the same time, Helen's entries in Joan's baby book also point to a more important truth about elite families, namely, that there were limits to their readiness to engage in the kind of parenting the baby book assumed. While middle-class parents increasingly organized their schedules around their children, elite parents did not. Indeed, Helen's journal from 1907 and family correspondence confirm that her routine and that of her husband prioritized the maintenance of social standing. Luncheons at the club, dinner parties, days at the races, yachting trips, European travel—these events came first, and time with the children was inserted into the interstices.[40] Helen and Payne Whitney, for instance, were on hand to throw a birthday party on the day in 1907 that Joan turned four, but they dined out that evening. In early July of the same year, they sailed for Europe without their children, only returning at the end of September, some six weeks after the third birthday of their son, Jock.[41] In 1912, they financed Jock's eighth birthday party, at which each guest received multiple gifts, including Brownie cameras.[42] Perhaps they hoped they would eventually see snapshots of the event, as they were traveling abroad on the day itself.

Rather than arrange their own schedules around their children, the Whitneys, like other elite parents, employed a surrogate (a nurse, Mary) to give their children the undivided attention they themselves could not provide. She was the one, for instance, who assured Helen that seven-month-old Joan was not worse for having ingested a rose leaf during an airing; as Helen reported to Payne (presumably trying to mimic the nurse's accent), Mary told her that "it came thro' all right & didn't bother her a bit."[43] Indeed, when Helen attempted to fill in the blanks in her copy of *Baby's Record*, she often found herself recording what Mary had told her about Joan's "firsts," including the child's first outing when she was three weeks old and the emergence of her first tooth at six months. Little surprise, then, that Helen's attention to the baby book was sporadic at best and that many of its pages remained untouched. The fact that she preserved the book is an indication that she appreciated the image of childhood it represented, but her routine simply did not align with the child-rearing practices it anticipated. This, then, was the conundrum of elite parenting: how to participate in the cult of the playful child while also pursuing the accumulation of social capital that was central to the life of elite adults. For many such families, the answer seemed to lie in providing a new, expanded range of child-centered spaces.

THE NURSERY SYSTEM REDUX

The conundrum of elite parenting was particularly acute on country estates, settings that were integral both to the accumulation of social capital and the accommodation of the playing child. At the same time, these large houses and their expansive grounds allowed elite parents to experiment with a range of spatial strategies that would facilitate their pursuit of both goals. Freestanding playhouses constituted one such strategy, allowing parents to eject the playing child from the main house, which could continue to be devoted to adult sociability. Yet, elite families often pursued multiple strategies, building playhouses while also incorporating a new range of spaces into the main house. Indeed, it is useful to think of these strategies as interrelated attempts to rethink the elite nursery, permitting elite parents to make their offspring visible in ways that had been unthinkable a generation earlier, while continuing to delegate the youngsters' care to others.

Well after middle-class families had abandoned the nursery system, elite parents continued to hire nurses and governesses to care for their young children. Yet, at the same time, they adjusted the physical location and spatial arrangement of the nursery suite in ways that signaled new patterns of domestic life. When Helen and Payne Whitney built Greentree, their country house on Long Island, architects d'Hauteville and Cooper provided interconnected day and night nurseries in an arrangement that would have been familiar in the last decades of the nineteenth century (Figures 4.4–4.6). This suite, however, was not tucked away on the topmost floor. Instead, it was situated in a prominent position just above the living room, accessible from the gallery that surrounded the double-height stair hall and located in close proximity to the parents' rooms. Indeed, the night nursery opened onto a short corridor that also provided access to Payne Whitney's dressing room and to the bathroom that Payne and Helen Whitney shared. (Although the architects labeled the large room above the dining room "Mrs. Whitney's room," Helen and Payne seem to have shared a bedroom; certainly, there was no room identified as "Mr. Whitney's room" and there was no indication of a bed in his dressing room.) Given the presence of the day nursery, it is unlikely that the Greentree living room was intended to accommodate children's play; instead, the terminology signals that Payne and Helen Whitney embraced a more relaxed style of entertaining in rooms devoted to adult sociability.[44]

Other elite families moved away from the practice of housing young children in shared day and night nurseries and abandoned the nursery nomenclature altogether. Nonetheless, they still maintained key aspects of what historian Jane Hamlett has aptly called "the nursery system," providing space for a nurse or governess, whose labor was integral to the smooth operation of the household.[45] At Sinnissippi Farm,

Figure 4.4. Exterior of Greentree, the Payne Whitney and Helen Hay Whitney estate, Manhasset, New York. The main house (in fact, an older house with a large addition) is on the right. The lower wing in the background was added circa 1914 to house tennis courts and a swimming pool. D'Hauteville and Cooper, architects, circa 1905. Photograph by the author.

architects Pond and Pond provided separate bedrooms for each of the four daughters of Frank O. Lowden and Florence Pullman Lowden.[46] Located on the same floor as their parents' suite and situated at the top of the formal stair, the children's bedrooms were arranged in pairs, each set sharing a small vestibule and a bath (Figures 4.7 and 4.8).[47] The largest (located just above the dining room) and the only one with a large bay seems to have served as the nursery in the sense that the term was used in middle-class houses—that is, the bedroom for the youngest child. Period photographs show that it was furnished with a high-sided crib, that the upper parts of its walls were covered with nursery rhyme wallpaper, and that its fireplace surround was ornamented with storybook tiles (Figure 4.9). Located adjacent to the service wing, it communicated with a servant bedroom through a closet, an arrangement that both facilitated and disguised the family's reliance on a nurse maid.

Highlawn, in Lenox, Massachusetts, was another country estate in which the location of the children's rooms was calculated to enhance their visibility. At the beginning of the project in 1908, W. B. Osgood Field and Lila Vanderbilt Sloane Field were the parents of two young sons (born in 1904 and 1905), and within two years

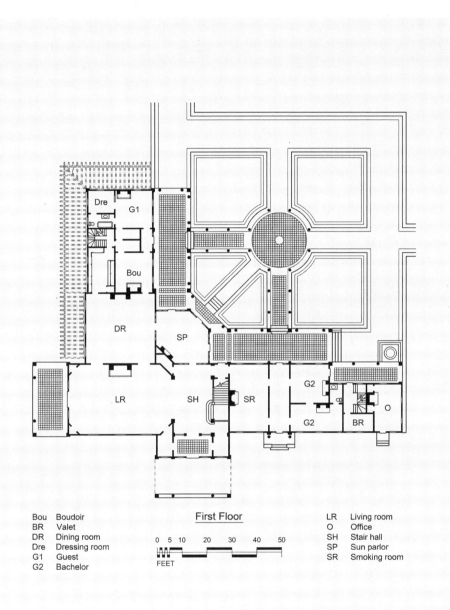

FIGURE 4.5. First-floor plan of Greentree, the Payne Whitney and Helen Hay Whitney estate, Manhasset, New York. The original house is on the right, its major rooms serving as a smoking room and bachelor quarters. To the left of the smoking room is the large new addition, including a stair hall open to the second floor and a living room comparable in area to the first floor of the original house. D'Hauteville and Cooper, architects, circa 1905. Drawing by Daniel De Sousa.

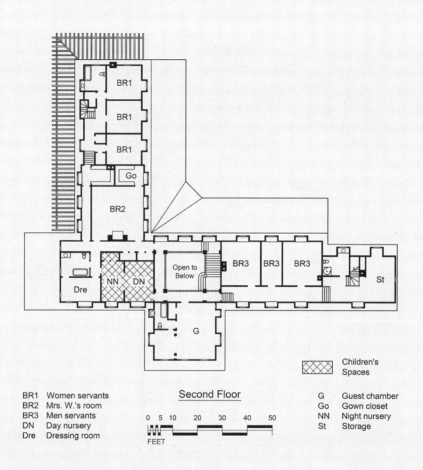

FIGURE 4.6. Second-floor plan of Greentree, the Payne Whitney and Helen Hay Whitney estate, Manhasset, New York. The nursery suite is in a prominent location directly above the living room and accessible both from the gallery overlooking the stair hall and the private passage leading to Mrs. Whitney's bedroom, Mr. Whitney's dressing room, and their shared bathroom. D'Hauteville and Cooper, architects, circa 1905. Drawing by Daniel De Sousa.

FIGURE 4.7. Exterior view, Sinnissippi Farm, the Frank O. Lowden and Florence Pullman Lowden estate, in Oregon, Illinois. Three of the four children's bedrooms had fireplaces, including one served by an unusual chimney stack that incorporated a window, visible in the center of this image. Pond and Pond, architects, 1904. Pond & Pond Collection, Ryerson and Burnham Art and Architecture Archives, Art Institute of Chicago. Digital file #200101.090515–22.

of completing the house in 1909, they also had two infant daughters.[48] Yet, the plans produced by architects Delano and Aldrich included neither day nor night nurseries, providing instead two rooms labeled "Child's Room No. 1" and "Child's Room No. 2," located on either side of a nurse's room (Figure 4.10). This last was furnished with, among other things, a rocker, a brass crib, and two brass beds, suggesting that it would serve as a night nursery for the youngest children. A bureau, chiffonier, and two tables finished in easily cleaned white enamel confirm that the room was furnished with young children in mind. The nurse's room was also more simply decorated than the children's rooms, each of which included a papered dado and frieze. The higher status of the children was further marked by the size of their rooms, the provision of a fireplace in each, and their ancillary spaces: vestibule, closet, and bathroom, which communicated with the nurse's room.[49] With its own hallway parallel to the main hallway, the children's zone also enjoyed pride of place, directly above the living room on the main axis of the house—a far cry from nurseries that had often been tucked away in attics or at the junction with the servants' wing. The children's

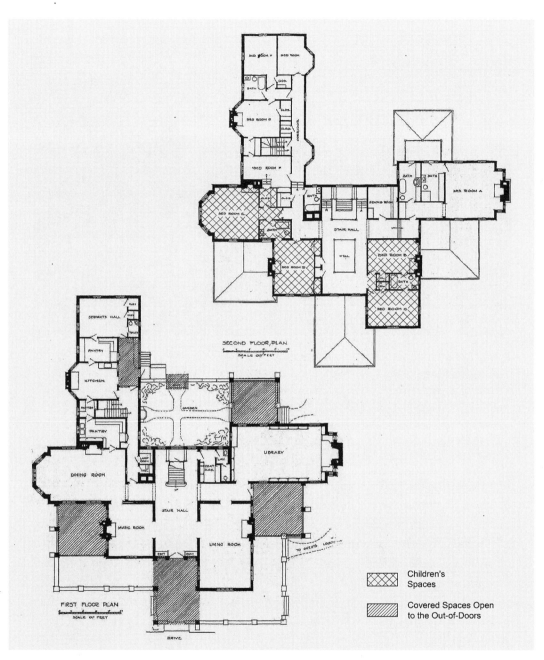

FIGURE 4.8. First- and second-floor plans of Sinnissippi Farm, the Frank O. Lowden and Florence Pullman Lowden estate, in Oregon, Illinois. The nursery is the large room with a bay window on the second floor, directly above the dining room. It was connected to a maid's room through a closet. Pond and Pond, architects, 1904. Pond & Pond Collection, Ryerson and Burnham Art and Architecture Archives, Art Institute of Chicago. Annotations by Daniel De Sousa.

Figure 4.9. Nursery at Sinnissippi Farm, the Frank O. Lowden and Florence Pullman Lowden estate, in Oregon, Illinois. A nursery in the twentieth-century meaning of the term, this is the bedroom of the youngest child in the family marked as especially childlike by its storybook tiles above the fireplace and nursery rhyme wallpaper. Pond and Pond, architects, 1904. Pond & Pond Collection, Ryerson and Burnham Art and Architecture Archives, Art Institute of Chicago. Digital file #200101.090805–43.

hall was accessed via a short set of wide steps, in part to ensure that the living room below had a lofty ceiling. At the same time, these steps were framed by an arch in an arrangement not unlike the chancel of a Christian church, announcing to houseguests the importance of the Field children. Indeed, three of the five guest rooms on the second floor stood opposite the arch framing the entrance to the children's zone, while another four on the third floor were accessible only from stairs in the children's zone.

The Field children were also made visible on the first floor, where they were provided with their own dining room, just off the main entrance to the house. While the room was furnished with an oval oak table and four side chairs of Spanish leather, it also included two rocking chairs and a bookcase, suggesting that the Field youngsters also used it as a sitting room of sorts.[50] However it was used, the room made their presence evident to visitors, while also ensuring that their meals and

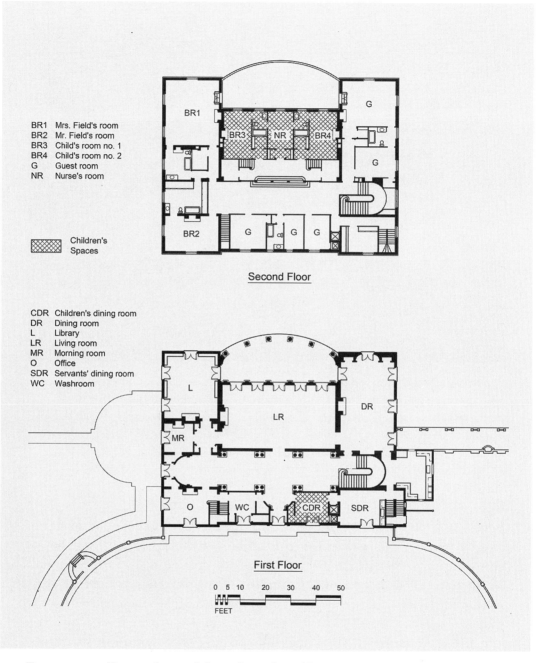

FIGURE 4.10. First- and second-floor plans of Highlawn, the W. B. Osgood Field and Lila Vanderbilt Sloane Field estate, in Lenox, Massachusetts. The design celebrated the spaces devoted to children's use, especially on the second floor, and ensured those spaces were visible to houseguests. Delano and Aldrich, architects, 1908–9. Drawing by Daniel De Sousa.

other activities did not impinge on the adult socializing that took place in the main dining room, a space that faced the back of the house. Indeed, there were still traces of the nineteenth-century tendency to locate children's spaces close to servants' quarters. At Highlawn, the children's dining room was adjacent to the servants' dining room, which was in turn separated from the main dining room by the house's grand staircase in an arrangement that neatly disguised the passage that connected the main house to the butler's pantry and the kitchen wing beyond.

Other elite families accommodated play more directly, as was the case at the Manor House, in Glen Cove, Long Island, a country house designed in 1910 by architect Charles A. Platt for John Teele Pratt and his wife, Ruth Sears Baker Pratt (Figures 4.11 and 4.12). As at Highlawn, the design and construction of the Manor House coincided with the Pratts' child-producing years; a son and two daughters were born between 1903 and 1908, followed by another son and daughter in 1912 and 1913, respectively.[51] Also like Highlawn, the Manor House had no nursery. Instead, individual bedrooms, some with private bathrooms, were clustered around a sitting room for the nurse, a bedroom for the governess, and a kitchenette. Although distinctly

FIGURE 4.11. Exterior of the Manor House, the John Teele Pratt and Ruth Sears Baker Pratt estate, Glen Cove, New York. The Georgian Revival was particularly popular for American country estates built in the early twentieth century, providing stately forms that also signaled the relatively modest tastes of their owners. Charles A. Platt, architect, 1909–11. The Mansion at Glen Cove.

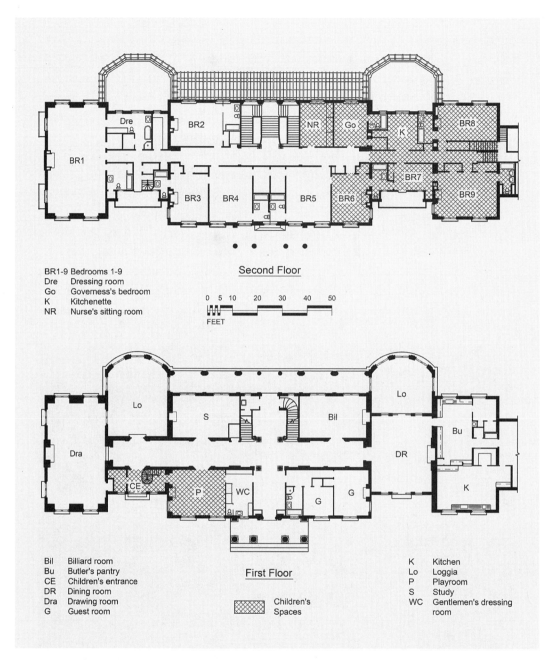

FIGURE 4.12. First- and second-floor plans of the Manor House, the John Teele Pratt and Ruth Sears Baker Pratt estate, in Glen Cove, New York. On the first floor, the playroom is located at the front of the house between the "gentlemen's dressing room" adjacent to the main entrance and the children's entrance, which also includes a stair that communicates with a hallway just outside the parents' bedrooms on the second floor. Charles A. Platt, architect, 1909–11. Drawing by Daniel De Sousa.

twentieth century in its provision of individual bedrooms for small children, this children's zone was situated in a conventional location: at the juncture of the main house and the servants' wing.

On the first floor, the Manor House also accommodated a purpose-built playroom, located on the house's main corridor, directly across from the study. Measuring 20 feet, 6 inches by 18 feet, 4 inches, this was a large room, almost the size of the study or the billiard room.[52] Like those rooms, the playroom communicated with the main corridor via double doors and was fitted out with a large fireplace, centered on one of its short walls. Unlike the adult spaces of the house, however, the playroom was designed to bring in natural light from two directions and was marked as children's space by the provision of a cozy window seat adjacent to the fireplace. If the playroom was in an unusually public part of the house—on the front façade and separated from the main entrance only by the "Gentlemen's Dressing Room" (a euphemism for the toilet facility provided for male visitors)—it was also connected to a children's entrance, which served to minimize the disruptions youthful play would inflict upon the main house. Fitted out with a spacious coatroom that may have served to store play equipment as well as outerwear, the children's entrance had its own private stairs, which led up to a narrow alcove that communicated with the passage to their parents' quarters. The Pratt children, then, could move from outside to the playroom to their individual bedrooms without using the main corridor on the first floor. Their playroom was always on display, as adults moved along the corridor between the drawing room and study at one end of the house to the billiard room and dining room on the other. If the Pratts maintained the practice of the men remaining in the dining room after dinner while the ladies withdrew to the drawing room, Ruth Pratt would have found it easy to show the playroom to her female guests, demonstrating that she had mastered the conundrum of elite motherhood by accommodating the play that was understood to be central to every child's well-being, while ensuring that her children were sleeping quietly upstairs in their rooms.

PLAYHOUSES AS DAY NURSERIES

On all these estates, the children's spaces within the house were supplemented by freestanding playhouses that served many of the functions of traditional day nurseries, albeit extracted from the main house and given their own architectural containers. Unlike mass-produced play sheds marketed to middle-class families, these were permanent, well-constructed buildings that could be used year-round. To be sure, manufacturers were eager to suggest that elite families purchased their products and often included testimonials from satisfied wealthy customers. Nonetheless, when the

E. F. Hodgson Company used one such testimonial from Isabel S. Rockefeller (wife of John D. Rockefeller's nephew, Percy Rockefeller), it revealed that she had not, in fact, purchased a play shed; instead, she had invested almost twice the price to buy one of their full-size cottages to serve as a playhouse for her daughters.[53]

Given that most elite playhouses were individually designed, their architectural forms varied widely. Single-story playhouses with one or two rooms were common before 1920 (Figure 4.13). One-room examples (often provided with small subsidiary spaces) include the first Field playhouse at Highlawn; the Phipps playhouse on the grounds of Westbury House, on Long Island's Gold Coast; the Coe playhouse on the grounds of Planting Fields in nearby Oyster Bay; and the Dows playhouse at Foxhollow Farm in Rhinebeck, New York. The Whitney playhouse at Greentree included two rooms, as did the Pratt playhouse at the Manor House. The Rogers playhouse at Black Point may have also featured two rooms; the building is no longer extant, but a photograph taken by Frances Benjamin Johnson seems to show an interior wall supporting a plate rack and creating front and back rooms. Although less common, there were also multistory playhouses as well. The 1896 Frick playhouse at Clayton in Pittsburgh had a bowling alley, a playroom (for daughter Helen), and workshop (for son Childs) on the first floor and a gymnasium and darkroom on the floor above (Figure 4.14).[54]

For all these differences, the heart of the playhouse was a spacious room, which was typically equipped with a fireplace, by this time a potent symbol of cozy domesticity. The Whitney playhouse at Greentree and the Phipps playhouse at Westbury House were fitted out with deep window seats as well (Figures 4.15 and 4.16). Indeed, the window seat, redolent of an unhurried existence that was understood to be carefree and yet also carefully cosseted, increasingly came to serve as a material sign of elite childhood.

Filled with the plethora of playthings gifted to children at Christmas and on their birthdays, playhouses were also like traditional day nurseries in providing spaces where younger children could spend some of their daylight hours, amusing themselves with books and toys, well away from the spaces occupied by adults. A period photograph of Helen Frick's playroom shows a simply finished space, not unlike an attic nursery, with what appears to be beadboard paneling on the walls and ceiling and what may be a floor cloth underfoot (Figure 4.17). Although a fireplace, fitted out with toy stove, provides coziness, the room was evidently furnished with a hodgepodge of elements typical of attic-level nurseries: doll-sized beds; a child-sized trunk, dresser, table and chairs; and a full-sized table, chair, screen, and corner sink.

Elite playhouses were like day nurseries in that they were spaces supervised under the watchful eye of governesses. Indeed, the notes governesses wrote to absent parents

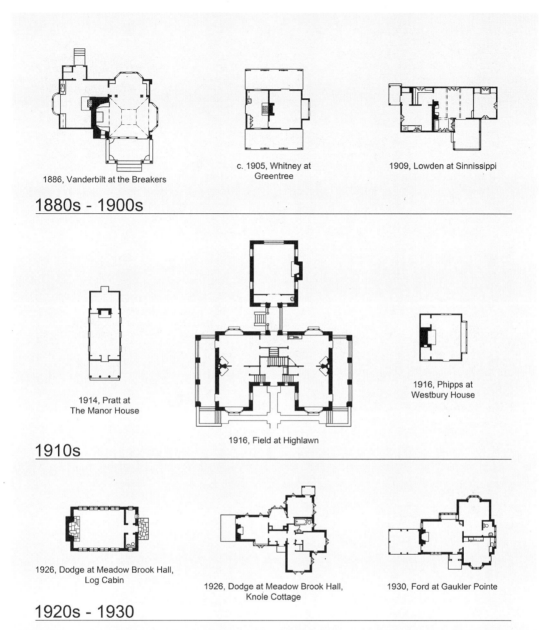

FIGURE 4.13. Plans of children's cottages and playhouses built in the United States between 1886 and 1930. Before 1920, cottages and playhouses tended to feature a single, relatively large, multipurpose room, often supplemented by a subsidiary space that accommodated cooking facilities. After the 1920s, playhouses for girls comprised several smaller, single-purpose rooms that both paralleled the spaces found in single-family houses and served to limit the range of activities their owners could pursue. In contrast, boys like Daniel Dodge enjoyed greater latitude in their play, which continued to take place in large multipurpose rooms. Drawing by Daniel De Sousa.

FIGURE 4.14. Exterior of the children's playhouse at Clayton, the Henry Clay Frick and Adelaide Childs Frick estate, in Pittsburgh, Pennsylvania. Although the building was called the children's playhouse, a bowling alley (just visible at the rear of the building) was primarily for adults. Alden and Harlow, architects, 1897. Photograph by the author.

(either in their own personae or assuming the voices of their young charges) are some of the few archival records of playhouse activities. In February 1898, Helen Frick's governess, Mlle. Marika Ogiz, appended a note to the letter the nine-year-old girl had written to her parents in New York, reporting that their daughter had been "a very good girl indeed," during their three hours of lessons and noting that it was so cold they would forgo their walk and would instead "just go down to the play house for a little while."[55] The following month, in a letter to her father, Helen mentioned another visit to the playhouse in the company of "Madle" (that is, Mlle. Ogiz) and her mother's maid, Pauline. Given that she used the letter to convey her mother's love to her father, it is clear Helen's days were overseen by the family's staff, even when her mother was in residence. Twenty years later, a governess employed at Highlawn wrote a similar note to Lila Vanderbilt Field in Washington, D.C. Adopting the voice of daughters May and Marjorie, she wrote (in French) that the previous afternoon "we" had played in and around "le 'Play House'" and that Anna (the governess) had played the phonograph.[56]

FIGURE 4.15. Exterior of the playhouse on the grounds of Greentree, the Payne Whitney and Helen Hay Whitney estate, in Manhasset, New York. Porches on two sides of the building allowed the children to spend time in the fresh air, while French doors in opposite walls ensured the main room had ample cross-ventilation. Architect unknown, circa 1905. Photograph by the author.

Freestanding playhouses offered significant advantages over traditional day nurseries. They tended to offer better daylighting, better cross-ventilation, and easier access to the out-of-doors than nurseries tucked away on upper floors of the main house. For elite parents familiar with professional advice and cognizant of the germ theory of disease, these were serious considerations. Nonetheless, freestanding playhouses needed to be sited with care, lest they detract from the estate landscape. The Frick playhouse at Clayton, for instance, was situated on the far side of the greenhouse to help minimize the visual impact of the brick bowling alley that extended from the rear of the building (Figure 4.18). More often, playhouses were sited to augment adults' experience of the landscape. At Highlawn, the first playhouse enhanced the formal approach to the main house, while the entrance to the second playhouse was aligned with the cross axis of a manicured garden nearby. At Greentree, the playhouse was nestled beneath the spreading branches of a yew tree, the focal point of a picturesque vignette visible from the curving drive that led to the main house. In other instances, the playhouse was set in its own precinct designed to

A Conundrum for Elite Parents 189

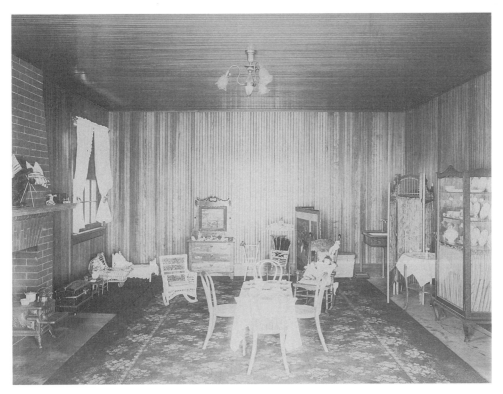

FIGURE 4.17. Helen Clay Frick's playroom in the children's playhouse at Clayton, the Henry Clay Frick and Adelaide Childs Frick estate, in Pittsburgh, Pennsylvania. Furnished with doll-sized, child-sized, and full-size furniture, the playroom accommodated a range of activities for a young girl. Alden and Harlow, architects, 1897. Courtesy of The Frick Collection / Frick Art Reference Library Archives.

complement the larger estate landscape. At Black Point, the Southampton, Long Island, estate of Henry Huddleston Rogers Jr., the playhouse stood within a children's garden that mimicked the formal design of other parts of the professionally designed landscape, albeit on a smaller scale (Figure 4.19). At Westbury House, also on Long Island, the Phipps playhouse was located within a fenced enclosure that featured plantings carefully selected for their small scale (Figure 4.20). Eye-catching elements in the landscape, freestanding playhouses could offer houseguests and other visitors visible evidence of parental commitment to facilitating children's play.

FIGURE 4.16. Interior of the playhouse on the grounds of Greentree, the Payne Whitney and Helen Hay Whitney estate, in Manhasset, New York. In the early twentieth century, the window seat often served as an architectural marker of childhood. In this case, the window seat looks toward a large stone-faced fireplace on the opposite wall. Architect unknown, circa 1905. Photograph by the author.

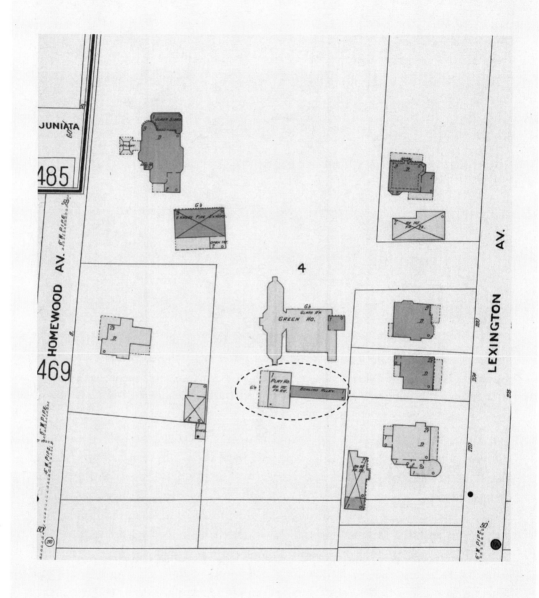

FIGURE 4.18. Site plan of Clayton, the Henry Clay Frick and Adelaide Childs Frick estate in Pittsburgh, Pennsylvania. The playhouse (in the dashed oval) is adjacent to the greenhouse, which blocks the view of the playhouse bowling alley from the main house. Sanborn Fire Insurance Map, 1905.

FIGURE 4.19. Exterior of the playhouse on the grounds of Black Point (also known as Villa del Mar), the Henry H. Rogers Jr. and Mary Benjamin Rogers estate in Southampton, Long Island, New York. Set within its own "children's garden," the playhouse seems to have had at least two rooms; an interior wall parallel to the front wall is visible through the open door. Walker and Gillette, architects, 1914–16. Frances Benjamin Johnston and Mattie Edwards Hewitt, photographers, circa 1916. Frances Benjamin Johnston Photograph Collection, Library of Congress, Prints and Photographs Division, LC-DIG-ppmsca-1687.

ANXIETIES ABOUT LUXURY AND CONSPICUOUS SIMPLICITY

If playhouses solved one conundrum for elite parents, they also foregrounded questions about what form the stuff of elite childhood should take. In important ways, these questions were a subset of concerns about the form of the objects with which elite adults surrounded themselves. The calls for reform were varied. As early as 1897, Edith Wharton and Ogden Codman Jr. used the pages of *The Decoration of Houses* to decry "the vulgarity of current decoration," untethered to the principles of architectural design. Although they blamed this state of affairs on "the indifference of the wealthy to architectural fitness," they also identified the rich as those best positioned

Figure 4.20. Exterior of the "English Cottage" on the grounds of Westbury House, the John Shaffer Phipps and Margarita Grace Phipps estate in Old Westbury, Long Island, New York. Thatching was unusual on children's cottages and playhouses in the United States and may have been a nod to the British connections of "Dita" Grace, who was living with her parents at Battle Abbey in East Sussex when she met and married "Jay" Phipps. Architect unknown, circa 1916. Photograph by the author.

to lead the reform. "When a rich man demands good architecture," they asserted, "his neighbors will get it too." To be sure, Wharton and Codman presented the classicism of fifteenth- to eighteenth-century Italy and France as the epitome of good taste, but they also advocated for (relatively) simple forms, noting that "simplicity is at home even in palaces."[57]

The cultivation of "taste" (once considered a quality of mind innate to those of wealth and status) was a central concern for Wharton and Codman, who argued that elite parents had a duty to surround their offspring with objects that would instill in them an appreciation of beauty. In their view, one of the obstacles to "the early development of taste" was the tendency to shower children with gifts at Christmas and on their birthdays. Indeed, they considered this practice as particularly hard on the children of the rich, who "suffer from the quantity as well as the quality of the presents they receive." For such children, "appetite is surfeited, curiosity is blunted, by the mass of offerings poured in with every anniversary." Their advice was to coordinate gift giving so that family and friends could pool their resources to present the child with "one thing worth having—a good edition, a first-state etching or engraving, or some object fitted to give pleasure at the time and lasting enjoyment through life."[58] In short, while Wharton and Codman believed taste had to be taught, they also recommended introducing rich children early on to the practices of connoisseurship and seeding private collections of luxury goods that would play a role in the performance of elite identity once the children grew to adulthood. Bibliophile William B. Osgood Field may have been motivated by a similar set of concerns when he built a studio in connection with a second playhouse at Highlawn. Fitted out with a fireplace and large window, the studio housed Field's bindery and could have facilitated attempts to share his collecting interests with his offspring (see Figure 4.13).

Increasingly, aesthetic reform was understood as more than a matter of taste. As Laurel J. Waycott has argued, in the early years of the twentieth century, it also became linked to a strategy of class self-preservation.[59] Debates about the gold standard (which before the establishment of the Federal Reserve in 1913 provided the greatest benefit to those with the most money already in the bank) unleashed pointed, even vitriolic, critiques of the wealthy, those whom William Jennings Bryant characterized as "idle hoarders of idle capital" in his 1896 "Cross of Gold" speech.[60] In the same years, Thorstein Veblen drew attention to the role of conspicuous leisure and conspicuous consumption as the primary means by which men of wealth secured their reputations. Indeed, the two were linked, as only those exempt from productive labor had the time for connoisseurship, "the cultivation of the aesthetic faculty" that allowed men of wealth "to discriminate with some nicety between the noble and the ignoble in consumable goods."[61] (This was precisely why Wharton and Codman looked to the rich to demand good architecture and why they encouraged coordinated gift giving for the young.) While Veblen insisted that his terms of analysis, especially "invidious comparison" and "conspicuous waste," were "used in a technical sense" and were "not to be taken in an odious sense," he also implicitly encouraged his readers to equate "noble" consumable goods with "waste."[62]

The responses of the wealthy varied. Some took up Andrew Carnegie's call for men of wealth to limit the amount they left to their descendants, establishing instead philanthropic foundations during their lifetimes so that they themselves could direct the distribution of their millions.[63] Others seem to have relied on publicists to help generate positive press, such as a 1914 article in the *Saturday Evening Post* that profiled a number of "average New York millionaires" to bolster the author's assertion that these men "live more simply and work much harder than the average individual."[64] As Waycott has argued, another strategy involved rejecting the aesthetics of affluence established by previous generations, a move that allowed elites to prove (to themselves as well as to the broader public) that they deserved their wealth. Eager to show they had the right kind of relationship to affluence, they set out to demonstrate that they were modest in their desires and spent their money prudently.[65] In reality, they continued to spend vast sums on huge, imposing houses that required large staffs to maintain them, but they increasingly chose to clothe those houses, especially their country houses, in the (relatively) simple forms associated with the Arts and Crafts movement and especially the Colonial Revival. The Georgian Revival in particular allowed elites to inhabit outwardly simple houses that spoke the language of both nationalism and white privilege.

Given the contemporary tendency to associate children with primitive simplicity, these aesthetic reforms seemed particularly appropriate in spaces devoted to the use of youngsters. Indeed, when Wharton and Codman articulated the principles to be followed in furnishing and decorating schoolrooms, nurseries, and the individual rooms of older children, their list of desiderata evoked many a Colonial Revival interior: white woodwork, "walls tinted in some bright color," hardwood floors with a removable rug or matting, windows "hung with either shades or curtains" (but not both), and "plain and substantial" furniture, including "a large, solid writing table."[66] Their aim was not only to create a "cheerful" space but also to instill important values in children. For instance, they asserted that a "well-designed bookcase with glass doors" would teach the child "respect for books by showing that they [that is, the books] are thought worthy of care."[67]

For many elite parents, the response was to provide their children with the ultimate toy—their own playhouse—but to clothe it in conspicuous simplicity. In some cases, the humbleness of the playhouse seems to have simply mirrored the architectural vocabulary of the main house. At Greentree, for example, there is a close family resemblance between the main house and the playhouse, which are both covered with clapboards, include chimneys made with river rock, and currently feature the same gray and white paint scheme (see Figures 4.4 and 4.14). Even there, the playhouse tended toward the quaint, thanks to its diamond pane windows and novelty clapboarding that mimicked shingles.

At Foxhollow Farm, the Dows playhouse was likewise a Colonial Revival building, in keeping with the architecture on the rest of the estate (Figure 4.21). Indeed, it was similar in form to the gardener's cottage: a low rectangular building, topped by a gable roof with its ridge parallel to the entrance façade and its eaves kicked out in an evocation of buildings associated with the region's early Dutch settlers.[68] Like the gardener's cottage, Fallsburgh (as the playhouse was known) was clad in white clapboards and its windows were fitted out with dark shutters. In both buildings, a porch ran the full length of the main façade. At the playhouse, the porch roof was supported by baseless Doric columns, paired at the two ends to give the porch sufficient visual strength. Here, architect Harrie T. Lindeberg used the classical orders to mark the playhouse as a genteel structure and to distinguish it from similar buildings

FIGURE 4.21. Exteriors of the playhouse (known as Fallsburgh) and gardener's cottage at Foxhollow Farm, the Tracy Dows and Alice Olin Dows estate in Rhinebeck, New York. As published in *American Country Houses of Today*, this pairing of images called attention to formal similarities between the two outbuildings, while the use of baseless Doric columns to support the playhouse porch roof signaled that building's greater gentility. Albro and Lindeberg, architects, 1908. Frank Miles Day, *American Country Houses of Today* (New York: American Book Publishing Company, 1912), 6.

inhabited by the family's employees. At the same time, the Doric, the most primitive of the Greek orders, may have seemed particularly appropriate for a building associated with children, especially in light of contemporary theories that held that the development of each individual involved the recapitulation of human evolution, with primitive children developing only gradually into a civilized adult state. In short, the exterior of the playhouse is based on a sophisticated architectural pun, which may explain why the playhouse was so often depicted in the architectural press and why it was pictured on the same page with the gardener's cottage in *American Country Houses of Today* in 1912.[69]

At the same time, the design of Fallsburgh's exterior also managed to give the impression that the playhouse was child-sized, while disguising the fact that its interior could easily accommodate adults. The well-proportioned Doric columns called attention to the building's reduced scale; when Tracy Dows photographed his six-year-old daughter standing between two columns in 1920, she was more than half their height. The placement of the windows also contributed to the impression that the building was child-sized. Photographs taken in 1909, soon after the playhouse was completed, reveal that the windows were set low enough in the wall that even three-year-old Margaret could peer through them. The porch roof drew attention away from the fact that the building's front wall rose well above the windows, creating an interior space that accommodated full-size furnishings. Indeed, the interior photographs of a family meal at the playhouse confirm that while the cooking range was on a small scale, the table was the correct height for Alice Dows. In contrast, her young son had to sit on the edge of his seat, his feet on a chair rung, in order to consume his meal.

On other estates, the distinction between the main house and the playhouse was even more overt, as at the Frick estate, where the redbrick playhouse (with its gambrel roof evoking Dutch colonial forms and minimizing the presence of its second floor; see Figure 4.14), contrasted sharply with the tawny brick main house with its eclectic forms, irregular footprint, vertical character, and spiky silhouette. The contrast was even more noticeable at Westbury House, where the main house was a brick-and-stone Georgian Revival mansion, while the thatch-roofed, half-timbered playhouse seemed to be a throwback to a simpler time entirely (see Figure 4.20).

Achieving this kind of conspicuous simplicity was particularly important for Frank O. Lowden, whose political aspirations depended on his reputation as a friend of the farmer. To be sure, he had grown up in poverty in rural Iowa and worked his way through school, eventually graduating from law school in 1887. Yet, in 1896, at age thirty-four, he had married twenty-six-year-old Florence Pullman, daughter of railroad car baron George Pullman. By 1903, the family included four children: George Mortimer Pullman Lowden (born 1897 and known as Pullman), Florence

Lowden (born 1898), Harriet Lowden (born 1900), and Frances Lowden (born 1903). Aware that being the son-in-law of a millionaire could be a liability in the political career he envisioned, Lowden ensured that published profiles mentioned that he and his family lived on his income and not on the Pullman millions.[70] This was not quite accurate, as the couple depended on Florence's money to buy land and build their large and comfortable house at Sinnissippi Farm.[71] The deception may have seemed small to Lowden; after all, having positioned himself as a friend of the farmer, it was imperative that he could demonstrate that he himself farmed.[72] In the early years of the twentieth century, his political star was rising. He served in the U.S. Congress from 1906 to 1911 and was elected governor of Illinois in 1916, an office he held until 1921. He had his eye on an even higher office, but it was not to be. He narrowly lost the Republican presidential nomination in 1920; declined an offer to run as vice president in 1924; and ultimately abandoned his White House aspirations in 1928, when he lost the presidential nomination to Herbert Hoover.[73] In 1936, his name was mentioned again, but the seventy-five-year-old (dubbed "the sage of Sinnissippi" by the Associated Press) offered no comment and sat out the convention at his Illinois farm.[74]

In this context, the design of the playhouse at Sinnissippi Farm in 1909 and its subsequent publication in 1918 suggest that Lowden understood its power to burnish or tarnish his reputation in the public sphere. Like the main house, the Lowden children's house (as it was called on the architectural plans) was designed by Pond and Pond. Like other playhouses, it took the form of a small-scale cottage (Figure 4.22). The Lowden playhouse was a more ambitious version of the type, especially in its treatment of interior space. The main entrance led into a room identified on plans as the living room (Figure 4.23; see Figure 4.13). Dominated by a large, open brick fireplace, the room was also distinguished by its vertical expansion and artfully carved roof trusses, composed of cross beams with both king and queen posts. Just to the left of the fireplace was a cozy inglenook that was set apart from the main room by its lower ceiling and built-in benches. On the wall above the fireplace, the ornamentation referenced the site as a place of play by depicting three children, rendered in silhouette, engaged in a game of I spy (what we might call hide-and-seek). One figure (seen in profile) was shown hiding by leaning against the fireplace, a second took a similar position against the king post, while the third, the seeker, faced out into the room on the other side of the king post. Below them, a door led to a pantry, which opened into a kitchen with what the *Western Architect* referred to as "a full complement of kitchen equipment . . . built to a child's scale."[75]

At the other end of the building was the boudoir (essentially a sitting room) set two steps above the floor level in the rest of the building. A railing carved with abstracted female figures (called maids in waiting in the *Western Architect*) marked the

FIGURE 4.22. Exterior of the children's house, Sinnissippi Farm, the Frank O. Lowden and Florence Pullman Lowden estate, in Oregon, Illinois. The balusters of the porch railing take the form of abstracted female figures, a motif also used on the interior. Pond and Pond, architects, 1909. Pond & Pond Collection, Ryerson and Burnham Art and Architecture Archives, Art Institute of Chicago. Digital file #200101.090805–45.

location of this level change without interrupting the view into the living room; at the same time, floor-to-ceiling curtains gave users the opportunity to provide visual separation, when desired. In short, this playhouse was a distinctly feminized space.[76]

Perhaps to offset the relative extravagance of the small building, every corner of its interior was informed by the aesthetic reforms of the Arts and Crafts movement, from the building's diamond-pane windows to its stenciled ceilings, dark-stained oak doors, and hammered-metal light fixtures. Associated with the simple life, these forms served to frame the Lowden children as modest, humble, and unaffected despite their wealth. The symbolic meanings of these forms overlapped with the messages conveyed by the Colonial Revival. Both helped signal that elites had adopted an appropriate relationship to affluence.[77]

In November 1918, the *Western Architect* published three photographs of the Lowden playhouse—one exterior photograph with a bit of the main house in the background

FIGURE 4.23. Interior of the children's house, Sinnissippi Farm, the Frank O. Lowden and Florence Pullman Lowden estate, in Oregon, Illinois. A railing decorated with abstracted silhouettes of so-called maids in waiting separates the raised boudoir in the foreground from the living room beyond. Pond and Pond, architects, 1909. Pond & Pond Collection, Ryerson and Burnham Art and Architecture Archives, Art Institute of Chicago. Digital file #200101.090805–51.

and two images of the living room, identified as the library and dining room in the captions. The timing of the article is worth noting, as the building was no longer new, and it seems likely that the daughters of the family had outgrown the cottage. Lowden's presidential ambitions, however, were at their brightest, which suggests that the governor and his wife saw the playhouse as a political asset. Since it also called attention to their wealth, the Lowdens must have known that the playhouse, for all its Arts and Crafts character, may have been a double-edged sword when it came to the reputation of the "friend of the farmer." Why run the risk by publishing it all? The photo captions suggest a possible answer, in that they characterize the playhouse as "a 'laboratory' in which the daughters of Governor and Mrs. Frank O. Lowden learned their lessons in domestic economy and practiced the arts of good housekeeping, social amenities, and service." Given that the Lowdens did not have the playhouse constructed until their only son was twelve years old, Pullman Lowden may not have made extensive use of the building. Whether or not he did is ultimately less informative than the fact that the senior Lowdens offered the playhouse as material evidence that they had raised their three daughters to embrace conventional gender roles combining housekeeping, the social graces, and (public) service. On the pages of the *Western Architect*, at least, the Lowdens had mastered the conundrum—in fact, both conundrums—of elite parenting.

PLAYHOUSES AS MATERIAL EVIDENCE OF PARENTAL CARE

In many ways, the elite parents who built extravagant playhouses in the early twentieth century fostered ambitions for their children that would have been familiar to the previous generation. They sought to prepare their offspring to take their place in society and thus to play their role in perpetuating the family's standing and in consolidating their wealth. They also used playhouses in ways that were not very different from the Gilded Age children's cottages that had preceded them, especially in providing a degree of parental control over their children's social connections, while simultaneously segregating the youngsters from the entertaining spaces of the main house. In short, these playhouses were still tools of elite culture, wielded toward dynastic ends.

At the same time, however, these small buildings speak to changes taking place in the wider context within which these wealthy families operated. In the previous generation, Gilded Age elites had tended to consider themselves as competitors with one another, vying, for instance, for entrée to New York's Four Hundred. In contrast, the next generation were more concerned with preserving the privileged status of their entire class, facing as they did both widespread criticism of the super wealthy as well as the looming specter of economic reforms that would impinge on their ability to amass even greater fortunes. More attuned to public opinion than their parents had been, they were also more likely to deploy their children and their domestic arrangements to craft public personae that would be palatable to the populace at large.

The campaign to justify great wealth was waged on several fronts, including aesthetics. Both for their country houses and especially for their children's playhouses, elite parents in the early twentieth century embraced an architecture of (relative) simplicity in order to demonstrate that they themselves had an appropriate relationship to money, that they were encouraging modest tastes in their offspring, and that they therefore deserved their wealth. Another part of their campaign, however, centered on presenting themselves as good parents, which in the early twentieth century involved paying attention to the advice of child study experts, all of whom emphasized the importance of play in child development. Thus, play activities that had once been corralled in day nurseries and kept well out of sight in the upper reaches of grand houses were given their own architectural containers and placed artfully in the landscape for visitors to admire. Even if wealthy parents were not able to organize their lives around their offspring—as their middle-class contemporaries sought to do—they could nonetheless ensure that their estates offered material evidence of their commitment to children's play.

In a sense, of course, they were following in the footsteps of Queen Victoria and Prince Albert, who had counted on the architectural arrangements at Osborne—particularly the Pavilion and the children's precinct—to serve as evidence of their attentiveness as parents. As at Osborne, the primary audience for these presentations of self were other social elites, notably the house guests who would have occasion to visit the upper floors of the main house and to stroll the grounds. Yet, Victoria had also come to see the benefits of using photography to ensure that the architectural evidence of her parental care was seen by a much wider audience. Frank O. Lowden and Florence Pullman Lowden were among the first—but by no means the last—American elites to follow suit.

As important as it was to these parents to encourage their offspring to play, the term itself meant different things for different children in different contexts. Despite scientific theories that posited the existence of innate play instincts, play professionals did not trust the children of recent immigrants from southern or eastern Europe to play correctly. Instead, they took it upon themselves to direct the play of these supposedly inferior youngsters, guiding them in activities that ignored their minds and focused instead on producing disciplined bodies accustomed to coordinated movement. In comparison, the play of elite, white, Anglo-Saxon, and Protestant children was largely self-directed, often with toys that encouraged the exercise of the imagination. Equally important, much of it also took place largely indoors, in settings specifically designed with the needs of particular youngsters in mind. Elite children may have been removed from the main house, but in their playhouses, they could each feel themselves to be the axis around which the world turned.

At the same time, the playhouses themselves provided the scripts for this seemingly self-directed play, inviting some behaviors, while discouraging others. Typically, these conspicuously humble settings encouraged the performance of homely virtues, performances that, initially at least, were gendered in surprising ways. Yet, by 1930, playhouses had changed, as a narrow playscript aimed specifically at girls was packaged with exquisite miniaturization.

FIGURE 5.1. Exterior of Knole Cottage, on the grounds of Meadow Brook Hall, the estate of Alfred Wilson and Matilda Dodge Wilson, in Rochester, Michigan. The image shows the building (initially called Hilltop Lodge) in its first location near the site's original farmhouse. Designed to be moved, it was relocated and renamed in 1929. Smith, Hinchman & Grylls, architects, 1926. Courtesy of Meadow Brook Hall Archives.

CHAPTER FIVE

Practicing Domestic Virtue

Gender Politics and the 1920s Playhouse

On 27 November 1926, Frances Dodge, daughter of one of the founders of the Dodge Brothers Motor Company, turned twelve. The festivities that day took the form of a housewarming party for a playhouse built on the grounds of Meadow Brook Farms in Rochester, Michigan (Figure 5.1). Initially called Hilltop Lodge but known since 1929 as Knole Cottage, the playhouse was a birthday gift from Frances's mother, Matilda Dodge Wilson. The next day, the society pages of the *Detroit News* covered the party, describing in detail its setting: "a model house, a bungalow, in miniature, although it is perhaps seven or ten feet by seven." The story continued:

> It is built of brick made especially in small size to conform with the little house; contains a living room, dining room, kitchen, two bedrooms and a bath, and is electrically heated and lighted, with especially designed fixtures. The furniture throughout the rooms has been especially made, with the exception of several small antiques such as a secretary, and the kitchen boasts of an electric stove and refrigerator.

According to the columnist, the playhouse "would be the envy or joy of any small miss."[1]

As a fully fitted-out house on a reduced scale, Knole Cottage differed in important ways from elite playhouses built in the first two decades of the twentieth century. Those earlier playhouses had been small, but not miniature; often included kitchen facilities, but did not attempt to mimic single-family houses; were used by both boys and girls; and offered multipurpose rooms in which youngsters could pursue a range of activities. In contrast, Knole Cottage and other playhouses built in the 1920s and 1930s were explicitly feminized spaces that offered elite girls a narrow play script, one focused exclusively on the housework required to maintain their complete, small-scale houses. While earlier playhouses had been the settings for play, in the 1920s and 1930s, playhouses also became the content of play, at least for girls.

This chapter traces the changing nature of the play accommodated in elite playhouses during the first thirty years of the twentieth century, with particular attention to the role of cooking, an activity pursued at children's cottages since the 1850s, when Victoria and Albert's offspring had prepared simple meals in the Swiss Cottage. In the early twentieth century, however, youthful cooking took on a new tone, as elite identity for both men and women came to incorporate activities that encouraged a modicum of self-sufficiency. Among these activities was camping. The earliest summer camps had been established in the 1880s and catered to elite boys, while private girls' camps began to spring up in the first decade of the twentieth century, with the goal of producing women who would take pleasure in the pursuits their husbands and sons enjoyed.[2] For many marriages formed in the early twentieth century, this proved to be the case, as elite women participated in extended hunting and fishing expeditions. Another important component of elite identity was the pursuit of higher education, which could require young men to live on their own and to prepare their own rudimentary meals.[3]

By the 1920s, the meaning and practice of youthful cooking among the very rich were further transformed by the Red Scare and the debates it engendered about housework, women's roles, and the future of the private home. These debates seem to have had particular resonance for the families of newly rich industrial magnates, who had a complicated relationship with cultural practices of social elites who had inherited their fortunes. On one hand, they were eager to announce their success by adopting many of the outward trappings of great wealth, notably building for themselves impressive estates. On the other, they were also inclined to celebrate the fact that their riches were earned, readily acknowledging their own modest backgrounds and highlighting the personal attributes they understood as responsible for their substantial achievements. Their parental ambitions, then, lay not just in ensuring that their children were prepared to function in society, but also in demonstrating that their offspring had inherited gender-appropriate proclivities for industriousness. Sons, for instance, were encouraged to demonstrate engineering prowess and managerial ability. In contrast, daughters were required to exhibit an interest in housekeeping and a willingness to turn their hands to domestic labor, ideally within the walls of a reduced-scale playhouse.

YOUTHFUL COOKING AT ELITE PLAYHOUSES IN THE EARLY TWENTIETH CENTURY

In the early twentieth century, elite playhouses accommodated a range of purposes. In addition to a bowling alley, the Frick playhouse at Clayton in Pittsburgh included a first-floor playroom filled with playthings for young Helen Clay Frick (see Figure 4.17), as well as a workshop for her older brother, Childs Frick. On the second floor were Childs's darkroom and a gymnasium that served as the headquarters for the Clayton Cadets, a drill team of neighborhood boys commanded by the Frick heir. Yet, like the children's cottage at the Breakers, the playhouse was also understood as an appropriate venue for homely activities. In May 1898, for instance, nine-year-old Helen wrote to her father: "Yesterday afternoon Madle [her governess, Mlle. Ogiz], Pauline and me went out to the play house and Madle read to us, while Pauline and me sowed." Pauline was presumably Pauline Turon, lady's maid to Helen's mother, Adelaide Frick, as she would have been well positioned to offer Helen instruction when the youngster attempted—with limited success, according to her letter—to mend her father's stockings.[4]

Cooking emerged as a particularly important activity in early twentieth-century playhouses, as evidenced by the writings of the renowned British horticulturalist and garden designer Gertrude Jekyll. In a 1901 *Country Life Illustrated* article, "The Children's Playhouse," she encouraged upper-middle-class parents to provide their children with a playhouse—"a real, well-built little house, with a kitchen and a parlour, where they can keep house and cook and receive their friends" (Figure 5. 2).[5] In *Children and Gardens,* a book published simultaneously in London and New York in 1908, Jekyll devoted a full chapter to the playhouse, supplementing her original text with detailed instructions for making salads, soups (julienne and two milk soups), toasted cheese, scrambled eggs, mustard and cress sandwiches, scones and fairy cakes—distinctly tea fare not unlike that enjoyed by Victoria's children fifty years earlier.

For Jekyll and her upper-middle-class readers, youthful cooking was inextricably associated with hospitality. She suggested that the sitting room be fitted out with glass-fronted cabinets to hold glasses and tea things, "for—who knows?—perhaps there might be an occasional luncheon party on birthdays or other great occasions."[6] Jekyll went on to write that "the elders would often be invited to tea," and later reminded young cooks that "when you have invited your elders, or on any other important occasion, you should have some freshly-made scones or little cakes."[7] From Jekyll's perspective, these events would help consolidate the child's sense of possession, which she understood as something "keenly enjoyed by children."[8] She encouraged parents to reward "a specially praiseworthy culinary effort or other evidence of good housewifeliness" with "a little gift of money, to be expended on the perfecting of the play-house's equipment."[9] In this sense, the youthful cooking of upper-middle-class children was less about preparing them for housework and more an avenue for introducing them to the ethos of consumerism. Here they came to understand that a house—even a playhouse—required continual elaboration and that purchasing "things both for use and ornament" was one of the great pleasures of life.[10]

mouth and gives one yell, and makes for that bit of cotton. 'E got there, for 'e would not be denied. 'E got there an' 'e couldn't get back. But 'e made a rush for it——"

"A divil he was on rushes," broke in Private Coolin, wiping his mouth nervously.

"'E's the pride of 'is 'ome and the bloomin' brigade, bar one, which is the Subadar Goordit Singh. For w'en the Subadar sees Connor in 'is 'ole, a cut across 'is jaw, doin' of 'is trick alone, away goes Subadar Goordit Singh and two of 'is company be'ind 'im for to rescue. 'E cut with 'is sword like a bloomin' picture. 'E didn't spare 'is strength, and 'e didn't spare the Osnum Digners. And 'e come back, an' he brought with him William Connor—that's all what come back!"

"How long did William live?" said Coolin. "He was a good frind to me was Connor, a thrue frind he was to me. How long did the b'y live?"

"'E lived long enough to 'ave McNeill shake 'im by the 'and. 'E lived long enough to say to the Subadar Goordit Singh, 'I would take scorn uv me to lave widout askin' y'r pardon, Subadar.' And the Subadar took 'is 'and and salaamed, and showed 'is teeth, which was meant friendly."

"What else did Connor say?" asked Coolin, eagerly.

"'E said 'is kit was for you that's spoilin' a good name in the condinsation of the commissaryat, Coolin."

"But what else?" said Coolin. "Nothin' about a drame at all?"

"Who's talkin' about dreams?" said Bagshot. "'E wasn't no bloomin' poet. 'E was a man. What 'e said 'e said like a man. 'E said 'e'd got word from Mary—which is proper that a man should do when 'e's a-chuckin' of 'is tent-pegs. If 'e aint got no mother—an' Connor 'adn't—'is wife or 'is sweetheart 'as the honour."

"Oh, my Gawd," said Coolin, "I wish I hadn't towld him —I wish I hadn't towld the b'y."

"Told 'im what?" said Bagshot.

PLAN OF A PLAY-HOUSE AND GARDEN.

But Coolin of the Commissariat did not answer; his head was on his arms, and his arms were on his knees.

THE CHILDREN'S PLAY-HOUSE.

IT may be safely said that there is no form of permanent plaything that can give intelligent children so much pleasure as a well-appointed play-house.

It must be confessed that it is a somewhat costly toy, but its value is so considerable, apart from the intense interest and delight that it is to the children, that it is well worth the consideration of parents whose means allow them to provide it.

It is a little house somewhere in garden or shrubland consisting of a kitchen and a sitting-room. If it can have an enclosed porch, so much the better. In the kitchen the children make and bake little scones and cakes and serve them at the tea that is laid in the adjoining sitting-room, and learn the elements of even more serious cookery, and jam-making and simple ways of cooking eggs, and any advance on these beginnings that their taste or capacity may seem to ask for. The little house would be provided with all necessary fittings: a cooking-stove in the kitchen, a dresser, a cupboard, and a stout little kitchen table with a drawer. If it can have a small pantry containing a water supply and a sink where the crockery is washed up and water drawn, and a round towel handy, it will be better than if these necessaries were in the kitchen itself.

The sitting-room would also have a fireplace, for though the little house might not be used for perhaps three winter months, yet by the time March comes with its long bright afternoons many would be the teas out at the play-house. The sitting-room would be appropriately fitted with two glass-fronted corner cupboards to hold the tea things and glasses, for—who knows?—perhaps there might be an occasional luncheon party on birthdays or other great occasions. There would also be a little

A MINIATURE COTTAGE.

FIGURE 5.2. Plan and elevation of a children's playhouse first published by renowned British horticulturalist Gertrude Jekyll in 1901. Jekyll republished the images and expanded the discussion of the playhouse and its uses in her book *Children and Gardens* (1908). Gertrude Jekyll, "The Children's Play-House," *Country Life Illustrated* 9, no. 230 (1 June 1901), 707.

Jekyll clearly assumed an upper-middle-class readership for both her article and her book: families who embraced child-centered parenting (in which a child's birthday was deemed a "great occasion") and who also had the means to forgo their children's labor, as well as home grounds of sufficient acreage that they could set aside part of the garden exclusively for the use of the youngsters. Nonetheless, her linking of children, gardens, and cooking harked back to the Swiss Cottage, which had been completed when Jekyll was ten years old and was regularly mentioned in books and articles about Queen Victoria's homelife throughout the early years of Jekyll's career. It may not be a coincidence that her *Country Life Illustrated* article appeared just a few months after the sovereign's death and the intense public attention that event had drawn to Osborne.[11] Although she did not mention Victoria, Jekyll was certainly aware of the connection between royal children and playhouses, as she illustrated her book with a photograph of a grown woman sitting in front of a thatched cottage, noting that "the pretty lady in the picture is a German Princess ... [who] has brought her work to the old play-house and is trying to think herself a child again, remembering all the happy hours she spent here a few years ago."[12] In short, the picture Jekyll painted of children using the fruits of their horticultural endeavors to make light fare they could share with their siblings and parents was framed in ways that allowed it to resonate in society's upper echelons.

To facilitate this mode of youthful cooking, elite playhouses built in the United States in the first twenty years of the twentieth century were typically provided with some sort of cooking stove. At Westbury House on Long Island, the Phipps's one-room playhouse was dominated by a broad fireplace fitted out with an open coal-burning range—an intentionally archaic cooking technology in 1916, in keeping with the building's half-timbered walls and thatched roof (Figure 5.3; see Figure 4.12). As an adult, Peggie Phipps recalled one attempt at using the range in her youth, when she and two friends set out to roast a chicken for their lunch. Given Peggie's admission that "none of us really knew how to cook," a governess or kitchen maid may have assisted their efforts. Indeed, the episode was memorable primarily for shining a light on the impish behavior of her younger brother, Michael, who used a hook and a stick to pull the chicken up through the chimney and abscond with it.[13]

More common was the provision of a separate kitchen, although those varied in their degree of elaboration. The kitchen in the Colonial Revival Whitney playhouse at Greentree on Long Island was relatively simple: the smaller of the playhouse's two rooms, it was fitted out with a full-sized range manufactured by the Cribben and Sexton Company of Chicago and a utility sink near the back door (see Figure 4.13). In contrast, the kitchen facilities at the Arts and Crafts Lowden playhouse at Sinnissippi Farm in Illinois comprised three rooms: a pantry, the kitchen proper, and a rear entry that also housed the refrigerator (Figure 5.4). Period photographs of the

FIGURE 5.3. Interior of "English Cottage," on the grounds of Westbury House, the John Shaffer Phipps and Margarita Grace Phipps estate, in Old Westbury, Long Island, New York. The cooking technology in this one-room, thatched-roofed playhouse was deliberately archaic: a small, open, coal-burning range, set into the fireplace. Architect unknown, circa 1916. Photograph by author.

kitchen highlight both its modern materials (notably the white sink and its white enameled drainboard) and its efficient layout, with a work triangle of sorts formed by the sink, range, and worktable (Figure 5.5). At the same time, the provision of a separate entrance—not just here, but also at Greentree, as well as at the second playhouse at Highlawn in Lenox and at Foxhollow Farm—suggests the presence of servants to do the heavy work.

Importantly, these playhouses and their kitchens were not understood as feminized spaces in the early twentieth century, although this would change abruptly in the 1920s. On 1 January 1913, Tracy Dows, a keen amateur photographer, documented aspects of his family's New Year's dinner at Fallsburgh, the classically detailed playhouse at Foxhollow Farm in Rhinebeck, New York (Figure 5.6). These photographs reveal that, like Vanderbilt cottages in the 1880s and 1890s, Fallsburgh was the setting for intergenerational socializing, with youngsters, including boys, playing host to their parents. Not only is eight-year-old Olin shown in three photographs preparing food on his own, but he also does so in ways that underscore his masculinity. Clad in a white toque, double-breasted white coat, and full-length white apron (the uniform

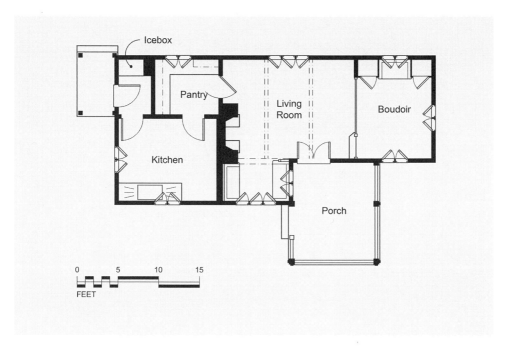

FIGURE 5.4. Plan of the children's house, on the grounds of Sinnissippi Farm, the Frank O. Lowden and Florence Pullman Lowden estate, in Oregon, Illinois. Like playhouses built after 1920, this building featured a number of single-purpose rooms, identified on the architect's plans as the kitchen, pantry, living room, and boudoir. Unlike later playhouses, it had no bedrooms. Pond and Pond, architects, 1909. Drawing by Daniel De Sousa.

favored by famous French chef Auguste Escoffier), Olin is shown playing the distinctly masculine role of professional chef de cuisine. One of the photographs shows the boy standing at the range, framed by the opening of an alcove in the rear wall of the playhouse. Looking directly at the camera with his hand on the knob of the range, he is poised and self-assured. Thanks to the photograph's low vantage point, which placed the boy's head at the top of the picture frame, young Olin is presented as a commanding figure. Other images in the family albums confirm that Olin continued to don this outfit when cooking at the playhouse well into 1915.

Cooking was also a favorite activity at the second playhouse at Highlawn, the William O. Field estate in Lenox, Massachusetts. Completed in 1917, this playhouse had four almost identical rooms on the main level (Figures 5.7 and 5.8). Each room included a window seat (by this time, firmly established as an architectural signifier of childhood), as well as a corner fireplace and its own door to one of the building's two porches. On one side of the building's central axis were two rooms, each identified as a "boy's room," suggesting that each of the Field sons could claim a room of his own for reading or playing games. Indeed, when the playhouse was still under

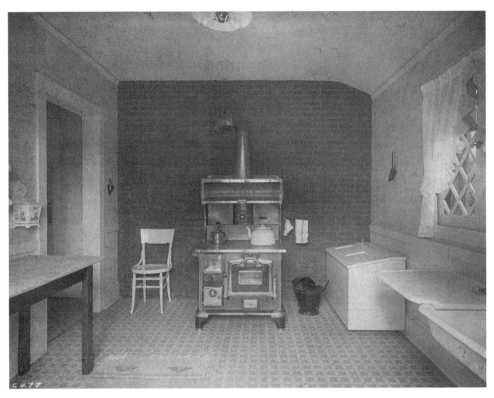

FIGURE 5.5. Kitchen of the children's house, Sinnissippi Farm, the Frank O. Lowden and Florence Pullman Lowden estate, in Oregon, Illinois. Like most children's cottages and playhouses built before 1920, it included a small (but not miniature) working range. Pond and Pond, architects, 1904. Pond and Pond Collection, Ryerson and Burnham Art and Architecture Archives, Art Institute of Chicago. Digital file #200101.090805–52.

FIGURE 5.6. Interiors of the playhouse (known as Fallsburgh) at Foxhollow Farm, the Tracy Dows and Alice Olin Dows estate in Rhinebeck, New York. Taken on New Year's Day in 1913 by Tracy Dows, two photographs show eight-year-old Olin Dows dressed in chef's whites, manning the stove. The third shows Olin, his six-year-old sister, Margaret, and their mother, Alice Olin Dows, at table. Albro and Lindeburg, 1908. Dutchess County Historical Society, Dows Collection.

construction, in September 1917, Field wrote to thirteen-year-old Osgood Field, who had just started his prep school education at Hotchkiss, to report that "the masons are all through at the play house and the plaster is all finished." He continued, "All the carpenters are there and your room has most of the wood work in place. It certainly looks fine. I am sure you will like it when it is done."[14] By default, the other side of the building was designed for the use of the Field daughters. Indeed, the rooms that mirrored the boy's rooms in plan were identified as the "girls' sitting room" and the kitchen, which was differentiated from the rest of the rooms only by the presence of a corner cupboard and small sink. To be sure, the girls did use the kitchen; in October 1921, ten-year-old Mary Field (known in the family as May) mentioned going to the playhouse "to make delicious candy" in a note to her parents.[15] Nonetheless, the boys also relished time spent in the kitchen. In 1921, for instance, seventeen-year-old Osgood (still at Hotchkiss) closed one of his regular letters to his sister Marjorie by suggesting that she "ask Mama, if I do get up to Highlawn, weather we can cook at the playhouse."[16]

FIGURE 5.7. Exterior of playhouse and studio at Highlawn, the W. B. Osgood Field and Lila Vanderbilt Sloane Field estate, in Lenox, Massachusetts. John C. Greenleaf, architect, 1916–17. William B. Osgood Field Estate records: [High Lawn Estate], 1908–1929, box 3, folder 29, Drawings and Archives, Avery Architectural and Fine Arts Library, Columbia University.

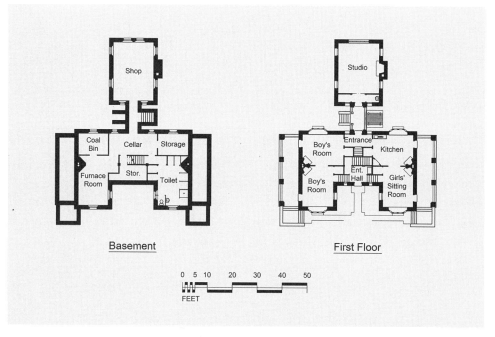

FIGURE 5.8. Basement and first-floor plans of the playhouse and studio at Highlawn, the W. B. Osgood Field and Lila Vanderbilt Sloane Field estate, in Lenox, Massachusetts. Each of the family's two sons has a multipurpose room of his own; the two daughters shared a sitting room. All the children, and sometimes their parents, cooked in the kitchen. The studio was designed to house the bookbinding equipment used by the children's bibliophile father. John C. Greenleaf, architect, 1916–17. Drawing by Daniel De Sousa.

On other occasions, the elder Fields joined their children for "picnics" at the playhouse, according to Frederick Field, the younger of their two sons. Writing in the early 1980s, when he himself was in his late seventies, Frederick recalled that the preparation for these events included "the butler carrying a large tray of silverware, plates and linen from the big house," while another servant was responsible for "carrying cooking utensils, eggs, cream, salt and pepper." The participants would "gather at the appointed hour around the electric stove, and the picnic would get underway." The events stood out in his memory for two reasons. First, "everyone was in a good humor," something the adult Frederick posited was because "we were, for a change, relatively on our own, away from the servants for a whole meal." Second, he recalled "lavish praise for the outstandingly delicious scrambled eggs my mother had managed to serve." The eggs, he remembered, "tasted better than eggs at the big house, because it was such fun to rough it at the playhouse." Having written his autobiography in order to explain how it was possible that he was simultaneously both a millionaire and a Communist, the adult Frederick also made a point of mentioning that a maid came out to the playhouse to clean up afterward, while the earlier procession returned to retrieve the accouterments of the meal.[17]

For whatever reason, the adult Frederick did not mention that his father also sometimes took the leading role in playhouse picnics. In June 1924, fourteen-year-old Marjorie described one such event in a letter to nineteen-year-old Freddy, who was camping in Alberta, Canada, with his brother Osgood:

> We had supper in the playhouse last night. It was oceans of fun. Papa made some pancakes. Cousin Tom ate only three or four. Papa put one on his head which Cousin Tom threw out into the bushes. I got it, and Mr. Smith put it in Cousin Tom's bed which gave him quite a scare.[18]

Marjorie's description confirms what the adult Frederick recalled: that meals at the playhouse featured simple fare more often associated with breakfast than with the multicourse dinners consumed in the main house and that the setting invited a relaxation of decorum—in this case, a descent into hijinks—that was unthinkable in the dining room.

Frederick Field was undoubtedly being somewhat facetious when he characterized eating scrambled eggs cooked on an electric stove and served on china plates in a heated, plumbed, and electrified building as "roughing it." Nonetheless, all the members of the Field family were avid outdoorsmen and -women, enjoying extended camping trips during which they hunted moose and fished for trout. The seniors Fields also regularly went camping in Canada for weeks at a time without their children, although they described their adventures in some detail in letters home. Sometimes these letters included parental sketches of the campsite, which made it clear that their expeditions were facilitated by the labor of others. For instance, a sketch Lila Field made for twelve-year-old Osgood in 1916 included three tents: the guide's tent, the cook's tent, and the tent in which she and her husband slept and took their meals (Figure 5.9). At the same time, she made it clear that the conditions were hardly luxurious. Her sketch indicated that the latrine (which she jokingly referred to as "the château") was "down in a hollow."[19] In short, elite adults in the early twentieth century were expanding the range of activities they enjoyed—activities in which a modicum of self-sufficiency, such as scrambling eggs and making pancakes, came in handy.

This type of self-sufficiency was also helpful when the younger generation pursued higher education. Both Field sons studied at Harvard University, while Marjorie Field attended Bryn Mawr; only May Field did not go to college. After graduating from Harvard, Frederick Field studied for a year at the London School of Economics, living in rooms with Joe Barnes, a friend from Harvard. In his seventies, Frederick

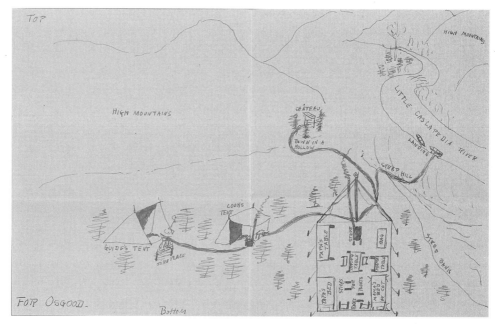

FIGURE 5.9. Sketch of campsite on the Cascapedia River in Quebec, Canada. Drawn by Lila Vanderbilt Sloane Field and included in a letter to son Osgood, dated 1 October 1916. Manuscripts and Archives Division, New York Public Library.

recalled that "the kitchen looked under equipped, but from it Anna Barnes [Joe's mother] produced splendid meals."[20] Letters written at the time suggest that Frederick was involved in meal preparation, however rudimentary. In 1927, his father wrote to say how "tremendously interesting" he found his son's letters, noting that he could "picture [Frederick] and Joe cooking." He went on to write, "I look back at the hours spent with you so intently watching over at the Playhouse, and absorbing what proves to be so essential at your present time and surroundings." From the older man's perspective, his son's culinary abilities were something that he himself was proud to have had a hand in. As he wrote, perhaps only partly in jest, "What it is to be well brought up!"[21]

THE POLITICS OF HOUSEWORK IN THE 1920S

By the 1920s, the meaning of domestic cooking and housework more generally had become highly politicized. As Dolores Hayden has shown, the Red Scare of 1918–19 unleashed a powerful backlash against any individuals or groups that advocated for reorganizing domestic arrangements in the interest of emancipating women from household drudgery. This backlash took many forms, including a spiderweb chart (developed by the War Department) that presented even moderate women's groups "as part of a 'red web,' aimed at destroying America through pacifism and socialism."[22] In the face of strikes and demonstrations in 1919, industrialists and politicians came to believe that the only way to secure growth and prosperity was to keep women out of the paid labor force and focused on maintaining their own homes. To this end, home ownership among workingmen increasingly seemed the best defense against Soviet socialism. In 1931, Herbert Hoover lent government support to these efforts by convening the Conference on Home Building and Home Ownership.

Home economists supported these efforts. In *Household Engineering: Scientific Management in the Home*, published in 1920, Christine Frederick advocated for Taylorism and the enhanced efficiency of the individual housewife, rather than cooperation. Positing parallels between the single-family house—especially its kitchen—and the factory, she introduced middle-class women to the principles of time management, encouraging them to play the dual role of supervisor and operative by counting their own steps and reducing any wasted movements. By the end of the decade, she had written *Selling Mrs. Consumer*, a book in which she encouraged marketing executives to see the cumulative purchasing power of ordinary families as the nation's most effective engine of economic growth, a prediction that became a reality after World War II.[23] Her vision depended on keeping women in the home and encouraging them to buy so-called laborsaving devices that succeeded in promoting ever-rising standards of household cleanliness (thus fueling demand for additional laborsaving devices), but such equipment ultimately failed to reduce the amount of time the average woman spent on housework.[24]

Less often acknowledged is the fact that children—or rather assertions about children—were deployed in these years to make it seem as if this nativist vision of a nation of single-family houses, each one maintained by a woman toiling in isolation, was not a product of politics but of nature. Progressive educators, for instance, encouraged middle-class women to see their homes as extensions of the kindergarten and to engage their children in housework as an educational endeavor. Not only did this approach increase the time women spent attending to their families in their own homes, but it was also predicated on the idea that girls were inherently interested in housework. In her 1920 book, *Children's Occupations*, Maude Cushing Nash asserted that "all small children like to play keeping house and delight in washing and keeping clean various things connected with their play." To be sure, she often used seemingly gender-neutral language, as when she suggested that "one of the best helps in training your child to enjoy domestic duties is doll play."[25] Yet, in the very next sentence, she made it clear that she was talking about girls: in her view, "every little girl should have her family of dolls and care for them." In contrast, she advised mothers to interest their small sons in helping to build the kitchen fire in the morning. Not only would this involve physical activity, but Nash also suggested that mothers use the materials of fire making as object lessons:

> Tell him that if he will bring you some wood from the woodshed you will tell him some interesting things about it, for instance, about the forests of California where there are great trees large enough in which to live.... Another time ask him to bring some coal, telling about the miners who go down into big holes in the ground and find all this black coal which was once wood.[26]

In this highly gendered approach, a boy's household chores could serve as a means of expanding his worldview, while those of his sister kept her focused on "domestic duties."

In short, in the 1920s, housework was firmly reinscribed as a woman's naturally ordained function in life. For her to disdain domestic labor was deemed by many to be both aberrant and un-American. To be sure, elite men and women (including newly rich industrialists raised in modest circumstances) continued to employ others to cook their meals, clean their houses, and launder their clothes. Nonetheless, they could not remain aloof from the politicized public debates that circulated around these and other forms of housework. In these same years, elite playhouses took on new forms at least in part to provide visible proof that those who commissioned them embraced the value system that placed domesticated women at the core of national identity.

CELEBRATING FEMINIZED HOUSEWORK AT THE FORD PLAYHOUSE

Throughout the 1920s, Henry and Clara Ford were deeply enmeshed in efforts to shore up the private home and the woman's place within it. Henry Ford, for instance, was the publisher of the *Dearborn Independent*, notorious as the platform for the automaker's virulent anti-Semitic views, as well as for his diatribes against "modern immigrants" who "pluck the country of its good things," bringing with them "destructive ideas" and "the danger of disease."[27] The War Department's spiderweb chart also appeared on the pages of the paper in 1924, as did slanderous articles claiming that women organizing to demand maternity benefits had direct links to the Bolsheviks. For her part, Clara Ford sat on the planning committee of the White House Conference on Home Building and Home Ownership.[28] Both Clara and Henry were also responsible for crafting model domestic environments that helped romanticize housework, albeit in very different settings.

Henry Ford's efforts have been widely recognized, as they were large scale and took place in highly visible venues that were open to the public, albeit privately controlled.

In these settings, he celebrated colonial kitchens, wrapping his reactionary views of housework in a nostalgic and distinctly nativist glow. In 1923, for instance, he purchased the Wayside Inn in Sudbury, Massachusetts, a site made famous by Henry Wadsworth Longfellow's *Tales of a Wayside Inn* (1863). After renovating the building to evoke his sense of the colonial past, Ford reopened the inn, providing guests with the opportunity to "consume a particularly engaging and participatory experience of history," according to cultural historian Abigail Carroll, an experience that included old-time dances and winter sleigh rides. The Old Kitchen was the centerpiece for these efforts and the setting for "Old Kitchen dinners" in which small groups of guests could enjoy a meal they had watched being prepared on the hearth by a costumed female cook. When used by Ford as a venue for his meetings with reporters, the Old Kitchen nodded to Ford's background as a farmer's son and evoked values the industrialist held dear: simple living, hard work, and patriotism.[29]

These values also informed Henry Ford's plans (announced in 1925) to build a museum housing early American artifacts near his home in Dearborn, Michigan. Although much of the Edison Institute (the formal name for the Henry Ford Museum and Greenfield Village) was dedicated to material celebrations of the ingenuity of American men (Ford's own as well as that of Thomas Alva Edison, in whose honor the institute was named), the automaker's larger goal was to "reproduce American life as lived" in the preindustrial age, which included women firmly ensconced in the domestic realm.[30] The eighteenth-century Secretary House served as a home economics laboratory for girls enrolled in the Edison Institute school, providing them with opportunities to practice "acting as hostesses, arranging meals, preparing them and caring for the rooms."[31] In this sense, Greenfield Village was a more far-reaching version of the Americanization programs sponsored by the Ford Motor Company.[32]

If Ford's motivation to establish Greenfield Village had a political component, his increasing devotion to the project also had corporate and personal elements. Indeed, Ford was unable to disentangle the two; from his perspective, he was the Ford Motor Company, even if his son, Edsel Ford, had assumed the president's title in 1919. In the mid-1920s, Henry Ford had become disenchanted with the direction in which consumer capitalism was moving. Particularly disturbing to him was the movement within his own company to participate in what design historian Penny Sparke has argued was "the feminization of . . . that most symbolically masculine of objects, the American automobile," that is, embracing beauty, comfort, and luxury in the form of streamlined design associated with Art Deco and the Moderne.[33] These qualities had had no place in the development of the Model T and remained anathema to Henry Ford.[34] In this sense, Greenfield Village was a means of recapturing a moment before things went awry. Yet, even Greenfield Village could not make up for the fact that Edsel supported the new, feminized approach to car design. If anything, by championing the development of the Model A, Edsel's actions only served to exacerbate Henry's concerns that his son was not man enough to succeed him. Intent on toughening up his son, Henry regularly used his authority at Ford Motor Company to humiliate the younger man in the workplace. At the same time, the elder Fords (for this included Clara Ford, who, like her husband, was raised on a farm) also looked askance at the life Edsel and Eleanor Ford led outside the office: their circle of wealthy friends in Grosse Pointe, an exclusive suburb on Detroit's east side; their interests in the arts and philanthropy; and their indulgence in speedboats and cocktail parties.[35] The very qualities that made Edsel gentlemanly and urbane in the eyes of his contemporaries rendered him weak, even effete, in the judgment of his parents.

In this context, Clara's decision in 1930 to give an imposing playhouse to her granddaughter, Josephine, on the girl's seventh birthday can be seen as a feminine parallel to her husband's efforts at Greenfield Village—feminine in that it was an ostensibly private and familial affair, yet like Greenfield Village in that it used a model domestic environment to address concerns in which the personal and the political were intertwined (Figure 5.10). Indeed, Clara had entered into the highly politicized debates on women and housework even before her work with the White House Conference on Home Building and Home Ownership: as she told the *Ladies' Home Journal* in 1923, "a woman puts her life into being a homemaker."[36] As the relationship

FIGURE 5.10. Exterior of playhouse at Gaukler Pointe, the estate of Edsel Ford and Eleanor Ford, in Grosse Pointe, Michigan. Robert O. Derrick, architect, 1930. Photograph by author.

between her husband and son deteriorated, she may well have wondered whether Edsel and Eleanor had drifted too far from the values she held dear and were either unwilling or unable to ensure that their only daughter was prepared to embrace what Clara Ford saw as her naturally ordained role in the domestic realm.

That Clara Ford sought to use the playhouse to exert influence over Edsel and his family is borne out by the fact that in order for Josephine to receive her grandmother's gift, the girl's parents had to agree to have the playhouse—designed by an architect not of their choosing—built on the grounds of their own estate, Gaukler Pointe, and accommodated in a naturalistic landscape plan recently completed to the designs of Jens Jensen.[37] In this sense, Josephine's playhouse was what cultural anthropologist Grant McCracken would characterize as a Trojan horse, a gift intended to manipulate the recipient (and, in this case, her parents) by carrying new meanings into their complement of material goods. Clara Ford may well have hoped that this gift would prompt Edsel and his family to seek cultural consistency by surrounding themselves with other material goods that would carry similar meanings and ultimately transform them.[38]

To be sure, the playhouse was not as intrusive as it might have been, as it was relegated to an area near the property line with other rectilinear features (including a playing field, a formal rose garden, and a tennis court), all of which were shielded from view from the main house by trees and other plantings. Jensen himself revisited the landscape design after the playhouse was completed, introducing a miniature kitchen garden and softening the sharp corners of the playground. Likewise, Robert O. Derrick, at this time the elder Fords' favorite architect, was sensitive to the existing ensemble of buildings. While he accommodated Henry and Clara's taste for the Colonial Revival at the Henry Ford Museum (the exterior of which evoked the forms of Independence Hall) and their new Greek Revival mansion at Richmond Hill, in Ways Station, Georgia, at Gaukler Pointe he used stucco and half-timbering to ensure the playhouse complemented the main house; both used Tudor Revival forms derived from British domestic architecture of the sixteenth and seventeenth centuries.[39] At the same time, his design evoked antiquated forms that seemed appropriate for children recapitulating the primitive phase of human evolution and that had by this time become redolent of childhood. This included the use of pargetting, an archaic plastering technique in which the modeling was done directly on the wall in the wet stucco.[40] In this case, the exterior ornamentation incorporated nursery rhyme motifs that also underlined the childlike quality of the playhouse. Mistress Mary Quite Contrary, Ride a Cock Horse to Banbury Cross, and Jack and the Beanstalk appeared in the gable above the bay window on the building's north side, while the Old Woman Who Lived in a Shoe, Humpty Dumpty, Baa, Baa, Black Sheep, and Little Miss Muffet graced the west façade (Figure 5.11).

FIGURE 5.11. Exterior detail of playhouse at Gaukler Pointe, the estate of Edsel Ford and Eleanor Ford, in Grosse Pointe, Michigan. Designed and executed by architectural sculptor Corrado Parducci, the bas-reliefs depict nursery rhymes: Mistress Mary Quite Contrary on the lower left; Ride a Cock Horse to Banbury Cross on the lower right; and Jack and the Beanstalk in the triangular gable above. Robert O. Derrick, architect, 1930. Photograph by author.

For all its formal consistency with the rest of the estate, the Ford playhouse represents a dramatic departure from elite playhouses built before 1920. For one thing, it was a complete house in the sense that it mimicked very closely the forms and arrangements of a middle-class, single-family dwelling (Figure 5.12). Sheltered by an entrance porch, the front door opened into a pine-paneled living room, which included a window seat—still an architectural signifier for childhood—as well as a formal fireplace flanked on one side by a long window and on the other by a French door that led out to a screened porch (Figure 5.13). The wall opposite the fireplace had two doorways, one leading to the kitchen, the other to the bedroom. The kitchen was supplied with the most up-to-date fixtures: a refrigerator, a (no longer extant) Hotpoint electric range, and a sink made of Monel metal, a nickel alloy that featured prominently in the ornamentation of Detroit's Art Deco skyscrapers. The bedroom was fitted out with a closet and two-fixture bath, the latter not part of the original plan but added early in the construction process.

The Ford playhouse also differed from early twentieth-century playhouses in that it was built on a consistently reduced scale. The doors, for instance, were 5 feet, 3 inches tall, requiring most adults to crouch in order to enter the building or to move between

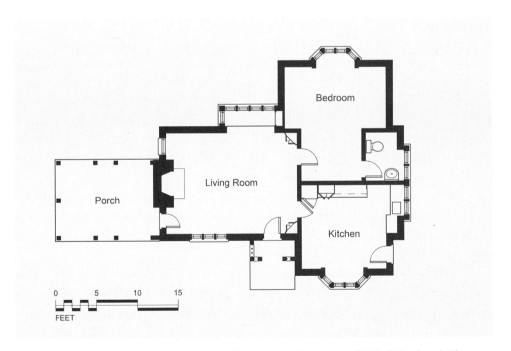

FIGURE 5.12. Plan of playhouse at Gaukler Pointe, the estate of Edsel Ford and Eleanor Ford, in Grosse Pointe, Michigan. Unlike children's cottages and playhouses built before 1920, this building contains the full range of room types found in middle-class houses, including a bedroom. Robert O. Derrick, architect, 1930. Drawing by Daniel De Sousa.

Figure 5.13. Living room of playhouse at Gaukler Pointe, the estate of Edsel Ford and Eleanor Ford, in Grosse Pointe, Michigan. In playhouses built after 1920, architecture and furnishings were built on a consistently reduced scale to support the fiction that the playhouse was the domicile of its young, and always female, owner. Robert O. Derrick, architect, 1930. Photograph by the author.

rooms. While her husband relied on nostalgia to romanticize women's domestic labor, Clara deployed what historian James E. Bryan calls the "peculiarly beguiling quality miniaturization can bestow" as a means to make "mundane tasks (what might even be classified as drudgery) interesting, appealing, and something to be looked forward to and embraced."[41] While Bryan was writing of nineteenth-century doll kitchens, his observations apply equally well to the Ford playhouse and others built in the 1920s and 1930s, structures that straddle the line between small houses and large dollhouses.

The effort and expense in carrying out this miniaturization were significant. Somewhat ironically, the architect had to provide many pages of full-size drawings of various details to help the carpenters maintain the building's small scale. The miniaturization was particularly challenging when it came to providing fully functional kitchen appliances and bathroom fixtures. The Hotpoint range was a standard model, albeit fitted out with legs reduced six inches in height.[42] At least in theory, reduced-scale toilets were more widely available, given the trend to provide child-sized bathroom facilities in public kindergartens and grade schools. By 1921, for instance, Crane was manufacturing five models of toilets that were available in a junior size, which varied between 13½ and 14 inches in height, as well as the "Baby" Vitroware siphon jet closet, which was just 10 inches tall. Securing such toilets was evidently not a simple matter. Initially, the architect made do with a toilet of the "approved type miniature fixture 13 inches high." Before the project was completed, that toilet was removed and replaced with an even smaller "miniature closet 10 inches high now in stock at Murray W. Sales Co."[43] Nor did such miniaturization come cheap. By the time Derrick issued his certificate authorizing the final payment to the contractor on 10 March 1931, a project originally budgeted at $12,000 ended up costing $14,772.41 (well over $286,000 in 2024 dollars).[44]

Unlike earlier playhouses, the Ford playhouse was an overtly feminized plaything, a birthday gift for a particular little girl, who was understood to be the mistress of the house.[45] Indeed, the architect participated in this fiction by listing seven-year-old Josephine Ford as the owner of the building on all the project bulletins (that is, documents used to record changes to the contract). Implicit in this ownership was the responsibility for upkeep, a message reinforced by the house itself, which provided a single script for Josephine's play, namely, to pretend that she inhabited the house. To be sure, Josephine could undertake a range of activities as part of that play script: bringing groceries in through the kitchen door, stocking the refrigerator, preparing simple meals, doing the dishes, greeting guests at the front door, giving them a tour of the house, inviting them to sit in the living room, keeping the entire place tidy, and ultimately retiring to bed at the end of the day. This is not to say Josephine actually followed that script closely; as an adult, for instance, she scoffed at the idea that she had ever slept in the playhouse, noting that "the bed was about half the size of the sofa." Instead, her memories were not too distant from those of May Field, as she and her governess "used to make tea and stuff there."[46] Nonetheless, the playhouse presented housework, and especially maintaining a single-family house, as the natural play activity for a young girl.

In an important sense, the playhouse, like the Wayside Inn and Greenfield Village, sought to celebrate and naturalize the distance between the domestic sphere where women nurtured their families and the corporate realm where men exercised executive authority. Yet the process of constructing the playhouse revealed the extent to which the corporate and the familial were intertwined. For one thing, the construction of Josephine's playhouse was overseen by officials at Ford Motor Company; early phases of the project came under the purview of B. R. Brown, the head of the company's Department of Power and Construction, the entity responsible for supervising the construction of factory buildings.[47] Even the nursery rhyme bas-reliefs had links to Ford's larger projects in that they were designed and executed by Corrado Parducci, a noted sculptor who had been deeply involved in the architectural ornamentation for a number of Art Deco skyscrapers in downtown Detroit. Chief among these was the Union Trust Building (now known as the Guardian Building), designed as the headquarters for a bank Henry Ford had helped organize in order to eliminate his dependence on Wall Street capital.[48]

It is worth noting that Edsel and Eleanor do not seem to have shared the highly gendered version of play materialized at the playhouse. When it was first completed, the main house included a range of play spaces in which any of the children, including Josephine, could choose the content of their play based on their age rather than their gender (Figures 5.14 and 5.15). On the third floor was a playroom for younger children still under the watchful eye of a nurse, who slept in the room next door. (This corridor also gave access to a kitchenette and an infirmary, where a sick child could be cared for in isolation from siblings.) On the first floor was a games room (now called the Modern Room), readily accessible from the children's entrance. At some point, a basement room was fitted out as a recreation room, presumably for older children who were encouraged to exert some independence from their elders.

FIGURE 5.14. Exterior of Gaukler Pointe, the estate of Edsel Ford and Eleanor Ford, in Grosse Pointe, Michigan. The children's entrance is the narrow door on the left, just below the double dormer window. Albert Kahn, architect, 1926–29. From the collections of Ford House (1986.2431.22).

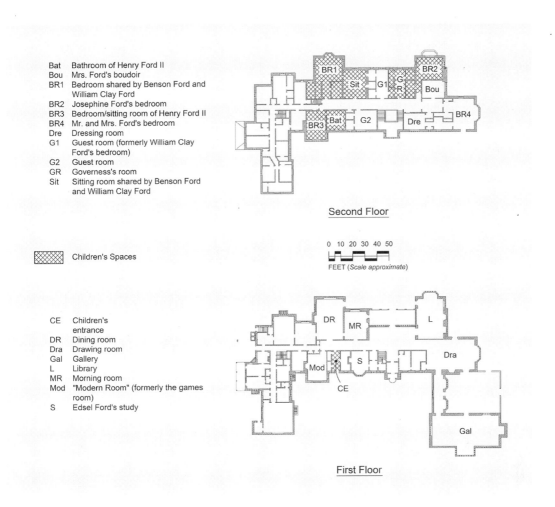

FIGURE 5.15. First- and second-floor plans of Gaukler Pointe, the estate of Edsel Ford and Eleanor Ford, in Grosse Pointe, Michigan. The room uses are those established in about 1934, in conjunction with design changes introduced by Walter Dorwin Teague. Albert Kahn, architect, 1926–29. Drawing courtesy of the Ford House with annotations by Daniel De Sousa.

In March 1932, almost exactly a year after the playhouse's completion, out-of-work Ford employees—an estimated 3,500 to 5,000 of them—marched from the Detroit city limits to the gates of the Ford plant at River Rouge to protest layoffs and call attention to working conditions. The Dearborn Police Department and Ford Motor Company security forces used tear gas and water cannons to suppress the demonstration and eventually opened fire on the marchers, resulting in five deaths.[49] Henry Ford was clearly in charge that day, but Edsel Ford, nominally president of the Ford Motor Company, was denounced in the Communist press for his failure to intervene.

Art historian Linda Downs has argued that he later sought to repair his reputation and that of the Ford name by enhancing his support of the Detroit Institute of Arts, notably by underwriting the plan to have noted Mexican artist Diego Rivera complete a monumental mural cycle celebrating the city's industrial prowess on the museum's walls.[50] In the short term, it is also possible to imagine him on the day of the Ford Massacre, retreating to Gaukler Pointe and seeking solace in its carefully designed grounds. Perhaps he found his way to Josephine's playhouse, where he could let himself become beguiled by its miniature forms and so distract himself, if only temporarily, from the hard truth of his life: that he had been party to a violent attack on workers whose labor had contributed so much to his wealth and that of his parents.

Or perhaps, just as events reminded Edsel Ford that his domineering father controlled his work life, the playhouse served to strengthen his resolve not to allow his mother to intervene—any more than she already had—in his home life as well. Certainly, within a few years, he had engaged industrial designer Walter Dorwin Teague to redesign all of his sons' bedrooms on the second floor, while Josephine's conventionally decorated bedroom remained untouched. A large guest room became a bedroom-cum-sitting-room for the eldest son and heir, Henry Ford II, who had been sharing a room across the hall with his next-younger brother, Benson Ford. William Clay Ford, the baby of the family, took Henry's place in that shared bedroom, which communicated with a sitting room also shared by the two younger brothers. With coved ceilings, indirect lighting, streamlined forms, and a calculated mix of wood and metal, the rooms were undoubtedly intended to familiarize the Ford sons with the Moderne aesthetics their father was helping to introduce into automobile design (Figure 5.16).

At the same time, the boys' rooms implicitly addressed the gender politics of industrial design, rejecting the association between the Moderne and the feminine and instead using streamlined forms to support a range of activities expected of sophisticated young men. Small desks built into windowed alcoves provided spaces for the Ford sons to complete their schoolwork, to carry out their correspondence, and to become acclimatized to the sedate character of executive action. Even more space was devoted to sitting areas supplied with built-in sofas and overstuffed chairs, where the Ford sons could read, play records, or listen to the radios built into low coffee tables. In short, these parents provided their sons with rooms that supported performances of the kind of relaxed urbane masculinity Edsel Ford enacted in other parts of the house, notably in the former games room Teague had redesigned, replete with a low cocktail table, a smoking stand, and a built-in cabinet, perhaps for cocktail fixings. Here one can imagine Edsel and Eleanor Ford modeling for their offspring the heterosocial conversational, sartorial, and libationary rituals of the

FIGURE 5.16. Bedroom/sitting room for Henry Ford II at Gaukler Pointe, the estate of Edsel Ford and Eleanor Ford, in Grosse Pointe, Michigan. With its coved ceiling, reliance on built-ins, and rounded corners and metal details, this room displays the Moderne aesthetics Edsel Ford was introducing into automotive design. Designed by Walter Dorwin Teague, circa 1934. Courtesy of Ford House.

cocktail hour—practices that were anathema to Edsel's parents but that were increasingly indispensable in elite social circles.[51]

Enmeshed in an intergenerational conflict that was both political and personal, the Ford playhouse was not just an expensive birthday gift from a fond grandmother. It was also certainly an attempt to use the charm of the miniature to make a certain mode of femininity—one firmly rooted in the domestic sphere—appealing. It may have also been intended to set off a chain reaction that would ripple out from the playhouse across the entire estate and, in the process, help transform Clara Ford's son and his family, aligning their values with those she and Henry held dear. If the Teague-designed rooms in the main house provide evidence that the playhouse failed to effect such a transformation, they also confirm the fact that newly rich Americans took seriously the role of the material world in helping their children navigate the changing nature of elite identity.

DESIGNING THE DODGE PLAYHOUSES

Some thirty miles from Gaukler Pointe stood another exquisitely miniature playhouse on the grounds of Meadow Brook Farm in Rochester, Michigan (see Figure 5.1). Although Knole Cottage was completed a few years earlier than the Ford playhouse, the two playhouses are comparable in multiple respects. Financed from the wealth of an auto baron and bestowed as a birthday gift upon a particular girl by a female relation, Knole Cottage was designed as a feminized site with a play script tightly focused on housework. At the same time, Knole Cottage engaged with contemporary concerns about women's roles in the domestic realm in complicated ways—both participating in the discourse that equated homemaking and normal womanhood, while at the same time allowing the woman who commissioned the playhouse to exert authority outside that domestic sphere.

The girl who received Knole Cottage as a birthday gift was Frances Dodge, the eldest of three children born to John Dodge, one of the cofounders of the Dodge Brothers Motor Car Company, and Matilda Rausch Dodge, the daughter of a saloonkeeper who had worked as the Dodges' secretary before marrying her widowed boss in 1907. By the time she turned twelve in 1926, Frances had lost her father and her uncle (both of whom died of influenza in 1920) and her little sister, Anna Margaret, who died in 1924 at the age of four from complications of measles. The following year, her mother had married lumber baron Alfred G. Wilson, soon after Matilda and her sister-in-law had sold Dodge Brothers for $146 million in cash (more than $2.6 billion in 2024 dollars). According to the New York Times, the payment was made via a check "said to be the largest ever drawn in a strictly cash industrial deal."[52]

Frances's playhouse stood on a property that John and Matilda Dodge had purchased in 1908 and where Matilda's parents, George and Margaret Rausch, oversaw the daily operations of the working farm.[53] In the years following John's death, Matilda increased her holdings to 1,400 acres, expanded the agricultural business, and began planning a grand house to be called Meadow Brook Hall. During a seven-week trip to Europe following their wedding, Matilda and Alfred Wilson devoted their days to visiting English manor houses looking for inspiration for their own Tudor Revival pile. Architect William Kapp, of the prominent Detroit architecture firm Smith, Hinchman & Grylls, began plans for the 110-room, 88,000-square-foot house in April 1926, and a formal groundbreaking took place on Matilda's forty-third birthday in October of that year. Construction began in earnest in December and lasted almost three years, during which time the family lived in the old farmhouse on the site (Figure 5.17).[54]

By the time construction began on the main house, two small outbuildings had been erected near the farmhouse. One was Knole Cottage, identified on the architects'

FIGURE 5.17. Exterior of Meadow Brook Hall, the estate of Alfred Wilson and Matilda Dodge Wilson, in Rochester, Michigan. Smith, Hinchman & Grylls, architects, 1926–29. Courtesy of Meadow Brook Hall Archives.

plan as a "playhouse for Miss Frances M. Dodge." The other was a "log cabin for Master Daniel Dodge" (Figure 5.18). Both were designed by Smith, Hinchman & Grylls, presumably by Kapp. Certainly, he was deeply involved in Frances's playhouse and may well have provided the initial design for Daniel's log cabin, given that early blueprints for both structures share the same date: 21 April 1926.[55] In essence, these buildings were pendant pieces, purposively different in character, their meanings sharpened when read in relationship to one another.

By the 1920s, log cabins had become increasingly associated with the performance of hardy masculinity, although that had not always been the case. As Alison Hoagland has argued, the log cabin carried multiple meanings in the nineteenth and early twentieth centuries, at times signifying abject poverty, at others evoking the political worthiness of a particular individual or suggesting the pioneer experience, which was understood to have had a broader impact, tempering effete Europeans into hardy Americans. Indeed, in the late nineteenth century, the form was often considered doubly worthy, intersecting as it did with both the Colonial Revival and its veneration of the past and also the Arts and Crafts movement and its celebration of handicraft.[56]

Elite parents selected the log cabin form for children's playhouses as early as 1882, when Joseph Sears and Helen Barry Sears had one such structure built on the

FIGURE 5.18. Exterior of Daniel Dodge's log cabin on the grounds of Meadow Brook Hall, the estate of Alfred Wilson and Matilda Dodge Wilson, in Rochester, Michigan. Smith, Hinchman & Grylls, architects, 1926. Courtesy of Meadow Brook Hall Archives.

grounds of their Prairie Avenue home on what was then Chicago's millionaire's row.[57] A small building with interior dimensions of just 11 by 12 feet, it nonetheless was fitted out with a covered porch along one long side, a split door, a fireplace, and glazed windows on two sides. A neighborhood playmate of young Philip Sears recalled that "we used to cook in it," suggesting that the structure functioned in much the same way as other Gilded Age children's cottages, providing a venue for boys as well as girls to prepare simple meals.[58]

In these same years, the Searses' neighbors, John J. Glessner and Frances Macbeth Glessner, had a similar log cabin playhouse built for their daughter, Fanny, on the grounds of the Rocks, their summer house in Bethlehem, New Hampshire (Figure 5.19).[59] Both the house and the playhouse were designed by Isaac Scott, a Chicago-based designer of art furniture who had become a family friend. The log cabin form was evidently understood as being appealingly antiquated; Mrs. Glessner recorded in her journal in September 1886 that she and her husband had bought "two old-fashioned door latches off of two old houses" in order to use them on the playhouse doors.[60] Far from being associated with rustic masculinity, the playhouse conveyed a level of gentility, especially inside, where the walls were lined with denim and where

FIGURE 5.19. Exterior of Fanny Glessner's house at The Rocks, the summer residence of John J. Glessner and Frances Macbeth Glessner, in Bethlehem, New Hampshire. Taken in about 1890, the photograph shows Fanny standing in the doorway with her dog, Hero, at her feet. Isaac Scott, architect, 1886. Courtesy of Glessner House, Chicago, Illinois.

Fanny had access to a child-sized chaise longue. Designed by Scott, it was upholstered in blue fabric (perhaps the same fabric that covered the walls), while its carved frame culminated in a stylized animal head (Figure 5.20). Scott also designed side chairs, two of which are preserved, along with the chaise, at the Glessner House in Chicago. Although small, the chairs are large enough to accommodate adults, suggesting that Fanny's playhouse was envisioned from the start as a site where the young girl could entertain her parents. Certainly, she tried her hand at cooking on the stove that had been purchased for the playhouse in New York. In August 1887, her mother recorded in her journal that her daughter and Miss Scharff (Fanny's paid companion) prepared peas, beans, chops, and coffee "at the little house."[61] The next month, Fanny and Miss Scharff "baked potatoes and made the coffee" for the family's dinner "in the little house," although Mrs. Glessner also reported that "the coffee was a failure on account of Fanny's being obstinate."[62]

By the early twentieth century, the symbolic meaning of the log cabin playhouse had started to shift, as is evident at Fort Ticonderoga, where in 1910 Stephen and Sarah Pell built a log playhouse for their young sons. Designed by Alfred Bossom in what he deemed, without evidence, to be "in the manner of the original homes of

FIGURE 5.20. Detail of chaise longue designed for Fanny's house at The Rocks, the summer residence of John J. Glessner and Frances Macbeth Glessner, in Bethlehem, New Hampshire. Designed to sit against a wall, the child-sized chaise was covered in blue upholstery, which may have matched the denim that lined the interior of the log structure. Isaac Scott, designer, circa 1886. Photograph by the author.

the settlers," the log cabin was dubbed the Y-D House—a site that said "Yes, do," to the Pells' young sons, who were so often told "No, don't" in the fort's historic Pavilion, a structure that had been renovated to serve as the family's summer residence.[63] Although the Y-D house included a kitchen for youthful cooking, it was also fitted out with rustic furniture and decorated with a print of a Native American man, a taxidermied ibex, and model sailboats—familiar tropes for hardy masculinity in the second half of the nineteenth century, when elite men had started socializing on all-male hunting expeditions (Figure 5.21).[64]

Daniel Dodge's log cabin was likewise a highly gendered setting, something made evident by a pencil drawing produced by Smith, Hinchman & Grylls early in the design process (Figure 5.22). In it, a man and boy stand at a little distance from the structure, which is shown set deep in the woods, the blue sky barely visible between closely set trees, its gabled façade adorned with a moose head over the door. In fact, the cabin was built on a treeless site near others of the farm's outbuildings, although

FIGURE 5.21. Interior of the Y-D (Yes, Do) House, on the grounds of the summer residence of Stephen H. P. Pell and Sarah Pell at Fort Ticonderoga, Ticonderoga, New York. Designed to allow the sons of the family free rein, this log cabin featured materials and decorative elements increasingly associated with hardy masculinity: exposed logs, inside and out; an enormous rustic fireplace; a taxidermied ibex; model sailboats; and a portrait of a Native American man. Alfred Bossom, architect, 1910. Fort Ticonderoga Museum Collection.

FIGURE 5.22. Preliminary design for the "Log Cabin for Master Daniel Dodge" for the grounds of Meadow Brook Hall, the estate of Alfred Wilson and Matilda Dodge Wilson, in Rochester, Michigan. Smith, Hinchman & Grylls, architects, 1926. Courtesy of Meadow Brook Hall Archives.

an early photograph shows the recently completed cabin surrounded by newly planted trees, suggesting an attempt to create something of the wooded feel of the pencil drawing. Given that moose had disappeared from Michigan's lower peninsula in the 1890s, the moose head is equally imaginative.[65] Particularly when juxtaposed with the pencil drawing of Frances's playhouse, the value of the sketch lay less in its ability to convey the reality of the cabin's setting or even its eventual form and more in its capacity to communicate the intention behind the cabin—to provide a setting for the performance of masculinity.

The rendering of Frances's playhouse is different in every respect (Figure 5.23). To be sure, the building itself contributes to the difference in tone. A T-shaped brick structure with half-timbering in one gable and diamond pane windows forming a bay at the reentrant angle, this is a Picturesque cottage—an idealized version of a rural peasant dwelling of the sort built in upper-middle-class American suburbs throughout the 1910s and 1920s. The building's charm is enhanced by its miniature scale, something easily gauged in reference to the human figures. At the same time, the

FIGURE 5.23. Preliminary design for the "Playhouse of Miss Frances M. Dodge" (later called Knole Cottage) for the grounds of Meadow Brook Hall, the estate of Alfred Wilson and Matilda Dodge Wilson, in Rochester, Michigan. Smith, Hinchman & Grylls, architects, 1926. Courtesy of Meadow Brook Hall Archives.

architect has chosen to present the building in a setting in which nature has been tamed. Flowers in boxes, shrubs and flowers at the cottage's foundation, a manicured lawn punctuated by flowering shrubs—all the plants have been placed by human hands, albeit to give the impression of natural informality. Even the two tall trees are part of the carefully arranged scene, echoing the location and height of the building's two chimneys. On one side of the house, there is a hint of a garden; on the other a glimpse of a striped awning, presumably for an outside area from which to enjoy a vista across a lake to a wooded area where trees obligingly grow to different heights in order to create an interesting backdrop. (Although there is no lake at Meadow Brook Hall today, early landscape plans did include such a feature. Thus, this drawing is less fanciful than it first appears.) The site is open to the sky where birds are in flight and where the sun shines down on a girl dressed in white, holding a doll, and a woman in a fashionable red dress and broad hat; both seem ready for a garden party. (In contrast, the man and boy in the drawing of the log cabin wear knickers and cloth caps appropriate for a hike.) In short, the drawing suggests that Frances's playhouse was designed for the leisured enjoyment of a cultured version of nature, a feminine pursuit that diverges sharply from rugged adventure promised by the depiction of Daniel's cabin.

Daniel's log cabin was larger than its nineteenth-century predecessors and included a vestibule at one end (flanked by a closet and a toilet) and a large stone fireplace at the other (see Figure 4.13). It was much simpler than Knole Cottage, both in terms of its form and in terms of the attention it required from the Wilsons and their design professionals.[66] Responsibility for translating the architect's drawings into reality fell to Leonard C. Vecelius, who maintained a log construction business in Hamburg, Michigan, some fifty miles west of Rochester. Costing $2,710 ($48,000 in 2024 dollars), the project was relatively inexpensive, at least in comparison to the sum of more than $21,000 (about $387,000 in 2024 dollars) spent on Frances's playhouse.[67] It was also executed quickly and without further input from the architect. Vecelius submitted his quote for the job on 4 August 1926, and by 29 September, the building was almost complete; the only items remaining were installing the light fixture, varnishing the floors, and making the windows operable.[68]

A photograph, taken at Christmas in about 1927, suggests Daniel Dodge used the cabin year-round, employing an electric heater and, at least on occasion, an open fire that left soot stains on the face of the stone fireplace (Figure 5.24). It is unlikely that Daniel attempted any cooking in this open hearth; a fireplace with a pot on a swinging arm was more evocative than useful, redolent of the campfire and masculine hardiness. Against this rustic backdrop, a modern drum set and freestanding Victrola strike a somewhat discordant note. Nonetheless, they point to the cabin's use as a place for Daniel to enjoy music—even forms of music that might disturb the rest of the family, if played in the farmhouse and eventually the Hall. The Christmas tree and a handful of toys and games (a toy car on the mantel, a toy truck under the tree, a toy cow riding backward on a toy goat on the floor near the fire, and a Poppin Ball board hanging on the wall) also suggest that the cabin served as a setting for a wide range of indoor activities. At the same time, the cabin's log walls and its decorative elements—notably the antlers displayed on the mantel and pennants from the resort towns of Harbor Springs and Mackinac Island—highlight Daniel's engagement in more active outdoor sports, something reinforced by the prominent display of snow skis and a fishing rod. A contemporary exterior photograph shows Daniel standing in the snow at the door of the cabin with his sled.

The cabin's later history confirms that Daniel did spend a great deal of time there and that his interests matched those suggested by the cabin. In 1937, when Daniel was nineteen, the log cabin received a large addition, allowing the Dodge heir to move from playing with toy trains to tinkering with full-scale vehicles. Despite the Depression, he had access to a 1937 custom Graham-Paige convertible coupe, a 1936 Indian motorcycle, a Lockheed Model 12A Electra Jr. plane, and a 1932 amphibian airplane.

Figure 5.24. Interior of Daniel Dodge's log cabin on the grounds of Meadow Brook Hall, the estate of Alfred Wilson and Matilda Dodge Wilson, in Rochester, Michigan. The photograph dates from about 1927. Smith, Hinchman & Grylls, architects, 1926. Courtesy of Meadow Brook Hall Archives.

Working away in this lab, located close to the estate's service buildings, Daniel grew up at ease with the men who worked for the family. Chief among them was Tom Compton, who had been hired by John Dodge in 1914 as the family's bodyguard and who became a boon companion to Daniel after his father's death. Tom taught Daniel to hunt, fish, and camp and accompanied him on trips into the great outdoors in the summers of 1929, 1930, and 1931.[69] In contrast, Frances preferred traveling to Europe with her mother and stepfather, even treating them to one such trip in 1934 to thank them for her lavish debutante ball, held on 27 December 1933; both the ball and the trip took place in the depths of the Depression.[70]

Far more extravagant than Daniel's cabin, Frances's playhouse was (like the Ford playhouse) essentially a miniature single-family house, built at approximately four-fifths the size of a full-sized dwelling (see Figure 5.1). Its interior doorways are 5 feet, 4 inches high, while in most rooms the ceilings are 6 feet, 3 inches high; the one exception is the living room, which is 7 feet, 3 inches high, purportedly to accommodate Alfred Wilson's tall frame. It was even constructed with smaller than normal bricks. Only some of the bathroom fixtures (notably, the toilet tank) were not quite to scale.

Matilda Dodge Wilson devoted substantial personal attention and financial resources to the playhouse, while also relying heavily on professional design expertise. In April 1926, Kapp developed at least two different plans, which differed only in the treatment of the entry sequence (Figure 5.25). Significantly, neither plan would have resulted in the elegantly simple massing of the cottage presented in Kapp's pencil sketch, suggesting that he had developed the sketch before discussing the details of the building's program with his client. Both plans make it clear that Matilda expected the playhouse to include all the room types found in a conventional single-family

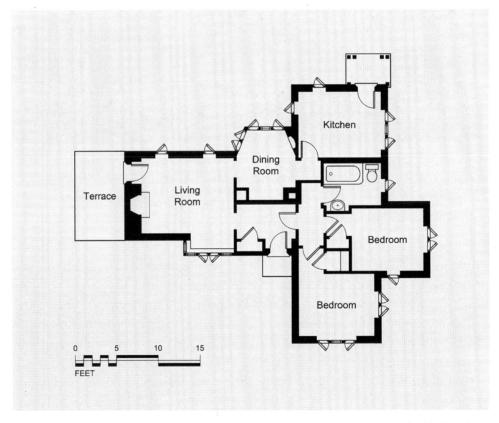

FIGURE 5.25. Plan of Knole Cottage at Meadow Brook Hall, the estate of Alfred Wilson and Matilda Dodge Wilson, in Rochester, Michigan. The plan shows the first iteration of the playhouse. After it was damaged during a move in 1928–29, changes were introduced, notably a half-timbered gable over the front door. Smith, Hinchman & Grylls, architects, 1926. Drawing by Daniel De Sousa.

house: entry hall (complete with a coat closet), living room, dining room, kitchen, two bedrooms, and a full bath. Once Matilda had selected the plan she preferred, Kapp developed detailed construction drawings that included designs for the interior and exterior doors in the hall, kitchen cabinetry details, and a finish schedule. No detail was too small for Kapp to discuss with his client; as the shell of the building was reaching completion in September 1926, he wrote to Matilda regarding the finishes on the playhouse switch plates.[71]

Matilda Dodge Wilson also worked closely with Arden Studios, professional interior decorators from New York City, who also provided design advice for Matilda's and Frances's bedrooms in the Hall proper.[72] The Arden Studios' involvement in the project was substantial, as they suggested, procured, and, in some instances, installed window treatments and wall coverings. They also provided custom-made bed linens and many of the playhouse furnishings, including the secretary, desk chair, upholstered

FIGURE 5.26. Living room of Knole Cottage, at Meadow Brook Hall, the estate of Alfred Wilson and Matilda Dodge Wilson, in Rochester, Michigan. Above the fireplace hangs a portrait of Matilda Dodge Wilson's youngest child, Anna Margaret Dodge, who had died in 1924 at age four. Smith, Hinchman & Grylls, architects, 1926. Courtesy of Meadow Brook Hall Archives.

wing chair, Italian side chair, and armchair for the living room (Figure 5.26). Throughout the process, Matilda always referred to the playhouse as Frances's and to the design decisions as hers, although she also weighed in at some length with her own views. Mother and daughter may well have made design decisions together, a process that would have helped guide Frances's taste and ensure that it was in line with her mother's.

Such personalized service was not inexpensive. In addition to the "curtain man," other Arden Studios employees also made the trek from New York to Rochester. Indeed, Matilda asked Arden Studios to send one of their "own men" to plaster and finish the walls in the entry hall and living room and to handle the silk material on the walls in the dining room.[73] Although Matilda curtailed costs somewhat by insisting that a local workman paint the woodwork and hang wallpaper in other rooms, she paid Arden Studios at least $2,000 (or more than $35,000 in 2024 dollars) for work on the playhouse.[74]

The results of these efforts were documented in a series of professional photographs that show what appears to be a comfortable, tasteful, servantless, middle-class house, perfect in all its details. A far cry from the lavishness of Meadow Brook Hall that was coming into being nearby, the playhouse was nonetheless meant to impress contemporary observers with its small size and its attention to detail. Given that the photographer was careful not to include any jarring full-scale elements, the images do not reveal the playhouse's reduced scale and can convey only part of the site's appeal. They excel at displaying the playhouse's range of domestic accouterments, whether the vase on the console table in the entrance hall, the desk set on the secretary in the living room, or the china and cookware in the fully stocked kitchen (Figure 5.27).

For the adults in Frances's life, such a splendid toy was not an extravagance but rather an investment in the girl's future. Matilda told newspaper reporters that she had built the playhouse "not only that Frances might have a place to play, but that she might learn from first-hand experience early in life the art of being a homekeeper."[75] Tellingly, on the day Frances took possession of the house, her stepgrandfather presented her with a poem he had composed in honor of the occasion. With one stanza for each year of her life, the twelve-stanza verse took as its theme the role of the playhouse in preparing the girl for the joyous embrace of housework in adulthood. The first four stanzas established Frances's happy present—her light tread, her merry laugh, her delight in time spent with her pony, her brother, and her playmates. The poem then turned to all she was doing to prepare for the next chapters of her life. After a single stanza celebrating the academic work that would lead her to college, the poem devoted five stanzas to housekeeping:

FIGURE 5.27. Front hall of Knole Cottage, at Meadow Brook Hall, the estate of Alfred Wilson and Matilda Dodge Wilson, in Rochester, Michigan. One of the building's two bedrooms is visible in the background. Smith, Hinchman & Grylls, architects, 1926. Courtesy of Meadow Brook Hall Archives.

And to further fit
For life's career
A housekeeper's task
She does not fear.

In a beautiful cottage
On the slope of a hill,
In miniature form
She works with a will.

Her curtains to hang,
Her rugs put in place,
And pictures on wall
And mantel to grace.

Her kitchen a wonder
With all things complete
Her marvels of cooking
To woo you to eat.

May this beautiful home,
A picture abide,
Of ease in the future
Where you will reside.

To ensure that Frances did not forget the purpose of the playhouse, a printed version of the poem was framed and given pride of place on the wall of the miniature living room.[76]

The narrative about the educational value of toys is one that parents had been telling themselves for at least a century. It helps explain the appeal of Nuremberg kitchens, the German doll kitchens mentioned in chapter 2. Often given as Christmas gifts, these well-appointed kitchens were in many families used only at Christmastime and were thus marked as special and carefully preserved. Passed from mother to daughter for generations, these highly gendered toys were understood to prepare girls for their future domestic roles. Neatly eliding housework and play, this narrative helped sustain the widely held expectation that women would gladly provide their families with a lifetime of domestic labor for free.

Toy historians have noted the flaws in interpreting Nuremberg kitchens as preparation for adult housework. Arranged for the convenience of play (rather than modeling the layout of real kitchens), these toy kitchens were provided with such abundance of cooking utensils that dishes, pots, and pans covered the floor space. Equally important, they allowed only for "cold cooking" (that is, mixing together foodstuffs that could be eaten cold). As Eva Stille points out, this process taught a girl "as little about cooking and keeping house as a boy learned about driving a car when he pushed a tinplate car through the room."[77] If such small-scale kitchens could not teach the practical aspects of domesticity, they nonetheless harnessed "the enchantment of the miniature" (to use another of James Bryan's apt phrases) in order to make housework seem appealing.[78] In this sense, they offered mothers a mechanism for responding to the pressure they undoubtedly felt "to encourage socially expected femininity in their daughters."[79]

Knole Cottage was, of course, different from a doll kitchen in many respects. With a working two-burner range in its small kitchen, it allowed for more than cold cooking. Indeed, as inhabitable space, it offered Frances a range of opportunities to practice household tasks with tools scaled to her small frame (Figure 5.28). She could wash dishes in the kitchen's working sink, sweep the floors with a small broom, or press tea towels on the flip-down ironing board in the kitchen. Knole Cottage (like the Ford playhouse) was akin to a Nuremberg kitchen in exploiting the appeal of miniaturization to make domestic femininity attractive. Like many such kitchens, it was also a gift from mother to daughter, offering material evidence of attentive and gender-appropriate parenting.

Matilda's commitment to using Knole Cottage to prepare her daughter for domestic responsibilities was such that she provided Frances with an account at a local bank and her own checkbook. Frances was responsible for ordering foodstuffs and supplies and paying for them herself. (This was a point of pride for Frances, who pointed out to reporters that her brother had a bank account, but no checkbook.)[80] Although the arrangement was unusual enough to merit comment in the newspaper, the checkbook can be seen as part of a longer practice of using material goods to train children to be responsible consumers. As early as the opening of the nineteenth century, authors such as Maria Edgeworth (writing in 1801) explicitly recommended that girls be supplied with pocket books to log their expenditures, although she made it clear that youngsters' pocket money was not to supply them with funds to buy "pretty, fashionable trifles."[81] Instead, the goal was to train children in restraint as they confronted the new world of consumerism. Frances's bank account and checkbook are presented in a similar vein, although their efficacy in teaching moderation may have been undermined by the context; her playhouse, after all, represents an extreme version of consumerism.

Knole Cottage was perhaps more important as a place for Frances to practice her skills as hostess. Although she received the almost completed playhouse as a gift on

Figure 5.28. Kitchen of Knole Cottage, at Meadow Brook Hall, the estate of Alfred Wilson and Matilda Dodge Wilson, in Rochester, Michigan. Fully functional plumbing fixtures were not always available at a reduced scale. In this case, the difference in scale between the small (but not miniature) sink and the miniature Hoosier cabinet just to its right is noticeable. Smith, Hinchman & Grylls, architects, 1926. Courtesy of Meadow Brook Hall Archives.

her twelfth birthday, the festivities on that day were not framed as a birthday party (at which Frances would have been the guest of honor) but as a housewarming. As Matilda's correspondence with Arden Studios confirms, mother and daughter imagined the affair as an event that Frances would host. The names recorded in the small, store-bought autograph book that served as the playhouse's guest book reveal that this was not a children's party for "twelve little girls" (as erroneously reported by the *Detroit News*). Rather, this was a multigenerational affair attended by Frances's maternal grandmother; her aunts Amelia and Mabel; and four other adult women, three of whom accompanied their own children to the party. The younger set included ten girls and four boys, ranging in age from six to eighteen.[82]

Given the difficulty of accommodating so many people in the playhouse's small living room, it is likely that Frances welcomed each guest at the door and invited them to tour the house on their own, perhaps even suggesting a route through the rooms that would minimize overcrowding. Alternatively, she may have guided small groups through the house in turn. Either way, Frances would have had the opportunity to greet each guest, to thank them for coming, and to say something that would facilitate their enjoyment of the house. The fact that her grandmother and aunts were the first names recorded suggests Frances was given the opportunity to practice her approach to these social tasks on family before engaging with friends. As Matilda did not sign the guest book, she may have served as Frances's cohostess, perhaps offering gentle guidance to her daughter as they received both male and female guests who varied significantly in age.

Seen from the perspective of the 1930s, Knole Cottage and Daniel Dodge's log cabin have a great deal in common. Both structures served to remove much of the children's play from the Hall. Both encouraged their respective proprietors to exercise a strong sense of ownership and control over the space. Both were designed to prepare their young owners for gender-specific future endeavors: the son for an active life of invention, adventure, and risk-taking, the daughter for a privileged version of domesticity in which entertaining would play a large role. Yet, it was not just the form of each structure that reinforced these gendered differences, but also the ways in which the child's autonomy was encouraged—or not. Not only was the log cabin designed to house a wide range of activities (playing with trains, tinkering with engines, listening to music, preparing for a day of sledding), but it also gave Daniel the latitude to choose what he would do at any given moment. Indeed, there was a loose fit between the cabin's large main room and its program, especially in comparison to Knole Cottage, where a series of small rooms were devoted to specific functions (see Figure 4.13). Daniel's cabin was also understood as a setting that would allow him to grow, something evident in his statement as a nine-year-old boy that he would use it "to smoke in" when he grew up. Indeed, many of the activities he pursued in the log cabin were not play at all, at least not in the sense of pretending to be something or someone he was not. Equally telling, the building was allowed to grow with him. The 1937 addition did not just provide him with more space; it also allowed him to tackle ever more ambitious mechanical projects. In that sense, Daniel's log cabin was not a toy but a tool he carried with him from boyhood to manhood.

In contrast, Knole Cottage offered Frances a more limited range of choices: the script in this setting was to play house. To be sure, she could have spent her time reading or listening to music, but the house's small scale was a constant reminder that this was home to her dolls and she their attentive mother. In that sense, she was always pretending (and thus always a child), even when the food she prepared was edible and the checks she wrote were honored by a real bank. The period photographs confirm this understanding of the playhouse: whereas Daniel's rustic cabin accommodated discordant elements (such as a modern Victrola), Frances's playhouse derived its appeal from the fact that nothing would disrupt her sense of this as a house and a home. While Daniel's cabin accommodated a certain level of messiness (note the toys on the floor in Figure 5.24), Frances's house, by its very nature, implored its young mistress to keep it tidy with every item of domestic utility and comfort in its designated place.

By virtue of its reduced scale, Knole Cottage was also a place Frances inevitably outgrew. When she returned later in life, she would have been confronted with the choice between two positions, two personas. She could remain an adult, peering in from the outside, looking in wonder at a miniature house and enthralled by its completeness. Or she could inhabit the space, but only by engaging in another form of play, pretending she was a child again. In that sense, it remained an exquisite, if complex, plaything—not a tool but a toy that could only serve to tether Frances to her youth.

Given that Frances would never be called on to sweep a floor or make a bed, it is impossible to take at face value her mother's assertions that she had built Knole Cottage to teach her daughter "the art of being a housekeeper." Instead, the playhouse is better understood as a visually arresting artifact that affirmed the daughter's attention to domestic matters and, notably, the mother's role in encouraging that attentiveness. Indeed, Matilda Dodge Wilson deployed the playhouse with great finesse in a carefully calculated campaign to get her own parenting skills into the public eye.

Matilda Dodge Wilson's most powerful tool in this publicity effort was the press. Initially, she used the society pages to amplify the visibility of social events focused on the playhouse. The *Detroit News*, for instance, covered the cottage's housewarming on Frances's twelfth birthday party, while the *Detroit Free Press* reported on the December 1926 meeting of the Historic Memorials Society in Detroit (an organization originally founded as the Mount Vernon Society of Detroit), held at Meadow Brook Farm.[83] According to the latter story, the business of the meeting was "dispatched quickly" so that the attendees could see "the interesting features of Mrs. Wilson's home, particularly the play house which is the delight of young Frances Dodge's heart." Although the paper mentioned that guests were impressed by the "huge fireplace and the balcony" in Daniel's log cabin, Frances's "miniature domicile" was described in much greater detail.[84] Equally telling, all 109 of those present signed the cottage's guest book, a process that undoubtedly took some time and encouraged a prolonged examination of the building's many details. For visitors, the act of registering their presence in one playhouse, but not the other, also helped ensure that Frances's cottage would resonate more profoundly in their memories of the day.

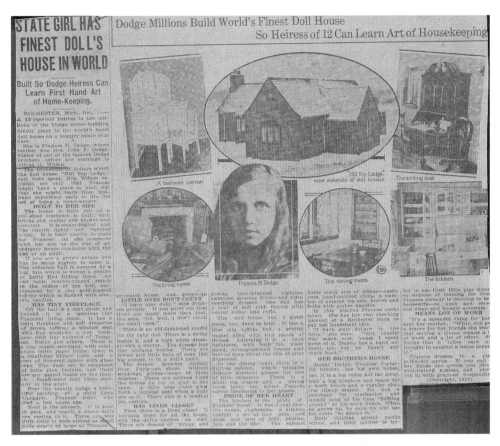

FIGURE 5.29. Feature story about Frances Dodge and her "Doll's House," syndicated by the Newspaper Enterprise Association. "State Girl Has Finest Doll's House in World," *Kalamazoo Gazette* (21 December 1926), 21. Courtesy of Meadow Brook Hall Archives.

Matilda Dodge also facilitated the publication of longer feature stories on Knole Cottage, giving reporters unusual access to her children and providing them with numerous professional photographs taken as soon as the playhouse was completed. One such story, illustrated with an exterior photograph, appeared in the *Detroit Free Press* on Christmas Day 1926, while a similar story was syndicated by the Newspaper Enterprise Association (NEA; Figure 5.29).[85] Replete with seven photographs (including five interiors and one of Frances), this story appeared in at least forty-two newspapers throughout North America between 20 December 1926 and 31 January 1927.

In addition to including Matilda's comments, the NEA story also quoted both Frances and Daniel, whose log cabin received just a brief mention and was not pictured. At moments, the piece presented Frances as a somewhat spoiled child whose material comfort had made her slightly out of touch with normal life. The story also commented approvingly on Matilda's parenting decisions, observing that "both children attend public school, and their mother is trying to use their little play houses as sources of training for them. Frances is already learning to be a housewife—to cook and sweep and clean and handle accounts."[86] In this sense, the playhouse served as material evidence of Matilda's dedication as a mother, someone who devoted time, attention, and substantial financial resources to ensure that her daughter was equipped with the domestic skills most women needed to have. Seen in this light, it was, perhaps, immaterial to Matilda and others whether Frances would use those skills or not.

An open question remains: if Matilda Dodge Wilson's publicity campaign was as deliberate as it appears to have been, why did she choose that precise moment to unleash it? Frances, after all, was twelve, and would soon outgrow the doll play that was scripted into the building. The fact that the *Kalamazoo Gazette* was the first Michigan newspaper to publish the NEA story suggests Matilda's actions may have had something to do with her stepson, John Duval Dodge, who had been briefly jailed in Kalamazoo before standing trial there in 1922 for reckless driving and violating prohibition laws. The charges stemmed from an incident in which the young man (already twenty-four years old and married) and a male friend offered three young women a lift home from a dance hall late one night. When Dodge instead drove out into the country to show how fast his car could go, one of the alarmed women leapt from the vehicle and was later found by another motorist, who took her to the hospital.[87] Although she recovered and Dodge was eventually acquitted on the reckless driving charge, the incident made sensational reading, especially when the young millionaire (as newspapers tended to identify him) was imprisoned the very next week in the Detroit House of Corrections on a separate speeding charge that had earned him a five-day sentence.[88] Michigan papers were almost gleeful in their descriptions of John Duval Dodge's fall from grace, as when the *St. Joseph Herald-Press* ran a front-page story with the headline "Millionaire Washes Dishes; John Duval Dodge Also Shoveling Coal at House of Correction."[89]

Immediately after his acquittal, John Duval Dodge made a public show of "turning over a new leaf," but also continued to make news as he pursued a larger share of the Dodge fortune.[90] Disowned by his disapproving father in 1917 when he had married at age nineteen, he challenged his father's will and in 1921 received a settlement of $1.6 million from the other heirs.[91] Far from satisfied, in April 1925, he attempted to claim part of the estate of Anna Margaret Dodge, Matilda's youngest child who had died a year earlier. Until that matter was settled, John Duval Dodge contended, his stepmother and aunt should not be allowed to sell the Dodge Brothers Motor Car Company, as the sale would impact Anna Margaret's estate.[92] Although the judge declined to issue a temporary injunction and the sale eventually went through as planned, the young man's legal action was front-page news across the country, thanks to another news syndicate, the Associated Press.[93] Only in January 1926 did newspapers report the court's finding that John Duval Dodge was not entitled to a share of Anna Margaret's estate.[94]

It is easy to imagine the displeasure Matilda Dodge Wilson felt in 1922 when her stepson brought the Dodge name into disrepute through his reckless behavior. By 1926, she may have also felt that news coverage of his legal actions called into question her fitness as a mother. Certainly, it called attention to the death of her young daughter. Would some readers think she might have prevented that tragedy? Seen in this context, it may be significant that a portrait of young Anna Margaret hangs over the fireplace in Knole Cottage (see Figure 5.26). Hard to ignore in this prominent location, the portrait was mentioned in the widely reprinted NEA story, helping to reassure readers that the dead child was cherished by her mother, who had also successfully instilled appropriately tender feelings in her surviving daughter.

Matilda Dodge Wilson might well have been concerned that news coverage of her 1925 legal battles with John Duval Dodge made her seem grasping and unfeminine in her efforts to retain control over the dead girl's estate. In fact, Matilda evinced no inclination to alter her own aspirations when it came to financial management. In 1928, the courts would, in fact, award the entirety of Anna Margaret's $7.5 million to her mother.[95] Three years later, the news media reported that Matilda had become "the first woman in America to be elected head of a major bank," further explaining that her experience directing the Dodge estate had "made her the best informed woman in high finance in the United States."[96]

In this sense, the publicity around Frances's playhouse takes on added significance. Through her careful campaign, Matilda presented herself as a mother committed to ensuring that her firstborn was prepared to assume a woman's proper place, even as she herself regularly stepped out of the domestic sphere. Thanks to her efforts at Knole Cottage, she all but invited the press to laud her daughter with the headline once used to shame her stepson: "Millionaire Washes Dishes."

THE CHANGING NATURE OF ELITE PLAY

The Ford and Dodge playhouses shed light on the dynastic ambitions of the adults involved—men and women who were enormously wealthy, but who had come also from modest backgrounds. Henry Ford certainly envisioned himself as the head of an industrial dynasty, one in which the leadership of the family business would pass from generation to generation through the male line. His doubts about Edsel's toughness notwithstanding, he appointed his son to the presidency of the Ford Motor Company while the young man was still in his twenties, and Edsel acquiesced to his father's vision. Not only did he persevere in the role despite his father's efforts to sabotage his effectiveness on the job, but he also prepared his own firstborn son to lead the company. Named for the paterfamilias, Henry Ford II assumed the company's presidency in 1945, well before his thirtieth birthday. Having sold her shares in the Dodge Brothers Motor Car Company, Matilda Dodge Wilson's dynastic ambitions were not directly tied to the company her husband had helped found. Nonetheless, she worked hard to ensure that her son (and not her stepson) was recognized as the rightful heir to the Dodge name and fortune. If young Daniel Dodge inherited his father's interest in machines, his mother nurtured his mechanical abilities by providing him with the space where he could explore the workings of increasingly complex engines. His early death at age twenty-one makes it impossible to know where that legacy might have led.[97]

In these families, daughters were less central to their parents' and grandparents' ambitions than they had been to Gilded Age social elites or their immediate descendants. To be sure, the girls were expected to function effectively in elite social circles. Among other things, this meant marrying men of a comparable social class and pursuing activities as adults that would confirm their wealth and social standing. As an adult, Josephine Ford focused on philanthropy, while Frances Dodge made a name for herself as a breeder of American Saddlebred horses. Yet, in important respects, the status and reputations of their families did not depend on their ability to land titled husbands.

In this context, elite playhouses continued to serve familiar functions, while also playing new roles. They remained an effective means for keeping children away from the adult activities that dominated the main house. They also continued to make visible parental acknowledgment of the importance of children's play, although that play took on a distinctly gendered quality that would have been unfamiliar to early twentieth-century elites. After all, the playhouses they had built offered their offspring—both boys and girls—the chance to try their hands at cooking, while also providing multipurpose rooms where the youngsters could read, play games, listen to music, or do nothing at all. In contrast, elite playhouses of the 1920s and 1930s responded to wider cultural trends by providing boys and girls with different types of play spaces. Boys could still choose from among any number of leisure activities (except cooking), while girls were provided with a complete, albeit small-scale, house that was theirs alone, but also theirs to maintain. In this way, the playhouses of the 1920s signaled a parental commitment to raising daughters who were not so far removed from their elders' modest beginnings that they had no interest in domestic matters.

Elite playhouses of the 1920s and 1930s also differed from their early twentieth-century predecessors in other ways. They no longer provided settings where girls in their teenage years could spend time before they came out in society. Indeed, the miniature scale of these playhouses ensured that their young owners would rapidly outgrow these extravagant birthday gifts. If anything, the exquisite miniaturization of these beguiling artifacts only amplified the extravagance involved in bringing them into being, another meaningful difference from the recent past. If the threat of financial reforms had informed the conspicuous simplicity of elite playhouses built in the early twentieth century by offering a tacit assertion that families with inherited wealth were modest in their desires, the 1920s and 1930s found families like the Fords and the Dodges in a very different frame of mind. Proud of their earned wealth and already confronting the reality of a federal income tax, they were happy to call attention to their fortunes. For them, miniature playhouses—fully plumbed and electrified—constituted a particularly conspicuous form of conspicuous consumption.

If Matilda Dodge Wilson was particularly adept at exploiting public interest in her daughter's charming playhouse for her own ends, she was not the first to do so. From the very beginning of the twentieth century, parents who could not claim a place among social elites began to build fairly extravagant playhouses for their children. Harboring very different ambitions for themselves and their children, they counted on these appealing buildings to attract public attention that would support their commercial endeavors in other realms. However unwittingly, they set into motion a process that transformed sumptuous playhouses into objects of desire for ordinary families and eventually undermined their value as tools of elite culture.

FIGURE 6.1. Patricia Ziegfeld's playhouse at Burkeley Crest, the suburban estate of Billie Burke and Florenz Ziegfeld in Hastings-on-Hudson, New York. The reduced-scale version of Mount Vernon was originally built as part of a movie set. Once moved to Burkeley Crest in about 1924, it became the frontispiece for a two-story structure, which is believed to have been fabricated by Bernie McDonald of the T. B. McDonald Construction Company. Courtesy of the Hastings Historical Society.

CHAPTER SIX

Objects of Middle-Class Desire

Playhouses in the Leisure Economy

I n 1924, the *Yonkers Statesman* declared that the finest playhouse in Westchester County, New York, was a reduced-scale replica of Mount Vernon with a forty-foot frontage (Figure 6.1). According to the news report, the front door of the playhouse was only 4 feet, 2 inches tall, but it led into a reception room with ten-foot-high ceilings, a working fireplace, and two staircases, each of which led to a second-story bedroom sitting above the main floor rooms that flanked the reception room; other sources identified these additional main-floor rooms as a library and a dining room. On both levels, the ceilings of these flanking rooms were reported to be about five feet high. Attached to the main house by a portico was an outbuilding that housed a kitchen fitted out with a red electric stove and a "full line of kitchen utensils."[1]

In many respects, this miniature Mount Vernon was akin to the playhouses built for the Dodge and Ford offspring: fully plumbed and electrified structures that mimicked full houses (complete with bedrooms) and each bestowed on a particular little girl. In this instance, the young owner was not the heiress to a vast fortune but seven-year-old Patricia Ziegfeld, the only child of actress Billie Burke and Broadway impresario Florenz Ziegfeld Jr. To be sure, Patricia's father spent lavishly, but he was also often broke. According to his friend comedian Eddie Cantor, "Zieggy had no notion of time, space, or money," to the extent that "sometimes there were as many process servers in front of the New Amsterdam Theatre as ticket-speculators."[2] He lost all of his money in the great stock market crash of 1929 and died just four years later deeply in debt, a situation that prompted the resourceful Burke to revive her movie career, memorably playing Glinda the Good Witch in *The Wizard of Oz* in 1939. In 1924, the couple were A-list celebrities in New York's theater world, their careers and their private lives providing fodder for feature articles in newspapers and magazines, including a number of heavily illustrated large-format theater journals that had sprung up in the early twentieth century.[3] Far from seeing this media attention as an intrusion into their privacy, Ziegfeld and Burke understood that the public consumption of their images was integral to maintaining their celebrity status, which could, in turn, be used to market an array of goods. Burke was featured in advertisements for cigarettes, silk, and beauty clay. While indulging in some of the luxuries enjoyed by the so-called idle rich, they were never isolated from the workings of the market. Even when at leisure, they were themselves marketable commodities.[4]

Burke and Ziegfeld were not alone in using their daughter's playhouses (there were two) to shape their public personas. Frank Lowden had done just that, deploying his daughters' playhouse as evidence that he valued conventional gender roles, a strategy Queen Victoria had a hand in crafting with the construction of the Swiss Cottage and that Matilda Dodge Wilson would subsequently pursue at Meadow Brook Hall. Yet it would be wrong to assume that Ziegfeld, Burke, and others who built extravagant playhouses in the early twentieth century were simply emulating elite practices or that they assigned identical meanings to their efforts. For one thing, playhouses built by social elites were long-term investments that were never intended to generate a financial return of any kind. Instead, they contributed to the complex process of transforming financial assets into symbolic capital—family prestige. In contrast, adults associated with the commodification of leisure deployed playhouses to very different ends. For these adults, costly playhouses were relatively short-term financial investments that would ultimately turn a profit, by encouraging punters to part with cash, whether backing a Broadway show, buying a movie ticket, or leasing a luxury house.

The emulation of elite practices was a more complex phenomenon. To be sure, some playhouses (such as the playhouse built by real estate developer Robert Burton) were attempts to secure entrée into elite social circles. For its part, the Ziegfeld playhouse seems to have played a dual role: speaking a language that was understood by the couple's well-to-do neighbors in Hastings-on-Hudson, New York, as well as dazzling theater colleagues with Ziegfeld's skill at producing lavish spectacles—the so-called Ziegfeld touch.[5] The relationship between expensive playhouses and elite culture was even more complicated in California, where movie stars were often characterized as Hollywood royalty. In important ways, the stars of stage and screen had supplanted social elites as trendsetters, initially in terms of fashion and eventually in terms of lifestyle choices as well.[6] Part of this had to do with the fact that film stars "diffused resentments formerly directed at the wealthy," in the words of cultural historian Lary May. "Universally loved because they were not socially powerful," film idols became "leisure experts" who helped demonstrate that luxury—far from undermining the work ethic—could fuel rising expectations among average consumers. In short, these "consumption idols" transformed "luxuries into necessities."[7] Especially when associated with Hollywood stars, extravagant playhouses became objects of desire, the stuff of daydreams for ordinary people.

THE PLAYHOUSE AND THE REAL ESTATE DEAL

Perhaps the earliest architect-designed playhouse to owe its existence to the profit motive was erected sometime before 1903 at Albro House, in Cedarhurst, New York, the Long Island estate of Robert L. Burton. A cotton manufacturer who turned his hand to real estate development, Burton was never a celebrity of any kind nor was he someone who sought to reach a mass market. Nonetheless, he recognized that leisure was emerging as a profitable commodity. In 1901, he had purchased 250 acres of land in the nearby town of Woodmere, intent on reinvigorating an area where, in the decades immediately following the Civil War, well-to-do New Yorkers had flocked to the then-gracious Woodsburgh Pavilion Hotel. (Other nineteenth-century resort hotels in nearby Lawrence Beach were called Osborne House and the Isle of Wight Hotel, names that confirm a fascination with Queen Victoria's maritime villa among American elites.) According to one contemporary chronicler, Burton's goal was to "emulate the style of Tuxedo Park [New York] and Lenox [Massachusetts], in making Woodmere the highest type of restricted suburban residential development."[8] In short, Burton's business plan was an ambitious one that relied for its success on racialized and religious social exclusivity.

Given that racial zoning was legal and regularly used to enforce residential segregation in the early twentieth century, it would have been a relatively simple matter to ensure that Woodmere remained an Anglo-Saxon preserve.[9] Burton does not seem to have used deed restrictions of the sort that became common in the 1920s, but he did retain ownership of the majority of the houses he built, renting them out on a seasonal basis.[10] Thus, he may well have used an informal screening process to carry out his stated goal: to prevent non-whites and Jews from summering in Woodmere.

The larger challenge for Burton was to attract Anglo-Saxon social elites whose race, class, and religion gave them almost unlimited choices of where to spend their summers. Providing the right kind of built environment was essential, and Burton reportedly spent more than a million dollars on improvements. In addition to laying out streets and installing gas, water, electricity, and telephone systems, he also began to assemble facilities that constituted the sine qua non of elite leisure: making plans for tennis courts, golf links, and a clubhouse, and dredging a deep-water channel to accommodate yachts. He also hired well-respected architects (Charles Barton Keen of Philadelphia, Ernest Flagg of New York, and Rossiter and Wright, also of New

York) to design gracious four- and five-bedroom houses with servants' quarters. Keen also designed Woodmere's elegant railroad station, its social pretensions made evident in the provision of a ladies' parlor and dressing room.[11]

Given this level of investment, the financial stakes were high, and Burton could not be certain that the quality of the development alone would garner Woodmere the kind of prestige required to make it a resounding commercial success. That depended, at least in part, on Burton's marketing himself as a man of taste and discernment—someone with whom wealthy social elites would be happy to associate. Thus, while the improvements at Woodmere were still on the drawing board, the developer used the architectural press to disseminate images and information about his own Cedarhust estate. Albro House was featured in a 1902 issue of the *Architects' and Builders' Magazine*, which devoted nine pages to the spacious Colonial Revival dwelling: two exterior images, six interiors, and ample descriptions of its furnishings and European art. Five years later, when several Woodmere houses were reaching completion, Albro House was again showcased in the architectural press, this time landing the inside cover of *American Homes and Gardens* and securing a lengthy and glowing analysis in the magazine's regular series Notable American Homes, written by Barr Ferree, one of the period's foremost authorities on country house design.[12]

In this context, the decision to commission Keen to design a playhouse for the grounds of Albro House can be seen as a strategic move on Burton's part, one aimed at signaling to New York's social elites that he and the architect most closely associated with Woodmere were both familiar with the full range of children's spaces that graced country estates, despite the fact that the material reality of such playhouses was not well known. The Dows playhouse, for instance, was not published until 1912, and then only in a single exterior image comparable to others used to call attention to the estate's many outbuildings. The Lowden playhouse was the topic of a freestanding article in the *Western Architect*, complete with both interior and exterior images, but not until 1918.[13] In contrast, detailed coverage of the Burton playhouse appeared as early as 1903, when *Scientific American Building Monthly* published not just an exterior image but also a plan and two interior photographs (Figure 6.2). The timing is significant, coinciding as it did with Burton's work on infrastructure improvements at Woodmere.[14]

The images published in *Scientific American Building Monthly* provide a remarkably clear picture of the playhouse, which was organized around a central chimney stack that serviced both a living room and a fully plumbed kitchen equipped with a working range. On the exterior, the building was a simple stucco box capped with a relatively steep, and therefore, eye-catching thatched roof. Interior photographs, especially those of the living room, reveal the impact of the Colonial Revival as it intersected with the Arts and Crafts movement: window and door trim painted white, wrought

FIGURE 6.2. Exterior, interiors, and plan of the playhouse at Albro House, the Robert L. Burton estate, in Cedarhurst, New York. Charles Barton Keen, architect, circa 1902. "A Child's Playhouse at Cedarhurst, N.Y.," *Scientific American Building Monthly* 36, no. 6 (December 1903), 117.

iron strap hinges on the doors and overmantel cabinet, wallpaper with a small repetitive pattern, sheer white curtains in the windows, and what may be a hooked rug on the wooden floor. In the center of the room was what the accompanying text characterized as "old-fashioned mahogany furniture"; a round tea table with scalloped edges was surrounded by four slat-back chairs with cane seats, while two chairs with arms flanked the fireplace. As was true of many elite playhouses erected around the turn of the century, the architectural expression of the Burton playhouse was conspicuous in its simplicity.

At the same time, other aspects of the Burton playhouse, especially its miniature scale, were all but unknown among elite playhouses built in the United States before 1920. If anything, Keen's design seems to be modeled quite directly on the more modest playhouse Gertrude Jekyll had published in *Country Life* in 1901 (see Figure 5.2). Both buildings sported thatched roofs (still a familiar sight in parts of the British countryside, but an exotic feature in the American context), entry porches that were at least partly integrated into the body of the house, and pantries tucked away on the far side of their chimney stacks. To be sure, Keen introduced a high degree of elaboration into his design, including establishing a hierarchy of finishes to distinguish the formal living room (with its plastered ceiling, papered walls, and painted woodwork) from the work-a-day kitchen (where the structural members of the walls and ceilings remained visible and the woodwork was stained, rather than painted). The Burton playhouse was also fully plumbed with hot and cold water, whereas Jekyll's design called for a wooden barrel to be positioned at the eave line to catch rainwater. For all these differences, Keen seems to have followed Jekyll's lead closely, suggesting that he may have had limited, if any, firsthand experience with elite playhouses. Likewise, Burton seems to have failed to grasp the fact that American elites embraced conspicuous simplicity in order to disguise the fact that their children's playhouses were, in fact, luxury goods. The text that accompanied the images (undoubtedly written with Burton's guidance, if not actually by his hand) repeatedly called attention to the luxurious character of the playhouse, referring to it as "the most luxurious of gifts" and noting that "the luxuries provided for the amusement of modern childhood are so rich and varied, and have, for so many years, exhibited a constant tendency toward luxury, that a playhouse built expressly for children . . . could not be long in the coming."[15] Interestingly, the text makes no effort to highlight Burton's efforts as a father and omits any mention of his children, who ranged in age from about twelve to nineteen in 1903. Instead, the playhouse is offered as evidence of a more general trend.

These missteps notwithstanding, Burton evidently remained confident in the public relations value of his playhouse, although the particulars of his strategy changed as his efforts at Woodmere became visible. In 1905, for instance, images of two buildings at

Woodmere—the railway station and a single-family house, both designed by Keen—were published in *Western Architect*, along with an interior and an exterior of the playhouse. Significantly, the text did not mention Burton as the owner of the playhouse, as he was no longer the primary entity being marketed. Instead, captions identified—or rather, misidentified—the location of the playhouse as Woodmere, a "mistake" that may have been calculated to enhance the social cachet of Burton's new development.[16]

Did Burton's strategy work? Yes and no. By 1907, the summer issue of the *Social Register* listed twenty-one prominent families that had opted to summer in Woodmere, among them bank presidents, heads of insurance and manufacturing firms, and several members of the New York Stock Exchange.[17] In these same years, the electrification of the Rockaway Beach branch of the Long Island Rail Road meant that Woodmere could appeal to year-round residents who needed to commute into Manhattan on a daily basis. While this change may have enhanced the value of Burton's investment, it may have also detracted from his dream of presiding over a development that would rival Tuxedo Park or Lenox in terms of social exclusivity.[18] In November 1909, Burton sold his interests in Woodmere to a consortium headed by real estate mogul Maximilian Morgenthau. According to the *New York Times*, the price was "said to be in the neighborhood of $3,000,000," making it "probably the largest real estate deal in the history of the New York suburban district."[19] In that sense, at least, investing in an architect-designed playhouse was sound business.

THE IMPRESARIO'S PLAYHOUSE

On the surface, Billie Burke and Florenz Ziegfeld had little in common with Robert Burton. They were, after all, celebrities whose association with the Broadway theater meant that they seemed to attract attention without trying. Their movements were reported in magazines and newspapers. Their faces were known. Yet, like Burton, they came to understand that their country house could serve as a powerful tool for transforming their private lives into public images that could enhance their professional endeavors. This was particularly so for Ziegfeld, whose goal, in Cantor's words, was to raise the theatrical revue "from a cheap vaudeville business to an affluent art."[20] At the same time, Burke and Ziegfeld deployed the very same estate in quite different ways, differences that speak to their discrete roles in their industry, as well as to gendered expectations they often challenged in surprising and effective ways. The playhouse built for their daughter, Patricia, is a case in point.

One way in which their family life ran counter to expectations was that Burke—and not her husband—provided the family home, having purchased the twenty-two-room house on fourteen acres of land not far from the center of Hastings-on-Hudson,

New York, in 1911, three years before the start of the couple's whirlwind courtship. Acquired at a cost of $60,000 (more than $1.9 million in 2024 dollars), the house was a clear sign of Burke's professional success.[21] In order to underscore her ownership, she dubbed the estate Burkeley Crest and had the name emblazoned in bronze on the stone pillars that stood at the head of the entrance drive. Often featured in magazine stories, the estate was typically offered as proof that the actress was just like the characters she played, described by an editor at *Harper's Bazaar* as "the sweet domestic type."[22] Despite the size of the house, the media highlighted its unpretentious quality. With its "light colors and joyous tones," it was presented as a setting where Burke, "an informal hostess," could indulge her love of "wide spaces and wood scents, the heart of quiet, and the companionship of the real in people and things."[23] In short, the house was a material expression of the supposed correlation between the actress's stage persona and her everyday self, giving Burke an authenticity and accessibility that resonated with her many fans.[24]

After her daughter's birth in 1916, Burke used Burkeley Crest to support her contention that acting and motherhood were complementary endeavors, despite having told a journalist in 1908 that she would give up the theater once she married.[25] Before Patricia's first birthday, a profile in *Good Health* presented Burke as a thoroughly "scientific" mother, who embraced the regularity and routine advocated by child-rearing experts of the behaviorist school.[26] According to *Good Health*, she never tickled or rocked the infant and refused to pick up the baby when she cried in a fit of temper. "This is the hardest thing to do," Burke told the interviewer, "but it must be done." The house was key to this rational approach to mothering, providing "quiet and peaceful" surroundings and supplying a nursery with "a sort of outdoor arrangement at one end where [the baby] can sleep in the freshest of this high Hudson air."[27] A few years later, *Theater Magazine* ran a series of photos of Burkeley Crest that included an interior view of the "charming little playroom of Billie Burke's small daughter" and an exterior glimpse of "the tree sheltered play house of baby Florenz Patricia Ziegfeld."[28] Although this playhouse is somewhat difficult to discern in the published image, other family photographs reveal that it was a one-room structure with a porch, akin to those play sheds manufactured by companies such as E. F. Hodgson or Mershon & Morley (Figure 6.3; see Figure 4.2). According to Burke's memoirs and those of her daughter, this play shed was on the grounds when the actress purchased the house in 1911, an assertion that is difficult to confirm. However it came to Burkeley Crest, this relatively modest play shed helped Burke maintain her public persona as sweet, domestic, unpretentious, and, perhaps above all, accessible.

For Ziegfeld, Burkeley Crest played a somewhat different role, highlighting his reputation as a visionary behind extravagant Broadway productions, while simultaneously presenting himself as a doting father. Indeed, this aspect of his public presentation

FIGURE 6.3. Billie Burke and Patricia Ziegfeld at the play shed at Burkeley Crest, the suburban estate of Burke and Florenz Ziegfeld in Hastings-on-Hudson, New York. This appears to be a mass-produced play shed similar to those manufactured by the Mershon & Morley Company (see Figure 4.2). The photograph dates from about 1922. Courtesy of the Hastings Historical Society.

of self became increasingly popular among male celebrities, especially, perhaps, for those, such as Ziegfeld, who were regularly unfaithful to their wives.[29] (Another example of this phenomenon is Harold Lloyd.)[30] One way Ziegfeld signaled his dedication to fatherhood was by agreeing to live full-time at Burkeley Crest. Before Patricia's birth, Ziegfeld had installed his bride in his Manhattan lodgings, an apartment in the elegant Ansonia Hotel. After their daughter was born, the family moved to Burke's estate, which provided the sunshine, fresh air, and closeness to the natural world that were understood to be the best setting for child-rearing.

Once ensconced in Hastings-on-Hudson, Ziegfeld set about to make his own, indelible, mark on his wife's "unpretentious" estate, which he eventually increased in size by purchasing additional acreage from a neighbor.[31] Some changes, such as the installation of three phones in his bedroom (including one that was a direct line to the theater) had little to do with his daughter. Many others, however, can be seen as part of Ziegfeld's campaign to transform Burkeley Crest into a Broadway producer's version of a child's paradise. There was a swimming pool (admittedly for the use of adults as well); a vast menagerie that included buffaloes, a baby elephant, lion cubs, a chimpanzee, ponies, a pair of Egyptian asses, ducks, pheasants, quail, pigeons, parrots, and many, many dogs; and a new playhouse.[32] According to Patricia, the modest play shed that had appeared in *Theater Magazine* "offended his sensibilities," as it was "small, cramped, and dingy, and Daddy liked things to be large, spacious, and beautiful."[33] In due course, it was swept away and replaced with a replica of Mount Vernon (see Figure 6.1).

In all these endeavors, the line between Ziegfeld's activities as a producer and his actions as a father was blurred. Many of the animals, for instance, had once been on stage; the buffaloes had been "fired" from a production of a play by J. P. McEvoy, a writer who contributed to the Ziegfeld Follies, while the elephant had worked for Ringling Bros. Ziegfeld also recruited Joseph Urban, the Austrian artist who designed many of the Follies sets, to design the swimming pool, as well as a glass-jeweled howdah for the elephant's back.[34] The playhouse had started life as a backdrop for the last scene of *Janice Meredith*, a 1924 silent film in which the titular heroine, played by Marion Davies (a former "Ziegfeld girl"), married her beloved at the home of General Washington. According to Patricia's memoirs, the set was trucked to Hastings-on-Hudson, where Bernie McDonald, "the T. B. McDonald Construction man who built most of Daddy's sets," fabricated the two-story structure that was attached to the Mount Vernon façade.[35]

Reports differ as to how Ziegfeld came to settle on Mount Vernon as the model for Patricia's playhouse. One thirdhand account suggests that it was a bit of serendipity: having gone to see Davies at work, he inquired about the set, learned that it would be scrapped once the film wrapped, and arranged to have it sent to Burkeley Crest.[36] In contrast, Patricia's 1964 memoir (which may or may not be accurate) gives her father full credit for the idea. According to this version of the story, when her mother asked her father what sort of playhouse he had in mind, his initial response was "Sunlight." Thinking aloud, he continued:

> "Big windows. Flowers blooming. I see white columns—a porch—" His voice trailed away. Suddenly he snapped his fingers in inspiration. "That's it! Why didn't I think of it before? . . . Mount Vernon."[37]

In Patricia's retelling, Ziegfeld's fatherly first instinct—to provide his offspring with healthy sunshine and fresh air—blossomed within seconds into the sort of full-blown theatrical production associated with the Ziegfeld name.

As unlikely as the choice may seem from a contemporary perspective, Mount Vernon was enjoying substantial public attention in the 1920s. To be sure, the campaign to protect the site had started much earlier and is often cited as the first nationwide effort at historic preservation.[38] By the 1920s, the historic preservation movement was coming into its own, thanks in part to the fact that historic sites became favorite destinations for Americans exploring the countryside in private automobiles. Almost 366,000 sightseers made the trek to Mount Vernon in 1924, the year *Janice Meredith* was released and part of its set presumably found its way to Hastings-on-Hudson.[39] For some visitors to Washington's home, the draw may well have been the one that had initially motivated the Mount Vernon Ladies' Association (MVLA) to purchase the site in 1859: the chance to venerate a national hero. Others may have been attracted by the opportunity to see for themselves the building that had inspired a number of replicas, notably the Virginia buildings at the 1893 World's Columbian Exposition in Chicago and the 1915 Panama–Pacific International Exposition in San Francisco. Indeed, by the second decade of the twentieth century, the building, characterized by one expert as "the finest example of Colonial architecture in the country," was at least as important as the man and became the most often copied historic building in the United States.[40] The MVLA concurred, moving its large collection of Washingtonia to a "relic house" in order to allow visitors to experience more fully the architecture and furnishings of the mansion house.[41] Lauded by another expert as "simple without severity and elegant without ostentation," the mansion also gained a reputation as an exemplary Southern plantation, where (according to the myth of the Old South, then in ascendance) supposedly contented slaves (to use the parlance of the time) supported their kind mistress in creating a "scene of an easy, graceful social life, based on opulent hospitality."[42] Given this set of associations, Mount Vernon was increasingly quoted in the design of elite houses in both North and South, among them Foxhollow Farm, the Dows house in Rhinebeck, New York. Little wonder, then, that it was chosen as the backdrop for the happy ending of *Janice Meredith*, where its instantly recognizable porticoed east façade could trigger a range of connotations that spoke to the patriotism, elegance, and grace of the film's elite white protagonists—all without recourse to the medium's intrusive and necessarily cryptic title cards.

In choosing Mount Vernon as the model for Patricia's playhouse, then, Ziegfeld was participating in multiple widespread cultural phenomena, especially the fad for building Mount Vernon replicas and the tendency to reference Washington's elegantly simple and hospitable house on the grounds of country estates. The site's patriotic associations may also have appealed to the son of a German immigrant given the intensity of anti-German sentiment following World War I.[43] Perhaps it had special resonance for Ziegfeld, who was often assumed to be Jewish and who may have embraced the symbolic associations of the site to claim an Anglo-Saxon racial identity in the face of widespread anti-Semitism.[44]

Ziegfeld's particular approach to his Mount Vernon replica is also consistent with his portrayal in the memoirs of friends and family: a visionary whose passion for lavish productions was innate, inexorable, and therefore on full display in every aspect of his existence. In Cantor's words, Ziegfeld "never splurged for effect—it was inherent with him."[45] In this understanding of Ziegfeld's life, Patricia's playhouse was simply another demonstration of these inborn talents and a further opportunity to inspire awe in the audience. Indeed, Patricia's "toy" was the first reduced-scale playhouse to mimic a conventional house, complete with bedrooms, having been built two years before the Dodge playhouse at Meadow Brook Hall. It also appears to have been the first reduced-scale playhouse to include a second floor. Ziegfeld's interest in impressing viewers was such that it outweighed his concern for historical accuracy. Rather than reproducing Mount Vernon's interior arrangements with a single-height central passage and double-pile plan, Ziegfeld provided Patricia's playhouse with a double-height reception room (which at this reduced scale created a space ten feet tall), ensuring that curious adults could step inside to marvel at the building's interior details.

Who would have had the opportunity to stare in awe at this one-of-a-kind playhouse? The local newspaper reveals that Burkeley Crest was often on view during Garden Days organized to raise funds for philanthropic endeavors, chiefly the Westchester County Children's Association, suggesting that Ziegfeld and Burke were happy to have their property showcased along with the estates of their well-to-do neighbors.[46] Ziegfeld's overarching goal at Burkeley Crest, and particularly in building Patricia's playhouse, had never been to secure a place among these social elites, as Robert L. Burton had hoped to do more than twenty years earlier on Long Island. Unlike Burton, Ziegfeld strove to present himself as sui generis, the undisputed master of his creative field—an endeavor that ultimately set him apart from the social elites who frequented his revues. Rather than behaving exactly like their neighbors, Ziegfeld and Burke called attention to their celebrity status, leveraging Burke's star appeal to boost attendance figures and enhance the success of fundraising efforts. In outlining the details for an upcoming event, for instance, one news story reminded readers that Mrs. Ziegfeld was "better known as Billie Burke" and held out the tantalizing possibility of meeting the famous actress: "it is hoped," although not guaranteed, "that Mrs. Ziegfeld will be at home, too."[47]

Patricia's striking playhouse would have been in evidence during these garden tours, but it and other changes Ziegfeld brought about at Burkeley Crest were not widely reported in the press. If they had been, they would have conflicted with the homely image of the estate described in Burke's publicity pieces, which were carefully crafted to help the actress cultivate an ever-growing fan base among people she would never meet in person. In contrast, Ziegfeld needed to reach a different audience, as the producer's livelihood depended on his ability to enhance his stature within his professional circles: especially his financial backers, but also the writers, composers, and designers on whom he depended to bring his vision to the stage, and, to a lesser extent, the performers he employed (and whom he was often accused of having "stolen" from his competitors). The couple ensured that these people had firsthand experience of Ziegfeld's efforts in Hastings-on-Hudson by making it a regular practice to host large gatherings on Sunday afternoons. During these events, their guests (friends, neighbors, a scattering of family, but "mostly professional theater people," according to Patricia) were free to do as they liked. They could pitch horseshoes, play croquet or tennis, or wander around the gardens and lawns, presumably taking in all the sights on offer, including the playhouse. At dinnertime, the assembly gathered in the dining room, where Ziegfeld made a show of carving the roast in a setting orchestrated to appeal to all the senses: "the table covered with fine china and silver, the shaded candles glowing, fresh flowers all about, wine in the crystal glasses, and the aroma of rich food in the air." As Patricia later remembered, her father "produced those Sunday dinners the way he produced his *Follies*."[48] The same might be said for the entire estate, the real star of those Sunday afternoon gatherings.

PLAYHOUSES IN HOLLYWOOD

The nascent film industry learned a great deal from Broadway—about the effectiveness of highlighting featured actors and actresses to attract audiences; about the importance of using large-format, highly illustrated magazines to give fans an inside look at the private lives of their favorite players; and about the necessity of making stars seem simultaneously glamorous and accessible. By the 1920s, Hollywood had transformed these patterns into something new, thanks in part to studio control over the production, distribution, and exhibition of films. Performers became, in the words of sociologist Joshua Gamson, "studio-owned-and-operated commodities," their public personas carefully crafted and tightly monitored by studio press agents.[49] At the same time, stars received enormous salaries, which most of them used to finance the construction of extensive estates, complete with opulent houses (often fitted out with home movie theaters) and some combination of facilities devoted to leisure: swimming pools, tennis courts, golf courses, areas for outdoor cooking, and, sometimes, children's playhouses. For all this attention to leisure-time activities, however, these estates were integral to the stars' working lives. Part of the apparatus that sustained the performers' celebrity status, they provided ample fodder for the endless stream of illustrated feature stories in newspapers and magazines that gave readers access—albeit vicariously—to the luxuries enjoyed by their film heroes. When fan magazines published maps that encouraged readers to "find the home of your favorite film star," they positioned these estates as something akin to sacred sites and fans as religious pilgrims of sorts, benefiting from physical proximity to their idols, even if long entrance drives ensured that there was little to see from the public road.[50]

In this context, Hollywood stars often found that their children could play an important role in enhancing their accessibility, offering living proof that they themselves took their parental responsibilities as seriously as did their middle-class fans. Arguably, this was easier for men than women, as studios frowned on pregnant female stars, especially those whose reputations hinged on sex appeal. Even the plucky but pure Mary Pickford, who controlled her own career as a founding member of United Artists, did not become a mother until she was almost forty, when she adopted children with her third husband.[51] Nonetheless, parenthood made good press. By surrounding their offspring with lavish versions of the material objects that were understood to underpin a "good childhood," Hollywood idols managed to give their lavish spending a sheen of wholesomeness. Luxuries deployed in the service of a happy childhood were easily construed as necessities.

One of the most opulent of these Beverly Hills estates was built by Harold Lloyd, the bespectacled comedian perhaps best remembered for hanging from a clockface several stories above street level in the 1923 film *Safety Last!* In the 1920s, he was the highest-paid movie star in Hollywood, outearning his friends Pickford and Charlie Chaplin, another founding member of United Artists. In 1922, he had followed their lead, using his early success to establish his own film studio, the Harold Lloyd Corporation (HL Corporation). Although no longer controlled by the studio system, Lloyd understood the importance of the movie-star home in maintaining his celebrity status. Thus, one of the first investments of the HL Corporation was the purchase of land not far from Pickfair, the estate of Pickford and her then husband Douglas Fairbanks. The timing also coincided with Lloyd's marriage to his leading lady Mildred Davis, who gave birth to the couple's first child, Gloria, in 1924. Design work for the property, dubbed Greenacres, began in 1925. By the time work was completed in 1929, the site featured a forty-four-room mansion modeled on an Italian Renaissance villa, a structure designed by the architectural firm of Webber, Staunton, and Spaulding. The grounds were designed by landscape architect A. E. Hanson and eventually encompassed a golf course (with a clubhouse, as well as a water hazard that did double duty as a canoe course), a tennis court, a barbeque building, multiple formal gardens, and play yard for young Gloria, complete with a thatched-roof playhouse (Figure 6.4). Within a year, Gloria was sharing her playhouse with an adopted sister, Peggy, and within a few more years with a brother, Harold Jr., born in 1931.[52]

According to Hanson, Lloyd's first priority was his private golf course, a feature that received a great deal of press coverage and that served to frame the star as an expert on leisure.[53] Gloria's playhouse seems to have followed soon after, suggesting that Lloyd was equally eager to present himself as a doting father. As early as May

FIGURE 6.4. Exterior of Gloria Lloyd's playhouse at Greenacres, the Harold Lloyd and Mildred Davis Lloyd estate in Beverly Hills, California. Gloria's name is carved into the wooden lintel above the door, while the bas-relief in the gable features a witch on a broomstick. Joseph Weston, architect, 1927. Library of Congress, Prints and Photographs Division, HABS CA-2192–19 16-CHIG, 33–2.

1926, *Motion Picture* magazine published "A Little Girl in a Big House," a feature story that provided a verbal description of the planned estate, including a playhouse "big enough for [Gloria] to entertain her little friends in." Not only was the story illustrated with a studio portrait of the titular "little girl," but it also suggested (admittedly somewhat tongue in cheek) that "she showed remarkable judgement in choosing her parents," who demonstrated their merit by "planning for her . . . a very large house in Beverly Hills."[54] Other accounts also underlined the Lloyds' parental conscientiousness by maintaining that they started with the playhouse early in the construction process so that Gloria would have somewhere to play while her mother and father were inspecting work in progress elsewhere on the site.[55]

In memoirs published almost sixty years after the fact, Hanson recalled that the idea for the playhouse came about in 1927 (the date engraved in the wooden beam above the door). The difference in the date is perhaps less significant than the fact that the landscape architect also took full credit for the idea:

> In the summer of 1927, when Harold Lloyd's daughter Gloria was three years old, I thought about what I would do if I were Harold Lloyd. If I had his money, I would build for Gloria a delightful fairyland for her very own. It would be something out of Mother Goose, or Cinderella, or Little Red Riding Hood. It would be a fairy-tale land.

In Hanson's telling, he reached out to architect Joseph Weston, who had already designed a folly for the Greenacres golf course in the form of an old mill, and suggested that they "do an Elizabethan house and farmstead, but on the scale of a three-year-old-child, rather than a six-foot adult. It would be a fairyland house." Weston was "all enthusiasm" and promptly made watercolor sketches that they then presented to Lloyd for approval. While Hanson did not claim credit for the design, he did characterize himself as "the orchestra leader." According to his memoir, if he "had not thought of the idea and gotten Harold Lloyd to spend the money, it would never have been done."[56]

Whoever thought up the idea, the built result was distinctly picturesque, in sharp contrast to the rectilinear formality of other components of the Greenacres garden. Located directly adjacent to the so-called Formal Garden, the play yard—sometimes also known as Gloria's farmyard—was defined by a rubble stone wall, fitted out with a pair of brass gates (Figure 6.5). Topping the gateposts were brass brownie figurines whose gestures of welcome were echoed in the ornamentation of the gates, which included the words "Come into my garden and play." Plans show three structures, all on a reduced scale: the stone cottage with a half-timbered gable and a thatched roof; a stone slide that sloped down from a clock tower in a gentle curve; and a stable and carriage house, which included a pony stall with a Dutch door, a pigeon loft, and access to a paddock, monkey house, and aviary (Figure 6.6). Period photographs also show a well near the cottage, its roof tiled to match those of the carriage house and clock tower. According to Gloria's daughter, Suzanne, who was raised at Greenacres, the playhouse included a living room, bedroom, kitchen, and bathroom, and was fitted out with heat, electricity, and hot and cold running water.[57] Hanson also credited Weston with designing the reduced-scale furniture, including a four-poster bed and a baby's crib, all of it "Elizabethan in character."[58]

The language Hanson used to describe the project highlights the extent to which new visual tropes of childhood were emerging in the 1920s. To be sure, Gloria's playhouse continued to reference simple cottages, deploying overtly archaic forms of the sort that had been associated with the architecture of childhood since the turn of the century. In the interwar years, however, these structures were increasingly framed in almost magical terms, as settings that allowed their young users to step into the pages of a fairy story. Fairy-book images abound in Gloria's play yard, from the brownies

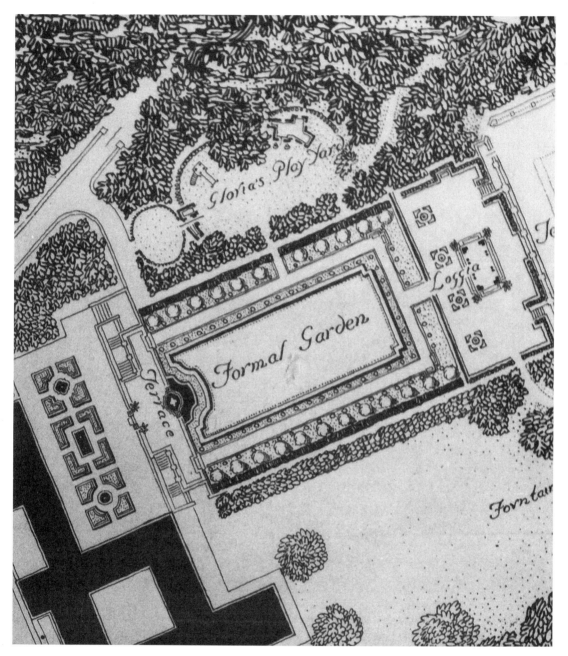

FIGURE 6.5. Plan of Gloria Lloyd's play yard, at Greenacres, the Harold Lloyd and Mildred Davis Lloyd estate in Beverly Hills, California. The play yard contained three structures: from left to right, the stable and carriage house; the clocktower-cum-slide; and the playhouse proper. A. E. Hanson, landscape architect, 1927. Architecture and Design Collection, Art, Design and Architecture Museum, University of California, Santa Barbara.

FIGURE 6.6. Stable and carriage house in Gloria Lloyd's play yard at Greenacres, the Harold Lloyd and Mildred Davis Lloyd estate in Beverly Hills, California. Joseph Weston, architect, 1927. Architecture and Design Collection, Art, Design and Architecture Museum, University of California, Santa Barbara.

on the gatepost mentioned earlier, to a cow jumping over the moon in the stable's steeple finial, to the weathervane on the slide in the shape of Old Father Time, to the witch on a broomstick soaring above the trees that march across the gable just above the playhouse door. Of course, these were the same years that full-sized middle-class houses were also designed to evoke "Old World" cottages. A notable early example, also in Beverly Hills, was the Spadena House, originally built in 1921 to house the dressing rooms and offices of the Willat Studio; in 1926, about the time that work began on Gloria's playhouse, it was moved to Beverly Hills and appeared twice in *The Home Designer and Garden Beautiful*.[59] Yet, the nomenclature used to characterize those single-family houses—sometimes described as being in the storybook style, at other times simply called Hansel and Gretel houses—made it clear they, too, were understood to be childlike and catered to adults who enjoyed the fantasy of inhabiting a fairy tale, especially after the horrors of World War I.

Translating this fantasy into reality, especially on a reduced scale, presented some challenges. While full-scale Hansel and Gretel houses were typically roofed with shingles or shakes used to create rolled eaves in imitation of thatch, Gloria's playhouse was to have a genuine thatched roof, an unusual feature that required Hanson to source suitable wheat straw and research the best methods for fireproofing the highly flammable material. Securing specially produced construction materials needed to maintain the ensemble's reduced scale was another detail in need of orchestration. For instance, Gladding, McBean, a northern California firm known for ornamental terra cotta, provided the small tiles that covered the steeple of the stable, allowing the builders to maintain a consistent scale throughout. According to Hanson, these challenges were relatively easy to resolve, as "every manufacturer was delighted to have a finger in the pie," having recognized "the advertising value of being able to say they had made the fixtures."[60] This was not the first time suppliers used their work for famous clients to generate advertising, a practice that also suited the celebrities who relished opportunities to keep their names (as well as their good taste and spending power) in the public eye. In 1922, for instance, the Quaker Lace Company ran a series of ads with the tag line "Billie Burke Selects Quaker Lace Curtains for Burkeley Crest."[61] Hanson's comments, however, suggest that the draw for suppliers was not just Harold Lloyd's celebrity status, but also the chance to be associated with a magical, miniature play yard for a young girl. Perhaps such a project took on special resonance in a metropolis associated with transforming fantasies into cash.

Even before the main house was finished, Gloria's playhouse was widely published. Sometimes, it was used as evidence that her famous father was Hollywood royalty, as in a November 1927 *Los Angeles Times* story that characterized the play yard as a place where the four-year-old could "play princess" on "an estate of her own."[62] The same month, the playhouse was described (although not pictured) in an article that reached a national audience through the pages of *Picture Play*, which also noted that "some of the Beverly Hills mansions are really comparable to the dwellings of princes and dukes."[63] The theme of stars as royals was also apparent in a two-page spread that appeared in 1930 in *New Movie Magazine* (Figure 6.7). Titled "The Play Yard that Laughs Built," it referred to Lloyd as "the comedy king" and pointed out that six-year-old Gloria, photographed framed by the colonnaded entrance to the main house, was wearing a black velvet coat and hat, trimmed in ermine, leaving unsaid that this was the type of fur traditionally used on royal robes in Europe.[64]

At the same time, these stories also offered the playhouse as proof of Lloyd's fitness as a father, an important move to make this Hollywood royal accessible to his fans. At times, this was accomplished obliquely, as when the *Los Angeles Times* characterized the play yard as a "fairyland," a term used in the headline and repeated

FIGURE 6.7. Photographs of Gloria Lloyd at Greenacres, the Harold Lloyd and Mildred Davis Lloyd estate in Beverly Hills, California. Published in a fan magazine, the images helped consolidate Harold Lloyd's public image as a loving father who could be admired for spending lavishly on his young daughter. "The Play Yard That Laughs Built," *New Movie Magazine* 1, no. 4 (March 1930), 76–77.

three times in the copy. Three photographs, all featuring Gloria alone or with two of the family's Great Danes, emphasized both her small size as well as the reduced scale of the "miniature old English house."[65] Here, the story implied, was a lucky little girl whose father made a point of cocooning her in a world of make-believe, far from the cares of adult life. The message was conveyed more directly when the Lloyds adopted young Peggy. Stories about the adoption in the *Beverly Hills Citizen* never failed to mention the playhouse, which served as evidence of the wonderful stuff of childhood her new parents were able to offer her.[66] In an important respect, Lloyd's devotion to Gloria (and later his other children) was offered as a justification for his lavish spending more generally, as in a photo spread published in the March 1929 issue of *Motion Picture Classic* that carried the punning headline "For Pleasure Unalloyd: Harold's New Estate Is a Paradise for Gloria and Golf."[67] In this framing of the estate, the golf course and the playhouse were two sides of the same coin, both luxuries, but ones that confirmed Lloyd's ability to channel his earnings appropriately, that is, toward wholesome leisure and familial responsibility.

MANAGING THE PUBLIC PERSONA OF THE CHILD STAR

Gloria Lloyd's playhouse received a further mention in 1935 when *Modern Screen* ran a long story about Shirley Temple that, among other things, made much of the day she and her mother were picked up in a chauffeur-driven car and taken to "the very top of a mountain," where they found both "a great house, like a palace" and, "wonder of wonders, a playhouse that looked like a picture in a fairy story and had the name 'Gloria' carved above the doorway." There, overseen by the Lloyd nurse, young Shirley reportedly spent the afternoon playing with the three Lloyd children and Jane Bannister, whose mother, actress Ann Harding, was fighting to retain custody of the girl.[68] The story did not mention the custody battle, of course, focusing instead on the fun the children had, both in the playhouse and later in the main house, where they watched a Mickey Mouse film, "just as if they were in a real theater." The story also quoted Gloria Lloyd's assessment of the young star: she is "just the way she is on the screen.... She doesn't seem to know that she's a movie star. Just like my father and Janie's mother. She doesn't seem to know that at all." Here Gloria and her playhouse contributed to the central message of the studio system's public relations machine: for all the luxuries that their film careers afforded them, these movie stars were just regular folks.

Lest *Modern Screen* readers worry that the young star was being somehow outclassed by Gloria Lloyd, the story's happy ending focused on Shirley's return to the studio, where she was surprised to find that "now, instead of her old dressing-room, she had a whole bungalow to herself. With a dove cote built into the roof, with a garden and a tree with a swing."[69] Like Gloria's playhouse, Shirley's four-room bungalow evoked a world of fairytales (Figure 6.8). The studio set designer who created it characterized it as a "Hansel and Gretel's cottage" with an interior that was "pure Sleeping Beauty." The living room was decorated with a mural of Shirley dressed as a fairy-tale princess and fitted out with furnishings in cherry red and white. The bedroom featured a sky-blue ceiling accented with silver stars.[70]

For all the supposed similarities between the two buildings, Shirley Temple's bungalow and Gloria's playhouse were as different as they could be. Neither a gift from her parents nor an extension of her family's domestic space, Shirley's bungalow was supplied by her studio bosses at Twentieth Century–Fox and stood on the studio lot. While Gloria's playhouse burnished the reputation of her movie star father, Shirley's bungalow supported her own celebrity status. She was, after all, one of the most popular film performers of the 1930s. And there was the rub. While adult stars enjoyed public personas that presented them as model consumers, especially of luxury goods, that path was not open to a child star. Shirley's celebrity status depended on her ability to remain a child in the eyes of her fans. On one hand, this meant she needed

Figure 6.8. Exterior of Shirley Temple's bungalow on the Twentieth Century–Fox Studios lot in Los Angeles, California. The bungalow predated Shirley's occupancy of the building, which began in fall 1934. Architect unknown. Courtesy Rita Dubas.

to be seen as enjoying "a good childhood," with all the material trappings implied by that term. Indeed, given her high salary, she deserved the best of everything. Yet, unlike adult stars who were celebrated as model consumers of luxury goods, she needed to remain isolated from the marketplace; it would have been unseemly for a girl of her tender years to indulge in an orgy of spending. Gifts offered a neat workaround, especially if the gift came from the studio's chief of production, Winfield Sheehan, acting in loco parentis.[71]

Yet Shirley Temple's bungalow diverged from Gloria's playhouse in another sense. After all, it was not a plaything, not a miniature house that encouraged its young mistress to pretend that she was a careful housewife. Instead, it facilitated labor of a different sort, namely, Shirley's very real work on the set. The kitchen was not a place where Shirley practiced cooking; it was where her mother prepared her lunch. In this sense, it can be understood as a time-management tool; instead of making her way to the commissary, Shirley could take her meals in her bungalow and devote her time to her studies, mandated by California law at three hours per day. Overseen by her tutor, Shirley's lessons took place at a school desk in a room (sometimes referred to as the bedroom, sometimes as the schoolroom) that also contained a bed where the young star could nap.⁷² In short, this small building was a star's bungalow masquerading as a child's playhouse, a deception perpetrated by the studio, which released images and information highlighting the fact that "all the furniture in the bungalow is scaled down to her size," from her "own little radio" in what they called the reception room, to the "diminutive dinette" in the kitchen (Figure 6.9).⁷³ By eliding the two kinds of cottages, the studio encouraged Shirley's fans to accept her work as a form of play, a message her mother reinforced when she assured interviewers that "motion picture acting is simply part of her play life." *Time* magazine gave credence to this interpretation, asserting in 1936 that the young star's "work entails no effort. She plays at acting as other small girls play at dolls."⁷⁴ The goal was to present Shirley as a joyful child—"just the way she is on the screen," to reuse the phrase attributed to playmate Gloria Lloyd.

In addition to her bungalow on the studio lot, Shirley had access to a number of playhouses built for her use over the years—a fact that points to other challenges involved in managing the public persona of a star so young. One was in the garden of the Temples' Santa Monica home and was a simple, one-room affair akin to mass-produced play sheds marketed to middle-class families and even smaller than Patricia Ziegfeld's original "small, cramped, and dingy" play shed. Yet, this modest play shed was the ideal adjunct to the many magazine stories in which Shirley's mother assured readers that "when my little girl became a film star, I saw to it that she did not become a star in the Temple home.... In spite of Shirley's financial success, she is not running the Temple household."⁷⁵ Shirley's public image depended on her being just like other little girls, and a modest play shed at home helped her achieve an important degree of accessibility. Indeed, Shirley and her modest play shed became all the more accessible when they were featured in a paper-doll set issued in 1935—a set that allowed little girls to own a version of Shirley's play shed and to imagine themselves as the carefree young star. The play shed was also visible in the press, including an article that appeared in the British magazine *The Sketch* in October 1934.⁷⁶ It included four photographs of Shirley at the play shed, two showing her dressed in overalls, suggesting the pictures were taken at the same time as unpublished photographs in which, clad in the same outfit, she was posed precariously on the structure's roof (Figure 6.10). Perhaps the rooftop images did not make the final cut because they would have revealed that the other, supposedly candid, shots of Shirley at play were also staged. To be effective, Shirley's accessibility also needed to seem authentic.

One indication that this strategy was successful was the increasing number of fans seeking out the Temple home in hopes of catching a glimpse of the young star. To secure the family's privacy, Shirley's parents purchased land in Brentwood and began construction on a new house that would shield their living space from public view.⁷⁷ There, beginning in 1936, Shirley had use of a fully plumbed and electrified playhouse, with glass block walls (to be discussed in chapter 7). Within a few years,

FIGURE 6.9. Interiors and exterior of Shirley Temple's bungalow on the Twentieth Century–Fox Studios lot in Los Angeles, California. Although it was a full-scale bungalow, the captions in a fan magazine highlight the small scale of the furnishings, including a "diminutive dinette" and the star's "own little radio." "That 4 O'Clock Let-down? Not for Shirley!" *Photoplay*, October 1936, 8.

SHIRLEY IN HER OWN DRESSING-ROOM AND PLAY-HOUSE.

Shirley Temple is nothing if not versatile, and she is here seen tinkering with her tricycle. She is appearing in "Now and Forever," at the Plaza, with Gary Cooper and Carole Lombard.

(Left) SHIRLEY TEMPLE, Fox Film starlet, bids you welcome to her play-house in the garden of her Santa Monica home.

"Will you take a walk with me?" says Shirley Temple as she wheels Raggedy Ann about the grounds surrounding her play-house.

(Right) Shirley Temple in working outfit attends to the irrigation of her play-house garden.

Just resting between scenes; that's Shirley Temple, who is the proud possessor of a dressing-room equipped, as befits a five-year-old, with gingham covers.

The eternal feminine! Finding a stage make-up table unoccupied, Shirley Temple decides to beautify herself; but the camera-man came along just then and caught her red-lipped.

FIGURE 6.10. Shirley Temple's play shed, in the yard of her family's house in Santa Monica, California. Early in the young actress's career, her modest play shed contributed to the public persona that was carefully crafted for her: a regular little girl, like any other. "Shirley in Her Own Dressing-Room and Play-House," *The Sketch*, 3 October 1934, 36. *Illustrated London News* / Mary Evans Picture Library.

George and Gertrude Temple commissioned an even more substantial building for Shirley's use. Although dubbed "the dollhouse," it was a full-size building that Shirley later described in her autobiography as "carved into the shoulder of a hillside, its appearance recalling an English stone farmhouse, with leaded glass windows, a steep roof sheathed in cedar shingles, and a turret with medieval window slits." If its architectural expression owed something to Gloria Lloyd's playhouse and other houses in the Storybook Style, the dollhouse was not a child's playhouse but a recreation facility for a teenager. Its principal room was a double-height space fifty feet long, with a stage and movie screen at one end and a soda fountain at the other. In the basement were a foreshortened bowling alley and storage areas: a vault where George Temple stored old documents and emergency rations of bottled water and canned food; a closet where Gertrude stored the costumes Shirley had worn in her films; and a room for Shirley's sizable doll collection.[78]

In an important sense, Shirley Temple's so-called dollhouse was more akin to the children's cottage at the Breakers than to the many imposing playhouses built in the twentieth century. Both were full-scale buildings that provided space for youngsters to socialize in settings separate from the main house. In both cases, the goal was to facilitate parental control, especially over teenage daughters who were central to their parents' aspirations. In Gilded Age Newport, the Vanderbilt playhouse helped safeguard the dynasty's social standing by ensuring that Gertrude, in particular, socialized with friends of whom her parents approved. In Depression-era Hollywood, the Temple dollhouse was designed to preserve the family's financial security by controlling the public persona of their highly remunerated daughter. But there the similarities ended. In order for Gertrude Vanderbilt to fulfill her parents' objectives, she needed to "graduate" from the children's cottage, make her debut, secure a socially prominent husband, and leave her parents' household. In contrast, Shirley Temple's mother used the dollhouse as a tool to keep her famous daughter close to home and under parental control. When, in 1945, seventeen-year-old Shirley married John Agar, her mother renovated the dollhouse into a full-time home for the newlyweds.[79]

PLAYHOUSES AS OBJECTS OF MIDDLE-CLASS DESIRE

In their architectural form, the impressive playhouses built by Hollywood stars and other adults enmeshed in the leisure economy had much in common with playhouses constructed by social elites. Products of professional design expertise, these fully plumbed and electrified structures were typically built on a reduced scale and often evoked archaic forms of peasant cottages or explicitly referenced fairy tales. Sometimes these design strategies were used in combination. After 1920, these elaborate playhouses also tended to follow another practice pursued by social elites, namely, bestowing upon a particular little girl a miniature version of a full-scale house, complete with a bedroom or two.

Yet, these playhouses, created by men and women who earned their livings by selling leisure, functioned quite differently in terms of parental ambitions. In fact, the aspirations they served varied with the adults' relationship to the leisure economy. Robert Burton's rationale for building a costly playhouse may have had the least to do with his parental role. Although he was the father of four children (three of whom survived infancy), none of his offspring were mentioned in published stories about his playhouse. This is not to say that he did not have ambitions for his children; his endeavors ensured that they were raised to become the sort of adults whose philanthropic efforts and social engagements were mentioned from time to time in the society pages of the *New York Times*.[80] The playhouse, however, was secondary to that process. Its primary purpose was to help Burton present himself to potential customers as someone who could be trusted to equip a socially exclusive seasonal community with every amenity. In this sense, it played a role in Burton's financial success at Woodmere, which ultimately enhanced his ability to finance his family's aspirational lifestyles.

In contrast, stars of stage and screen were more interested in using impressive playhouses to publicize their parental efforts. They were content—even eager—to have their children mentioned by name in the press and often ensured that the youngsters' smiling faces appeared there as well. Even in these cases, the motivations for building such playhouses were quite distinct from those of social elites. For one thing, social elites tended to play a long game. They invested in splendid playhouses (and the many other trappings of elite culture) to help ensure that their children were prepared to take their own places in society and so continue their parents' determined pursuit of symbolic capital, securing the family's reputation among other social elites. As much as Florenz Ziegfeld and Harold Lloyd doted on their children, they had no expectation that their offspring would eventually step into their shoes or enhance the family name. Their goals were much more short term: to consolidate public personas that depended on their demonstrated ability to enjoy life to the fullest and to bring joy to everyone in their ambit, most especially their children. Patricia Ziegfeld certainly seems to have understood her upbringing in just these terms; despite the fact that her father died deeply in debt when she was sixteen, she gave her memoir the subtitle *Confessions of an Abnormally Happy Childhood*. In this context, the primary role of an ostentatious playhouse was to provide visibly compelling evidence of this delirious happiness. Especially in Hollywood, such a building served as fodder for the voracious public relations machines that needed constant feeding in order to secure a star's fan base, sell tickets, and justify enormous salaries.

Far from using the playhouse (as did social elites) to keep children separate from adult spaces and activities, stars of stage and screen regularly broke down the boundaries between the two realms. By her own account, Patricia Ziegfeld was very much a part of the Sunday afternoon gatherings at which her parents entertained. Harold Lloyd went even further, designing the main house to accommodate fun for the whole family, including the home theater where Shirley Temple watched Mickey Mouse cartoons with the Lloyd offspring in 1935. Twenty years later, he devoted large parts of the main house to the celebration of Christmas, a holiday that had become strongly associated with childish wonder. According to a granddaughter who was raised at Greenacres, the household celebrated Christmas 365 days a year, as the Christmas tree (in reality, three trees combined into one fireproof tree and decorated with five thousand ornaments) had become too big to take down.[81] When his own children were young, Lloyd also made sure he was photographed in Gloria's play yard. Soon after it was finished, he was shown emerging from the miniature house with his eldest daughter; a few years later, he posed with his wife and all three children—all five of them evidently shouting with glee—on the nearby slide. How better for a grown man to exude joy than to become a child at play again?

In short, Gloria Lloyd's playhouse was an integral part of Greenacres and its role in sustaining Harold Lloyd's public persona. In its size, in its forms and in its range of amenities, the estate confirmed that the movie star lived in the lap of luxury. At the same time, the playhouse provided evidence that Lloyd pursued a version of child-centered family life that validated the priorities of his middle-class admirers. In that sense, his lifestyle was simultaneously extravagant and accessible. Few of his fans had the wherewithal to build similar buildings for the use of their children, but in their daydreams they could certainly imagine themselves following his lead. In that sense, his efforts helped transform the meaning of elaborate playhouses from artifacts of elite culture to objects of middle-class desire.

Shirley Temple's playhouses were another matter. The small house built for her use on the studio lot was not a gift from her parents. Indeed, it was not a playhouse at all, despite the many visual tropes of childhood incorporated into its decorative scheme. If anything, the building's appearance was calculated to disguise the fact that it was a movie star's bungalow, a building designed to maximize Shirley's effectiveness as a hardworking actress. Between takes, she could go there to rest, take her meals, learn her lines, practice dance steps, and keep up with the private tutoring mandated by state law. While her studio bosses and her parents often asserted that her work was play, her bungalow revealed that her play was, in fact, work. When the young star eventually received an impressive playhouse of her own in 1936, it was the product of a very different set of economic forces, ones far removed from any ambitions her parents may have had for her.

FIGURE 7.1. Shirley Temple at the glass block playhouse built by the Owens-Illinois Glass Company on the grounds of the Temple family home in Brentwood, California, circa 1937. Courtesy Marc Wanamaker / Bison Archives.

CHAPTER SEVEN

For Movie Stars and Princesses

The 1930s Celebrity Playhouse

More than five thousand miles separate the two photographs, but in many respects they are remarkably similar. Both date from the mid-1930s. Both use a miniature playhouse to create a charming backdrop for a portrait of a young girl. Both take as their subject a recognizable youngster, a celebrity of sorts. One shows Princess Elizabeth of York (later Queen Elizabeth II) at her playhouse on the grounds of Royal Lodge, the country house of her parents, the Duke and Duchess of York, in Windsor Great Park (see Figure I.1). The other shows Shirley Temple, one of the biggest stars in Hollywood, later dubbed by one of her biographers as an American princess. Plainly accustomed to radiating joyful wholesomeness for the camera, the young actress sits in front of her glass block playhouse in the backyard of her parents' suburban house in Brentwood, California (Figure 7.1). Although they inhabited very different worlds, both girls appealed to a wide swath of the public in their fresh-faced innocence. They were quite literally adorable.

The playhouses with which they were pictured were directly related to their celebrity status. Y Bwthyn Bach To Gwellt (Welsh for The Little Thatched Cottage) was presented as a birthday gift to Princess Elizabeth in the spring of 1932 when she turned six, ostensibly as a token of loyalty from the people of Wales. Shirley Temple received her glass block playhouse from the Owens-Illinois Glass Company in 1936, nominally the year she turned seven. (In reality, Shirley was eight; her age had been misrepresented starting early in her career to make her seem even more precocious than she was.)[1] In each instance, the gift was not simply an attempt to make a beloved young girl happy; it was also a strategic move to leverage the girl's fame to bolster a particular segment of the construction industry and to encourage consumer spending that might help end the Depression.

If the two playhouses were originally motivated by similar goals, they came to serve different ends. A key difference was that Princess Elizabeth's parents recognized the playhouse as a powerful tool in crafting their public image as a warm, loving, tight-knit nuclear family, something that became even more important to them after Elizabeth's uncle Edward VIII abdicated in December 1936. Not only did her father unexpectedly become King George VI, but Princess Elizabeth found herself heir presumptive, on the path to becoming queen. While she eventually outgrew her playhouse, she was daily growing into the woman who would be the most important public figure in Great Britain. Tellingly, images of her playhouse were popular at important points in that journey, especially at the time of her marriage in 1947 and the time of her coronation in 1953. At these moments, Y Bwthyn Bach offered evidence that Elizabeth's life was built on the firm foundation of a happy childhood that had prepared her to embrace marriage and motherhood, as well as royal responsibilities.

In contrast, Shirley Temple's glass block playhouse was a relatively small part of her public persona, in part at least because it was a reminder that once she outgrew the playhouse, she would also have outgrown the adorable girlhood that was central to her star appeal. If anything, her mother was more concerned with using a very different kind of playhouse (the so-called dollhouse discussed in chapter 6) to maintain some sort of control over Shirley's social life as she entered her adolescence. To be sure, Owens-Illinois tried to make the most of their experiment in celebrity endorsement, including providing "an exact replica" for the New York World's Fair in 1939. By that time, Shirley's popularity had started to wane, and the replica playhouse, struggling to attract visitors in the somewhat tawdry atmosphere of Children's World, lost whatever air of luxury and exclusivity the original may have enjoyed in the backyard of the Temples' Brentwood house. In that sense, it helped bring the era of the elaborate playhouse to a close.

Y BWTHYN BACH TO GWELLT

By the time Y Bwthyn Bach was placed on its permanent site on the grounds of Royal Lodge in May 1932, it was well known throughout Britain and beyond. As early as May 1931, British newspapers were reporting on a plan to present Princess Elizabeth with a "miniature house" on her sixth birthday in April 1932.[2] Within six months, the *Illustrated London News* had commissioned renowned architectural illustrator Cyril A. Farey (who was not otherwise involved in the project) to create perspective renderings of the house (Figure 7.2).[3] Farey's section looked so much like a dollhouse that when it was published in September 1931, the paper included a headline for its extended caption that started with the words "Not a Dolls' House, but a Habitable Home, Built on a Scale Adapted to a Child of Six." Soon afterward, the completed house had gone on tour and been displayed at the Ideal Home and

FIGURE 7.2. Section of Y Bwthyn Bach To Gwellt (Welsh for The Little Thatched Cottage), eventually installed at Royal Lodge, Windsor Great Park. The *Illustrated London News* commissioned renowned architectural draftsman Cyril A. Farey to draw the section, which accurately depicts the misalignment of the central chimney on the roof and the fireplace on the end wall of the sitting room. The drawing was published on 12 September 1931, while the cottage was still under construction in Cardiff. Morgan Willmott, architect, 1931–32. *Illustrated London News* / Mary Evans Picture Library.

Building Trades Exhibition in Cardiff in late October and early November 1931 and at the Brighter Homes Exhibition, sponsored by the *Birmingham Gazette* in February 1932.

The American press also covered Y Bwythn Bach. In February 1932, the *New York Times* published photographs of the house with a detailed story that may have caught the attention of financier E. F. Hutton and his heiress wife, Marjorie Merriweather Post.[4] Within two years they had engaged Charles M. Hart (the architect responsible for the 30,000-square-foot Tudor Revival mansion at Hillwood, their Long Island estate) to return to the site to design a miniature playhouse (Figure 7.3). Called Deen-Wee (after their daughter, Nedenia, known later in life by her stage name, Dina Merrill, and Post's granddaughter, Marjorie, known as Marwee), the building did not imitate the English example directly.[5] Its front door opened directly into the main room, without a foyer or hallway (Figure 7.4). The building's reduced scale, its thatched roof, the completeness of its furnishings, and especially the inclusion of a second floor fitted out with a bedroom and a small bathroom—all these features suggest that Deen-Wee was inspired by Y Bwthyn Bach.

FIGURE 7.3. Exterior of Deen-Wee on the grounds of Hillwood, the estate of E. F. Hutton and Marjorie Merriweather Post in Brookville, Long Island, New York. The front door and the side door both led into a living room, while the door at the back of the outdoor seating area provided access to a small kitchen. Charles M. Hart, architect, circa 1934. Courtesy of Kenneth Mensing.

FIGURE 7.4. Interior of Deen-Wee on the grounds of Hillwood, the estate of E. F. Hutton and Marjorie Merriweather Post in Brookville, Long Island, New York. The stair led to a bedroom and bathroom on the second floor. Charles M. Hart, architect, circa 1934. Courtesy of Kenneth Mensing.

In mid-March 1932, Y Bwthyn Bach had been brought back to Cardiff, where it had been officially presented to the Duke and Duchess of York, who also visited the Royal Infirmary, where they unveiled a tablet above the infirmary cot endowed with funds raised by the exhibition of the model house.[6] Within days, the small house had been on its way to London, but caught fire when an errant spark from the steam engine used to allow the lorry to tow its heavy load ignited the thatched roof. Both the fire and subsequent repair efforts made dramatic copy, with the local paper highlighting the "Welsh loyalty and determination" involved in the "day and night rush to complete repairs" in time to display the house at the Daily Mail Ideal Home Exhibition in London in early April, as originally planned. Even the *New York Times* ran the story; although it offered no comment on Welsh fortitude in the face of adversity, it described the cottage as Princess Elizabeth's "wonder house."[7]

During these months, Y Bwthyn Bach was increasingly characterized as "a gift from the people of Wales," glossing over the extent to which the undertaking was the brainchild of a relatively small group of men from Cardiff. Likewise, most of the published statements treated the desire to express "sturdy loyalty and warm affection" for "the universally loved little Royal lady" as wholly natural, masking the fact that the gift was also intended to leverage public interest in the young princess in order to bring attention to South Wales businesses involved in building and outfitting middle-class houses.[8] Indeed, it seems a prescient move. While the country was in the throes of a significant shift to a consumer economy, Welsh MPs, at least in the early 1930s, remained focused on reviving the coal industry, without recognizing the employment opportunities that could be provided by industries that made radios and refrigerators.[9] For all its quaint rusticity, Y Bwthyn Bach was firmly connected to a new vision for the Welsh economy.

Yet, even at the time, the commercial character of the project was apparent. For one thing, the Publicity Club of Cardiff, a booster organization, provided the organizational expertise for the complicated undertaking, which included arranging for the house to be exhibited to raise funds for Welsh charities. For another, news stories rarely called the cottage Y Bwthyn Bach and never referred to it as a playhouse. Instead, the most common designation was "Princess Elizabeth's model house," a term that evoked the nomenclature and display techniques of commercial home shows. Indeed, when Y Bwthyn Bach was put on display at the Ideal Home and Building Trades Exhibition in Cardiff, the "woman correspondent" for the *Western Mail & South Wales News* lauded the house as "an ambassador of commerce," an object that "wherever it goes, will take the message of Cardiff and show what South Wales firms can do toward the erection of full sized 'ideal homes.'"[10] Little wonder that this story shared the page with thirteen advertisements, all of which were placed by firms that had contributed materials, furniture, or fittings to the project. Among the Cardiff concerns were All-British Initials Ltd., "the only all-British firm making raised foundation initials and designs for embroidery"; Express Hemstitching Company, which produced the curtains; Kleen-e-ze Brush Company; Richard Beere, a purveyor of "modern furniture"; Lermons Limited, makers of the princess's writing desk; Western Radio & Supplies Ltd., which provided a wireless set; William Blake, who claimed to have supplied the "Perfect Plumbing for a Perfect House"; and Page & Stibbs, whose ads identified them simply at "'THE' Electricians." A few months later, Lord Mayor C. W. Melhuish confirmed the extent to which the involvement of "the people of Wales" was a convenient fiction, while also revealing additional ways Y Bwthyn Bach could serve the local economy. At the annual dinner of the Incorporated Cardiff and District Retail Meat Traders' Association in February 1932, he referred to "Princess Elizabeth's present of a model house" as coming "from the City of Cardiff," and boasted that in exchange the city had been given a stand at the upcoming London exhibition, which would provide "an opportunity for Cardiff to advertise the facilities the city offered to foreign firms seeking sites for new factories."[11]

At the same time, the royal acquiescence upon which the plan depended required some finesse, given that members of the royal family were not allowed to accept gifts from private individuals; hence the importance of framing Y Bwthyn Bach as an expression of loyalty from the Welsh nation. Mindful of the delicacy of the situation, organizers had initially considered following an established precedent by presenting the princess with a true dollhouse, along the lines of the one that had been created for her grandmother, Queen Mary, in the 1920s. Designed by architect Edwin Lutyens and remarkable for the completeness of its fittings, that dollhouse had been framed as both an expression of widespread affection for the "home-loving" queen and also as a historical document that would provide "a lifelike memorial for future times of the sort of way in which people of our own days found it desirable and agreeable to live."[12] At the same time, Queen Mary's dolls' house (as it was and is still known) was also understood to have a charitable component. Before it was presented to the queen toward the end of 1924, it was displayed for six months at the British Empire Exhibition at Wembley Park, where some 1.5 million visitors had paid to see it, resulting in an estimated £80,000 for charity—the equivalent of over £6 million or $7.7 million in 2024.[13] In Cardiff, the dollhouse idea had been floated by E. R. Appleton, the director of the Western Regional Station of the BBC, who envisioned something that would "have a real cultural and educational value for the children to whom it would be exhibited."[14] Not only did he imagine a didactic function for the project, but he also assumed that the finished product—like Queen Mary's dolls' house—would be widely displayed before reaching its young owner. Although Appleton is somewhat notorious for opposing Welsh language broadcasting, he was committed to providing programming with Welsh content, which in the winter of 1930 included a series of talks, *Life in Bygone Wales.* Thus, he may have had Welsh folklife in mind when he proposed something of "real cultural value."[15]

The project took a different turn when Morgan Willmott, a well-respected Cardiff architect, suggested that they produce instead a habitable house on a reduced scale, in this case a two-story structure twenty-two feet long and fifteen feet deep. Nonetheless, Y Bwthyn Bach was influenced by the example of Queen Mary's dolls' house. Although it avoided the regal magnificence of that earlier gift—"making no attempt to obtrude or impress"—it embraced a similar attention to detail, both in the consistency of its reduced scale and also in its completeness.[16] With ceilings just four to eight feet high, its dimensions required most adults to crouch as they moved from room to room, except on the stairway landing, where visitors between five and six feet tall could stand up straight, with their shoulders reaching the level of the upper floor. (In contrast, most adult visitors to Frances Dodge's Knole Cottage had to stoop somewhat to move through doorways but were able to stand comfortably in any room.) Each of the cottage's four rooms—kitchen, sitting room (sometimes also called the living room), bedroom, and bathroom—was fitted out not only with appropriately scaled furniture and window treatments, but also with an impressive array of movable objects, both useful and decorative. Some were utensils for cooking and cleaning, including a pastry board, a rolling pin, brushes, and mops. Others were for serving meals, with distinct services for breakfast, dinner, and teas. The writing desk was stocked with notepaper emblazoned with Princess Elizabeth's crest, which was also embroidered on the sheets, blankets, and towels in the fully stocked linen cupboard. The decorative objects included an original oil portrait of the Duchess of York, given pride of place over the mantel in the sitting room (Figure 7.5). The artist was Margaret Lindsay Williams, a student of John Singer Sargent who had already painted the Prince of Wales and who would within a few years go on to create a widely reproduced dual portrait of Princesses Elizabeth and Margaret.[17] The cottage was also fitted out with consumables, from tinned goods and a birthday cake in the kitchen, to soap, toothpaste, and bath salts in the bathroom upstairs. Such was the drive for completeness that Y Bwthyn Bach came with a small-scale vellum deed and a small-scale fire insurance policy—another nod to Queen Mary's dolls' house, where a Householder's Comprehensive Insurance Policy had been filed away safely in its miniature library.[18]

THE WELSH CHARACTER OF Y BWTHYN BACH

The rationale behind modeling Princess Elizabeth's playhouse on a Welsh cottage was not as self-evident as it might first appear. Social elites had long associated children with cottages, at times using the nomenclature to describe full-sized buildings devoted to the use of the young and at others dressing miniature playhouses in forms borrowed from storybook cottages. Yet the cultural specificity of a Welsh cottage carried particular associations, which were in flux. In the nineteenth century and into the twentieth, health officials condemned the cottages of rural Wales as dank, unsanitary dwellings where the proximity of pigs and fowl contributed to the ever-present dung heap at the door. Yet, in the same years, the Welsh cottage was also the focus of intense nostalgia, especially among those who had moved from their homes in the countryside to urban settings.[19] Thatched roofs took on a particularly strong association with familial warmth and coziness, as in an enormously popular folk song first published in 1878 in which the narrator remembered his grandmother's

FIGURE 7.5. Sitting room, Y Bwthyn Bach To Gwellt, Royal Lodge, Windsor Great Park, with Margaret Lindsey Williams's original oil portrait of the Duchess of York, Princess Elizabeth's mother, on the chimneypiece. Morgan Willmott, architect, 1931–32. Photograph by the author.

"little straw-thatched cot" as "a peaceful dwelling . . . a heavenly home."[20] Indeed, the title of that song, "Y Bwthyn Bach To Gwellt," became the favorite phrase for evoking this idealized version of the Welsh cottage and would have carried these associations when attached to Princess Elizabeth's model house. By the early twentieth century, travel guides singled out the thatched houses of Carmarthenshire and Cardiganshire as "the quaintest and most picturesque cottages in the world," drawing particular attention to the roof as "a thing of joy and a work of art."[21] By the 1920s and 1930s, the disappearance of these simple dwellings became a topic of concern. After singing the praises of the thatched cottages of Carmarthenshire, one commentator for the *Western Mail & South Wales News* asked plaintively, "Is there no way of preserving 'Y bwthyn bach to gwellt' of Wales's biggest county?"[22] Equally troubling, expert thatchers seemed to be on the verge of extinction; they were, in the words of the *Western Mail & South Wales News*, "champions of a dying industry."[23] Faced with such losses in the folkways of rural Wales, the National Museum of Wales opened a "Welsh Bygones" gallery in 1926.[24]

In an important sense, then, Princess Elizabeth's model house benefited from this larger preservation movement and, ostensibly at least, also contributed to it. Its roof, for instance, was provided by Thomas James David, a fifth-generation thatcher and reportedly one of only three or four qualified thatchers in the country.[25] Likewise, Willmott turned to the collections of the National Museum of Wales to bring a degree of authenticity to the cottage's furnishings. According to the *Western Mail & South Wales News*, "Museum authorities have taken great interest in the making of the various pieces and have given all facilities for making working drawings."[26] These pieces included a Welsh dresser, a long table and chairs with rush seats for the sitting room, a corner cupboard in the hall, and a settle that served as both a bench and table for the landing; all except the settle are visible in Figure 7.2. The souvenir guidebook underlined the Welsh character of the project by referring to the sitting room as the "Siamber Fach," or "Little Chamber," and the exterior dormers as "gapolyns," features that imitated "the poke and ruffle of an old Welsh bonnet."[27] When the Duke and Duchess of York accepted the cottage on their trip to Cardiff, the ceremony was given a distinctly Welsh flavor when the duchess received a bouquet of flowers from seven-year-old Jean Blake, dressed in the costume traditionally worn by rural women of Wales, complete with its distinctive tall hat.[28] On a more whimsical note, the president of the Welsh Terrier Association ensured that Y Bwthyn Bach came with a live dog; rather than giving the pup a name from Welsh folklore, they dubbed him Ianto Fullpelt, after a character that appeared in cartoons published in the *South Wales Football Echo and Express*; images of the presentation ceremony reveal that Ianto's doghouse was also thatched.[29]

For all this attention to authenticity, Willmott also used Welsh material culture selectively in his design for Y Bwthyn Bach. For one thing, he neatly skirted any reminder of the squalid cottages that had so bothered nineteenth-century reformers by modeling the princess's miniature house on estate cottages, dwellings commissioned by large landowners both to house their workers and "to provide a picturesque incident to an estate—to delight the eye rather than prompt a reforming frown," in the words of historian Richard Suggett and architectural historian Greg Stevenson.[30] The balanced arrangement of Y Bwthyn Bach's front façade and its neat thatched roof with swept eyebrows above the second-floor windows are features reminiscent of well-kept estate cottages, such as those at Merthyr Mawr, a manor owned by Sir John Nicholls in the nineteenth century and located some twenty miles from Cardiff.[31] If anything, Willmott exaggerated the tidiness of Princess Elizabeth's model house by providing a perfectly symmetrical composition, calling attention to the central axis by aligning the front door with a central chimney that bore no relation to the location of the one interior fireplace, which was built into an end wall of the sitting room.

At the same time, Willmott's design for Y Bwthyn Bach combined otherwise distinct regional building methods with modern techniques and materials. The tidy thatched roof was typical of Glamorgan, where thatchers used reed straw combed to lie in the same direction; elsewhere in Wales, the use of crushed straw gave the thatch a shaggier appearance.[32] In contrast, the modern wood-frame walls of Y Bwthyn Bach were finished with Petrumite imitation stone paint, simulating clay-walled, lime-washed rural cottages common in west Wales and disregarding the common use of unplastered stone in Glamorgan (including at the Merthyr Mawr estate cottages).[33] In short, at Y Bwthyn Bach, Willmott fused regional differences inherent in folk building practices with modern techniques and offered the amalgam as an invented "Welsh" national style.

Inside was a different story altogether. Despite the assertion in the souvenir booklet that "the dream house of the Princess follow[ed] a simple Welsh cottage interior," Y Bwthyn Bach bore little resemblance to vernacular houses in plan or room use.[34] As furniture historian Richard Bebb has argued, the *cegin* was the defining feature of rural homes in Wales from the mid-seventeenth into the twentieth century for all groups below the landed gentry (Figure 7.6).[35] Typically accessed directly from outside and dominated by a large open hearth, often with an adjacent settle, the *cegin* was the larger of a cottage's two rooms and the center of domestic life, the space where the family prepared and consumed their meals and completed a variety of household tasks. At the same time, the *cegin* was also a public space, described in the 1840s as "the theater of the Welsh farmer's domestic life."[36] Here the family displayed its

FIGURE 7.6. *Cegin* of farmhouse in Betws-y-coed, Caernarfonshire, Wales. The *cegin* was both a place of work and also a room for entertaining and for the display of the family's best goods, which in this case included a tall case clock and a large Welsh dresser. Artist unknown, 1883. Richard Bebb Collection.

best pewter and earthenware on large, elaborately carved, and highly polished oak dressers—"prestigious pieces," in Bebb's words—typically acquired to celebrate a marriage and often passed down for generations.[37] By the early twentieth century, the particular form—with open shelves sitting atop an enclosed cupboard—was so closely associated with Wales that it was known as the Welsh dresser. Indeed, just such a dresser figured prominently in the Welsh farmhouse kitchen that was part of the Welsh Bygones gallery, both when it was first opened in 1926 and also after it was moved to the museum's new wing and reopened in 1931, just as Y Bwthyn Bach was being built.[38]

Willmott ensured that Y Bwthyn Bach had its Welsh dresser as well as a longcase clock, another prized possession often on display in many rural *cegins*. Yet, the *cegin* was nowhere to be found. The service functions of the *cegin* were accommodated in the kitchen, although a gas stove took the place of the *cegin*'s open hearth. In contrast, the *cegin*'s public functions, especially entertaining and the display of luxury goods, took place in the sitting room/living room/"Siamb[e]r Fach"; there again an electric fireplace displaced the *cegin*'s open hearth (see Figure 7.5). A central hall not only introduced a spatial buffer between these two zones but also housed a stairway. In addition to announcing the existence on the upper floor of a third zone devoted to family privacy in the bedroom and bathroom, the stair also provided an additional degree of seclusion for that family-only precinct (Figure 7.7). In short, with its careful demarcation and complete separation of family, public, and service rooms, Y Bwthyn Bach relied on a mode of spatial organization that was foreign to Welsh cottages but had been a defining feature of respectable bourgeois homes since the eighteenth century.[39]

If this spatial organization somewhat undermined the cultural value of Y Bwthyn Bach as a window into the rural life of Wales, it was nonetheless centrally important to the project's other important goal: to showcase the quality of the goods and services that respectable bourgeois visitors could procure to outfit and update their own houses. To this end, Y Bwthyn Bach needed to be recognizably modern—comfortable and convenient. Not only was the house plumbed and electrified, but it also was equipped with a wide range of fully functional modern appliances: a refrigerator, cook stove, and washing boiler (all gas powered) in the kitchen; an electric fire and a radio set in the sitting room; and a telephone in the hall. While every effort was made to work with Welsh businesses, the project also revealed the extent to which homeowners interested in the most up-to-date products and materials would have to look beyond the borders of Wales. The Cardiff Gas Light and Coke Company, for instance, "presented" the cottage's miniature gas cooker and gas washing boiler, but both appliances had been manufactured by John Wright and Company, a well-established Birmingham concern. If homeowners wanted brand-name products, they had to go even farther afield. The cottage's gas-operated Freezolux refrigerator was manufactured by Electrolux, a company with central offices in London, while the brand-name paints (Petrumite, Dulux, and Nobel Enamel Paint) all came from Nobel Chemical Finishes Ltd., headquartered in Slough, not far from Windsor.[40]

At times, the desire to display the latest household equipment seems to have taken priority over other considerations. The miniature indicators in the kitchen are a case in point. Wired to doorbells at the front door and the tradesman's entrance (which was just a step away from the indicator) and to call buttons in the sitting room, bedroom, and bathroom, they complicated Princess Elizabeth's relationship to her house. Was she the "busy little Royal Housekeeper" evoked in the souvenir booklet, someone who "with the fine independence of youth, [would] scorn all help and do her own household tasks"? If so, who would summon her to other parts of the house, especially to the bedroom and bathroom, where the unstinting use of her crest made manifest her ownership? Rather than engage that question and imagine the princess in the role of servant, organizers instead noted that "if a lucky maid should serve a royal mistress here," she would be able to respond to the bells with "cheerful speed."[41]

FIGURE 7.7. Interior of stair hall of Y Bwthyn Bach To Gwellt, Royal Lodge, Windsor Great Park, as seen from kitchen. Morgan Willmott, architect, 1931–32. Photograph by the author.

Y BWTHYN BACH AT ROYAL LODGE

Unlike other elite parents, the Duke and Duchess of York had not initiated the idea of providing an extravagant playhouse for the use of their elder daughter. Nonetheless, they embraced the project, not least for the pleasure it would bring Elizabeth and her sister. In April 1932, the royal couple invited Willmott to Windsor to discuss the siting of the cottage at Royal Lodge.[42] In its final location, the cottage fronted its own small-scale garden, where the formality of the straight paths, which intersected at a sundial on axis with the front door, was softened by the irregular placement of trees (see Figure I.1). Set at an angle to the orthogonal lines of the larger site, the cottage also served as the focal point of a picturesque vignette, just visible through the trees to guests arriving at the formal entrance to the main house.

Almost immediately, the Yorks ensured that Y Bwthyn Bach was also visible to a wider audience, using this same photograph of Elizabeth with the cottage in the background for their Christmas card in 1933. Yet, their use of the cottage in the service of their public image took on a new intensity three years later, as a constitutional crisis began brewing over the relationship between the new king, Edward VIII, and Wallis Simpson. During these critical months, the cottage figured prominently in several of the photographs used to illustrate *Our Princesses and Their Dogs*, a slim volume that celebrated the Yorks' devotion to their canine companions and that offered Royal Lodge as evidence that "our British Royalty is most royal in its simplicity."[43] These images were the product of Lisa Sheridan's first photo shoot with members of the royal family; working under the professional name Studio Lisa, she would continue to photograph British royals for the next thirty years, revolutionizing the genre of royal family portraiture by capturing her subjects in intimate and relaxed moments.[44] *Our Princesses and Their Dogs* included several images focused on the princesses, each on her own and together. The frontispiece featured the entire family at the cottage, offering the British public a reassuring glimpse of the Duke of York, now the heir presumptive, as a steady, family-oriented royal, who enjoyed the company of his wife and children. In December 1936, the *Illustrated London News* reported on the movements of the Duke of York in the tense days leading up to the abdication—a hasty return from Scotland, a visit to his mother at Marlborough House, a conference with his brother at Buckingham Palace, and Sunday services at the Royal Chapel in Windsor Great Park during a snowstorm. Although the situation was dire, the story was given an uplifting note by its almost full-page illustration—a colorized version of Sheridan's frontispiece photograph, showing the family of four smiling and bathed in spring sunshine (Figure 7.8).[45] Given that Edward VIII had just the month before toured the part of Wales hardest hit by unemployment and offered comments understood as a tacit critique of Whitehall's inaction in the face of Welsh suffering, the

DEC. 12, 1936 — THE ILLUSTRATED LONDON NEWS — 1047

A ROYAL HOUSEHOLD CLOSELY CONCERNED IN THE CONSTITUTIONAL CRISIS.

FROM A PHOTOGRAPH BY STUDIO LISA IN "OUR PRINCESSES AND THEIR DOGS," BY MICHAEL CHANCE. REPRODUCED BY COURTESY OF THE PUBLISHER, JOHN MURRAY. (SEE REVIEW ON THE OPPOSITE PAGE.)

THE DUKE AND DUCHESS OF YORK WITH THEIR CHILDREN, PRINCESS ELIZABETH (AT THE BACK) AND PRINCESS MARGARET ROSE, AND SOME OF THEIR DOGS: A DELIGHTFULLY INFORMAL GROUP AT PRINCESS ELIZABETH'S MINIATURE HOUSE.

On the death of King George and the accession of King Edward VIII., the Duke of York became Heir Presumptive and first in the order of succession to the Throne, while his two daughters, Princess Elizabeth and Princess Margaret Rose, became respectively second and third. Consequently, the crisis over King Edward's projected marriage affected them very closely. The Duke and Duchess of York, who had returned to London from Scotland, travelling by the night express from Edinburgh to Euston, visited Queen Mary at Marlborough House soon after their arrival on December 3, and later the Duke went to see King Edward at Buckingham Palace. The Duke and Duchess spent the week-end (December 5—7) at their country home, Royal Lodge, Windsor Park. On the Sunday morning, accompanied by their daughters, they walked in a storm of sleet and snow to attend Divine Service at the Royal Chapel. It was in the rose garden of Royal Lodge that the above family group was taken, at the entrance to the miniature house presented by the people of Wales to Princess Elizabeth on her sixth birthday. Over the door is inscribed its Welsh name, Y Bwthyn Bach (The Little House). In a note on one of the other charmingly informal photographs in the same book ("Our Princesses and Their Dogs") the author writes: "Many are the days spent by the dogs in this house as they watch their young mistresses busying themselves with its practical appliances."

FIGURE 7.8. Princess Margaret, Princess Elizabeth, and the Duke and Duchess of York at Y Bwthyn Bach To Gwellt, Royal Lodge, Windsor Great Park. Taken in the spring of 1936, the photograph by Lisa Sheridan of Studio Lisa initially served as the frontispiece of the book *Our Princesses and Their Dogs,* then was reprinted in the *Illustrated London News* in December of that year, just days before the abdication of Edward VIII. *Illustrated London News* / Mary Evans Picture Library.

image may also have been intended as a signal that his brother would not forget "the people of Wales" who had presented his daughter with such a charming gift.[46]

Once the Duke of York ascended to the throne as George VI, a new kind of attention focused on his elder daughter. Eager to present the new heir presumptive as a normal, down-to-earth girl, the palace press office deployed Y Bwthyn Bach as material evidence that Elizabeth took naturally to her assigned gender role and did so without expecting the trappings of state. A case in point is a *Sunday Mirror* story from December 1937 that carried the headline "Princess Elizabeth Is Little Mother in 'Toy' Gift House: Scrubs Floors and Washes Up." According to the story, "Y Bwthyn Bach is the greatest passion of the Princess's life," proving that "no task in the cleaning up is too menial for the heir-presumptive to the throne."[47] Of course, the strategy was not new; Matilda Dodge Wilson had demonstrated its effectiveness in the 1920s. In this context, however, the stakes were considerably higher.

As the cottage took on a special resonance among the royal family's middle-class admirers, manufacturers were prompted to offer a range of Y Bwthyn Bach playthings, allowing British girls to emulate the shining example set by the future queen. Lines Brothers, for instance, produced two versions of a dollhouse fashioned after Y Bwthyn Bach (Figure 7.9). The deluxe model was 47½ inches long and included a garage, while a smaller version was 30 inches long and sold for 56 shillings (the equivalent of almost £230 or $294 in 2024). A less expensive option was a paper cutout version, akin to the paper-doll set of Shirley Temple and her modest play shed issued a few years before. Published by Dean's and priced at just 6 pence, this option made up for its flimsy materials by offering a level of detail not available in the dollhouse. In addition to "disclosing the rooms inside . . . just as they are used by the Princesses," advertisements also called out elements that had featured in published photographs of Elizabeth at her model house, notably the sundial, dolls' pram, and "favourite dogs."[48]

So integral was Y Bwthyn Bach to Elizabeth's public persona that Dean's reissued the cutout book at the time of her marriage in 1947 and again for her coronation in 1953. This later version included a twelve-page booklet in which children's author Arthur Groom provided a lively account that explained the cottage's origins, described its contents, and affirmed Elizabeth's affection for "her very own little house." The text rehearsed the narrative of Elizabeth and her sister as regular little girls who enjoyed keeping house: "how busily the little Princesses bustled around with their washing-up, sweeping, and dusting . . . just like real housewives."[49] In this paper form, Y Bwthyn Bach and its evocation of a fully domesticated Elizabeth traveled easily to all parts of the British Commonwealth. In 1949, the Toronto Branch of the Canadian Junior Red Cross (JRC) mailed a copy to one of their school-based branches, perhaps as a prize or an incentive to participate in a JRC activity.[50] In 1953, when the new

PRINCESS ELIZABETH'S DOLLS' HOUSE
3146
A model of the dolls' house presented to Princess Elizabeth by the Welsh people. Double-fronted, with four rooms, hall, staircase and landing. Opening metal windows. Imitation thatched roof. Four electric lights, less batteries. Front hinged in two parts. Length 30". Height 23¾".

3147
No. 2. (Not illustrated.) Larger model. Four rooms. Five electric lights. Bathroom with dummy bath, kitchen with dummy sink and gas stove. Garage with opening doors. Otherwise similar to No. 1. Length 47½". Height 31½".

FIGURE 7.9. Advertisement for Princess Elizabeth's Dolls' House, produced by Lines Bros. Ltd., 1937. According to the text, the larger model included a garage, which was not a feature of Y Bwthyn Bach To Gwellt at Royal Lodge. Courtesy of Brighton Toy and Model Museum, Brighton, U.K.

queen visited New Zealand, the cutout book with the booklet containing Groom's text was widely available; a copy now in the collections of Te Papa Tongarewa / Museum of New Zealand was purchased that year in Wellington as a Christmas gift for a young girl.[51]

SHIRLEY TEMPLE'S GLASS BLOCK PLAYHOUSE

About the same time Lisa Sheridan was taking photographs of the Yorks at Y Bwthyn Bach in 1936, the Owens-Illinois Glass Company presented Shirley Temple with a glass block playhouse (see Figure 7.1). Substantially more impressive than the modest play shed that had featured in earlier photospreads documenting the young star's supposedly normal childhood (see Figure 6.10), this playhouse was twenty feet long and twelve feet deep, and thus had a footprint comparable to Princess Elizabeth's model house. Its interior arrangements (with a living room, kitchen, and small bedroom area, all arranged on a single floor) were more akin to those of Gloria Lloyd's playhouse. With its six-foot-high ceilings and its distinctly industrial quality, Shirley's playhouse also looked quite different from the consistently reduced-scale and overtly archaic quaintness of the thatched cottages built for Gloria Lloyd and Princess Elizabeth. Nonetheless, the glass block playhouse was ornamented with what *Architectural Forum* described as "a candy pole porch column and murals depicting various story-book characters," suggesting that Owens-Illinois attempted to give the building a childlike atmosphere.[52] Period photographs confirm that the playhouse was fully furnished; they also make it clear that Owens-Illinois did not provide the range of utilitarian and decorative objects that filled Y Bwthyn Bach.

For all their differences, Y Bwthyn Bach and Shirley Temple's glass block playhouse functioned in similar ways. In each case, the playhouse was a strategic move on the part of commercial interests to use the celebrity of its well-known mistress to draw attention to their products or services. In both, the fame of the girl served to enhance the beguiling quality of miniaturization (to paraphrase historian James E. Bryan), even as the reduced scale of the environment augmented the charm of the adorable girl. In both cases, the combination of the small girl and miniature house was calculated to deliver captivating content for visually appealing human-interest stories, which promoted the associated products and services without seeming to advertise them. Indeed, by using her gift, each girl seemed to offer an endorsement of the products and services that had brought her little house into being.

In the case of Shirley Temple's playhouse, the goal was to promote Insulux glass blocks, an innovative material Owens-Illinois had brought to market in 1935. That this "gift" was first and foremost a business decision was acknowledged at the time, with *Architectural Forum* recognizing the company's willingness to embrace innovative advertising trends, including what the unnamed author referred to as "promotion methods customarily used to bolster the sales of cigarettes, cosmetics, and breakfast foods." Despite the periodical's deprecating tone, its story also conceded that the approach had merit, given that "the small cinema star" possessed a "magnetic personality [that had] already helped pull the doll business and other large industries out of the depression."[53]

Nonetheless, the corporate decision to build a small-scale domestic environment seems curious, at least in retrospect, given that glass block soon became one of the go-to materials for updating storefronts in a far-reaching campaign to "modernize Main Street."[54] Perhaps in 1936, however, decision-makers at Owens-Illinois were still persuaded by the economic insights Christine Frederick had articulated in her 1929 book, *Selling Mrs. Consumer*—namely, that the cumulative purchasing power of ordinary families, especially as they built and maintained single-family houses, was the most powerful engine of economic growth. What better way to encourage middle-class parents to embrace glass block for home use than to associate it with a reduced-scale playhouse for a young star? Domesticity, the stuff of childhood, the enhancement of the miniature, and the magic of Hollywood: a small-scale playhouse for Shirley Temple ticked all the boxes. At the same time, the material did not lend itself to the storybook forms that increasingly constituted the visual language of childhood in the 1920s and 1930s. With its column of glass block rising from a circular bench to support one end of the structure's flat roof, Shirley Temple's playhouse instead highlighted the potential for using Insulux blocks to create volumetric forms, an approach to the new material that had been evident in the company's experimental structure at the 1933 Century of Progress Exposition in Chicago.[55]

This innovative marketing strategy depended on making images of Shirley and her playhouse widely available, and Owens-Illinois arranged for at least three photoshoots between 1936 and 1938. The first took place when the playhouse was under construction and resulted in images of the young star interacting with members of the crew and even wielding a mason's trowel (Figure 7.10). These images appeared in a variety of publications, including newspapers, industry journals (such as *American Builder and Building Age*), and fan magazines. In December 1936, *Movie Mirror* published three photographs under the punning title "A Little Glass Temple for Shirley."[56] While the caption highlighted the innovative building material—noting that the glass blocks were translucent, but not transparent—it made no mention of Owens-Illinois's involvement in the project. Images of Shirley using the completed playhouse appeared in the spring of 1937 (she wore a dark cardigan) and again in 1938 (she wore a pale dress trimmed with stripes) around the time of her birthday in late April (Figure 7.11; see Figure 7.1). While these images were published in a wide range of newspapers, the stories that accompanied them tended to focus on Shirley and used

FIGURE 7.10. Shirley Temple and a mason during construction of her glass block playhouse on the grounds of the Temple family home in Brentwood, California, 1936. Courtesy Rita Dubas.

the playhouse in ways that would have been familiar to the British royal family and American social elites: as evidence that she enjoyed housekeeping tasks and had remained unchanged by her success. Few referenced Owens-Illinois or the Insulux trade name.[57] In short, the project may have succeeded in generating general interest in glass block as a building material, but its advertising value for Owens-Illinois is unclear.

Perhaps in an attempt to make up for the somewhat lackluster performance of their innovative marketing strategy, Owens-Illinois officials were persuaded to provide a replica of Shirley Temple's glass block playhouse for Children's World at the New York World's Fair of 1939.[58] The driving force behind the project was Narcissa Cox Vanderlip, a well-to-do and philanthropically inclined woman who served for decades as president of the New York Infirmary for Women and Children.[59] Her idea was to charge a modest admissions fee, with all of the proceeds going to finance the construction of a new hospital. Of course, the strategy was not new and Vanderlip

FIGURE 7.11. Shirley Temple in the bedroom alcove of her glass block playhouse on the grounds of the Temple family home in Brentwood, California, 1938. Courtesy Rita Dubas.

may have been aware of the sums raised by the exhibition of Queen Mary's dolls' house in the 1920s. Whether or not she knew of that example, she would have certainly read in the newspapers about the plans of the New York City Visiting Committee of the State Charities Aid Association to raise funds at the World's Fair through the display of Titania's Palace, a dollhouse owned by Sir Neville Wilkinson and reportedly the inspiration for Queen Mary's dolls' house.[60] In a similar vein, Y Bwthyn Bach had also been displayed to raise funds for hospitals before it was delivered to Royal Lodge. Given that a photo mural of Princess Elizabeth's little thatched house adorned the walls of the exhibition building in which the replica glass block playhouse was displayed at the World's Fair, Mrs. Vanderlip seems to have been well informed about the precedents she was attempting to follow.[61]

As it happened, the project did not enjoy great success, perhaps in part because it was a last-minute addition to Children's World. Although the fair opened officially on 30 April, the director of concessions executed a concession agreement with the New York Infirmary for Women and Children only on 22 May; the playhouse did not open officially until 7 June. Given this timing, it may have been difficult to find a space for the playhouse in a section of the fair that had been in the works for the previous two years. A report issued after the completion of the 1939 season reveals that it was located "on the passageway leading back from an entrance between the donkeys and the fortune tellers" and "very unattractively arranged." According to the assistant director of amusements, who wrote the report, "There was little reason for anyone to be induced to patronize the project."[62] Of course, the overall timing of the fair was an issue as well. After several months at the helm of the operation, Mrs. Vanderlip told a *New York Times* reporter about "the anxiety with which parents inquire the price and reluctantly turn away from the 10-cent or even the Children's Day admission of 5 cents." Her conclusion was that "the whole country is poorer than the economists has [sic] guessed."[63]

To salvage the situation, Vanderlip pursued a range of strategies, some of which exposed her own class assumptions. The dedication, for example, was open to children from a wide range of backgrounds, including 150 children from the Protestant, Jewish, and Catholic orphanages. Yet, the same event was also attended by "a group of society women and their children," with the youngsters assigned to act as "hostesses" to the orphaned children. Photographed by the fair's Public Relations unit, the orphans' visit was intended to advertise the fact that the playhouse could be enjoyed by all, but also inadvertently revealed limits to the site's inclusivity. For one thing, official photographs of this and other special events at the replica playhouse show only white children. For another, by identifying the "society children" as "hostesses," this event framed the well-to-do children as the symbolic owners of the playhouse and gave their attendance at the fair an air of noblesse oblige. In contrast, the orphaned children were cast in the role of neophytes in need of guidance about the deportment demanded in this strange new environment. Official photographs were carefully arranged to confirm that the orphans were adept pupils who had quickly learned the play behaviors expected of them. One image, for instance, showed two girls seated primly, providing tender, motherly care for Shirley Temple dolls, while simultaneously smiling up at a boy at the window; he, in turn, deported himself admirably by doing nothing to disrupt the girls' sedate, feminized play.[64] The youngsters' calm demeanor and girls' grateful smiles helped reassure viewers that these disadvantaged children were worthy recipients of the altruistic efforts made on their behalf.

On other occasions, Vanderlip lured children to the replica playhouse with giveaways. On the day of its dedication, a sign on the exhibition building referred to the structure inside only as "Her Playhouse" and offered a "free lollipop if you guess her name." Later in the season, Vanderlip organized a drawing in which youngsters who had previously paid to visit the playhouse and also signed its guestbook (a class-inflected practice) received autographed baseballs (if boys) and Shirley Temple dolls (if girls). For one official photograph, the caption supplied by the fair's Public Relations unit provided street addresses in Long Island, the Bronx, and Queens for the three pictured recipients.[65] While the caption may have been intended to highlight the fact that youngsters from all parts of the city benefited from the drawing, it also glossed over the racial homogeneity of the event. All the prizewinners pictured were white.

Another photograph taken on the day of the doll giveaway raises questions about how young visitors experienced the playhouse (Figure 7.12). Taken in the kitchen, the image shows both the full-size elements (notably the door and ceiling height) that allowed adults to access the interior, as well as the small-scale furniture and fittings meant to entice youngsters. Low counters, for instance, accommodated a small working sink positioned in front of a window set low in the wall. Yet, none of the small girls pictured seem particularly interested in the small-scale wonders enjoyed by the Hollywood star, focusing instead on the Shirley Temple dolls being doled out by Mrs. Vanderlip. Three of the girls are deeply engrossed in examining their new playthings, while the fourth stands with hands on hips, seemingly unhappy with the toy offered to her; perhaps she had her eye on the bigger doll seated on the chair in the foreground. Despite the differences in their reactions, all four girls demonstrate their expertise as consumers, whether casting an appraising eye over a new acquisition or expressing frustration triggered by the thwarted desire for material goods. In each case, they seem more interested in securing the mass-produced, widely advertised, and lasting things they would be able to carry home with them than they were in savoring the extraordinary, albeit fleeting, enchantment of the miniature house or the chance to imagine themselves as figuratively sharing space with Shirley Temple.

For Movie Stars and Princesses 307

FIGURE 7.12. Kitchen in the replica of Shirley Temple's playhouse at Children's World at the New York World's Fair in 1939. The woman handing out Shirley Temple dolls is Narcissa Cox Vanderlip, president of the New York Infirmary for Women and Children; Vanderlip sponsored the project in hopes of raising funds for the infirmary. Manuscripts and Archives Division, New York Public Library.

By the end of the 1939 season, the replica of Shirley Temple's glass block playhouse had grossed more than $2,400 in admissions and another $65 in sales. Yet, it had cost more than $4,300 to operate, a sum that included attendants' salaries, insurance, and electricity but not the approximately $5,000 it had cost to erect the building. That sum was covered by Mrs. Vanderlip.[66] Although the replica playhouse was displayed again in the 1940 season of the fair, there was no notion that it would serve as a fundraiser. In its new location in the America at Home Building, it was exhibited for free, before being raffled off in October.[67]

Despite its short life, the replica of Shirley Temple's playhouse may well have had a lasting if somewhat indirect impact on the history of the type. Thanks to its inclusion in the 1939 World's Fair, it undoubtedly came to the attention of Frank W. Darling, who served for a time as president and managing director of Children's World, Inc. (officially a concession at the fair). Both before and after his involvement with the fair, he was also the director of Playland, the first municipally run amusement park in the United States. Opened in Rye, New York, in 1928, Playland was conceived by the Westchester County Park Commission as a wholesome alternative to Coney Island, a new kind of park in which an orderly and unified physical environment (designed by architects Walker and Gillette and landscape architect Gilmore D. Clarke) would attract upper-middle-class white families whose presence, the commissioners believed, would enhance the site's respectability and its capacity to moderate working-class behavior.[68]

To attract these genteel patrons, Darling paid particular attention to Kiddyland over the course of the 1930s, transforming what had started out as an uninspiring supervised playground into a lively area featuring smaller versions of rides found elsewhere in the park: Kiddy Coaster, Kiddy Ferris Wheel, Kiddy Carousel, Kiddy Whip, and Junior Fly-A-Plane, among others. Eventually Kiddyland also included a miniature playhouse, designed to evoke the storybook forms that had been popular in the 1920s (Figure 7.13).[69] In that sense, the architecture of the Kiddyland playhouse bore little resemblance to Shirley Temple's glass block play structure. Nonetheless, official photographs of the living room and bedroom show small rooms,

FIGURE 7.13. View of play area at Kiddyland at Playland in Rye, New York. The playhouse is on the right; the octagonal building on the left is a monkey cage. Architect unknown, circa 1940. Courtesy of Westchester County Archives.

reduced-scale fittings, and rectangular windows with sheer white curtains, all elements familiar from the replica playhouse Darling would have seen at the World's Fair. Even more telling are the human figures shown inhabiting these spaces. In the living room, a young white girl wearing a stylish halter dress appraises her appearance in a mirror, inviting viewers to admire her likeness to Shirley Temple, with her blonde hair carefully coiffed into ringlets (Figure 7.14). A different blonde girl in the bedroom mimics the young Hollywood star less overtly but still looks into a mirror and fusses with her hair. Both photographs presented the Kiddyland playhouse as a site where girls—at least, white girls—could imagine themselves as pretty and carefree, just as Shirley Temple always seemed to be.

If the Kiddyland playhouse, like the replica of Shirley Temple's playhouse, was presented as a white space, its association with other forms of social exclusivity was undermined by the sheer number of people who visited the park each year. In 1932, in the midst of the Depression (although admittedly a few years before the playhouse was probably built), annual attendance was more than 3.8 million.[70] Respectable the playhouse may have been, but it could not claim the same sort of social

FIGURE 7.14. Interior of Kiddyland playhouse at Playland in Rye, New York. Architect unknown, circa 1940. Courtesy of Westchester County Archives.

cachet enjoyed by, say, the Whitney playhouse on the grounds of the Greentree estate, located just thirty miles away in Manhasset, on Long Island (see Figure 4.15). No longer the sole purview of patrician families, habitable playhouses had been transformed—gradually, but fully—into objects of everyday life for a wide swath of the American public.

Elite playhouses have often been dismissed as beguiling little buildings with negligible connections to the adult sphere. Indeed, structures such as Y Bwthyn Bach were typically designed to convince viewers they were nothing more than places for cherished (or, perhaps, cossetted) children to escape into a world of their own. Yet, despite their relatively small size, these buildings were typically well-built and weathertight buildings, designed by professional architects, furnished with care, and often plumbed and electrified as well. Equally important, these buildings were never isolated from adult concerns. They contributed in important ways to the functioning of the country estates on which they stood, often allowing the main house to retain its character as a site devoted to adult sociability. At the same time, luxurious playhouses were also central to the ambitions of the parents who devoted time, energy, and financial resources to bring them into being.

These parental aspirations were distinctly dynastic for British royals and American aristocrats. They built cottages, at least in part, to control their children, minimizing opportunities for their offspring to form damaging social connections and thus preserving their potential for making marriage alliances advantageous to the family's social standing. These cottages, too, helped elite children take their privileges for granted, by providing them a space in which they were nominally in control, especially over the adults employed by their parents. Equally important was the fact that cottages helped frame domestic tasks as a form of recreation, an optional activity that elite youngsters could enjoy, secure in the knowledge that (unlike the adults who served them) they would never be required to undertake such chores, if they preferred not to do so.

The cottages were also integral to the efforts of elite parents to craft their own public presentations of self. Being seen as a caring parent resonated across the social spectrum and was perhaps especially important for Queen Victoria and her descendants, who were eager to demonstrate that they embraced familial values their middle-class subjects claimed as their own. In the American context, children's playhouses became important in this regard in the twentieth century, initially as a means for social elites who had inherited vast fortunes to signal their appropriate relationship to wealth, as well as their attentiveness to the science of child study, with its emphasis on the importance of children's play. Later, and particularly in the wake of the Red Scare, a new kind of playhouse—one that mimicked a complete middle-class house in miniature form—allowed newly rich industrialists to spend lavishly, while simultaneously acknowledging their modest backgrounds and also signaling their commitment to raising daughters who embraced conventional gender roles, even if they themselves did not.

By the 1920s, celebrities in the burgeoning entertainment industry began to build impressive playhouses for the use of their children. While they could spend lavishly, they were not focused on the sorts of dynastic concerns that motivated social elites. Less worried about protecting the main house from youthful boisterousness, they nonetheless readily embraced the public relations potential of charming playhouses. Such miniature structures helped movie stars present themselves to their audiences as devoted parents, while simultaneously confirming that they lived happy, carefree lives of leisure. In the process, sumptuous playhouses came within the reach of adoring fans, even if only in their daydreams, as they lived vicariously through their movie idols.

The 1930s saw important changes in the form and meaning of lavish playhouses. The decade opened with plans to create a small-scale, habitable house for a royal princess, a girl poised at the very apex of the social ladder. Within ten years, such habitable playhouses had become fixtures in landscapes that were imagined as democratic, although they were typically more welcoming to white users. Arguably, such playhouses still stood on the boundary that separated social elites from everyone else, but instead of policing that border as they had once done, they increasingly breached and blurred it.

Even Y Bwthyn Bach inhabited this liminal zone. If considered as an artifact of a specifically royal childhood, the model house might be considered a direct descendant of the Swiss Cottage at Osborne, just as Princess Elizabeth descended in a direct line from Bertie, the young Prince of Wales, who had in 1853 laid the first stone of the building where he and his siblings would eventually cook, take tea, and display shells collected on the nearby beach. Yet, the Swiss Cottage was not a miniature house, and the domestic activities the royal children pursued there were unconnected to the world of make-believe. When Bertie and his siblings enjoyed the simple meals they themselves had cooked, they did just that, without pretending to be anything. They were what they were: privileged royal youngsters relishing an opportunity to escape the formalities of court life.

In contrast, Y Bwthyn Bach was fully embedded in twentieth-century practices that were largely disconnected from royal existence. In its form, it was directly comparable to the miniature houses presented as birthday gifts to the young heiresses of American automobile fortunes. Like those playhouses, Y Bwthyn Bach pretended to be a middle-class house, complete with a bedroom and a full bath. Like those playhouses, it also offered Princess Elizabeth precisely the same play script extended to Josephine Ford and Frances Dodge—namely, to make believe that she was a grown woman, mistress of her own home and mother to her dolls. In the way it was regularly and self-consciously pushed into the public eye, Y Bwthyn Bach was also akin to playhouses built by celebrities in the entertainment business, providing material proof that the young recipients' fathers were home-loving family men. Finally, in its origin, Y Bwthyn Bach was even more like Shirley Temple's glass block playhouse—a clever ploy to draw attention to a particular sector of the construction industry. At least when using her model house, then, Princess Elizabeth was closer to the Hollywood star than she was to her royal predecessors. By the end of the 1930s, neither the Princess of York nor "America's princess" could count on their habitable playhouses to set them apart from the countless little girls at play in Kiddyland.

From 1853 to 1936, a relatively small number of adults expended a good deal of time, energy, and expense in order to provide their children with splendid cottages and playhouses. While their particular forms varied, these relatively small buildings were typically designed to suggest that they were integral to providing their young users with a good childhood, cocooning them in a playful, carefree, innocent realm untouched by adult concerns. Yet nothing could be further from the truth. Initially understood as integral to the reproduction of class privilege, these cottages and playhouses eventually made their way down the social register, providing fodder for fan magazines, where they became objects of desire for middle-class moviegoers (and others). Even as these buildings lost much of their power as tools of elite culture, they were nonetheless always carefully considered architectural manifestations of adult concerns.

Acknowledgments

This project is the work of many years, having been started in July 2006, when I thought (naively, as it turns out) that a single summer would be sufficient time to conduct archival research on the children's cottage at the Breakers, the Newport mansion of Cornelius and Alice Vanderbilt. In the end, that research required several years and was not published in article form until 2011. By that time, I had taken on a full-time administrative role at Connecticut College, work that was enormously satisfying in many respects but also limited the time I could devote to primary research. Once I completed a term as Dean of the Faculty in June 2018, I returned to the project with enthusiasm, conducting both site visits and archival research for the next eighteen months. I am grateful to Connecticut College for providing me with a yearlong sabbatical in 2018–19 and with regular research funding throughout my tenure as Dayton Professor of Art History. I am also deeply appreciative of the Fulbright Scholar award that supported my research at Osborne on the Isle of Wight and offered me an intellectually stimulating institutional base at the University of York in the fall of 2019.

On my return to the United States, full-time retirement gave me plenty of time in which to work, but almost immediately the Covid pandemic complicated subsequent research. This was true for most scholars, of course, but particularly so for those of us who rely heavily on a firsthand examination of the built environment. Although progress was slow, many librarians, archivists, and fellow scholars were open to remote inquiries and generous with their time and expertise. Eventually, I was able to take advantage of in-person visits, as archives and sites began to reopen. I felt fortunate to be able to submit a full manuscript for peer review in June 2022.

Given that timeline, I find myself more deeply indebted to a wider range of individuals than with any other research endeavor I have previously undertaken. Chief among them are the curators, site managers, and other stewards of the buildings at the heart of this study. John Tschirch and Janice Wiseman of the Preservation Society of Newport County provided unfettered access to the children's cottage at the Breakers and to the society's files. At the Edsel and Eleanor Ford House, Julie Cook was an engaging and knowledgeable guide, and both she and Lisa Worley responded readily to my many follow-up questions. At Meadow Brook Hall, Madelyn Chrapla was unstinting with her assistance, both during the multiple days that I was on site and afterward. Michael Hunter was equally generous with his time and expertise, welcoming me to Osborne, orienting me to the estate and its complicated history, and giving me access to the many reports produced under the aegis of English Heritage, including his own careful study of changing room uses. Lorraine Gilligan enriched my visit to Old Westbury Gardens by sharing everything in her files, including the Phipps family's home movies. Andrea Crivello of the Planting Fields Foundation served as a ready guide to Coe Hall. At the Frick Pittsburgh, Dawn Brean and Kim Cady went out of their way to give me access to every inch of the playhouse, despite its current use as staff offices. Beth Hill was equally welcoming at Fort Ticonderoga; only the deteriorated state of the playhouse restricted my access. I was fortunate to participate in a behind-the-scenes tour of the third floor at the Breakers, organized by Leslie Jones, curator and director of museum affairs for the Preservation Society of Newport County, and Jason Bouchard, archivist for members of the Vanderbilt family. Nigel Manley, of the Forest Society, shared his deep understanding of the former Glessner estate in Bethlehem, New Hampshire, during a time when construction closed the site to the public. Facilitating my visits to sites that are not usually open to the public were Nicole Ward, who hosted my visit to the Greentree estate, and Jarron Jewell, who arranged my tour of the playhouse on the Post Campus of Long Island University.

    I am grateful for the assistance of those with family connections to some of these playhouses. Flora Biddle and Pam Le Boutillier gave me access to their mother's girlhood diaries and shared their memories of the Breakers cottage. Lila Berle spoke with me at length of her memories of the second playhouse at Highlawn in Lenox, Massachusetts. Barry Sears organized a pleasant visit to Kenilworth, Illinois, to see a log cabin that both he and his father before him had used as boys. Robin Culbertson shared what she knew about how the 1909 playhouse built by Frank Lowden and Florence Pullman Lowden had been used since the 1950s.

    The librarians, archivists, and curators who were integral to my research are too many to name and in some cases never identified themselves to me; they simply assisted me as part their professional responsibilities. I am grateful to them all. I also express my gratitude to the library staff at Connecticut College, who figured out how to get library materials into the hands of readers during the depths of the pandemic, when the library was closed. Emily Aylward and Lisa Dowhan deserve special thanks for maintaining an exceptional interlibrary loan service, and I will forever be indebted to Kathy Gehring for ensuring that I had online access to Queen Victoria's journals.

Farther afield, I am deeply appreciative of the assistance I received from the staff of the Royal Collection Trust (RCT). Sally Goodsir was particularly helpful in giving me a much-needed primer about the various entities responsible for royal palaces. I am also obliged for her persistence in securing permission for me to visit Y Bwthyn Bach, which is not normally accessible to the public. I am also grateful for the help I received from others at the RCT: Catlin Langford, who helped coordinate my visits to the Royal Archives, Photographs Collection and the Print Room at Windsor Castle; Carly Collier, who facilitated my use of prints and drawings; Helen Trompeteler, who gave me access to her research on Disdéri's *Osborne Album*; and Lucy Peter, who shared what she had learned of children's spaces at Buckingham Palace while preparing *Queen Victoria's Palace*, an exhibition for the palace's 2019 summer opening. I am equally obliged to Claudia Williams of Historic Royal Palaces for giving me an individual tour of *Victoria: A Royal Childhood*, an installation she curated at Kensington Palace.

In the United States, my in-person archival research was facilitated by Lisa Long at the Redwood Library; Kimberly Tomey at the Newport Historical Society; Susan Kriete at the New-York Historical Society; Janice Chadbourne and Ceil Gardner at the Boston Public Library; Susan Lewis at the Boston Architectural College; Emily Guthrie at the Winterthur Library; Pamela Casey and Mathieu Pomerleau at the Avery Drawings and Archives at Columbia University; Christine Weideman and Stephen Ross in Manuscripts and Archives at the Sterling Library at Yale University; and Tal Nadan and the rest of the team at the Brooke Russell Astor Reading Room for Rare Books and Manuscripts at the New York Public Library. During the pandemic, I was fortunate that many archivists and volunteers at local historical societies were willing to provide remote assistance, including Patrick Raferty at the Westchester County Historical Society; Jackie Graziano at the Westchester County Archives; Natalie Barry at the Hastings (New York) Historical Society; Bill Jeffway at the Dutchess County (New York) Historical Society; Felicity Frisch at the University of California, San Diego's Art, Design, and Architecture Museum; and Phil Savenick at the Beverly Hills Historical Society. I am equally grateful to Sara Beth Mouch, at the Ward M. Canaday Center for Special Collections at the University of Toledo's William S. Carlson Library, who consulted the Owens-Illinois Glass Company corporate records on my behalf; and to Benjamin Diego, who served as my able research assistant for collections housed in Hanna Holborn Gray Special Collections Center at the University of Chicago and at the Chicago History Museum. Bill Tyre, executive director of the Glessner House, has been a friend of this project in multiple ways:

sharing his knowledge of all things Glessner; providing access to family papers, period photographs, and pieces of furniture designed for Fanny Glessner's log playhouse; alerting to me to the existence of the Lowden and Sears playhouses; and putting me in touch with family members who knew both sites well.

My research was also enhanced by many people who shared with me the fruits of their own careful research. David Silverman, David Picasso, Melissa Tonnessen, and Rita Dubas gave me access to their extensive collections of Shirley Temple materials, while Ken Mensing and David Byars were equally generous with their holdings on Deen-Wee and Foxhollow Farm, respectively. Keith Morgan replied to my questions about Charles Platt's work at the Manor, while Anne Walker offered similar assistance on the work of Harrie T. Lindeberg, architect of Foxhollow Farm. Cornelia Gilder brainstormed with me about where to look for children's cottages in the Lenox area, as did Gary Lawrence for estates in the Hamptons. Sue Wilson was a knowledgeable correspondent on the Swiss Cottage phenomenon in Georgian Britain. Mimi Hellman fielded my questions about furniture history and alerted me to the scholarship of Dena Goodman, who, in turn, provided PDFs of her work when libraries were closed during the pandemic. Laura Jenkins shared her innovative work on Vanderbilt houses in New York. Sarah Glassford offered useful guidance for exploring the activities of the Canadian Red Cross, while Kara Schlichting alerted me to key aspects of the history of Playland. Oriel Prizeman and Chris Williams both supplied welcome advice on sources about early twentieth-century Wales.

With a good deal of serendipity, my Fulbright award brought me to the U.K. during the bicentennial year of Victoria and Albert's births, an occasion that prompted not just the theme of the Buckingham Palace summer opening but also a valuable international conference, "Victoria and Albert at Osborne," sponsored by English Heritage. Organized by Andrew Hann, the conference introduced me to a cadre of scholars whose expertise was integral to my understanding of the Swiss Cottage. Among them were Annie Gray, an expert on food history who has a deep knowledge of the cooking undertaken by the royal children; John Davis, who enhanced my understanding of Albert's intellectual life; Rosemary Yallop, who shared her insights into the Italianate style in Britain; and Michael Turner, who knows more about the architecture of the Osborne estate than anyone and was generous enough to engage in a lengthy email discussion about how we might understand an 1856 plan of the first floor at the Swiss Cottage there (he may not agree with my interpretation, but I know I benefited from seeing the plan through his eyes).

I am grateful for opportunities to present research in progress at a number of venues, including conferences organized by the Society for the History of Childhood and Youth (Norrköping, Sweden, 2007) and New England Chapter of the Vernacular Architecture Forum (Sturbridge, Massachusetts, 2009); at both events, colleagues offered important feedback on my interpretation of the children's cottage at the Breakers. My thinking about the Swiss Cottage has benefited from discussions that followed two presentations in 2019. The first was in the History of Art Research Seminar Series at the University of York, attended by colleagues who welcomed me so warmly into the department, including chair Michael White; my fellow Fulbrighter Amy Werbel; and especially Helen Hills, who nipped in the bud my initial instinct to write a separate book about the spaces that Victoria and Albert provided for their children. The second presentation was part of The English Country House symposium, cosponsored by the Birkbeck Eighteenth-Century Research Group and the Architecture Space and Society Research Centre at Birkbeck College in London. I am especially grateful to Leslie Topp for suggesting this event and for introducing me to Kate Retford, whose work on family portraiture was a revelation.

A very special thanks goes to those colleagues who read parts of the book in draft form and offered valuable feedback. Chief among them are my fellow Uptonians Annmarie Adams, Swati Chattopadhyay, and especially Marta Gutman. Kate Solomonson also deserves special mention, as she has been a trusted thought-partner on this project and others for many years. All of them inspire me by the example of their own fine scholarship, while also offering pointed commentary that challenges me to produce my very best work. Kate Retford shared a number of ways in which George III set important precedents for Victoria in her role as monarch-as-parent and saved me from the erroneous assumption that these practices were inventions of the nineteenth century. Rachel Delman's fascinating scholarship on the spaces of late medieval British queens gave her unique insights into my project; I will be forever grateful that she urged me to think more seriously about what role the Swiss desk may have played in the lives of the royal children. Rosemary Yallop proved a wonderful sounding board for a range of themes, chief among them the transformation of British education in the nineteenth century and how we understand the term *middle class* in a British context. Elizabeth Narkin's reading of my Osborne chapters opened a productive discussion about the role of pastoral play for royal children in France and Britain. Laura Jenkins reminded me to articulate an insight so central to my work that I often leave it unspoken—namely, that the architecture of childhood is never solely about children.

As I prepared my work for publication, Tom Hubka and Jamie Jacobs helped me think about the book's art program, while Dan De Sousa cheerfully took on the monumental task of producing plans to a consistent scale. Indeed, Dan measured and drew the children's cottage at the Breakers back in 2007, when he was an undergraduate at Connecticut College. I am enormously grateful that, now a seasoned professional, he was willing to help bring the project to completion several years later.

I am indebted to the team at the University of Minnesota Press, especially senior editor Pieter Martin, who offered sound advice on the structure of the book at a critical, early moment. He oversaw the long process of transforming the manuscript into a finished book, including finding two astute readers willing to lend expertise to the almost-final product and to offer constructive advice for improvement.

On a personal note, it is a pleasure to acknowledge the love and support of the many friends who helped the project along, in ways both direct and oblique. Marta Gutman and Gene Sparling hosted me on a number of research trips to New York, as did Mike Waters and Emily Morash. Christine Conklin and Jay Kistler warmly welcomed me to their house in the Berkshires, while Chris also facilitated key introductions to those with a deep knowledge of the Lenox area. Barry Kernfeld was patient when Sally McMurry let me try out my nascent ideas on her. Lisa Wilson was equally attentive during weekly Zoom dates that we initiated during the long months of the pandemic. Before and after the shutdown, she and Dave Kanen regularly provided the food, wine, and laughter that were integral to the success of the project. Brenda and Dave Verdolino played a remarkably similar role. Indeed, Brenda has been my stalwart supporter and my partner in crime since the late 1970s, when we shared a library carrel at Smith College. As always, my biggest thanks go to Mitch Favreau, my beloved and my mainstay.

Notes

INTRODUCTION

1. Although *Peter Pan* was published in 1904, the term *Wendy house* in reference to a child's playhouse first appeared in print in 1949. "Wendy house, n.," OED Online, December 2022, Oxford University Press. https://www.oed.com/view/Entry/227809 (accessed 13 February 2023).

2. Clair Price, "'Most Important Little Girl in the World': Elizabeth, Queen of English Childhood, Prepares for the Day When She May Become Queen of the Greatest Empire," *New York Times*, 20 December 1936, SM6.

3. Michèle Lamont and Annette Lareau, "Cultural Capital: Allusions, Gaps and Glissandos in Recent Theoretical Developments," *Sociological Theory* 6 (Fall 1988), 159.

4. Nicola Beisel, *Imperiled Innocents: Anthony Comstock and Family Reproduction in Victorian America* (Princeton, N.J.: Princeton University Press, 1997), 8.

5. Mary Suzanne Schriber, *Writing Home: American Women Abroad, 1830–1920* (Charlottesville: University of Virginia Press, 1997), quoted in Maureen E. Montgomery, "'Natural Distinction': The American Bourgeois Search for Distinctive Signs in Europe," in *The American Bourgeoisie: Distinction and Identity in the Nineteenth Century*, ed. Sven Beckert and Julia B. Rosenbaum (New York: Palgrave Macmillan, 2010), 35.

6. Sven Beckert, *The Monied Metropolis: New York City and the Consolidation of the American Bourgeoisie, 1850–1896* (Cambridge: Cambridge University Press, 2001), 2 and 6–9.

7. Frederic Cople Jaher, *The Urban Establishment: Upper Strata in Boston, New York, Charleston, Chicago, and Los Angeles* (Urbana: University of Illinois Press, 1982), 2–3.

8. Clifton Hood, *In Pursuit of Privilege: A History of New York City's Upper Class and the Making of a Metropolis* (New York: Columbia University Press, 2017), xi–xii.

9. Marta Gutman and Ning de Coninck-Smith, "Good to Think with—History, Space, and Modern Childhood," in *Designing Modern Childhoods: History, Space, and the Material Culture of Children*, ed. Marta Gutman and Ning de Coninck-Smith (New Brunswick, N.J.: Rutgers University Press, 2008), 3–4.

10. Karen Sánchez-Eppler, *Dependent States: The Child's Part in Nineteenth-Century American Culture* (Chicago: University of Chicago Press, 2005), xviii.

11. Beisel, *Imperiled Innocents*, 19.

12. My understanding of Bourdieu's framing of cultural capital has benefited from Lamont and Lareau, "Cultural Capital," 153–68.

13. Beisel, *Imperiled Innocents*, 20.

14. B. H. Friedman, *Gertrude Vanderbilt Whitney* (Garden City, N.Y.: Doubleday, 1978), 14–17.

15. Steven Watts, *The People's Tycoon: Henry Ford and the American Century* (New York: Alfred A. Knopf, 2005), 362–63.

16. Hood, *In Pursuit of Privilege*, 25–27.

17. John Archer, *The Literature of British Domestic Architecture, 1715–1842* (Cambridge, Mass.: MIT Press, 1985), 59 and 68; see also Amy F. Ogata, *Art Nouveau and the Social Vision of Modern Living: Belgian Artists in a European Context* (Cambridge: Cambridge University Press, 2001), 67–68; Daniel Maudlin, *The Idea of the Cottage in English Architecture, 1760–1860* (London: Routledge, 2015), especially chapters 7 and 8.

18. Ogata, *Art Nouveau*, 76–77.

19. Abigail A. Van Slyck, *A Manufactured Wilderness: Summer Camps and the Shaping of American Youth, 1890–1960* (Minneapolis: University of Minnesota Press, 2006), 8–9. See also Gail Bederman, *Manliness and Civilization: A Cultural History of Gender and Race in the United States, 1880–1917* (Chicago: University of Chicago Press, 1995), chapter 3; and Dorothy Ross, *G. Stanley Hall: The Psychologist as Prophet* (Chicago: University of Chicago Press, 1972).

20. The Historic American Building Survey has documented a number of homemade playhouses, some of which featured ornate exteriors that imitated the main house or other buildings on a given property. These include a playhouse on the Stafford Plantation in Saint Marys, Georgia (ca. 1820); a playhouse-cum-dovecote at the Angelina Plantation near Mount Airy, Louisiana (probably from the 1830s); the Handwerker playhouse in Memphis, Tennessee (1890s); the playhouse at the Peleg Brown Ranch, near Reno, Nevada (ca. 1900); the playhouse on the former Joyce estate in Grand Rapids, Minnesota (ca. 1927, now part of the Chippewa National Forest); and a playhouse at the Borough House Plantation in Stateburg, South Carolina (ca. 1927). I am grateful to Catherine Lavoie for drawing my attention to these buildings. I am obliged to Andrew Dolkart for sharing his images of the Houseman playhouse in Austerlitz, New York (1875, originally located in Chatham, New York) and the so-called Dietz Doll House in Seguin, Texas (1910); and to Bill Tyre for alerting me to the playhouse at the Park–McCullough house in North Bennington, Vermont (ca. 1880s?; https://www.parkmccullough.org). Another nineteenth-century example, this one attributed to architect Lucas Pfeiffenberger, is the Haskell playhouse in Alton, Illinois (1885). Ruth Means and P. H. Poehner, "Haskell Playhouse," National Register of Historic Places Inventory Nomination Form, surveyed 1967. Charles Dana Gibson also built a children's house for his grandchildren on 700 Acre Island off Islesboro, Maine (ca. 1920s; photograph in the collection of the Maine Historical Society). A playhouse built for the granddaughter of John Philip Sousa (a child born ca. 1926) stands in Sands Point, New York, on Long Island. In Centerville, Massachusetts, on Cape Cod, there is a playhouse commissioned by Mrs. Daniel H. Hamilton in the early 1920s; originally designed with three rooms (playroom, studio, and theater), it is now a single-family home. Thomas

Hunt, "A Playhouse and Study Designed by Mr. and Mrs. Thomas Hunt for the Children of Mrs. Daniel H. Hamilton, Centerville, Cape Cod, Massachusetts," *Architectural Record* 51 (May 1922), 521–28.

1. RAISING ROYALS IN AN AGE OF SENTIMENT

1. Margaret Homans, *Royal Representations: Queen Victoria and British Culture, 1837–1876* (Chicago: University of Chicago Press, 1998), 43–57.

2. The addition of the Durbar Wing in 1890–91 brought greater balance to the composition. While it is notable for a state reception room with remarkable Indian-style fittings designed by Lockwood Kipling (father of the author) and elaborate plasterwork created from wooden molds designed and carved by Bhai Ram Singh of the Lahore School of Art, it played no role in the lives of the royal offspring when they were still themselves youngsters and so will not feature in the analysis of the site that follows.

3. Peel's role and the property negotiations are laid out in Tyler Whittle, *Victoria and Albert at Home* (London: Routledge & Kegan Paul, 1980), 6–12.

4. Quoted in Michael Turner, *Osborne*, revised reprint (London: English Heritage, 2016), 37.

5. Whittle, *At Home*, 6–15; Turner, *Osborne*, 37–39.

6. Gill Perry, Kate Retford, and Jordan Vibert, with Hannah Lyons, eds., *Placing Faces: The Portrait and the English Country House in the Long Eighteenth Century* (Manchester: Manchester University Press, 2013), 12.

7. Perry et al., *Placing Faces*, 3.

8. The sale of the Royal Pavilion to the town of Brighton was completed in 1850. Amanda Foreman and Lucy Peter, *Queen Victoria's Buckingham Palace* (London: Royal Collection Trust, 2019), 43.

9. Jonathan Marsden, ed., *Victoria & Albert: Art & Love* (London: Royal Collection Publications, 2010), 83 and 91.

10. Letter to King Leopold I of the Belgians, dated 25 March 1845, quoted in Marsden, *Art & Love*, 22.

11. Leonore Davidoff, *Thicker than Water: Siblings and Their Relations, 1780–1920* (Oxford: Oxford University Press, 2021), 79–85.

12. Biographies of Victoria's children are numerous and include Hannah Pakula, *An Uncommon Woman: The Empress Frederick, Daughter of Queen Victoria, Wife of the Crown Prince of Prussia, Mother of Kaiser Wilhelm* (New York: Simon & Schuster, 1995); Miranda Carter, *The Three Emperors: Three Cousins, Three Empires and the Road to World War One* (London: Fig Tree/Penguin, 2009); Jane Ridley, *Bertie: A Life of Edward VII* (London: Chatto & Windus, 2012); David Duff, *Hessian Tapestry: The Hesse Family and British Royalty* (Newton Abbot, U.K., North Pomfret, Vt.: David and Charles, 1979); Jon Van der Kiste and Bee Jordan, *Dearest Affie: Alfred, Duke of Edinburgh, Queen Victoria's Second Son, 1844–1900* (Stroud, Gloucestershire: Sutton, 1984); Seweryn Chomet, *Helena: Princess Reclaimed; The Life and Times of Queen Victoria's Third Daughter* (New York: Begell House, 2000); Jehanne Wake, *Princess Louise: Queen Victoria's Unconventional Daughter* (London: Collins, 1988); Noble Frankland, *Witness of a Century: The Life and Times of Prince Arthur Duke of Connaught, 1850–1942* (London: Shepheard-Walwyn, 1993); Charlotte Zeepvat, *Prince Leopold: The Untold Story of*

Queen Victoria's Youngest Son (Stroud, Gloucestershire: Sutton, 1998); and Matthew Dennison, *The Last Princess: The Devoted Life of Queen Victoria's Youngest Daughter* (London: Weidenfeld & Nicolson, 2007). Collective biographies include Daphne Bennett, *Queen Victoria's Children* (New York: St. Martin's Press, 1980); John Van der Kiste, *Queen Victoria's Children* (Stroud, Gloucestershire: Sutton, 1986); and Jerrold M. Packard, *Victoria's Daughters* (New York: St. Martin's Griffin, 1998).

13. Ariès's claim that this understanding of childhood had started to emerge in the seventeenth century has been disputed by subsequent scholars, some of whom have also critiqued what Kate Retford has characterized as his tendency to draw "an overly simplistic and direct link between pictures and society" (397) and to interpret the absence of images of children in the medieval period as evidence that childhood was unknown. Kate Retford, "Philippe Ariès's 'Discovery of Childhood': Imagery and Historical Evidence," *Continuity and Change* 31:3 (2016), 391–418. Nonetheless, *Centuries of Childhood*, first published in French in 1960, remains a touchstone in the history of childhood, both for encouraging scholars to take the history of childhood seriously and also for exploring various methods for examining historically variable attitudes toward children. Philippe Ariès, *Centuries of Childhood: A Social History of Family Life*, trans. Robert Baldick (New York: Vintage Books, 1962).

14. Ariès, *Centuries of Childhood*, 400.

15. Marta Gutman and Ning de Coninck-Smith, "Introduction: Good to Think with—History, Space, and Modern Childhood," in *Designing Modern Childhoods: History, Space, and the Material Culture of Childhood*, ed. Marta Gutman and Ning de Coninck-Smith (New Brunswick, N.J.: Rutgers University Press, 2008), 3.

16. Johan Zoffany is the artist most closely associated with these images of George III's family. Simon Schama, "The Domestication of Majesty: Royal Family Portraiture, 1500–1850," *Journal of Interdisciplinary History* 17:1 (Summer 1986), 170–73.

17. Schama, "Domestication of Majesty," 157.

18. Schama, "Domestication of Majesty," 157.

19. Kate Retford, *The Art of Domestic Life: Family Portraiture in Eighteenth-Century England* (New Haven, Conn.: Yale University Press, 2006), 209.

20. Given that Victoria was the product of this race among the sons of George III to produce a legitimate heir, the competition is part of every biography of Victoria and is detailed in A. N. Wilson, *Victoria: A Life* (New York: Penguin Books, 2014), 23–30. Victoria's girlhood at Kensington Palace is examined in Lynne Vallone, *Becoming Victoria* (New Haven, Conn.: Yale University Press, 2001).

21. RA VIC/MAIN/M/12/14. This and other documents in the Royal Archives are used with the permission of His Majesty King Charles III.

22. In *A Vindication of the Rights of Women*, Wollstonecraft argued that "the wife . . . who is faithful to her husband, and neither suckles nor educates her children, scarcely deserves the name of wife and has no right to that of a citizen." Quoted in Sandrine Bergès, *The Routledge Guidebook to Wollstonecraft's "A Vindication of the Rights of Woman"* (London and New York: Routledge, 2013), 152. Yet, as Bergès points out, "Wollstonecraft is not merely giving an instrumental argument for educating women—she is not saying that unless we teach her a little morals and politics, a woman will not educate her sons properly. . . . She is saying that the progress of

humanity as a whole will be halted unless it concerns the whole of humanity, be it women or not who are excluded." Bergès, *Guidebook to Wollstonecraft*, 24.

23. RA VIC/MAIN/M/12/14.

24. Robert Filmer, *Patriarcha: or the Natural Power of Kings* (London: Richard Chiswell, 1680), 12. https://oll.libertyfund.org/titles/221, accessed 11 November 2020. For the impact on the concept of Adamic descent on royal portraiture in the early modern period, see Schama, "Domestication of Majesty," esp. 163–64.

25. For an extended comparison of Elizabeth and Anne and their attempt to deploy symbolic maternity, see Toni Bowers, *The Politics of Motherhood: British Writing and Culture, 1680–1760* (Cambridge: Cambridge University Press, 1996), 65–74.

26. Bowers, *Politics of Motherhood*, 42.

27. Homans, *Royal Representations*, 9.

28. Homans, *Royal Representations*, 19.

29. Homans, *Royal Representations*, 2.

30. Homans, *Royal Representations*, 2.

31. Although she does not analyze the images directly, literary scholar Elizabeth Langland argues that "early portraiture of Victoria cast her as a mother—of a nation, of a family, of a nation as family." Elizabeth Langland, "Nation and Nationality: Queen Victoria in the Developing Narrative of Englishness," in *Remaking Queen Victoria*, ed. Margaret Homans and Adrienne Munich (Cambridge: Cambridge University Press, 1997), 23. Other scholars have noted that her maternal image survived her own childbearing years. By the time of her jubilees in 1887 and 1897, Victoria was celebrated as an ideal wife and mother, so much so that child rescue activists sought to attract charitable donations by claiming "a natural affinity" between the queen and their cause. Shurlee Swain, "A Motherly Concern for Children: Invocations of Queen Victoria in Child Rescue Literature," in *Children, Childhood and Youth in the British World*, ed. Shirleene Robinson and Simon Sleight (Basingstoke: Palgrave Macmillan, 2016), 27–40 (quoted passage appears on 29).

32. Norbert Elias, *The Court Society*, trans. Edmund Jephcott (Oxford: Basil Blackwell, 1983), 50.

33. Freya Gowrley, *Domestic Space in Britain, 1750–1840: Materiality, Sociability and Emotion* (London: Bloomsbury Visual Arts, 2022), 2.

34. Leonore Davidoff points out that siblings in "long families" often fell into clusters, depending on their spacing and gender, and that the youngest might be treated almost as an only child. The thematic groupings of Thornycroft's portraits suggest the composition of these clusters among the royal offspring and the special place Beatrice (tellingly known as "Baby") occupied in this family structure. Davidoff, *Thicker than Water*, 88–91.

35. For the dates and occasions on which the marble originals were bestowed as gifts, see Marsden, *Art & Love*, 457–59. According to the Royal Collections Trust website, both plaster and parian ware versions of the set are displayed at Frogmore House, while a bronze version of Louise as "Plenty" is at Buckingham Palace (https://www.rct.uk/collection/search#/30/collection/53090/albert-edward-prince-of-wales-1841-1910-as-winter, accessed 15 January 2021; https://www.rct.uk/collection/search#/9/collection/53206/princess-alice-1843-1878-as

-spring, accessed 15 January 2021; https://www.rct.uk/collection/search#/41/collection/2171/princess-louise-1848-1939-as-plenty, accessed 15 January 2021).

36. Victoria's role in commissioning the sailor suit is recorded on the Royal Collection Trust website: https://www.rct.uk/collection/themes/trails/royal-travel/king-edward-vii-1841-1910-when-albert-edward-prince-of-wales.

37. Susanne Groom and Lee Prosser, *Kew Palace: The Official Illustrated History* (London: Historic Royal Palaces, in association with Merrell Publishers, 2006), 74.

38. Richard Ormond and Carol Blackett-Ord, *Franz Xaver Winterhalter and the Courts of Europe, 1830–70* (London: National Portrait Gallery, 1988), 41.

39. One of the Staffordshire Pottery's earthenware figurines is in the collections of the National Trust at Attingham Park in Shropshire.

40. I am grateful to Kate Retford for alerting me to the biscuit porcelain figures based on Zoffany's portrait. A group of the four eldest sons is held in the Royal Collections, RCIN 37021.

41. Clare Rose, "What Was Uniform about the Fin-de-Siècle Sailor Suit?" *Journal of Design History* 24:2 (2011), 107. Rose also notes that sailor suits for children were not widely worn until the 1860s, when manufacturers advertised them as appropriate dress for seaside holidays. Clare Rose, *Making, Selling and Wearing Boys' Clothes in Late-Victorian England* (Farnham, Surrey: Ashgate, 2010), 187–89.

42. Ormond and Blackett-Ord, *Winterhalter*, 39–41.

43. For the details of Victoria and Albert's dress and honors, see Marsden, *Art & Love*, 78, 324–25, and 329.

44. At the time of her marriage, Victoria was dismayed to find that the order of precedence put her uncles—all English princes—before her husband, who was merely the younger son of the duke of a small German principality. The couple found this particularly galling, given that a king's female consort was automatically given the rank and title of queen and took precedence over everyone except her husband. When Victoria failed to get Parliament to address Albert's status, she resorted to issuing letters patent specifying that Albert had precedence immediately after her. This decree, however, was valid only in her realm; European courts were not obliged to honor the arrangement. As they began to consider Vicky's marriage into a European royal family, Victoria and Albert must have also anticipated traveling more regularly to a foreign court, where Albert's dignity was especially fragile. Even at home, children approaching their majority posed challenges for their parents. Once Bertie came of age, as heir he could demand to take precedence immediately after his mother and insist that his siblings do the same. In 1856, when Bertie was fifteen, Victoria again tried and failed to secure Parliamentary assistance and again resorted to letters patent, this time bestowing upon Albert the title of Prince Consort of the United Kingdom and Ireland. As an English prince, he could—at last—claim precedence after Victoria at home and in any European court. Gillian Gill, *We Two: Victoria and Albert; Rulers, Partners, Rivals* (New York: Ballantine Books, 2009), 153–54, 322–24.

45. QVJ 18 December 1846.

46. Retford, *Art of Domestic Life*, 129.

47. Gill, *We Two*, 310–14.

48. Had Vicky been a working-class girl, she might well have been caring for her infant sister in earnest. Later in the century, it was not uncommon for small girls to function as

"little nurses" to their younger siblings. Anna Davin, *Growing Up Poor: Home, School and Street in London, 1870–1974* (London: Rivers Oram Press, 1996), 89–90.

49. RA VIC/MAIN/M/12/1; VIC/MAIN/M/12/5; and QVJ 1 December 1840.

50. After Vicky's birth, Victoria mentions both "Mrs. Pegley (the monthly nurse for the Baby)" and "Mrs. Lilly (my monthly nurse)." QVJ 1 December 1840. Mrs. Lilly is mentioned in connection with the birth of all the other children, although Victoria noted that an assistant monthly nurse was brought in to help her when Beatrice was born in 1857, "Mrs. Lilley being old, & having been so ill last year." QVJ 29 April 1857.

51. QVJ 19 February 1841.

52. RA VIC/MAIN/M/12/5.

53. Melisa Klimaszewski, "Examining the Wet Nurse: Breasts, Power, and Penetration in Victorian England," *Women's Studies* 35:4 (2006), 326–27.

54. RA VIC/MAIN/M/12/5.

55. Gill, *We Two*, 181.

56. Klimaszewski, "Examining the Wet Nurse," 334. Suspicion of wet nurses' alcohol consumption was so pervasive that it can now be difficult to discern the facts of their role for the royal family. Gill (*We Two*, 181) notes that Vicky's colic was understood as connected to her wet nurse's diet of heavy beer and cheese, while a lithograph from the early 1840s in the Wellcome Collection, *Royal Dry Nursing Extraordinary* (https://wellcomecollection.org/works/s9fay8sp/images?id=a9u2msd4, accessed 29 September 2020), shows Victoria and Albert bursting into the nursery, aghast at the sight of a drunken wet nurse giving the infant Bertie alcohol. There were also reports that drinking heavy liquor was a factor in the dismissal of Bertie's first wet nurse, Mary Ann Brough, just two months after his birth. Yet, it is not clear how reliable such reports were, given that they only appeared in the newspaper twelve years later, when, in 1854, Mrs. Brough was tried for the gruesome murder of her six children, a crime for which she was acquitted by reason of insanity. For the Brough case, also known as the Esher murders, see Kayla Jo Seppelt, "Inside Queen Victoria's Household: The Ladies of the Royal Nursery and Schoolroom, 1839–1889" (master's thesis, University of Northern Iowa, 2017), 85–96. I am grateful to Elisabeth Narkin for pointing out anxieties about "overlaying."

57. Worries about alienation of the child's affections were possibly more acute in situations in which the suckling child went to live with the wet nurse. These worries are encapsulated in George Morland's painting *Visit to the Child at Nurse* (ca. 1788). Held in the collection of the Fitzwilliam Museum, it is set in the wet nurse's humble country cottage and focuses on a child recoiling from his own elite mother and reaching instead for the rosy-cheeked nurse. I am grateful to Kate Retford for bringing the painting to my attention.

58. RA VIC/MAIN/M/12/5.

59. A. N. Wilson, *Prince Albert: The Man Who Saved the Monarchy* (New York: HarperCollins, 2019), 214. Robert Rhodes James, *Prince Albert: A Biography* (New York: Alfred A. Knopf, 1984), 118, 127.

60. Wilson, *Prince Albert*, 114–17.

61. Seppelt, "Inside Queen Victoria's Household," 141.

62. RA VIC/MAIN/M/12/5.

63. Van der Kiste, *Queen Victoria's Children*, 12.

64. Lady Sarah Lyttelton, *Correspondence of Sarah Spencer, Lady Lyttelton, 1787–1870*, ed. Mrs. Hugh Wyndham (London: John Murray, 1912), 318–19.

65. RA VIC/MAIN/M/12/55.

66. Miss Hildyard's arrival and departure are noted in Victoria's diaries (QVJ 16 February 1847 and QVJ 28 February 1865). Born in 1810 to an Anglican clergyman and his wife, she had lost both her parents by 1838 and may have worked as a governess before coming to Stockmar's attention in 1846. Seppelt, "Inside Queen Victoria's Household," 113–14.

67. In 1847, the French governess was Mlle. Rollande, who served until 1859 (QVJ 17 April 1847; QVJ 20 January 1859). The German governess was Fräulein Gruner, who started sometime before February 1845 and stayed until her marriage in 1850, when she was replaced by Fräulein Illhardt (QVJ 1 February 1845, QVJ 20 July 1850, and 12 July 1850).

68. RA VIC/MAIN/M/12/55.

69. RA VIC/MAIN/M/12/55.

70. Henry French and Mark Rothery, *Man's Estate: Landed Gentry Masculinities, 1660–1900* (Oxford: Oxford University Press, 2012), 46–47.

71. Leonore Davidoff, *The Best Circles: Women and Society in Victorian England* (Totowa, N.J.: Rowman and Littlefield, 1973), 51.

72. The application of the Prussian system in British schools in the 1870s and 1880s is discussed in Deborah E. B. Weiner, *Architecture and Social Reform in Late-Victorian London* (Manchester: Manchester University Press, 1994), 104–11. At Eton in 1861, for instance, nineteen of the twenty-eight boys in the highest division of the lower school were over fourteen years of age. Malcolm Seaborne, *The English School: Its Architecture and Organization, 1370–1870* (Toronto: University of Toronto Press, 1971), 245.

73. French and Rothery, *Man's Estate*, 47. Albert's own interest in educational reform is evident from the contents of his private library, which was cataloged in about 1860. Franz Bosbach, John R. Davis, and Karina Urbach, eds., *Common Heritage: Documents and Sources Relating to German-British Relations in the Archives and Collections of Windsor and Coburg*, vol. 2, *The Photograph Collections and Private Libraries* (Berlin: Duncker & Humblot, 2018), 524–30.

74. Van der Kiste, *Queen Victoria's Children*, 30–31.

75. RA 715, copy at Osborne House.

76. French and Rothery, *Man's Estate*, 48.

77. Susanne Groom and Lee Prosser, *Kew Palace: The Official Illustrated History* (London: Historic Royal Palaces in association with Merrell Publishers, 2006), 83–84.

78. French and Rothery, *Man's Estate*, 3.

79. French and Rothery, *Man's Estate*, 41–43.

80. Charles Vaughn, headmaster of Harrow, from an open letter to Viscount Palmerston (1853), quoted in John Chandos, *Boys Together: English Public Schools, 1800–1914* (London: Hutchinson, 1984), 242.

81. Birch's successor, Frederick Gibbs, recorded these outbursts, which occurred over a two-day period in February 1852, in his diary. Quoted in Ridley, *Bertie*, 26.

82. RA VIC/MAIN/M/12/55.

83. Brindle, ed., *Windsor Castle*, 369.

84. Peter Inskip + Peter Jenkins Architects and Debois Landscape Survey Group, "Osborne House Conservation Plan: Analysis 1—The House" (report commissioned by English Heritage, October 2000), 12.

85. Turner, *Osborne*, 30–31.

86. Details of the work of Cubitt's crews at Osborne are provided in Hobhouse, *Cubitt*, especially 383 and 389–90.

87. Whittle, *At Home*, 7. Marsden, *Art & Love*, 22–24.

88. Michael Turner, "From Coburg to Osborne via Naples: Prince Albert and Architectural Inspiration at Osborne," in *Art in Britain and Germany in the Age of Queen Victoria and Prince Albert*, ed. Franz Bosbach and Frank Büttner (Berlin: De Gruyter, 1998), 26–27.

89. Rosemary Yallop, "Villa Rustica, Villa Suburbana: Vernacular Italianate Architecture in Britain, 1800 to 1860" (Ph.D. diss., University of Oxford, 2016), 157–58.

90. Yallop, "Villa Rustica," 162.

91. William Kent's 1734 design for the Treasury in Whitehall is often considered the first governmental building in England to follow this architectural precedent. Nikolaus Pevsner, *A History of Building Types* (Princeton, N.J.: Princeton University Press, 1970), 47.

92. In 1954, Henry-Russell Hitchcock opined that "the prominent use of Palladian motifs on these low wings and along the long side façade [of the main and household wings] makes evident, even more than that clumsiness of the original block [that is, the Pavilion], how little either Albert or Cubitt grasped the true character of [Charles] Barry's Italianism." Henry-Russell Hitchcock, *Early Victorian Architecture in Britain*, 2 vols. (New Haven, Conn: Yale University Press, 1954), 1:183.

93. Mark Girouard, *The Victorian Country House* (New Haven, Conn.: Yale University Press, 1979), 149.

94. Mark Girouard, *Life in the English Country House* (New Haven, Conn.: Yale University Press, 1978), 230.

95. Girouard, *Victorian Country House*, 35.

96. Robert Kerr, *The Gentleman's House; or, How to Plan English Residences from the Parsonage to the Palace*, 2nd ed. (London: John Murray, 1865), 107. A smoking room was added for Bertie's use in 1866, but it was attached to the far side of the household wing and only accessible from the outside.

97. Turner, *Osborne*, 11.

98. Girouard, *Life*, 238.

99. Girouard, *Life*, 234.

100. Turner, *Osborne*, 14.

101. QVJ 7 March 1843.

102. QVJ 3 March 1843.

103. Girouard, *Life*, 286.

104. Jill Franklin, *The Gentleman's Country House and Its Plan, 1835–1914* (London: Routledge & Kegan Paul, 1981), 80–81.

105. QVJ 14 September 1846.

106. Desmond Shawe-Taylor, *The Conversation Piece: Scenes of Fashionable Life* (London: Royal Collection, 2009), 112.

107. Affie's sixth birthday, celebrated at Osborne, followed just this pattern: "We went to fetch him down & wish him joy. The table with his presents, was in the Breakfast Room, & was covered with toys. What delighted him most, was a little violin, which his dear Father gave him. The 4 little girls were all in white, & so was I, & little Arthur in ¾ clothes!—All, out together.—Mama took leave of us before 12" (QVJ 6 August 1850).

108. Shawe-Taylor, *Conversation Piece*, 112.

109. QVJ 24 May 1844; 10 February 1852; 10 February 1853; 10 February 1854.

110. Untitled article, *The Builder* 6:303 (25 November 1848), 565.

111. QVJ 10 August 1857.

112. Commissioned in 1844 as a pendant to Emil Wolff's statue of Albert in classical garb (commissioned in 1841 and completed in 1849), the original was installed in Buckingham Palace. The version at Osborne (also by Gibson) was a birthday gift from Victoria to Albert in 1849. Marsden, *Art & Love*, 70 and 72.

113. Martina Droth, Jason Edwards, and Michael Hatt, eds., *Sculpture Victorious: Art in an Age of Invention, 1837–1901* (New Haven, Conn.: Yale University Press, 2014), 205–7.

114. Elias, *Court Society*, 53.

115. For a discussion of the principles in laying out the nursery, see Kerr, *Gentleman's House*, 144–47.

116. Girouard, *Life*, 279 and 286.

117. Birch served from 1849 to early 1852, when he was replaced by Frederick Gibbs. Bennett, *Queen Victoria's Children*, 52–54. QVJ 22 April 1849.

118. Foreman and Peter, *Buckingham Palace*, 43–44.

119. The functions of these rooms (and others discussed later) changed over time. This analysis relies on Michael Hunter, "The Occupation of Rooms in the Main and the Household Wings (1848–1901)," an unpublished report produced by the curator of Osborne House in May 2007 and preserved in the Osborne House files.

120. Carter, *Three Emperors*, 38–39.

121. According to Ruth Colton, "The idea of claiming land by observing it was critical to the colonial enterprise," and not only for the royal family. Colton notes that raised terraces incorporated into public parks in late Victorian Britain allowed park users, including children, to experience "visual mastery" over the surrounding landscape and so to become "petty imperialists." Ruth Colton, "Savage Instincts, Civilized Spaces: The Child, the Empire, and the Public Park, c. 1880–1914," in *Children, Childhood and Youth in the British World*, ed. Shirleene Robinson and Simon Sleight (Basingstoke: Palgrave Macmillan, 2016), 255–70 (quoted passage appears on 258).

122. Andrew Lambert, "A Palace on the Ocean: Osborne, the Victorian Monarchy and the Seapower State," presentation at a conference titled *Victoria and Albert at Osborne*, Osborne House, 8 November 2019.

123. The royal couple specified the subject matter as appropriate for the fresco, which (as Albert's secretary George Anson told the painter) they considered "a kind of dedication picture of the building (the Marine Residence of the Queen of England.)" Dyce had originally suggested a subject from Boccaccio's *Decameron*. Marsden, *Art & Love*, 24.

124. Turner, *Osborne*, 14.

125. The vestibules in the main wing are largely invisible today as they were the logical place to install the elevators required when the wing became part of the Edward VII Convalescent Home for Officers serving in His Majesty's Forces in the early twentieth century.

126. Mrs. Steuart Erskine, ed., *Twenty Years at Court: From the Correspondence of the Hon. Eleanor Stanley, Maid of Honour to her Late Majesty Queen Victoria 1841–1862* (London: Nisbet, 1916), 115.

127. Quoted in Whittle, *At Home*, 28.

128. QVJ 24 June 1856.

129. QVJ 20 February 1846.

2. A PASTORAL PARADISE FOR YOUNG ROYALS

1. A frequent visitor to Osborne, Leitch taught Victoria for almost twenty years. Carly Collier, *Victoria & Albert: Our Lives in Watercolour* (London: Royal Collection Trust, 2019), 4 and 29–34.

2. Collier, *Our Lives in Watercolour*, 8–9.

3. William White, *History, Gazetteer, and Directory of Hampshire and the Isle of Wight* (Sheffield: William White, 1859), 623.

4. Seventy years later, Victoria and Albert built themselves a similar "place of Refuge" on the grounds of Buckingham Palace. In 1842, Victoria referred to the building in her diary as "the little Cottage that is being built in the Mound." Within a few years, however, Albert claimed the site as a laboratory of sorts for encouraging British artists to take up fresco painting, a technique he deemed appropriate for the new Houses of Parliament, then under construction. Thereafter, the building was often called the Garden Pavilion or the Comus Pavilion (in a nod to the depiction of John Milton's masque in the structure's central octagonal room), although Victoria continued to call it "the cottage." The building was demolished in 1928. Marsden, *Art & Love*, 21–22; QVJ 5 November 1842; QVJ 11 November 1844.

5. Dates for the components of the children's precinct come from Turner, *Osborne*, 30–35.

6. Hermione Hobhouse, *Thomas Cubitt: Master Builder* (London: Macmillan, 1971), 392.

7. Groom and Prosser, *Kew Palace*, 84.

8. Turner, *Osborne*, 30–31. As much as this might be true, the garden's individual plots did nothing to maximize crop production. Instead, the arrangement maintained the children's birth order—although notably not the order of succession—and made it easy to see which children were paying attention to their garden plots and which were not. This insistence on direct comparison of the children was not uncommon in nineteenth-century Britain. According to Lenore Davidoff, middle-class parents accepted "the arrival of numerous children as inevitable" and "had little compunction about comparing and marking out certain children." Nonetheless, the practice seems to have been particularly hard on the Prince of Wales, who had none of his older sister's intellectual spark and was considered backward and lazy by his parents. Davidoff, *Thicker than Water*, 97–98.

9. QVJ 5 May 1853.

10. QVJ 27 May 1853.

11. *The Osborne Album: Thirty-three Photographic Views of the Queen's Maritime Residence at Osborne* (London and Paris: [André Adolphe-Eugène] Disdéri, 1867), ix.

12. By the mid-1950s, the story that the Swiss Cottage "was brought in sections from Switzerland" was included in the official guide to the site. John Charlton, *Osborne House* (London: Her Majesty's Stationery Office, 1955, reprinted 1957), 22. Mark Girouard relied heavily on Charlton's guide for his treatment of Osborne, having done "no documentary research into the history of Osborne." Thus, he asserted that "a Swiss chalet was shipped over in pieces." Girouard, *Victorian Country House*, 448n1, 152. The story was often elaborated upon, as when Matson claimed that "a Swiss chalet arrived, imported in sections and speedily erected on the site." John Matson, *Dear Osborne: Queen Victoria's Family Life in the Isle of Wight* (London: Hamish Hamilton, 1978), 50. (In fact, over three months after laying the cornerstone, Victoria noted that "The Swiss Cottage is getting on nicely but slowly." QVJ 15 August 1853. She only noted that the Swiss Cottage was "up" another three months after that. QVJ 26 November 1853.) Sarah Ferguson, Duchess of York, gave the claim a new spin in 1991, asserting that the cottage "was assembled from ready-made wooden sections, incidentally making it one of the first prefabricated buildings in England." HRH The Duchess of York, *Victoria and Albert: Life at Osborne House* (London: Weidenfeld and Nicolson, 1991), 108.

13. P. F. Robinson, *Rural Architecture, or a Series of Designs for Ornamental Cottages* (London: Rodwell and Martin, 1823), design no. VIII.

14. Stockhammer was interviewed about his research for two English-language publications: "Typical Swiss Chalets 'Not Actually Swiss,'" *The Local* (8 September 2016), https://www.thelocal.ch/20160908/typical-swiss-chalets-not-actually-swiss-says-researcher, accessed 31 December 2020; and Astrid Tomczak-Plekawa, "The Swiss Chalet—Not Quite So Swiss," *Horizons: The Swiss Magazine for Scientific Research* 28:110 (September 2016), 35.

15. QVJ 26 November 1853.

16. Turner, *Osborne*, 32.

17. "Inventory of the Swiss Cottage, 1904," privy purse copy consulted at St. James's Palace.

18. In 2009, English Heritage commissioned food historian Annie Gray to research cooking and eating at the Swiss Cottage to inform their public presentation of the site. While Gray's study ("Cooking and Dining at Swiss Cottage, Osborne House, Research Report") was not published, that research informed her treatment of the Swiss Cottage in her book on Victoria's relationship with food. Annie Gray, *The Greedy Queen: Eating with Victoria* (London: Profile Books, 2017), 160–73.

19. Turner, *Osborne*, 33. The locally made furniture gives the lie to Bell's assertion in *The Osborne Album* that "the furniture, ornament, and decorations for [the Swiss Cottage], were expressly imported from Switzerland," ix.

20. Michael Turner, "From Coburg to Osborne via Naples: Prince Albert and Architectural Inspiration at Osborne," in *Art in Britain and Germany in the Age of Queen Victoria and Prince Albert*, ed. Franz Bosbach and Frank Büttner (Berlin: De Gruyter, 1998), 35.

21. QVJ 20 August 1845.

22. Victoria was so committed to the myth of Albert's happy childhood that after his death in 1861 she directed the compilation of a book about his youth that highlighted her husband's love for Rosenau: "the principal scene, as it was, of what he always fondly looked back to as a most happy childhood." Charles Grey, *The Early Years of His Royal Highness the Prince Consort* (New York: Harper & Brothers, 1867), 106.

23. A. N. Wilson, *Prince Albert: The Man Who Saved the Monarchy* (New York: HarperCollins, 2019), 36–37.

24. Daniel Maudlin argues that classically educated British elites were well aware of Pliny's idea that the countryside was a place for quiet contemplation, but also notes that "an appreciation of rural retreat . . . was not just an intellectual pursuit, but also a social strategy." Daniel Maudlin, *The Idea of the Cottage in English Architecture, 1760–1860* (London and New York: Routledge, 2015), 17–18.

25. Kate Heard, "The Print Room at Queen Charlotte's Cottage," *British Art Journal* 13:3 (Winter 2012/13), 53.

26. Groom and Prosser, *Kew Palace*, 76.

27. Maudlin, *Idea of the Cottage*, 59.

28. The *London Magazine*'s August 1774 characterization of the "elegance and humour" of the prints is quoted in Heard, "Print Room," 54.

29. Ann Bermingham, "Gainsborough's *Cottage Door*: Sensation and Sensibility," in *Sensation and Sensibility: Viewing Gainsborough's "Cottage Door,"* ed. Ann Bermingham (New Haven, Conn.: Yale Center for British Art, 2005), 10.

30. Polly Putnam, "'The Tasteful Genius of Princess Elizabeth': The Furnishing of Queen Charlotte's Cottage in Kew in 1805," *Furniture History* 53 (2017), 112.

31. QVJ 15 May 1856.

32. Although the question has not received scholarly attention, it is worth asking if the emergence of Swiss cottages on aristocratic and royal estates in the early years of the nineteenth century may have also been a response to political events of the 1790s, when, according to art historian John Barrell, "the image of the cottage had become thoroughly involved in questions of the morality of the war with the French Republic, popular radicalism and the movement for parliamentary reforms, and the declining standard of living of the poor under the burden of wartime taxation." John Barrell, "Spectacles for Republicans," in Bermingham, *Sensation and Sensibility*, 58. By evoking cottages that were not native to the British Isles, British elites could retreat, not just from the city, but also from contemporary political debates.

33. In the most comprehensive treatment of the theoretical roots of the Swiss garden cottage, Sue Wilson highlights a range of authors who laid the groundwork for Rousseau, among them Albrecht von Haller, who wrote the didactic ode "Die Alpen" in 1732. Sue Wilson, "'The Poetry of Architecture': The Historical and Theoretical Roots of the Swiss Garden Cottage (1760–1864)" (PhD diss., University of Bristol, 2010), 5–7.

34. Quoted in Felicity Rash, "Early British Travellers to Switzerland 1611–1860," in *Exercises in Translation: Swiss-British Cultural Interchange*, ed. Joy Charnley and Malcolm Pender (Oxford and Bern: Peter Lang, 2006), 111.

35. Referencing Horace Walpole's discussion of a "forest or savage garden," Wilson repeatedly uses the term "savage Picturesque garden." Wilson, "Poetry of Architecture," 65.

36. For the main house, see Derek Linstrum, *Sir Jeffry Wyatville: Architect to the King* (Oxford: Clarendon Press, 1972), 88–95; and Maudlin, *Idea of the Cottage*, 172–74.

37. J. Britton and E. W. Brayley, *Devonshire and Cornwall Illustrated* (London: H. Fisher, R. Fisher & P. Jackson, 1832), 56.

38. Britton and Brayley, *Devonshire*, 56.

39. It was rumored at the time that Landseer was the father of the duchess's youngest child, Rachel. Clare Sherriff, *Swiss Cottage, Endsleigh: History Album* (report commissioned by the Landmark Trust, 2014), 15–18.

40. Linstrum mentions those at Claverton Manor, Langold Park, and Virginia Water in passing. Linstrum, *Wyatville*, 95. Wyatt's association with Bulstrode is mentioned in Charnley and Pender, *Exercises in Translation*.

41. "Railway Rambles," *Penny Magazine* 11:669 (3 September 1842), 351.

42. Robinson was born in 1776 and published multiple editions of eight distinct books between 1823 and 1853. For a review of Robinson's publishing career, see John Archer, *The Literature of British Domestic Architecture, 1715–1842* (Cambridge, Mass.: MIT Press, 1985), 735–50.

43. "Old Warden Park (including the Swiss Garden)," https://historicengland.org.uk/listing/the-list/list-entry/1000474, accessed 23 September 2019.

44. "Singleton Park and Sketty Hall," CADW/ICOMOS Register of Parks and Gardens of Special Historic Interest in Wales. https://coflein.gov.uk/en/site/28736/details/singleton-abbey-and-sketty-hall-gardens-sketty-swansea, accessed 2 February 2021.

45. "Some Account of the Colosseum, in the Regent's Park," *Mirror of Literature, Amusement, and Instruction* 13:352 (17 January 1829), 36.

46. Kata Phusin, "The Poetry of Architecture," *Architectural Magazine* 5:48 (February 1838), 57–58.

47. Archer, *Literature*, 742–45.

48. According to his biographer, Dickens was working on *The Mystery of Edwin Drood* in the chalet on the last day of his life. Peter Ackroyd, *Dickens* (New York: HarperCollins, 1990), 955–56, 1076–77.

49. QVJ 3 May 1845.

50. QVJ 8 September 1842.

51. Meredith Martin, *Dairy Queens: The Politics of Pastoral Architecture from Catherine de' Medici to Marie-Antoinette* (Cambridge, Mass.: Harvard University Press, 2011), 11.

52. Martin, *Dairy Queens*, 7.

53. Martin, *Dairy Queens*, 10, 208.

54. British dairies are discussed in Meredith Martin, "Interiors and Interiority in the Ornamental Dairy Tradition," *Eighteenth-Century Fiction* 20 (Spring 2008), 357–84.

55. Martin, "Interiors and Interiority," 363.

56. Among the innovations incorporated into the Royal Dairy at Frogmore were double windows and cavity walls to maintain a consistent interior temperature and "the most modern system available" for ventilation. G. E. Fussell, *The English Dairy Farmer: 1500–1900* (London: F. Cass; New York: A. M. Kelley, 1966), 153–54. (Page numbers are from the American edition.)

57. "Taymouth Castle, Dairy," https://canmore.org.uk/site/24953/taymouth-castle-dairy, accessed 2 February 2021. (Canmore is the National Record of the Historic Environment in Scotland.)

58. Maudlin notes that William Chambers was the leading British theorist of the primitive hut, but that Thomas Rawlins was the first to make a direct connection between the primitive hut as a neoclassical ideal and the cottage as a site for pastoral retreat in 1768. The result was

a number of "early pattern books on cottage-retreats ... characterized by a strict adherence to geometry and thatch." Maudlin, *Idea of the Cottage*, 33–37.

59. Thomas Dick Lauder, *Memorial of the Royal Progress in Scotland* (Edinburgh: A. and C. Black, 1843), 320.

60. Martin, "Interiors and Interiority," 368.

61. Lauder, *Memorial*, 347.

62. She may not have been alone. The Duchess of Bedford built both a Swiss cottage and an ornamental dairy at Endsleigh, as well as an ornamental dairy at her other estate, Woburn Abbey.

63. Wilson, "Poetry of Architecture," 3.

64. Gray, *Greedy Queen*, 164–65.

65. White, *History, Gazetteer, and Directory*, 623.

66. QVJ 8 September 1854.

67. QVJ 8 and 10 August 1857.

68. QVJ 15 August 1857.

69. QVJ 14 July 1861; 3 August 1861; and 13 August 1861.

70. Martin, "Interiors and Interiority," 378–80.

71. Feodora's letter notes that the Swiss cottage built for her children had "one room and a kitchen." Quoted in Gray, *Greedy Queen*, 161.

72. Albert's visit to Shrublands is mentioned in Turner, *Osborne*, 32. The pre-1840 date of the Shrublands Swiss cottage is given on the Shrubland Hall page of the Historic England website: https://historicengland.org.uk/listing/the-list/list-entry/1000155, accessed 31 August 2020.

73. QVJ 4 June 1850.

74. QVJ 14 May 1851.

75. M. Digby Wyatt, *The Industrial Arts of the Nineteenth Century*, 2 vols. (London: Day and Son, 1851–53), 2, Plate CXXX.

76. Royal Commission for the Exhibition of 1851, *Great Exhibition of the Works of Industry of All Nations, 1851: Official Descriptive and Illustrated Catalogue*, 3 volumes (London: Spicer Brothers, 1851), 2:844 and Plates 143 and 144.

77. Maudlin, *Idea of the Cottage*, 21.

78. Royal Commission, *Great Exhibition of the Works of Industry of All Nations*, 3:1281, Plate 43.

79. Royal Commission for the Exhibition of 1851, *Great Exhibition of the Works of Industry of All Nations, 1851: Reports of the Juries on the Subjects in the Thirty Classes into Which the Exhibition Was Divided*, 2 volumes (London: William Clowes & Sons for the Royal Commission, 1852), 550 and cix.

80. Royal Commission, *Reports of the Juries*, 544–45.

81. *The World's Fair; or Children's Prize Gift Book of the Great Exhibition of 1851. Describing the Beautiful Inventions and Manufactures Exhibited therein; with Pretty Stories about the People who have made and sent them; and how they live when at home* (London: Thomas Dean & Son, [n.d.]), 95.

82. Marsden, *Art & Love*, 251–52.

83. *Children's Prize Gift Book*, 37.

84. *Children's Prize Gift Book*, 37–39.

85. Gill, *We Two*, 311.

86. Martin, "Interiors and Interiority," 378–80.

87. This analysis of the *secrétaire* and its cultural implications, especially in contrast to the *bureau plat*, draws extensively from Dena Goodman, "The *Secrétaire* and Integration of the Eighteenth-Century Self," in *Furnishing the Eighteenth Century: What Furniture Can Tell Us about the European and American Past*, ed. Dena Goodman and Kathryn Norberg (New York: Routledge, 2007), 183–203. The quoted phrase appears on 183.

88. Goodman, "The *Secrétaire*," 183.

89. Goodman, "The *Secrétaire*," 191–92.

90. *The Young Lady's Book: A Manual of Elegant Recreations, Exercises, and Pursuits* (London: Vizetelly, Branston, 1829). The chapter titled "The Escrutoire" runs from page 313 to page 346.

91. *The Young Lady's Book: A Manual of Elegant Recreations, Arts, Sciences, and Accomplishments; Edited by Distinguished Professors* (London: Henry G. Bonn, 1859), 379.

92. *Young Lady's Book* (1859), 380.

93. *Young Lady's Book* (1859), 383.

94. *Young Lady's Book* (1859), 383.

95. Hannah Pakula, *An Uncommon Woman: The Empress Frederick, Daughter of Queen Victoria, Wife of the Crown Prince of Prussia, Mother of Kaiser Wilhelm* (New York: Simon & Schuster, 1995), 106–7.

96. Roger Fulford, ed., *Dearest Child: Letters between Queen Victoria and the Princess Royal, 1858–1861* (New York: Holt, Rinehart and Winston, 1964), 1 and 4.

97. Pakula, *Uncommon Woman*, 108.

98. QVJ 16 May 1857.

99. QVJ 17 December 1857.

100. QVJ 18 December 1857.

101. QVJ 19 December 1857.

102. QVJ 24 May 1860.

103. Victoria described Affie with his air pump and steam engine in an 1858 letter to Albert (visiting Vicky in Potsdam); quoted in Tyler Whittle, *Victoria and Albert at Home* (London: Routledge & Kegan Paul, 1980), 96.

104. Ann Taylor Allen, *The Transatlantic Kindergarten: Education and Women's Movements in Germany and the United States* (Oxford: Oxford University Press, 2017), 44.

105. As Michael Lewis notes, Milton Bradley dominated the market in Froebel products, but also introduced a number of pseudo-Froebel toys. Michael J. Lewis, *Toys That Teach* (Montreal: Canadian Centre for Architecture, 1992), 14–16.

106. Allen, *Transatlantic Kindergarten*, 70–72.

107. According to one of Albert's earliest biographers, that youthful collection formed the kernel of the Ernst-Albert Museum, originally located in Coburg, but by 1864 moved to purpose-built rooms in the Festung. C. Grey, *The Early Years of His Royal Highness the Prince Consort* (New York: Harper & Brothers, 1867), 107.

108. VIC/MAIN/M/17/7. Albert and Victoria did not always treat their children with the kindness Combe advocated, but they certainly retained his report.

109. Prince Albert expressed these views in a speech he gave at a banquet hosted by the Lord Mayor of London on 21 March 1850. Known as the Mansion House speech, it was published

in *The Principal Speeches and Addresses of His Royal Highness the Prince Consort* (London: John Murray, 1862), 109–14, https://www.gutenberg.org/files/61205/61205-h/61205-h.htm#Page_109, accessed 3 February 2021. See also Paul Young, *Globalization and the Great Exhibition: The Victorian New World Order* (Basingstoke: Palgrave Macmillan, 2009), 51–53.

110. Juliet Chippindale and James Ford, "Swiss Cottage Museum Research Report" (2011), 5. Osborne House records.

111. Among them were a birch-bark wallet (RCIN 84296), carved dolls (RCIN 84303), a number of birch-bark mats with porcupine quills (including RCIN 84341, RCIN 84322, RCIN 84323, RCIN 84324), and a beaded collar (RCIN 84311). www.rtc.uk, accessed 21 February 2021.

112. RCIN 84606. www.rtc.uk, accessed 21 February 2021.

113. RCIN 42089. www.rtc.uk, accessed 21 February 2021.

114. RCIN 83638. www.rtc.uk, accessed 21 February 2021.

115. Tony Bennett, *The Birth of the Museum: History, Theory, Politics* (London and New York: Routledge, 1995), 63-68.

116. RCIN 83629. www.rtc.uk, accessed 21 February 2021.

117. Chippindale and Ford, "Swiss Cottage Museum," 7–8.

118. Charles Lyell to Lady Lyell, 8 May 1863, quoted in Chippindale and Ford, "Swiss Cottage Museum," 5.

119. Jehanne Wake, *Princess Louise: Queen Victoria's Unconventional Daughter* (London: Collins, 1988), 32.

120. Gray, *Greedy Queen*, 165.

121. Gray, *Greedy Queen*, 166.

122. QVJ 25 July 1860.

123. QVJ 14 April 1866.

124. QVJ 24 May 1856.

125. QVJ 18 March 1859.

126. QVJ 25 May 1861.

127. QVJ 6 August 1858.

128. QVJ 25 May 1959.

129. QVJ 14 April 1861.

130. QVJ 25 April 1864.

131. QVJ 24 July 1864.

132. QVJ 7 April 1871.

133. QVJ 10 February 1862.

134. QVJ 10 February 1869.

135. QVJ 15 April 1874.

136. QVJ 4 August 1879.

137. QVJ 27 December 1878.

138. QVJ 3 February 1888.

139. John Chalmers Morton, *The Prince Consort's Farms: An Agricultural Memoir* (London: Longman, Green, Longman, Roberts & Green, 1863), 22–23.

140. See, for example, "Foreign Gossip," *Detroit Free Press*, 1 October 1865, 3, and "Over the Ocean," *The Cecil Whig* [published in Elkton, Md.] (30 November 1872), 1.

141. *Osborne Album*, ix–x.

142. Disdéri patented the carte de visite portrait in November 1854 and by 1857 had begun producing photographs of French celebrities, chief among them members of the French imperial family and their entourage. Elizabeth Anne McCauley, *A. A. E. Disdéri and the Carte de Visite Portrait Photograph* (New Haven, Conn.: Yale University Press, 1985), 27, 54–55, and 206–7.

143. Homans, *Royal Representations*, 46.

144. *Osborne Album*, x.

145. James E. Bryan, "Material Culture in Miniature: Nuremberg Kitchens as Inspirational Toys in the Long Nineteenth Century," in *Childhood by Design: Toys and the Material Culture of Childhood, 1700-Present*, ed. Megan Brandow-Faller (New York: Bloomsbury Visual Arts, 2018), 227.

146. Turner, *Osborne*, 33.

147. "Queen Victoria," *Indiana Progress*, 26 September 1878, 11.

148. John Oldcastle, "An English Princess," *Merry England* 3:14 (June 1884), 125.

149. G.H.P., "The Crown Prince and Princess of Germany," *Leisure Hour* (May 1887), 320.

150. "In a Royal Garden," *The [Guernsey] Star*, 22 September 1891, 1.

151. QVJ 15 May 1856.

152. QVJ 19 September 1881.

153. QVJ 20 December 1881.

154. QVJ 19 September 1881.

155. QVJ 20 December 1881.

156. The 1851 census of England, Hampshire, registration district Isle of Wight, subdistrict Cowes, enumeration district 2b, Whippingham parish, folio 217, page 14, household 54 (https://www.ancestry.co.uk/imageviewer/collections/8860/images/HAMHO107_1662_1662-0430?ssrc=&backlabel=Return&pId=5846958, accessed 22 February 2021; citing PRO HO 107/1662).

157. Royal Commission, *Reports of the Juries*, lviii.

158. Henry Roberts, *The Model Houses for Families, Built in Connexion with the Great Exhibition of 1851* (London: Society for Improving the Condition of the Labouring Classes, 1851), 7–8. S. Martin Gaskell, *Model Housing from the Great Exhibition to the Festival of Britain* (London: Mansell, 1986), 19–23.

159. It seems likely that the building did not originally include a W.C.; toilet facilities were available close by in a washhouse. Perhaps in deference to Mrs. Farley's age, the W.C. was added when the second bedroom was created. Certainly, the 1856 plan shows the location of plumbing lines, including a cold-water supply connecting the Swiss Cottage to the washhouse and waste pipes that connected both buildings to their respective cesspools. An interior lobby was added to room C at the same time, so that all members of the household could access the W.C. without impinging on the privacy of the marital bedroom.

160. The Hon. Eleanor Stanley to her mother, Lady Mary Stanley, 28 July 1848, quoted in *Twenty Years at Court: From the Correspondence of the Hon. Eleanor Stanley*, ed. Mrs. Steuart Erskine (London: Nisbet, 1916), 173.

161. The Hon. Eleanor Stanley to her father, 26 July 1852, quoted in Erskine, *Twenty Years at Court*, 211.

162. Roy Porter, "Heritage Statement in Support of a Listed Building Consent and Planning Application Concerning the Swiss Cottage Quarter, Osborne House," prepared under the auspices of English Heritage, December 2012.

163. Guy Laking, *An Illustrated Guide to Osborne. The Royal House, incorporating the Durbar Room and the various other places of interest, with Catalogue of the Pictures, Porcelain and Furniture in the State Apartments. Also Notes on the Swiss Cottage and the Swiss Cottage Museum* (London: His Majesty's Stationery Office, 1919), 16.

164. Laking, *Illustrated Guide to Osborne*, 16.

165. Laking, *Illustrated Guide to Osborne*, 17.

166. Philip Mansel, "Once upon a Time in Wolfsgarten," *Architectural Digest* 10 (October 1988), 276, 280, and 284.

167. Paul Rem, "De chalets van koningin Wilhelmina in de paleisparken van Het Loo (1881–1882) en Soestdijk (1892)," *Bulletin KNOB* 110:2 (2011), 49–58. I am beholden to Marte Stinis for alerting me to the existence of these chalets.

168. Mary Spencer Warren, "The Childhood and Girlhood of the Queen of the Netherlands," *English Illustrated Magazine* 170 (November 1897), 129.

3. MAKING AMERICAN ARISTOCRATS IN THE GILDED AGE CHILDREN'S COTTAGE

1. "Building Notes," *Newport Mercury* 129 (3 July 1886), 1. A native of Nova Scotia, McNeil was a prolific builder in the Boston area who worked on a wide variety of projects, from triple-deckers to Commonwealth Avenue mansions. Keith Morgan, personal communication, 9 June 2010.

2. The conversion of 1885 dollars into 2024 dollars comes from the CPI Inflation Calculator: https://www.in2013dollars.com/us/inflation/1885?amount=200000, accessed 4 June 2024.

3. Public fascination with the Vanderbilts has been fueled and slaked by popular books published for more than a century. Among the earliest is W. A. Croffut's *The Vanderbilts and the Story of Their Fortune* (Chicago: Belford, Clarke, 1886); others include Wayne Andrews, *The Vanderbilt Legend: The Story of the Vanderbilt Family, 1794–1940* (New York: Harcourt, Brace, 1941); B. F. Friedman, *Gertrude Vanderbilt Whitney* (New York: Doubleday, 1978); Barbara Goldsmith, *Little Gloria . . . Happy at Last* (New York: Dell, 1980); and Jerry E. Patterson, *The Vanderbilts* (New York: Harry N. Abrams, 1989). The Vanderbilts themselves have participated in this process, authoring a number of books that are part memoir, part biography: Consuelo Vanderbilt Balsan, *The Glitter and the Gold* (New York: Harper & Brothers, 1952); Cornelius Vanderbilt Jr., *Queen of the Golden Age: The Fabulous Grace Wilson Vanderbilt* (New York: McGraw-Hill, 1956); Arthur T. Vanderbilt II, *Fortune's Children: The Fall of the House of Vanderbilt* (New York: William Morrow, 1989); Flora Biddle Miller, *The Whitney Women and the Museum They Made: A Family Memoir* (New York: Arcade Publishing, 1999). A granddaughter of Gertrude Vanderbilt Whitney, Flora Biddle Miller also collaborated on the research for Friedman's biography of her grandmother.

4. The architectural partnership between Robert Swain Peabody (1845–1917) and John Goddard Stearns Jr. (1843–1917) was established in 1870. Wheaton A. Holden, "The Peabody

Touch: Peabody and Stearns of Boston, 1870–1917," *Journal of the Society of Architectural Historians* 32:2 (May 1973), 114.

5. Wayne Craven, *Gilded Mansions: Grand Architecture and High Society* (New York: W. W. Norton, 2009), 152–55.

6. Vanderbilt, *Fortune's Children*, 187.

7. Holden, "The Peabody Touch," 120–21; Arnold Lewis, *American Country Houses of the Gilded Age* (New York: Dover, 1982), plate 33; Annie Robinson, *Peabody and Stearns: Country Houses and Seaside Cottages* (New York: W. W. Norton, 2010), 42–45.

8. Cornelius II and Alice Vanderbilt's first child, Alice, had died in 1874 at the age of five. Brief biographies of the Vanderbilt offspring are included in Armin Brand Allen, *The Cornelius Vanderbilts of the Breakers* (Newport: Preservation Society of Newport County,1995; rev. 2005), 45, 47, 51, 63, 83, 95, 103.

9. By the time they began to renovate the Breakers, Peabody and Stearns were already responsible for the design of six such houses in Newport and would go on to design seven others there (including Rough Point for Frederick W. Vanderbilt, one of Cornelius II's younger brothers). Holden, "The Peabody Touch," 115–16, 128–29.

10. According to Wright, Chicago developer Samuel Eberly Gross "built and sold over seven thousand houses, all between 1880 and 1892," including "$3,000–$4,000 houses for middle-class families." Gwendolyn Wright, *Building the American Dream: A Social History of Housing in America* (Cambridge, Mass.: MIT Press, 1983), 100.

11. While the purchase of the Breakers and breaking ground on Elm Court took place in 1885, the year of William Henry Vanderbilt's death, Vanderbilt involvement with both estates began in the months before his fatal stroke in December of that year. Richard S. Jackson Jr. and Cornelia Brooke Gilder, *Houses of the Berkshires, 1870–1930* (New York: Acanthus Press, 2006), 99–104. See also Robinson, *Peabody and Stearns*, 110–13.

12. Neither the teahouse nor the bowling alley are represented among the many surviving drawings of the estate's original outbuildings, also designed by Hunt, which suggests that they may have been later additions. The main house burned in 1899 and its replacement (sometimes called Idle Hour II) was designed by Hunt's son, Richard Howland Hunt. Robert B. Mackay, Anthony Baker, and Carol A. Traynor, eds., *Long Island Country Houses and Their Architects, 1860–1940* (New York and London: Society for the Preservation of Long Island Antiquities, in association with W. W. Norton, 1997), 224–25 and 227–28.

13. "Idle Hour, The W.K. Vanderbilt Estate," pamphlet, ca. 1967, in the collection of the Oakdale Historical Society.

14. Balsan, *The Glitter and the Gold*, 14.

15. Hunt's other Vanderbilt houses include Biltmore in Asheville, North Carolina (1892–95), for George Vanderbilt and three houses for William K. Vanderbilt: Idle Hour, 660 Fifth Avenue (also known as the Petit Chateau) in New York City (1878–82), and Marble House in Newport (1888–95).

16. The transformation of the landscape is well documented in John R. Tschirch, "The Evolution of a Beaux-Arts Landscape: The Breakers in Newport, Rhode Island," *Journal of the New England Garden History Society* 7 (Fall 1999), 1–14.

17. Craven, *Gilded Mansions*, 170–83. See also Paul Baker, *Richard Morris Hunt* (Cambridge, Mass.: MIT Press, 1980), 364–72; David Chase, "Superb Privacies: The Later Domestic Commissions of Richard Morris Hunt, 1878–1895," in *The Architecture of Richard Morris Hunt*, ed. Susan R. Stein (Chicago: University of Chicago Press, 1986), 151–71; and Robert B. King, *The Vanderbilt Homes* (New York: Rizzoli, 1989), 38–45.

18. Only two architectural historians have commented on the children's cottage in print. One was Wheaton A. Holden, whose interest in the structure was limited to the light it could shed on the design process of Robert Swain Peabody. In a paragraph devoted to the firm's Newport work, Holden included a period photograph of the Breakers' playhouse (as he called it) next to an image of the English almshouses he had identified as the model for its design. He ventured no explanation as to why an almshouse would have been an appropriate source of inspiration for a cottage designed for the children of a millionaire. Holden, "The Peabody Touch," 121. The other is Annie Robinson, who mentions it as the only extant building designed by Peabody and Stearns at the Breakers site. Robinson, *Peabody and Stearns*, 44.

19. Pierre Bourdieu, "The Forms of Capital" (1983; trans. 1986), *The Routledge Falmer Reader in Sociology of Education*, ed. Stephan J. Ball (New York: Routledge Falmer, 2004), 21.

20. Bourdieu, "Forms of Capital," 22.

21. Thorstein Veblen, *The Theory of the Leisure Class* (1899), quoted in Rebecca Edwards, *New Spirits: Americans in the Gilded Age, 1865–1905* (New York: Oxford University Press, 2006), 97. Although Edwards uses the Vanderbilts (specifically, Cornelius's sister-in-law Alva and her daughter, Consuelo) as examples of this kind of conspicuous consumption, she does not extend her analysis to younger children.

22. Consider the experience of Caroline Astor, the gatekeeper of American high society in this period. Mrs. Astor (as she was always called) had no intention of recognizing the notorious Alva Vanderbilt (wife of Cornelius II's brother William K.) until her youngest daughter set her heart on attending a particularly lavish costume ball to be held at the Vanderbilts' New York house in 1883. When Alva upheld the social convention that precluded her issuing an invitation to the daughter until the mothers were on calling terms, Mrs. Astor was forced to recognize Alva and thus admit her into the highest echelons of New York society. Arthur T. Vanderbilt, II, *Fortune's Children*, 100–106.

23. Architectural historians—guided by the work of Mark Girouard and Dell Upton—have developed sophisticated means for interpreting buildings as mechanisms through which social identities and especially social hierarchies are communicated, naturalized, and reproduced. Yet, such work has tended to understand social identity as a fixed quality that exists prior to the building, which in turn is understood largely as an expression of the social order. Bringing Judith Butler's theories to bear upon their work, I adopt the language of performance to signal my understanding of social identify as a less stable quality that is always in the process of construction, performed every moment by each individual. Thus, social identity does not exist in any fixed way prior to the buildings designed to support and sustain those performances. Mark Girouard, *Life in the English Country House* (New Haven, Conn.: Yale University Press, 1978); Dell Upton, *Holy Things and Profane: Anglican Parish Churches in Colonial Virginia* (New York: Architectural Foundation; Cambridge: MIT Press, 1986); Judith Butler, *Gender Trouble: Feminism and the Subversion of Identity* (New York: Routledge, 1990).

24. For the development of Vanderbilt Row, see Robert A. M. Stern, Thomas Mellins, and David Fishman, *New York 1880* (New York: Monacelli Press, 1999), 578–601. For the Hyde Park house, see Peggy Albee, Molly Berger, H. Eliot Foulds, Nina Gray, and Pamela Herrick, *Vanderbilt Mansion: A Gilded-Age Country Place; A Historic Resources Study* (Boston: National Park Service Northeast Museum Services Center, 2008), 93–94. See also King, *The Vanderbilt Homes*.

25. As recently as 2009, Wayne Craven referred to the building campaign as a major component of "the social poker game" between Alice and Alva. Craven, *Gilded Mansions*, 133.

26. Richard Morris Hunt is perhaps the premier example of an architect who understood the extent to which American aristocrats were still in the process of defining their domestic requirements. While it is easy to assume that any architect would leap at the opportunity to design enormous, costly houses, Hunt seems to have been willing to engage with the requirements of the commissions at a different level. George Vanderbilt was so grateful for his efforts (and those of Frederick Law Olmsted) that he commissioned full-length portraits of the architect and landscape designer to hang at Biltmore.

27. The term *Knickerbocker* was in use by the 1870s to describe New York's social elites, many of whom were descendants of the city's original Dutch settlers. Craven implies that Knickerbockers disdained the tendency of new millionaires to flaunt their wealth in part because they themselves were not excessively wealthy. Craven, *Gilded Mansions*, 13.

28. In his well-documented history of Gilded Age mansions in New York and Newport, Craven traces the rise of the grand gala and the emergence of new room types, but he does not consider the disappearance of the parlor. Craven, *Gilded Mansions*, chapter 1.

29. King, *Vanderbilt Homes*, 11–13.

30. For a comparable experiment on the West Coast with creating new forms of domestic space, see Diana Strazdes, "The Millionaire's Palace: Leland Stanford's Commission for Pottier & Stymus in San Francisco," *Winterthur Portfolio* 36:4 (Winter 2001), 213–43.

31. Stern et al., *New York 1880*, 578–89.

32. Annmarie Adams, *Architecture in the Family Way: Doctors, Houses, and Women, 1870–1900* (Montreal: McGill-Queen's University Press, 1996), 78–79.

33. According to Stephanie Coontz, American fertility rates dropped 40 percent between 1855 and 1915, a trend accompanied by other changes in family life: families that "revolved more tightly around the nuclear core" and parents who "became more emotionally involved in child-rearing." Stephanie Coontz, *The Social Origins of Private Life: A History of American Families, 1600–1900* (London: Verso, 1988), 259–60.

34. In Sánchez-Eppler's reading of these temperance stories, incest was always in the background, as the young child's erotic appeal heightened the efficacy of his or her redemptive power. Sánchez-Eppler, *Dependent States*, chapter 2.

35. A fifth son, Allen Vanderbilt, died in 1846, before his first birthday. Find a Grave, database and images (https://www.findagrave.com/memorial/180677058/allen-vanderbilt, accessed 20 May 2024); memorial page for Allen Vanderbilt (11 December 1846–20 November 1847), Find a Grave Memorial ID 180677058, citing Vanderbilt Family Cemetery and Mausoleum, New Dorp, Richmond County, New York, USA; Maintained by Stories Of The Gilded Age (contributor 46959922).

36. Consuelo and the 9th Duke of Marlborough separated in 1906 and eventually divorced in 1921, just before her marriage to Louis Jacques Balsan. Vanderbilt, *Fortune's Children*, 285; Friedman, *Gertrude Vanderbilt Whitney*, 444.

37. Vanderbilt, *Fortune's Children*, 152–75.

38. After eleven years, Alice eventually acknowledged her daughter-in-law, but the reconciliation came too late for her husband, who had died in 1899. Vanderbilt, *Fortune's Children*, 202–16, 303–4.

39. Rebecca Edwards noted that 115 heiresses married noblemen between 1874 and 1911, and quoted turn-of-the-century commentator May Lease, who decried the practice as "selling our children to titled debauchees." Edwards, *New Spirits*, 101.

40. "Children of the Vanderbilts: How They are Trained, Dressed, and Educated," *Ladies' Home Journal* 7:11 (October 1890), 7.

41. As Annmarie Adams notes, nurseries also separated middle-class and elite women from their children, freeing their time to pursue the charitable works that were a notable component of Victorian culture. Adams, *Architecture in the Family Way*, 140–45.

42. According to Mark Girouard, the book functioned primarily as "tempting bait to rich clients." Kerr eventually published two expanded editions, one in 1865 and another in 1871. Mark Girouard, *The Victorian County House* (Oxford: Clarendon Press, 1971), 20, 121.

43. Robert Kerr, *The Gentleman's House or, How to Plan English Residences, From the Parsonage to the Palace*, 2nd ed. (London: John Murray 1865), 144.

44. Kerr, *Gentleman's House*, 144–45.

45. In contemporary critical theory, the concept of the abject explains the revulsion caused by dead bodies, excrement, rot, and decay—that which is neither subject nor object and so stands outside the symbolic order. According to Julia Kristeva, the abject is especially associated with the maternal body. Julia Kristeva, *Powers of Horror: An Essay on Abjection*, trans. Leon S. Roudiez (New York: Columbia University Press, 1982); Julia Kristeva, *Tales of Love*, trans. Leon Roudiez (New York: Columbia University Press, 1987). The plans depict Bear Wood (1865–74), the Berkshire house Kerr designed for John Walter, chief proprietor of *The Times*. Girouard, *Victorian County House*, 121–24.

46. Kerr, *Gentleman's House*, 147. Children were not the only members of the household to experience gender segregation. In Figure 3.7, note the stairway near the nurse's room; not accessible from this level, it connected bedrooms for male servants on the floor above to their workspaces on the floor below. Other stairs are identified as for the use of "women" (female servants), "young ladies," and "bachelors," and served to segregate the household by gender, as well as by class and marital status.

47. While it was unheard of to have the children themselves at social events, the senior Vanderbilts were nonetheless keen to acknowledge the existence of the next generation, an important first step in the long process of identifying appropriate mates and continuing the family line. Thus, bronze silhouette portraits by Augustus Saint-Gaudens ensured that likenesses of Gertrude, Bill, and Neily were on view to the Vanderbilts' dinner guests from 1882 on; a similar bronze portrait of Gladys, executed by H. LeGrand Cannon in 1890, may have also graced the Vanderbilts' New York City dining room. The double portrait of William and Neily is in the collection of the Metropolitan Museum of Art in New York, while the

individual portrait of Gertrude is in the collection of the Crystal Bridges Museum of American Art in Bentonville, Arkansas. The portrait of Gladys is reproduced in Armin Brand Allen, *The Cornelius Vanderbilts of the Breakers* (Newport, R.I.: Preservation Society of Newport County, 1995), 103.

48. The basement, ground-floor, and second-floor plans of the 1882 version of the house seem to have been lost, which explains to some extent why this iteration has received so little attention from architectural historians. Third- and fourth-floor plans preserved in the collections of the New-York Historical Society provide a rare view into the arrangement of spaces for the Vanderbilt children and their parents' house guests.

49. Craven, *Gilded Mansions*, 136–49.

50. Far from the setting for erotic encounters, the boudoir was, according to Kerr, "a Private Parlor for the mistress of the house," akin to "the Lady's Bower of the olden times"—that is, a quiet retreat from the social activity that dominated the rest of the house. Kerr, *Gentleman's House*, 114. On the fourth floor, the designation of two rooms as "Mrs. Vanderbilt's maid's room" and "Miss Vanderbilt's maid's room" confirm the architect's careful attention to providing parallel accommodation for mother and elder daughter.

51. Laura Jenkins, "Bathing the Civilised Body: From Venus to Vanderbilt," in "Civilising Decoration: French Interiors in the American Gilded Age" (Ph.D. thesis, Courtauld Institute of Art, University of London, 2024), chapter 4.

52. The architect's notation on plans dated 1894 ("Mr. Vanderbilt, Jr.") evidently refers to Neily, as Bill had contracted typhoid fever and died in May 1892, just after the remodeling project began.

53. The mantelpiece is now in the collection of the Metropolitan Museum of Art in New York; https://www.metmuseum.org/art/collection/search/9195, accessed 27 February 2023.

54. Perhaps because he is thinking of the house only in terms of its adult users, Craven does not recognize the existence of the third-floor boys' room. Instead, he says that the entrance hall fireplace was reinstalled in "the family sitting room on the second floor" (139) and misidentifies period photographs of the boys' room as "the billiard room on the second floor" (142–43). Craven, *Gilded Mansions*.

55. The Lorillards had two sons and two daughters: Emily (b. 1858), Pierre Jr. (b. 1860), Griswold (b. 1863), and Maude Louise (b. 1876). *The World Almanac and Encyclopedia 1906* (New York: Press Publishing Company, 1905), 157.

56. The phrase is Bowditch's, quoted in Tschirch, "Evolution of a Beaux-Arts Landscape," 5.

57. In addition to the carriage house and stable, the service area included greenhouses, identifiable in figure 3.12 by the "fingers" of their distinctive footprint.

58. Tschirch, "Evolution of a Beaux-Arts Landscape," 6.

59. Alva wrote in a draft of her memoirs that she felt herself "the most hated woman on earth," on Consuelo's wedding day. Vanderbilt, *Fortune's Children*, 176.

60. According to Holden, Peabody's published commentaries in professional journals confirm his role as "an early advocate of Colonial Revival forms." Holden, "Peabody Touch," 117.

61. Holden, "Peabody Touch," 120–21.

62. "Almshouses at Guildford," *Building News and Engineering Journal* 37:2 (4 July 1879), 8 and 10. "A Group of Almshouses at Guildford," *British Architect* 24 (18 December 1885). Holden

noted that a copy of the sketch published in *British Architect* is among the papers of Julius A. Schweinfurth, who "at the time was a rising young architect on the [Peabody and Stearns] office staff." The Schweinfurth papers are preserved at Northeastern University. Wheaton Arnold Holden, "Robert Swain Peabody of Peabody and Stearns in Boston: The Early Years (1870–1886)" (Ph.D. diss., Boston University, 1969), 94.

63. Robert Peabody's travel diaries are preserved in the papers of Wheaton Holden in Special Collections of Brown University.

64. Irony seems the least likely explanation, as neither Cornelius II nor Alice Vanderbilt possessed a whimsical nature; one lifelong acquaintance observed that he had never once seen Cornelius II smile. Vanderbilt, *Fortune's Children*, 177.

65. Ogata is primarily interested in the idea of the cottage as manifested in the work of Belgian architects associated with the Art Nouveau at the turn of the century. Nonetheless, she documents the longer development of an international fascination with the cottage, which she describes as "a culturally constructed idea that embodied an enduring, even prehistoric, tradition, intimately associated with the rural landscape, comfort, economy and rational planning" (66–67). She also discusses at length European and American admiration for the English cottage in particular, a phenomenon that was "pervasive during the second half of the nineteenth century" (79). Amy F. Ogata, *Art Nouveau and the Social Vision of Modern Living: Belgian Artists in a European Context* (Cambridge: Cambridge University Press, 2001).

66. For the cottage's characteristic elements, see Ogata, *Art Nouveau and the Social Vision of Modern Living*, 71–72.

67. The British almshouses originally included approximately twenty-four figural porch posts, several of which were saved when the buildings were pulled down in the 1970s to make way for a modern facility that is still called Hillier House. Twelve of the porch figures were incorporated in a garden folly still standing on the grounds, while two others now grace a bus stop nearby. The symbolic meaning of these figures is not clear. Some are vaguely classical, including a male Dionysian figure holding grapes and two female figures holding a lyre and a cornucopia. Others are vaguely medieval, including a man—perhaps a pilgrim—carrying a lantern. Two other figures—a bare-breasted woman carrying a water jug on her shoulder and a bare-chested man wearing a necklace and earrings—seem to represent Africans, or perhaps the African continent. It is not clear if Peabody was privy to the meaning Ernest George and Harold Peto attached to these figures; no mention of their meaning was included in *British Architect*.

68. It is not clear if these meanings were originally attached to the porch figures in Newport, as the building's symbolic content was not recorded in nineteenth-century documents. Given their link to the English almshouses, however, these attributions seem more likely than the explanation published by the Preservation Society of Newport County in 1952, namely, that they are "figures from Dutch folklore." Holbert T. Smales, *"The Breakers": An Illustrated Handbook* (Newport: Preservation Society of Newport County, 1952; 33rd printing, 1975), 32.

69. According to Craven, as a young man, the first Cornelius Vanderbilt "scorched the New York waterfront with his fists and his foul language." Even as a mature man and a millionaire, the Commodore remained "famous for his profanity." Craven, *Gilded Mansions*, 82, 84.

70. I am grateful to my colleague Robert Baldwin, who used his knowledge of Italian Renaissance villa culture to suggest this reading of the gable panel.

71. Mark Girouard, *Sweetness and Light: The Queen Anne Movement, 1860–1900* (New York: Oxford University Press, 1977; New Haven, Conn.: Yale University Press, 1984), 139–51.

72. Richardson & Boynton catalog, 1886, n.p.

73. The farm, which Vanderbilt called "Oakland," supplied eggs, chickens, milk, and vegetables used at the Breakers. Yet, it also provided sites for leisure. According to the *Mercury*, "The lawn is well trimmed, the beeches are noble in proportion and ample in shade, forming a continuous bower suggestive of lunches all day long. Not far off is a twenty-acre grove of oaks that Mr. Vanderbilt intends to make a veritable pleasure park, with drives, and paths, and seats, and rustic houses, such a gem of forestry as the island cannot boast elsewhere." "Fashion and Its Votaries at Newport," *Newport Mercury*, 6 September 1890, 4.

74. Gertrude Vanderbilt, diary entries, 20 July 1890 and 10 August 1890, Whitney Museum of American Art, Gertrude Vanderbilt Whitney Papers, gift of Flora Miller Irving.

75. Martha Falow's name appears on the passenger list of a ship carrying the Vanderbilts in 1889, when her age was listed as thirty-five. I am grateful to Jeroen van den Hurk for tracking down this information.

76. Preserved in the collections of the Redwood Library, the photographs are unsigned.

77. Laura Jenkins, "The Gilded Interior: French Style and the American Renaissance," *Architectural History* 64 (2021), 102. Alva Vanderbilt likewise embraced the fashion for eighteenth-century French furnishing, which she used to express her lofty social aspirations by purchasing pieces with royal provenance, notably a commode and *secretaire* once owned by Marie-Antoinette. See also Yurio Jackall, "American Visions of Eighteenth-Century France," in *America Collects Eighteenth-Century French Painting* (Washington, D.C.: National Gallery of Art, 2017), 11–15.

78. Mimi Hellman, "Furniture, Sociability, and the Work of Leisure in Eighteenth-Century France," *Eighteenth-Century Studies* 32 (1999), particularly 415–16.

79. As a future hostess, Gertrude may have benefited from understanding the complex workings of the Breakers kitchen, but the spatial logic of the estate—which worked to maintain the invisibility of service spaces, at least to the family and their guests—precluded her from trespassing into that realm.

80. As Steward points out, "This kind of playacting at being of a lower class was a complex commentary on class and social relationships." Yet, the effectiveness of such images depended on their use of conceptual connections (in this case between children and peasants) that viewers found appropriate. James Christen Steward, *The New Child: British Art and the Origins of Modern Childhood, 1730–1830* (Berkeley: University Art Museum and Pacific Film Archive, 1995), 87–88.

81. Given Greenaway's influence on children's clothing—including the "Greenaway dress" sold at Liberty of London—the "white dress" Gertrude Vanderbilt lent to Sybil Sherman might well have been the kind of simple cotton or muslin dress donned during the day by many a young woman of fashion as a symbol of her innocence and simplicity. For Greenaway's impact on children's fashion, see *Encyclopedia of Children and Childhood in History and Society*, 1st ed., s.v. "Greenaway, Kate (1846–1901)."

82. Hall is credited with coining the term *adolescence*, which is also the title of his best-known work, *Adolescence: Its Psychology and Its Relations to Physiology, Anthropology, Sociology, Sex, Crime, Religion and Education* (New York: Appleton, 1904), 2 vols. See also Dorothy Ross, *G. Stanley Hall:*

Psychologist as Prophet (Chicago: University of Chicago Press, 1972), and Gail Bederman, *Manliness and Civilization: A Cultural History of Gender and Race in the United States, 1880–1917* (Chicago: University of Chicago Press, 1995), chapter 3.

83. Balsan, *The Glitter and the Gold*, 14.

84. Alva Vanderbilt Belmont memoirs, quoted in Vanderbilt, *Fortune's Children*, 125.

85. In an interview with the author, one of Gertrude Vanderbilt's granddaughters recalled going to the cottage in the 1920s with a large number of young cousins. Interview with Pam Le Boutillier, 31 May 2007.

86. Friedman, *Gertrude Vanderbilt Whitney*, 55–56; Vanderbilt, *Fortune's Children*, 202–23.

87. Friedman, *Gertrude Vanderbilt Whitney*, 26–27.

88. Leonore Davidoff, Megan Doolittle, Janet Fink, and Katherine Holden, *The Family Story: Blood, Contract and Intimacy, 1830–1960* (London: Longman, 1999), 168–69.

4. A CONUNDRUM FOR ELITE PARENTS

1. The parallels between Mount Airy and Highlawn include devoting one outbuilding to family use and one to service activities. At both sites, those who worked in the service outbuilding were rendered invisible, either by their race and enslaved status (at Mount Airy) or by a screen created by a pergola and teahouse (at Highlawn). Mount Airy's entry sequence is analyzed in Dell Upton, *Holy Things and Profane: Anglican Parish Churches in Colonial Virginia* (New York: Architectural History Foundation; Cambridge, Mass.: MIT Press, 1986), 206–7 and 216–18. The screening of the Highlawn service yard is discussed in Samuel Howe, *American Country Houses of To-Day* (New York: Architectural Book Publishing Company, 1915), 192–97.

2. G. Stanley Hall, introduction to Alice Minnie Herts Heniger, *The Kingdom of the Child* (New York: E. P. Dutton, 1918), 2; quoted in Robin Bernstein, *Racial Innocence: Performing American Childhood from Slavery to Civil Rights* (New York: New York University Press, 2011), 184. Bernstein notes that Heniger had established a children's theater on the Lower East Side of New York in 1903 in order to use the power of imaginative play to Americanize the children of recent immigrants and through them their parents. In *The Kingdom of the Child*, she also encouraged native-born Americans to encourage imaginative play by pretending right along with their children. Bernstein, *Racial Innocence*, 184–85.

3. Gail Bederman, *Manliness and Civilization: A Cultural History of Gender and Race in the United States, 1880–1917* (Chicago: University of Chicago Press, 1995), 25–26.

4. No longer extant playhouses built by elite families include a rustic treehouse at Windy Gates, the Baltimore estate of railroad executive Joseph W. Jenkins (circa 1890), and a playhouse at Trygveson, the Andrew Calhoun and Mary Trigg Calhoun estate in Atlanta, Georgia (circa 1919). See Mac Griswold and Eleanor Weller, *The Golden Age of American Gardens: Proud Owners, Private Estates, 1890–1940* (New York: H. N. Abrams, in association with the Garden Club of America, 1991), 146–47 and 215. In the Philadelphia area, there was once a log cabin on the grounds of Grey Arches, the Chestnut Hill estate of William J. Latta (1890s); a playhouse at Stonehurst, the Charles Wolcott Henry and Sallie Houston Henry estate, also in Chestnut Hill (circa 1900; photograph in the collection of the Chestnut Hill Conservancy and Historical Society); and a thatched cottage built by Thomas Pym Cope Jr. at Awbury in

Germantown (circa 1900; photograph in the collection of the Awbury Arboretum). On Long Island, William May Wright and Cobina Wright had a miniature playhouse built for their daughter at their Sands Point estate, Casa Cobina (circa 1920s). Cobina Wright, *I Never Grew Up* (New York: Prentice-Hall, 1952), 187 and 190.

There are extant playhouses that are not discussed in this chapter, notably an outbuilding erected in 1905 for J. Levering Jones at a Chestnut Hill property he called Homecroft; although identified on later Sanborn maps as a playhouse, it may have been originally designed as a smoking retreat. Chestnut Hill Historic District Inventory, 245; see also James B. Garrison, *Houses of Philadelphia: Chestnut Hill and the Wissahickon Valley, 1880–1930* (New York: Acanthus Press, 2008), 77–82. Another is a derelict miniature house on the grounds of what was once Muttontown Meadows, a Long Island estate built by Bronson Winthrop in the early twentieth century and given to his brother Egerton Winthrop in about 1910. As Bronson was childless, the miniature house was presumably built by Egerton. "Muttontown Meadows/Nassau Hall," *Old Long Island* blog post, 16 June 2008, http://www.oldlongisland.com/2008/06/muttontown-meadow-nassau-hall.html. Also in a derelict state is the so-called Doll House (built around 1912) at Sabattis Adventure Camp, formerly Tarnedge, the Charles and Florence Goodyear Daniels estate, at Long Lake, New York. Richard Longstreth, *A Guide to Architecture in the Adirondacks* (Keesville, N.Y.: Adirondack Architectural Heritage, 2017), 366. See also "What Is Happening with Sabattis Adventure Camp?" on the Sabattis Group website (https://www.sabattisgroup.org/info), updated in 2022. In Tarrytown, New York, Rose Cottage was built for Helen Gould Shepard and Finley J. Shepard in 1916; although it still stands on the grounds of Lyndhurst, it has a particularly sparse archival record. Personal communication with Krystyn Silver, 13 March 2019.

5. Gertrude Vanderbilt Whitney may also have had a playhouse built for her children at her Long Island estate in Old Westbury, New York. Certainly, her niece, Gloria Vanderbilt, remembered "a little house" at the edge of the garden when she was living there in the early 1930s. In her memoirs, Gloria described its exterior as "painted all white," while "inside there was just one room—a perfect little room with just enough in it for two people to sit and have a tea party." Given that its simple forms are similar to those of the playhouse at Greentree, it too may have dated from the early years of the twentieth century when Gertrude's children were young. Gloria Vanderbilt, *Once upon a Time: A True Story* (New York: Alfred A. Knopf, 1985), 64.

6. "'The Master Mind of Standard Oil': Personality and Business Career of Henry H. Rogers Whose Death Marks the Close of a Memorable Era in the Creation of Gigantic Industrial Enterprises," *New York Times*, 23 May 1909, SM1. The Black Point playhouse is mentioned in Edith Crouch, *Walker & Gillette: American Architects; From Classicism through Modernism, 1900–1950s* (Atglen, Pa.: Shiffer, 2013), 143–44, although the text misidentifies the owner of the house as Henry H. Rogers, "William Coe's father-in-law," who was long dead when Black Point was started in 1914. The playhouse at Coe Hall is mentioned in Henry B. Joyce, *Guidebook to Coe Hall* (Oyster Bay, N.Y.: Planting Fields Foundation, 2018), 76.

7. The playhouse at the Manor House is referenced in Keith N. Morgan, *Charles A. Platt: The Artist as Architect* (New York: Architectural History Foundation, 1985; Cambridge, Mass.: MIT Press, 1985), 106; and Robert B. MacKay, Anthony K. Baker, and Carol A. Traynor, eds., *Long Island Country Houses and Their Architects, 1860–1940* (New York: W. W. Norton, 1997), 349.

8. The Frick playhouse received a brief mention in "Interesting Brick Architecture in Pittsburg, Pa. Domestic," *Brickbuilder* 2:2 (November 1902), 228; and in Margaret Henderson Floyd, *Architecture After Richardson: Regionalism Before Modernism—Longfellow, Alden and Harlow in Boston and Pittsburgh* (Chicago: University of Chicago Press, 1994), 185. The playhouse on the grounds of Westbury House is pictured in Richard Cheek (photographer), *Old Westbury Gardens* (Long Island, N.Y.: Old Westbury Gardens, 1985), 22, where it is identified as a "tea cottage." Jay Phipps's brother, Henry Carnegie "Hal" Phipps, built a similar, if not identical, thatched playhouse on the grounds of Spring Hill, also in Old Westbury, New York. In 2008, it was still standing, but in a ruinous state. "Spring Hill Playhouse/Playground," *Old Long Island* blogpost, 20 August 2008, http://www.oldlongisland.com/2008/08/spring-hill-playhouse-playground.html.

9. The playhouse at Foxhollow Farm appeared in Frank Miles Day, *American Country Houses of Today* (New York: American Book Publishing, 1912), 6; was pictured in David Byars, *Our Time at Foxhollow Farm: A Hudson Valley Family Remembered* (Albany: State University of New York Press, 2016), 58; and received the briefest acknowledgment in Peter Pennoyer and Anne Walker, *Harrie T. Lindeberg and the American Country House* (New York: Monacelli Press, 2017), 56. Three images of the playhouse at Sinnissippi were published in *Western Architect* 27 (November 1918), plates 4–6.

10. Quoted in Howard P. Chudacoff, *Children at Play: An American History* (New York: New York University Press, 2007), 98.

11. As Viviana Zelitzer has argued, it is not just that mechanized vehicles were making the streets more hazardous for playing children, but that adults increasingly deemed the increasingly economically "useless" child as "emotionally" priceless. Viviana A. Zelizer, *Pricing the Priceless Child: The Changing Social Value of Children* (Princeton, N.J.: Princeton University Press, 1994).

12. Many scholars have written about the organized playground movement in the United States, but few have put it into its international context. Doing so would reveal that American playgrounds omitted the gardens that were often a component of outdoor gymnasia in early nineteenth-century Germany; as Sun-Young Park argues, these sites "emphasized the garden space as a key pedagogical realm . . . [intended to] cultivate mind, body and spirit." Devoid of gardens, American playgrounds were more akin to the gymnasiums in mid-nineteenth-century Paris, where "gymnastics, once depicted as a joyful mix of games and exercise in a verdant garden, appears to have devolved into a set of formulaic drills." Sun-Young Park, *Ideals of the Body: Architecture, Urbanism, and Hygiene in Postrevolutionary Paris* (Pittsburgh: University of Pittsburgh, 2018), especially 50–51, 210. For American playgrounds, see Dominick Cavallo, *Muscles and Morals: Organized Playgrounds and Urban Reform, 1880–1920* (Philadelphia: University of Pennsylvania Press, 1981); Peter C. Baldwin, *Domesticating the Street: The Reform of Public Space in Hartford, 1850–1930* (Columbus: Ohio State University Press, 1999); Elizabeth A. Gagen, "Playing the Part: Performing Gender in America's Playgrounds," in *Children's Geographies: Playing, Living, Learning*, ed. Sarah L. Holloway and Gill Valentine (London: Routledge, 2000), 213–229; Sarah Jo Peterson, "Voting for Play: The Democratic Potential of Progressive Era Playgrounds," *Journal of the Society of the Gilded Age and Progressive Era* 3:2 (April 2004), 145–75; Chudacoff, *Children at Play*, 73, 111–16; Marta Gutman, *A City for Children: Women, Architecture, and the Charitable Landscapes of Oakland, 1850–1950* (Chicago: University of Chicago Press, 2014), 217–25; and Michael Hines,

"'They Do Not Know How to Play': Reformers' Expectation and Children's Realities on the First Progressive Playgrounds of Chicago," *Journal of the History of Childhood and Youth* 10:2 (Spring 2017), 206–27.

13. Lisa Jacobson, *Raising Consumers: Children and the American Mass Market in the Early Twentieth Century* (New York: Columbia University Press, 2004), 162–63.

14. Chudacoff, *Children at Play*, 98–125.

15. Bryn Varley Hollenbeck, "Making Spaces for Children: The Material Culture of American Childhoods, 1900–1950" (Ph.D. diss., University of Delaware, 2008), 243–44.

16. *Illustrated Descriptive Catalogue of Portable Houses* (Buffalo, N.Y.: National Construction Company, 1907), 10.

17. *M. & M. Portable Houses* (Saginaw, Mich.: Mershon & Morley, n.d.), 10–13.

18. *Hodgson Portable Houses* (Boston: E. F. Hodgson, 1916), 36–39. The conversion of 1916 dollars into 2024 dollars comes from the CPI Inflation Calculator: https://www.in2013dollars.com/us/inflation/1916?amount=150, accessed 22 May 2024; and https://www.in2013dollars.com/us/inflation/1916?amount=273, accessed 22 May 2024.

19. By the early 1930s, 46 percent of the houses owned by professional parents had backyard swings, while 58 percent had sandboxes. Gary Cross, *Kids' Stuff: Toys and the Changing World of American Childhood* (Cambridge, Mass.: Harvard University Press, 1997), 128.

20. Hanna Tachau, "The Boy's Room," *House Beautiful* 37 (May 1915), 190–91.

21. Cross, *Kids' Stuff*, 127–29; Jacobson, *Raising Consumers*, 165–69.

22. Karin Calvert, *Children in the House: The Material Culture of Early Childhood, 1600–1900* (Boston: Northeastern University Press, 1992), 131.

23. Agnes Rowe Fairman, "The Child's Own Room," *Good Housekeeping* 60 (March 1915), 287–89; and Nina Tachau, "The Child's Own Room," *House Beautiful* 37 (April 1915), 156–57.

24. Calvert, *Children in the House*, 130.

25. As Bryn Hollenbeck demonstrates, the transition was not without its detractors. Especially in the early years of the twentieth century, some commentators continued to see the parlor as an adult sanctuary, Hollenbeck, "Making Space," 100–12.

26. Miriam Formanek-Brunnell was perhaps the first scholar to take seriously the fact that girls often intentionally broke their dolls, acts she interpreted as self-conscious challenges to patriarchal authority. More recently, Robin Bernstein has connected doll play to large-scale racial projects, such as slavery, abolition, and antiblack violence, arguing that the materiality of black dolls helped "script" their abuse in performances of childhood that helped coproduce racist culture. Miriam Formanek-Brunnell, *Made to Play House: Dolls and the Commercialization of American Girlhood, 1830–1930* (New Haven, Conn.: Yale University Press, 1993), 30–33. Robin Bernstein, *Racial Innocence: Performing American Childhood from Slavery to Civil Rights* (New York: New York University Press, 2011).

27. Cross, *Kids' Stuff*, 79–81.

28. John R. Gillis notes that the transformation of Christmas began in the mid-nineteenth century, as Father Christmas (a figure akin to grim Father Time) was reinvented as jovial Santa Claus. By the early twentieth century, Christmas was firmly established as "a children's feast." According to Gary Cross, the holiday had long been associated with overindulgence, which granted parents permission to give extravagantly to their children in an act that transformed

money earned in the market into an expression of family sentiment understood to be "radically separate from that market." John R. Gillis, *A World of Their Own Making: Myth, Ritual, and the Quest for Family Values* (New York: Basic Books, 1996), 98–104; Cross, *Kids' Stuff*, 44–45.

29. "Books for Children," *Book Notes: A Monthly Literary Magazine and Review of New Books* 1 (July–December 1898), 418; "New Holiday Gifts for All" [advertisement], *Book Notes: A Monthly Literary Magazine and Review of New Books* 1 (July–December 1898), 350. The conversion of 1898 dollars into 2024 dollars comes from the CPI Inflation Calculator: https://www.in2013dollars.com/us/inflation/1898?amount=5, accessed 22 May 2024.

30. Gary Cross, *The Cute and the Cool: Wondrous Innocence and Modern American Children's Culture* (Oxford: Oxford University Press, 2004), 33–35.

31. Even when urban children were "doing nothing," child savers interpreted their lack of purposeful play as "the first step on the road to gambling, thievery, vandalism and fighting." Chudacoff, *Children at Play*, 110.

32. Hollenbeck makes this point directly about class, if not about race. Hollenbeck, "Making Space," 99–100.

33. "Miss Helen Hay," *Harper's Weekly* 45: 2348 (21 December 1901), cover.

34. Biographical information is drawn from E. J. Kahn Jr., *Jock: The Life and Times of John Hay Whitney* (New York: Doubleday, 1981), 1–15 and 22–26.

35. For *Beasts and Birds* and *The Little Boy Book*, see *The Bookseller* 5:2 (June 1900), 138; for *Verses for Jock and Joan*, see *Publishers Weekly* 68:1764 (18 November 1905), 1330; for *The Punch and Judy Book*, see *Publishers Weekly* 70:1814 (3 November 1906), 1247; for *The Bed-Time Book*, see *A.L.A. Booklist* 4:1 (January 1908), 116.

36. Helen Hay, *The Little Boy Book* (New York: R. H. Russell, 1900), n.p.

37. Helen Hay, *Verses for Jock and Joan* (New York: Fox, Duffield, 1905), 15.

38. Hay, *Little Boy Book*, n.p.

39. Clara Stone Hay to Helen Hay Whitney, 11 July 1903, John Hay Whitney and Betsey Cushing Whitney Family Papers (MS 1938), Manuscripts and Archives, Yale University Library.

40. For Americans like the Whitneys, European travel could serve as "an extension of communal behavior at home, . . . enabl[ing] them to extend and consolidate networks of kin, friends and acquaintances on both sides of the Atlantic." In Paris, such travelers acquired culture and high-end consumer goods, while devoting their time in London to "socializing and strengthening close ties with members of the aristocracy." Maureen E. Montgomery, "'Natural Distinction': The American Bourgeois Search for Distinctive Signs in Europe," in *The American Bourgeoisie*, 31 and 33.

41. Journal of Helen Hay Whitney, 5 February 1907, 17 August 1907, 28 September 1907, John Hay Whitney and Betsey Cushing Whitney Family Papers (MS 1938), Manuscripts and Archives, Yale University Library.

42. Joan Whitney described Jock's party in a letter to her parents, who were in London. The activities she mentioned included sack races, barrel races, hoop races, and three-legged races. In addition to the cameras, presents given to the guests included guns (which both Jock and Joan received), ring tosses, tennis rackets, "and lots of other things." Joan Whitney to Payne Whitney and Helen Hay Whitney, 20 August 1912, John Hay Whitney and Betsey Cushing Whitney Family Papers (MS 1938), Manuscripts and Archives, Yale University Library.

43. Helen Hay Whitney to Payne Whitney, 1 September 1902, John Hay Whitney and Betsey Cushing Whitney Family Papers (MS 1938), Manuscripts and Archives, Yale University Library.

44. The published plans of Greentree show a secondary door adjacent to the main entrance leading into a space labeled "present hallway," suggesting that the Whitneys had hired d'Hauteville and Cooper to expand an existing house. "Summer Home of Payne Whitney, Esq., Manhasset, L.I.," *Architects' and Builder's Magazine* 36:9 (June 1904), 393–96.

45. Jane Hamlett, *Material Relations, Families and Domestic Interiors in England, 1850–1910* (Manchester: Manchester University Press, 2010), 111.

46. The Lowdens may have turned to Pond and Pond because of Irving K. Pond's work on Pullman, Illinois, as he was employed by architect Solon S. Beman from 1880 to 1887, working initially on George Pullman's company town and later designing details for the Pullman Building in Chicago, where he and his brother Allen Pond rented office space when they formed their own architectural firm in 1887. Allen Pond's friendship with Jane Addams and the firm's work on Hull House and other Chicago settlement houses may have also been a factor. At the time of her engagement to Frank Lowden in 1896, the *New York Times* reported that Florence Pullman took "a keen interest in the Hull House work of Jane Addams." After they designed the house at Sinnissippi, the Ponds sometimes encountered the Lowdens socially at the Eagle's Nest Camp, an artists' colony on the Rock River, near the Lowden estate in Oregon, Illinois. Irving K. Pond, *The Autobiography of Irving K. Pond: The Sons [sic] of Mary and Elihu*, ed. David Swan and Terry Tatum (Oak Park, Ill.: Hyoogen Press, 2009), 82–91, 139, 175–85, and 361–63. "Frank O. Lowden and Miss Florence Pullman: They Are to Be Married in Chicago Next Month," *New York Times*, 22 March 1896, 26.

47. William Herbert, "The House of Col. Frank O. Lowden, at Oregon, Ill.," *Architectural Record* 22:4 (October 1907), 299–303.

48. Biographical information on the Field family is drawn from a finding guide compiled in 2006: Megan O'Shea, "William B. Osgood Field Papers, 1610–1952, n.d., MssColl 6090," Manuscripts and Archives Division, Humanities and Social Sciences Library, New York Public Library.

49. Information about finishes and furniture are drawn from an invoice issued on 1 August 1910 by the Department of Decorations of W. & J. Sloane, a New York rug and furniture store. The original is preserved in the William B. Osgood Field Estate Records, Department of Drawings and Archives, Avery Architectural and Fine Arts Library, Columbia University.

50. W. & J. Sloane invoice, 1 August 1910, preserved in the William B. Osgood Field Estate Records, Department of Drawings and Archives, Avery Architectural and Fine Arts Library, Columbia University.

51. Biographical information is drawn from the Wikipedia entry on John Teele Pratt, https://en.wikipedia.org/wiki/John_Teele_Pratt, accessed 31 August 2021.

52. Mackay et al. assert that the room labeled billiard room on the plan was in fact Ruth Pratt's study. It may well be that she claimed this room as her study after her husband's death in 1927, using it for this purpose during her service in the U.S. Congress from 1929 to 1930 and until her death in 1965. However, its proportions, its regular rectangular form, and its location near the dining room suggest that it was indeed designed as a billiard room, if it was only used

that way for a relatively short period of time. Mackay, Baker, and Traynor, *Long Island Country Houses*, 350. For the location and form of the billiard room in a British context, see Jill Franklin, *The Gentleman's Country House and Its Plan, 1835–1914* (London: Routledge & Kegan Paul, 1981), 55–56; and Robert Kerr, *The Gentleman's House*, 119–20.

53. The cottage Isabel Rockefeller purchased for Owenoke Farm in Greenwich, Connecticut, appears to be a version of the two-room cottage (catalog number 1602), which in 1916 cost between $420 and $475, depending on size. *Hodgson Portable Houses*, 7.

54. In an 1896 letter to her son, Adelaide Frick reported that "Papa has promised to have a play house built for [Helen] this summer and she wants an up stairs to it and a whole lot of rooms." Correspondence between architects Alden and Harlow and Henry Clay Frick reveals that the building was constructed in 1897 and makes reference to the "little girls room, first floor" and "second story, future dark room." Adelaide Frick to Childs Frick, 1 March 1896, Childs Frick Papers, The Frick Collection/Frick Art Reference Library Archives. The 1897 Alden and Harlow correspondence is quoted in UDA Architects and Robbins Grulke Architect, "The Playhouse at Clayton: Restoration of the West Porch," unpublished report, March 1989, 2.

55. Marikia Ogiz to Adelaide Frick, 2 February 1898. Henry Clay Frick Papers, The Frick Collection/Frick Art Reference Library Archives.

56. Anna [surname unknown] writing on behalf of Marjorie Field and Mary (May) Field, 30 September 1918. William B. Osgood Field Papers, series IX, Lila Vanderbilt Sloane Field, 1889–1938, Manuscripts and Archives Division, Humanities and Social Sciences Library, New York Public Library.

57. Edith Wharton and Ogden Codman Jr., introduction to *The Decoration of Houses* (New York: Scribner, 1902; repr., New York: W.W. Norton, 1978), n.p.

58. Wharton and Codman, *Decoration of Houses*, 177.

59. Laurel J. Waycott, "Reflective Creatures: Goldfish, Affluence, and Affect in Gilded Age New York," *Winterthur Portfolio* 54:2/3 (Summer/Autumn 2020), 151–52.

60. Quoted in Waycott, "Reflective Creatures," 161.

61. Thorstein Veblen, *The Theory of the Leisure Class: An Economic Study of Institutions* (1899; repr., New York: Augustus M. Kelley, 1975), 74.

62. Veblen, *Theory of the Leisure Class*, 97.

63. Carnegie's essay "The Gospel of Wealth" was first published in 1889 but reprinted in 1901. Waycott, "Reflective Creatures," 167. See also Abigail A. Van Slyck, *Free to All: Carnegie Libraries and American Culture, 1890–1920* (Chicago: University of Chicago Press, 1995), 19–24. The Rockefeller Foundation, for example, was started in 1913.

64. Isaac F. Marcosson, "The Simple Life among the Rich: The Diet and the Method behind Million Making," *Saturday Evening Post*, 3 January 1914, 8–10, 40–41.

65. Waycott, "Reflective Creatures," 151.

66. Wharton and Codman, *Decoration of Houses*, 178, 180–82.

67. Wharton and Codman, *Decoration of Houses*, 181.

68. Although buildings such as the Dows playhouse are typically labeled Dutch Colonial Revival, the structures they referenced were sometimes the work of Huguenot and German Palatine immigrants to North America (and so not always Dutch) and were often built after the Dutch colony of New Netherlands ceased to exist (and so not strictly colonial). Jeroen van

den Hurk, "Imagining New Netherland: Origins and Survival of Netherlandic Architecture in Old New York" (PhD diss., University of Delaware, 2006), 3.

69. Day, *American Country Houses of Today*, 6.

70. See William H. Crawford, "Frank O. Lowden," *North American Review* 225:840 (February 1928), 145.

71. A history of Camp Lowden (the Boy Scout camp on the site) confirms that "Mrs. Lowden purchased the house and the land on May 20, 1899." http://www.camplowdenhistory.org/spotlights/lowden_frank.html, accessed 2 September 2021.

72. A brochure "prepared and published by friends of Frank O. Lowden" included a section called "Goes Back to the Farm" and discussed at length "his unflagging interest in agriculture." *Frank O. Lowden, Governor of Illinois* (Chicago: Allied Print, 1919), n.p.

73. Lowden's biographical information is drawn from "Guide to the Frank O. Lowden Papers circa 1870–1943," Hanna Holborn Gray Special Collections Research Center, University of Chicago Library, https://www.lib.uchicago.edu/e/scrc/findingaids/view.php?eadid=ICU.SPCL.LOWDENF, accessed 2 September 2021.

74. "Lowden Sticks Quietly to His Farm in Illinois, Refusing to Talk on All Presidential Rumors," *New York Times*, 7 June 1936, 332.

75. *Western Architect* 27 (November 1918), plate 6.

76. Ted Newcomen claimed that the playhouse was "a present for [Lowden's] two daughters following their recovery from polio." Yet, the timeline does not bear out this interpretation; the plans carry a date of June 1909, while the letters and telegrams the girls' mother received during their illness arrived in October and November 1910. Ted Newcomen, "The Hopi House: 'The Children's Playhouse' designed by Pond and Pond at 'Sinnissippi', Rock River, Illinois," unpublished typescript (February 1997), 2, housed in the Art Institute of Chicago Archives. The Pullman–Miller family papers at the Chicago History Museum include a file of "Letters and telegrams received during illness [infantile paralysis/polio] of Florence and Harriet October and November 1910." Jane McCarthy, "Pullman–Miller papers, ca. 1823–1988: Descriptive Inventory for the Collection at Chicago History Museum, Research Center" (2005): http://chsmedia.org/media/fa/fa/M-P/Pull-Miller.htm, accessed 2 September 2021.

77. According to Ted Newcomen, the Lowdens dubbed the building "Hopi House," suggesting that they saw parallels between the style of their playhouse and contemporary use of Native American motifs in buildings that played on contemporary understanding of American Indians as noble savages, standing outside evolutionary time. Perhaps they were aware of Hopi House, a 1905 building at the Grand Canyon designed by architect Mary Colter. That there was some family connection to Arizona is borne out by the fact that Frank O. Lowden had retired to Tucson by 1927. Newcomen, "The Hopi House."

5. PRACTICING DOMESTIC VIRTUE

1. Helen Le Baron Whiteley, "Bobbed-Haired Girls Rare Among 'Debbies'—Only Seven Eschew Long Tresses—Frances Dodge Entertains in Unique Playhouse—Army-Navy Game Lures Many," *Detroit News*, 28 November 1926. Clipping preserved in Meadow Brook Hall Archives.

2. Abigail A. Van Slyck, *A Manufactured Wilderness: Summer Camps and the Making of American Youth, 1890–1960* (Minneapolis: University of Minnesota Press, 2006), 8–14. See also W. Barksdale Maynard, "'An Ideal Life in the Woods for Boys': Architecture and Culture in the Earliest Summer Camps," *Winterthur Portfolio* 34 (Spring 1999), 3–29.

3. As architectural historian H. Horatio Joyce argues, Harvard took the lead in assuming responsibility for creating an American leadership class, and soon New York was home to Harvard House and other alumni clubhouses that served as visible traces of the amalgamation of upper-class male identity with an emerging American alumni culture. H. Horatio Joyce, "New York's Harvard House and the Origins of an Alumni Culture in America," in *Experiencing Architecture in the Nineteenth Century*, ed. Edward Gillin and H. Horatio Joyce (New York: Bloomsbury, 2018), 89–100.

4. Helen Frick to Henry Clay Frick, 5 May 1898. Henry Clay Frick Papers, Frick Collection/Frick Art Reference Library Archives.

5. See Gertrude Jekyll, *Children and Gardens* (1908; repr., Woodbridge, Suffolk: Antique Collectors' Club, 1990), 25.

6. Jekyll, *Children and Gardens*, 26.

7. Jekyll, *Children and Gardens*, 27 and 36.

8. Jekyll, *Children and Gardens*, 28.

9. Jekyll, *Children and Gardens*, 27.

10. Jekyll, *Children and Gardens*, 26.

11. Gertrude Jekyll, "The Children's Play-House," *Country Life Illustrated* 9:230 (1 June 1901), 707–8.

12. Jekyll, *Children and Gardens*, 27.

13. Peggie Phipps Boegner and Richard Gachot, *Halcyon Days: An American Family Through Three Generations* (New York: Old Westbury Gardens and Harry N. Abrams, 1986), 161.

14. William B. Osgood Field to William Osgood Field, 25 September 1917, William B. Osgood Field Papers, Manuscripts and Archives Division, New York Public Library.

15. May Field to William B. Osgood Field and Lila Vanderbilt Sloane Field, postmarked 10 October 1921, William B. Osgood Field Papers, Manuscripts and Archives Division, New York Public Library.

16. Osgood Field to Marjorie Field, 21 April 1921, William B. Osgood Field Papers, Manuscripts and Archives Division, New York Public Library.

17. Frederick Vanderbilt Field, *From Right to Left: An Autobiography* (Westport, Conn.: Lawrence Hill, 1983), 20–21.

18. Marjorie Field to Frederick Field, postmarked 29 June 1924, William B. Osgood Field Papers, Manuscripts and Archives Division, New York Public Library.

19. William B. Osgood Field to William Osgood Field, 1 October 1914, William B. Osgood Field Papers, Manuscripts and Archives Division, New York Public Library.

20. Frederick Field, *From Right to Left*, 66.

21. William B. Osgood Field to Frederick Field, 9 November 1927, William B. Osgood Field Papers, Manuscripts and Archives Division, New York Public Library.

22. Dolores Hayden, *The Grand Domestic Revolution: A History of Feminist Designs for American Homes, Neighborhoods, and Cities* (Cambridge, Mass.: MIT Press, 1981), 281.

23. Hayden, *Grand Domestic Revolution*, 283–86.

24. Summarizing decades of feminist scholarship, Ellen Lupton could assert that "standards of cleanliness and child care rose dramatically between 1920 and 1960, leaving women with *more* work rather than less. In the domestic economy of 'labor-saving' devices, work saved on one task often diverts to another." Ellen Lupton, *Mechanical Brides: Women and Machines from Home to Office* (New York: Cooper-Hewitt Museum of Design and Princeton Architectural Press, 1993), 15.

25. Lucy Wheelock, ed., *The Kindergarten Children's Hour* (Boston: Houghton Mifflin, 1920), vol. 2, *Children's Occupations*, by Maude Cushing Nash, 78.

26. Nash, *Children's Occupations*, 78–79.

27. For over two years in the early 1920s, for instance, the front page of the *Dearborn Independent* ran a weekly series titled "The International Jew: The World's Problem." Although the Federal Council of Churches and other American leaders condemned the series, Ford offered an apology only in 1927, after he was sued for libel (he claimed he was not aware of what the paper was publishing). Steven Watts, *The People's Tycoon: Henry Ford and the American Century* (New York: Alfred A. Knopf, 2005), 376–97. For Ford's views on immigrants, see "What Makes Immigration a 'Problem'?" *Ford Ideals, Being a Selection from "Mr. Ford's Page" in the Dearborn Independent* (Dearborn, Mich: Dearborn Publishing, 1922), 401–4.

28. Hayden, *Grand Domestic Revolution*, 281 and 286.

29. For Ford's activities at the Wayside Inn, see Abigail Carroll, "Of Kettles and Cranes: Colonial Revival Kitchens and the Performance of National Identity," *Winterthur Portfolio* 43:4 (Winter 2009), 335–37, 344–49, and 354–55. See also Patricia West, *Domesticating History: The Political Origins of America's House Museums* (Washington, D.C.: Smithsonian Institution Press, 1999), 96.

30. Ford quoted in West, *Domesticating History*, 97.

31. *A Guide Book for the Edison Institute Museum and Greenfield Village* (Dearborn, Mich.: Edison Institute, 1937), 46.

32. For Americanization efforts, see Stephen Meyer, "Adapting the Immigrant to the Line: Americanization in the Ford Factory, 1914–1921," *Journal of Social History* 14:1 (Autumn 1980), 67–82.

33. Penny Sparke, *As Long as It's Pink: The Sexual Politics of Taste* (1995; repr., Halifax: Press of the Nova Scotia College of Art and Design, 2010), 92–93.

34. For Ford's resistance to these design changes, see West, *Domesticating History*, 96–97, and Watts, *People's Tycoon*, 366–75.

35. Watts, *People's Tycoon*, 358–66.

36. Quoted in Watts, *People's Tycoon*, 305.

37. For Jensen's work at Gaukler Pointe, see Robin Karson, *A Genius for Place: American Landscape of the Country Place Era* (Amherst: University of Massachusetts Press, in association with the Library of American Landscape History, 2007), 239–64. Jensen was also involved in the landscape design for Fair Lane, but came into conflict with the senior Fords when Clara hired another landscape architect to install the formal rose garden in the middle of one of Jensen's signature meadows. Robert E. Grese, *Jens Jensen: Maker of Natural Parks and Gardens* (Baltimore: Johns Hopkins University Press, 1992) 100–102.

38. Grant McCracken, *Culture and Consumption: New Approaches to the Symbolic Character of Consumer Goods and Activities* (Bloomington: Indiana University Press, 1990), 126.

39. For Derrick's work at the Henry Ford Museum, see Watts, *People's Tycoon*, 406–7; and Wes Hardin, William S. Pretzer, and Susan M. Steele, eds., *An American Invention: The Story of Henry Ford Museum and Greenfield Village* (Dearborn, Mich.: Henry Ford Museum and Greenfield Village, 1999), 14–15. The Richmond Hill house was constructed from materials the Fords salvaged from the Hermitage, on the outskirts of Savannah. Two brick slave quarters from the Hermitage were disassembled and reconstructed at Greenfield Village. Ford Bryan, *Friends, Families, and Forays: Scenes from the Life and Times of Henry Ford* (Detroit: Wayne State University Press, 2002), 404–5.

40. According to sculptor Corrado Parducci, the process started in the studio, where he made clay models and cast them. Once on-site, the plasterer applied the cement grounds, and Parducci copied the models he had made in the studio. As he told an interviewer, "That's one of the very few occasions I had to work directly on a building. It's a very rare, the thing, I mean it dates ways back." Corrado Parducci, interview by Dennis Barrie, 17 March 1975, transcript, Archives of American Art, Smithsonian Institution, Washington, D.C.

41. James E. Bryan, "Material Culture in Miniature: Nuremberg Kitchens as Inspirational Toys in the Long Nineteenth Century," in *Childhood by Design: Toys and the Material Culture of Childhood, 1700–Present*, ed. Megan Brandow-Faller (New York: Bloomsbury Visual Arts, 2018), 220.

42. These instructions were written on an ad for the range in a note that also mentioned budgeting an additional $2.50 for freight to Detroit. Ford House Archives.

43. *Architect's Bulletin* 1 (9 July 1930), 2; and *Architect's Bulletin* 12 (18 December 1930). Henry Ford Office Papers, Accession 285, Benson Ford Research Center.

44. The conversion of 1931 dollars into 2024 dollars comes from the CPI Inflation Calculator: https://www.bls.gov/data/inflation_calculator.htm, accessed 2 June 2024.

45. The playhouse is regularly described as a birthday gift and the contract was certainly let around the time of Josephine's birthday in July. The project files suggest, however, that the senior Fords came to look upon the playhouse as a Christmas gift, given that they approved overtime for the painting crew, "in order to complete the Decorating before December 24, 1930." *Architect's Bulletin* 12 (18 December 1930), 2. Henry Ford Office Papers, Accession 285, Benson Ford Research Center.

46. Josephine Ford, interview with Hadley French, 22 April 1996, Edsel and Eleanor Ford House Archives.

47. Fredric L. Quivik, *The Ford Motor Company's Richmond Assembly Plant, a.k.a. The Richmond Tank Depot*, historical report prepared for National Park Service, Rosie the Riveter World War II Homefront National Historic Park, 2 September 2003, 19–21.

48. Michael G. Smith, *Designing Detroit: Wirt Rowland and the Rise of Modern American Architecture* (Detroit: Wayne State University Press, 2017), 170–71.

49. Richard Bak, *Henry and Edsel: The Creation of the Ford Empire* (Hoboken, N.J.: Wiley, 2008), 200–203.

50. Linda Downs, *Diego Rivera: The Detroit Industry Murals* (Detroit: Detroit Institute of Arts, in association with New York: W. W. Norton, 1999), 30–32. See also Linda Downs, "Diego Rivera's Portrait of Edsel Ford," *Bulletin of the Detroit Institute of Arts* 57:1 (1979), 46–52.

51. According to Jennifer Hawkins Opie, cocktail drinking—once part of the "dangerously raffish atmosphere of the 1920s"—had by the 1930s become respectable and bounded by social conventions that defined the timing of the cocktail hour, the length of the cocktail dress, and the associated furnishings, namely, the home cocktail bar, the gramophone, and the radio, as well as smartly designed cigarette and bar accessories. Jennifer Hawkins Opie, "Cocktail Culture," in *Elegant Eating: Four Hundred Years of Dining in Style*, ed. Philippa Glanville and Hilary Young (London: V&A Publications, 2002), 30–31. See also Bak, *Henry and Edsel*, 160.

52. Charles K. Hyde, *The Dodge Brothers: The Men, the Motor Cars, and the Legacy* (Detroit: Wayne State University Press, 2005), 19, 44–45, 117, 123, 178. "Dodge Shares Drop; Deal Closes Today; Active Trading Indicates Underwriting Syndicate Has Withdrawn Market Support. Sale Has Been Widespread. Title to Property to Pass to New Owners on Receipt of $146,000,000 Check," *New York Times*, 1 May 1925, 28. The conversion of 1925 dollars into 2024 dollars comes from the CPI Inflation Calculator: https://data.bls.gov/cgi-bin/cpicalc.pl?cost1=146%2C000&year1=192505&year2=202401, accessed 4 June 2024.

53. John B. Cameron, *Meadow Brook Hall: Tudor Revival Architecture and Decoration* (Rochester, Mich.: Meadow Brook Art Gallery, Oakland University, 1979), 2, 16–19.

54. The family had their first meal in the dining room of Meadow Brook Hall in September 1929. Cameron, *Meadow Brook Hall*, 2–4.

55. These blueprints, Kapp's pencil drawings, and period photographs are all preserved in the Meadow Brook Hall Archives.

56. Alison K. Hoagland, *The Log Cabin: An American Icon* (Charlottesville: University of Virginia Press, 2018), chapters 2, 3, and 4, especially 150–56.

57. The Sears log cabin playhouse was moved in 1891 to the family's home in Kenilworth, Illinois, a planned community Sears established on land he bought in 1889. In 1945, it was moved to the Northbrook, Illinois, property of Sears's son, Alden. In 1968, it was moved again to public land in the center of Kenilworth. Colleen Browne Kilner, *Joseph Sears and His Kenilworth: The Dreamer and the Dream* (Kenilworth, Ill.: Kenilworth Historical Society, 1969), 291. Barry Sears, personal communication, 29 January 2019.

58. The playmate, Carl Keith, was quoted in Kilner, *Joseph Sears and His Kenilworth*, 98.

59. The Glessners are best known for commissioning Henry Hobson Richardson to design their Chicago house, built between 1885 and 1887. A few years earlier, in 1883, they hired Isaac Elwood Scott to design the "Big House" at the Rocks. Beginning in 1889, Charles Allerton Coolidge of Richardson's successor firm, Shepley, Rutan and Coolidge, redesigned the house in the Shingle style. Some of the estate's outbuildings were designed by Hermann Valentin von Holst. Bryant F. Tolles Jr., *Summer Cottages in the White Mountains: The Architecture of Leisure and Recreation, 1870 to 1930* (Hanover, N.H.: University Press of New England, 2000), 108–13.

60. Frances Macbeth Glessner, journal, 30 September 1886, Chicago History Museum.

61. Frances Macbeth Glessner, journal, 7 August 1887, Chicago History Museum.

62. Frances Macbeth Glessner, journal, 21 September 1887, Chicago History Museum.

63. Richard Longstreth, *A Guide to Architecture in the Adirondacks* (Keesville, N.Y.: Adirondack Architectural Heritage, 2017), 146–49; Bossom is quoted on 149. Hoagland, *The Log Cabin*, 168–69. See also *Exiting Condition Report for Fort Ticonderoga Y-D House, Ticonderoga, New York* (Albany, N.Y.: John G. Waite Associates, Architects, 2016).

64. Although Currier and Ives made the Adirondacks famous for such expeditions as early as the 1860s, Michigan's Upper Peninsula and nearby Ontario also attracted elite hunters and campers. Wealthy Detroiters established the Huron Mountain Shooting and Fishing Club, forty miles north of Marquette, Michigan, in 1889. In 1929, Henry and Clara Ford engaged Derrick to design a cabin (in fact, a large house that could accommodate twelve people) for their use at the club. Bryan, *Friends, Families, and Forays,* 414–17. For Currier and Ives and the Adirondacks, see Georgia B. Barnhill, *Wild Impressions: The Adirondacks on Paper* (Blue Mountain Lake, N.Y.: Adirondack Museum; Boston: Godine, 1995), 87.

65. Michigan Department of Natural Resources, "History of Moose in Michigan," https://www.michigan.gov/dnr/0,4570,7-350-79135_79218_79619_84917-256178--,00.html, accessed 19 December 2018

66. The Meadow Brook Hall Archives included two versions of the floor plan for Daniel's log cabin, both dated 21 April 1926. The only difference between them is that one includes a low cabinet under one bank of windows and a "table for trains" under the other.

67. Preserved in the Meadow Brook Hall Archives is a final reckoning of costs, up to 31 December 1929; it lists Frances's playhouse at $21,587.69. The conversion of 1929 dollars into 2024 dollars comes from the CPI Inflation Calculator: https://www.bls.gov/data/inflation_calculator.htm, accessed 2 June 2024.

68. Vecelius's written quote to build the log cabin for $2,710, dated 9 August 1926, is preserved in the Meadow Brook Hall Archives, which also contain a letter (dated 29 September 1926) from H. J. Gallagher (Matilda's business manager) transmitting to Vecelius a check in the amount of $1,500, which, he said, "makes a total of $2500 you have received." Gallagher's letter also noted that the balance remaining was $210 and outlined the work that still needed to be completed. Although similar to the initial design, the cabin differed from those drawings in some of its details. The sketch provided by Smith, Hinchman & Grylls, for instance, showed the logs at the corners all cut to the same length in an even vertical line; in the cabin as built, however, the corner logs taper inward from the foundation up to the eave line. Vecelius also inserted a cantilevered gabled roof immediately over the door, instead of having the eave line of the front gable step out, as the architect had drawn it.

69. Details of Daniel's youth are documented in Madelyn Rzadkowolski, "Great Expectations: The All-Too-Short Life of Daniel G. Dodge," *Meadow Brook Magazine,* Fall 2015, 10–15.

70. According to Karen Bond Lucander, the ball, held at the Book-Cadillac Hotel, cost about $25,000. The European trip lasted six months. Karen Bond Lucander, *Riding on the Edge: Frances Dodge and Dodge Stables* (Rochester, Mich.: Meadow Brook Press, 2017), 25–27.

71. William Kapp to Matilda Wilson, 13 September 1926, Meadow Brook Hall Archives.

72. According to *Vogue* magazine, the firm had been established in 1915 to "induce artists of distinction and ability to turn their attention to the designing of furniture, hangings, and bibelots, and to cooperate with the studios in producing furnishings of the highest type of individual design." Associating their work with art and seeking to "avoid that commercializing of designs which has been the ruin of so much excellent arts and crafts work in this country," the studios maintained galleries where they hosted exhibitions of "decorative art of high standard, both foreign and American." By the mid-1920s, the firm was located on Fifth Avenue and its work was often featured in *The Spur,* a society periodical that eventually adopted the tag

line "a magazine of the good things in life." Either the work of Arden Studios or their exhibitions were mentioned eleven times in *The Spur* between 1 August 1921 and 15 May 1928.

73. Matilda Wilson to Mrs. Rogerson, Arden Studios, 2 October 1926, Meadow Brook Hall Archives. In addition, Mrs. Rogerson herself may have visited the site in September; certainly, Kapp indicated to Matilda that he was available to meet Mrs. Rogerson at the playhouse on Friday, "if it is your intent to have any of the furnishings made by the Arden Studios." William Kapp to Matilda, 13 September 1926, Meadow Brook Hall Archives.

74. It is difficult to know exactly how much Arden Studios received for their work. Invoice 2299, dated 6 December 1926, has a grand total of $2516.75, although it includes $510 for painters to travel to Rochester to plaster and prepare the living room and entry hall walls, work Matilda wanted completed by a local painter; these items do not have check marks next to them, indicating that Matilda may have questioned those charges, as she did the $35 charge for one pair of living room curtains and the travel time and expenses for the curtain man. Another invoice, dated 10 December 1926, resubmitted the curtain man's expenses, while on 14 December 1926, the Arden Studios acknowledged an order for portières at $100. Meadow Brook Hall Archives. The conversion of 1926 dollars into 2024 dollars comes from the CPI Inflation Calculator: https://www.bls.gov/data/inflation_calculator.htm, accessed 2 June 2024.

75. "State Girl Has Finest Dolls' House in World; Built So Dodge Heiress Can Learn First Hand Art of Home-Keeping," *Kalamazoo Gazette*, 21 December 1926, 21.

76. While there are no period photographs of the poem in the playhouse, Meadow Brook Hall Director of Curatorial Services Madelyn Rzadkowolski notes that the poem, in a historic frame, was part of the Knole collection donated by the family in 1972.

77. Eva Stille, *Doll Kitchens, 1800–1980* (West Chester, Pa.: Schiffer, 2007), 16.

78. Bryan, "Material Culture in Miniature," 215.

79. Bryan, "Material Culture in Miniature," 218.

80. "State Girl Has Finest Doll's House."

81. Dyer, "Training the Child Consumer," 35. Maria Edgeworth and Richard Lovell Edgeworth, *Practical Education* (New York: Self, Brown, 1801), 2:276; quoted in Dyer, "Training the Child Consumer," 35.

82. The guestbook is preserved in the Meadow Brook Hall Archives. The identity of Frances's adult guests (listed in the guest book only with the title Mrs. and a surname) and the parentage and ages of Frances's younger guests (listed in the guest book by first and last name) were established from census records of 1920, 1930, and 1940, Familytreenow.com, accessed 17 November 2018. In 1922, the membership roster of the Detroit Riding and Hunt Club included Mrs. J. F. Dodge (as Frances's mother was known before her marriage to Alfred G. Wilson in 1925), Joseph A. Braun (whose children Josephine and Julien attended Frances's twelfth birthday celebration), and A. J. Stahelin (whose daughters Betty and Alberta were among Frances's guests). Grace Booth Wallace and Florence Earle (whose daughters attended the party) were members of the Twentieth Century Club with Mrs. Dodge. *The Social Secretary of Detroit* (Detroit: Social Secretary, 1922), 223 and 255–57. Other guests (Jean MacDonald, Josephine Braun, Betty Stahelin, and Alice Osterman) are included in a 1927 class picture of the sixth, seventh, and eighth grades at the Bloomfield Hills School, Meadow Brook Hall Archives.

83. Helen Le Baron Whiteley, "Bobbed-Haired Girls Rare among 'Debbies'—Only Seven Eschew Long Tresses—Frances Dodge Entertains in Unique Playhouse—Army–Navy Game Lures Many," *Detroit News*, 28 November 1926, clipping preserved in Meadow Brook Hall Archives.

84. Untitled article on the "Society Page," *Detroit Free Press*, 5 December 1926, 5.

85. Although its headline varied from paper to paper, the story appeared in the *Kalamazoo Gazette* as "State Girl Has Finest Dolls' House in World; Built So Dodge Heiress Can Learn First Hand Art of Home-Keeping," *Kalamazoo Gazette*, 21 December 1926, 21.

86. "State Girl Has Finest Dolls' House in World," 21.

87. "Millionare in Michigan Prison; Two Young Women Bring Charges Against John Duval Dodge," *News and Observer* (Raleigh, N.C.), 14 March 1922, 8.

88. For his acquittal, see "Dodge Freed by Kalamazoo Jury; Acquitted of Driving Automobile While Intoxicated, Causing Injury to Girl; Faces Another Charge; Held on Charge of Possessing, Transporting and Distributing Liquors," *Enquirer and Evening News* (Battle Creek, Mich.), 23 March 1922, 7. He was, however, found guilty of breaking prohibition laws. See "Dodge Convicted Again; Youth Is Found to Have Had Liquor on Automobile When Girl Was Hurt," *New York Times*, 20 April 1922, 7. For his incarceration in Detroit, see "Bartlett Sends Millionaire to Jail Five Days; John Duval Dodge Spends First Night on Cot in Jail Corridor at Detroit; Donned Prison Garb; Former Battle Creek Man Who is Detroit Judge Shows No Mercy with Speeder," *Enquirer and Evening News* (Battle Creek, Mich.), 17 March 1922, 1.

89. "Millionaire Washes Dishes; John Duval Dodge Also Shoveling Coal at House of Correction," *St. Joseph (Mich.) Herald-Press*, 18 March 1922, 1.

90. "Time to Turn Over a New Leaf Dodge Decides; Says He'll Show Detroit He Is Made of 'Right Kind of Stuff,'" *Detroit Free Press*, 26 March 1922, 1.

91. Hyde, *The Dodge Brothers*, 178.

92. "John F. Dodge's Son Sues to Halt Auto Firm Sale," *St. Louis Post-Dispatch*, 4 April 1925, 1.

93. "Dodge Bros. Sale Is Not Affected; Action Begun by John Duval Dodge Has No Bearing on Purchase of Auto Plant by Dillon, Read & Co.," *Burlington (Vt.) Free Press*, 6 April 1925, 1.

94. "John D. Dodge Loses Verdict in Estate Suit," *Miami Daily News and Metropolis*, 20 January 1926, 8.

95. "Daughter's $7,500,000 to J.F. Dodge's Widow," *New York Times*, 4 April 1928, 31.

96. "Bank Head," *Standard Union* (Brooklyn, N.Y.), 7 July 1931, 25.

97. Daniel Dodge died in 1938 at the age of twenty-one. While on his honeymoon at his hunting lodge on an island in Lake Huron, he and others were injured when old sticks of dynamite exploded. As they traveled by boat to get medical attention for the wounded, Daniel fell overboard into choppy water and drowned. Rzadkowolski, "Great Expectations," 15.

6. OBJECTS OF MIDDLE-CLASS DESIRE

1. "Miss Patricia Ziegfeld Has Finest Playhouse in County," *Yonkers Statesman*, 4 August 1924, 5. The library and dining room are mentioned in Patricia Ziegfeld, *The Ziegfelds' Girl: Confessions of an Abnormally Happy Childhood* (Boston: Little, Brown, 1964), 50.

2. Eddie Cantor and David Freedman, *Ziegfeld: The Great Glorifier* (New York: Alfred H. King, 1934), 45, 96.

3. In New York, these publications included *The Theatre* (founded in 1901) and *Play-goer* (1902); in London, *Play Pictorial* (1902) and *Playgoer and Society Illustrated* (1909). Michele Majer, "Staging Fashion, 1880–1920," in *Staging Fashion, 1880–1920: Jane Harding, Lily Elsie, Billie Burke*, ed. Michele Majer (New York: Bard Graduate Center, 2012), 37 and 46.

4. The couple's biographical details are drawn from Grant Hayter-Menzies, *Mrs. Ziegfeld: The Public and Private Lives of Billie Burke* (Jefferson, N.C.: McFarland, 2009), especially 123–78. This framing of the working of celebrity draws on Majer, "Staging Fashion," 26.

5. One biography defines "the Ziegfeld touch" as a form of "theatrical genius [that] lay in transforming popular but plebian dramatic forms into art without losing their mass appeal." Richard and Paulette Ziegfeld, *The Ziegfeld Touch: The Life and Times of Florenz Ziegfeld, Jr.* (New York: Harry N. Abrams, 1993), 12.

6. In the early twentieth century, women of all classes, including social elites, copied the costumes they had seen on the stage. Marlis Schweitzer, *When Broadway Was the Runway: Theater Fashion and American Culture* (Philadelphia: University of Pennsylvania Press, 2009), 164–66. See also Majer, "Staging Fashion," 28–31.

7. Lary May, *Screening Out the Past: The Birth of Mass Culture and the Motion Picture Industry* (New York: Oxford University Press, 1980), 190–98.

8. Alfred H. Bellot, *History of the Rockaways from the Year 1685 to 1917* (Far Rockaway, N.Y.: Bellot's Histories, [circa 1918]), 67. Other information on Woodmere's history comes from Millicent D. Vollono, "Brief History of the Village of Woodsburgh" (typescript issued in conjunction with the Village's Centennial Anniversary, 2012), n.p.

9. Even after the Supreme Court declared such city ordinances unconstitutional in 1917, restrictive covenants—essentially privately negotiated contracts—were used to maintain residential segregation. The Supreme Court only ruled against these restrictive covenants in 1948 and then with only partial success. George Lipsitz, *The Possessive Investment in Whiteness: How White People Profit from Identity Politics*, rev. and expanded ed. (Philadelphia: Temple University Press, 2006), 25–26.

10. In her research on Woodmere, Millicent Vollono did not come across any deeds with restrictive covenants in public records. Millicent Vollono, personal communication, 3 June 2024. See also Millicent D. Vollono, "Robert Burton's Woodmere," in *Gardens of Eden: Long Island's Early Twentieth-Century Planned Communities*, ed. Robert B. Mackay (New York: W. W. Norton, 2015).

11. Houses designed by Keen were published in *American Architect and Building News* 94:1708 (16 September 1908), n.p., while those by Flagg and by Rossiter and Wright appeared in the next issue: *American Architect and Building News* 94:1709 (23 September 1908), n.p. See also Vollono, "Brief History," n.p.

12. "Residence of Mr. R. L. Burton at Cedarhurst, L. I.," *Architects' and Builders' Magazine* 4:2 (November 1902), 43–51. This article lists Joseph H. Taft as the architect, but local architectural history aficionados believe Charles Romeyn designed the original house and that Burton hired Taft to undertake renovations: http://www.oldlongisland.com/2012/06/albro-house

.html, accessed 19 January 2022. Barr Ferree, "The House of R. L. Burton, Esq., Cedarhurst, Long Island," Notable American Homes, *American Homes and Gardens* 4:3 (March 1907), 85–90.

13. "The 'Play' House of the Daughters of Governor and Mrs. Frank O. Lowden," *Western Architect* 27 (November 1918), plates 4–6.

14. Frank Miles Day, *American Country Houses of Today* (New York: Architectural Books, 1912), 5–7. "A Child's Playhouse at Cedarhurst, N.Y.," *Scientific American Building Monthly* 36:6 (December 1903), 127 and plate.

15. "Child's Playhouse," 127.

16. *Western Architect* 4 (September 1905), plates following p. 8.

17. *Social Register*, Summer 21:66 (June 1907), 11, 22, 44, 45, 68, 72, 81, 115, 150, 155, 160, 180, 182, 201, 205, 215, 225, 238, 245, 249, 261.

18. Vollono, "Brief History," n.p.

19. "Morgenthau Buys a Town. Pays $3,000,000 for Land and Houses in Long Island Suburb," *New York Times*, 10 November 1909, 1.

20. Cantor and Freedman, *Ziegfeld*, 16.

21. The conversion of 1911 dollars into 2024 dollars comes from the CPI Inflation Calculator: https://www.in2013dollars.com/us/inflation/1911?amount=60000, accessed 4 June 2024.

22. Billie Burke, "Under My Own Vine and Fig Tree," *Harper's Bazaar* 48:2 (August 1913), 10.

23. Ada Patterson, "The Lady of Burkeleigh Crest," *Theatre* 17:143 (January 1913), 28–30.

24. Rebecca Parry, "Billie Burke: The Press," in Majer, *Staging Fashion*, 164–68.

25. Ada Patterson, "A Sunday Morning Chat with Billie Burke," *Theatre* 8:93 (November 1908), 300–304.

26. Chief among these experts in the early decades of the twentieth century were Dr. Luther Emmett Holt, author of *The Care and Feeding of Children* (1896), and Mrs. Max West, who echoed Holt's precepts in *Infant Care*, a pamphlet published by the Children's Bureau in 1914. Susan Strasser, *Never Done: A History of American Housework* (New York: Pantheon Books, 1982), 232–35.

27. "Billie Burke as a Mother," *Good Health* 52:3 (March 1917), 30.

28. "'Burkeley Crest,' the Hastings New York Home of Billie Burke (Mrs. Florenz Ziegfeld, Jr.) has a charm all its own," *Theatre Magazine* 36:246 (September 1921), 186.

29. According to one of Burke's biographers, "Flo was a loving husband who appreciated his wife . . . but who had the signal failing of being unable to resist sleeping with other women." Hayter-Menzies, *Mrs. Ziegfeld*, 89.

30. Lloyd's extramarital affairs are discussed in Jeffrey Vance and Suzanne Lloyd, *Harold Lloyd, Master Comedian* (New York: Harry N. Abrams, 2002), 54. Later in life, his hobby was taking three-dimensional photographs, hundreds of thousands of which were of "beautiful young women, all of them naked," according to another biographer, Tom Dardis, who also asserts that "it is likely that Harold had sexual relations with many of the young models." Tom Dardis, *Harold Lloyd: The Man on the Clock* (New York: Viking Press, 1983), 271.

31. According to the press, Ziegfeld bought an additional twelves acres, bringing the total acreage to forty. These figures, however, do not tally with those offered by Burke's biographer, who reported that Burke originally purchased fourteen acres. "Ziegfeld Adds to Estate," *New York Times*, 27 July 1920, 31.

32. Ziegfeld, *Ziegfelds' Girl*, 46–48, 53, and 64–75.

33. Ziegfeld, *Ziegfelds' Girl*, 49.

34. Ziegfeld, *Ziegfelds' Girl*, 65–67.

35. Ziegfeld, *Ziegfelds' Girl*, 50. Although one of Burke's biographers claims the set was shipped from Hollywood, *Janice Meredith* was filmed in New York City and upstate New York. Hayter-Menzies, *Mrs. Ziegfeld*, 93. "Story of a Production," *New York Times*, 24 August 1924, X2.

36. Kate Kelly, "Westchester Power Couple: Billie Burke and Flo Ziegfeld," *Westchester Historian* 88:3 (Summer 2012), 78.

37. Ziegfeld, *Ziegfelds' Girl*, 50.

38. Shaun Eyring, "Special Places Saved: The Role of Women in Preserving the American Landscape," in *Restoring Women's History through Historic Preservation*, ed. Gail Lee Dubrow and Jennifer B. Goodman (Baltimore: Johns Hopkins University Press, 2013), 38–41.

39. Lydia Mattice Brandt, *First in the Homes of His Countrymen: George Washington's Mount Vernon in the American Imagination* (Charlottesville: University of Virginia Press, 2016), 83.

40. Mildred Stapley, "The Home of George Washington, Country Gentleman," *Country Life in America* 26 (May 1914), 29, quoted in Brandt, *First in the Homes*, 91. For more on copies of Mount Vernon between the 1890s and 1920s, see Brandt, *First in the Homes*, 81–126.

41. Although the idea of a separate museum building first came up in 1889, the first "relic house" was opened in the structure then known as the carpenter's shop in early 1923, while a purpose-built "relic house" was completed in 1928. Brandt, *First in the Homes*, 85–90.

42. Paul Wilstach, *Mount Vernon: Washington's Home and the Nation's Shrine* (New York: Doubleday, Page, 1916), 276 and 75, quoted in Brandt, *First in the Homes*, 92. For Mount Vernon and the Old South myth, see Brandt, *First in the Homes*, especially 93–95.

43. For anti-German sentiment during World War I and the conjunction of anti-Semitism and the Red Scare of 1919, see John Higham, *Strangers in the Land: Patterns of American Nativism, 1860–1925* (1955; repr., New York: Atheneum, 1966), 194–202 and 279–86.

44. Many people close to the man, including his cousin Richard Ziegfeld, claimed that Ziegfeld's father was Lutheran and his mother Catholic. Nonetheless, it appears to have been widely assumed that he was Jewish, perhaps because many Jews played prominent roles in financing and producing Broadway shows and perhaps because he was a longtime benefactor of the Israel Orphan Asylum in New York and supported Zionist causes, such as the Palestine Relief Fund. Certainly, caricatures of him published during his life time, like that drawn by Alex Gard, deployed facial features (a large hooked nose, full lips, hooded eyes) widely used to signify Jewishness. Ziegfeld and Ziegfeld, *The Ziegfeld Touch*, 13. Heather Hester, "Florenz Ziegfeld, Jr.," http://www.immigrantentrepreneurship.org/entries/florenz-ziegfeld-jr/, accessed 3 February 2022. For Gard's caricature, see Sidney Skolsky, *Times Square Tin Types* (New York: Ives Washburn, 1930), opposite 1. For a discussion of cartoon representations of Jews, see Matthew Baigell, *The Implacable Urge to Defame: Cartoon Jews and the American Press, 1877–1935* (Syracuse, N.Y.: Syracuse University Press, 2017), 11–14.

45. Cantor and Freedman, *Ziegfeld*, 25.

46. "Lure of Fine Gardens: Notable Westchester Estates Opened for County Charities," *New York Times*, 25 May 1924, X9; "Visiting Country Gardens: Show Estates in Suburbs to Be Opened to Aid Philanthropic Institutions," *New York Times*, 27 April 1930, 129.

47. "Untermyer, Ziegfeld and Other Large Estates to Open Gardens to Public," *Yonkers Herald*, 26 April 1930.

48. Ziegfeld, *Ziegfelds' Girl*, 55–58.

49. Joshua Gamson, *Claims to Fame: Celebrity in Contemporary America* (Berkeley: University of California Press, 1994), 22–28.

50. See, for instance, "The New Movie's Own Map of Beverly Hills: Find the Home of Your Favorite Film Star," *New Movie Magazine* 1:4 (March 1930), 34–35.

51. For the intersection between Pickford's screen roles and her public persona, see May, *Screening Out the Past*, 118–46.

52. Jeffrey Vance and Suzanne Lloyd, *Harold Lloyd, Master Comedian* (New York: Harry N. Abrams, 2002), 52–63; Dardis, *Harold Lloyd*, 140–41, 145–46, 217–23.

53. A. E. Hanson, *An Arcadian Landscape: The California Gardens of A. E. Hanson, 1920–1932*, ed. David Gebhard and Sheila Lynds (Santa Monica, Calif.: Hennessey & Ingalls, 1985), 19–24.

54. C. H. Phillips, "A Little Girl in a Big House," *Motion Picture* 31:4 (May 1926), 54.

55. Vance and Lloyd, *Harold Lloyd*, 59.

56. Hanson, *Arcadian Landscape*, 38–39.

57. *Harold Lloyd's Legacy* (Beverly Hills, Calif.: Beverly Hills Historical Society), documentary film, circa 2015. https://vimeo.com/113470172, accessed 19 February 2022.

58. Hanson, *Arcadian Landscape*, 39.

59. Arrol Gellner and Douglas Keister, *Storybook Style: America's Whimsical Homes of the Twenties* (New York: Viking Studio, 2001), 13–15.

60. Hanson, *Arcadian Landscape*, 38.

61. "Miss Billie Burke Selects Quaker Lace Curtains for Burkeley Crest," Quaker Lace Company advertisement in *Country Life* (May 1922), 112.

62. "Little Girl Plays Princess in Her Own Fairyland with Dog Guardians," *Los Angeles Times*, 28 November 1927, A1.

63. Edwin and Elza Schallert, "Hollywood High Lights," *Picture Play* 27:3 (3 November 1927), 53.

64. "The Play Yard that Laughs Built," *New Movie Magazine* 1:4 (March 1930), 76–77.

65. "Little Girl Plays Princess," A1.

66. "Her Dreams Come True with Dolls, Playhouse," *Beverly Hills Citizen*, 4 September 1930; "They Rule Lloyd Home Now," *Beverly Hills Citizen*, 27 November 1930; both clippings in the collection of the Beverly Hills Public Library.

67. "For Pleasure Unalloyd: Harold's New Estate Is a Paradise for Gloria and Golf," *Motion Picture Classic* 29:1 (March 1929), 56–57.

68. "Calls Ann Harding Not a Fit Guardian: Bannister Asks Court to Take Custody of Their Girl, 6, from the Film Star," *New York Times*, 23 January 1935, 19; "Ann Harding Keeps Child: Court Sustains Sole Custody, but Permits Visits by Bannister," *New York Times*, 25 October 1935, 24.

69. Roberta Ormiston, "Shirley Temple's First Six Years," *Modern Screen* 11:1 (June 1935), 115.

70. Anne Edwards, *Shirley Temple: American Princess* (1988; repr., Guilford, Conn.: Lyons Press, 2017), 77.

71. According to Anne Edwards, Sheehan authorized the fitting out of Shirley's bungalow just before he left the studio, forced out as the result of a merger that created 20th Century–Fox. Edwards, *Shirley Temple*, 77.

72. If Shirley fell behind in her studies, her tutor had the authority to pull her from the set. Lester David and Irene David, *The Shirley Temple Story* (New York: G. P. Putnam's Sons, 1983), 67–68.

73. "That 4 O'clock Let-Down? Not for Shirley!," *Photoplay*, October 1936, 8.

74. Gertrude Temple's statement is quoted in Edwards, *Shirley Temple*, 76. "Pee Wee's Progress," *Time*, 27 April 1936, 42.

75. Gertrude Temple, "Bringing Up Shirley," *American Magazine* 119 (February 1935), 92–93.

76. "Shirley in Her Own Dressing-Room and Play-House," *Sketch*, 3 October 1934, 36.

77. David and David, *Shirley Temple Story*, 65–66. The first mention of the glass block playhouse appeared in late summer 1936, in a United Press story purportedly dictated by Shirley. Shirley Temple, "Shirley Temple Wasn't Fooling," *Southeastern Oklahoma Citizen and the Bryan County Democrat*, 3 September 1936.

78. Shirley Temple Black, *Child Star: An Autobiography* (New York: McGraw-Hill, 1988), 309.

79. Black, *Child Star*, 382.

80. Burton's daughters were Mrs. Stephen H. Philbin, who was active in philanthropic efforts, and Mrs. W. P. Blagden, who summered in the Hamptons. Coverage of their activities includes "Garden Tea Is Given to Help Hospital: Mrs. Stephen H. Philbin Hostess in Behalf of New York Eye and Ear Institution," *New York Times*, 12 May 1937, 20; and "C. S. Cuttings Hosts at Southampton: Have a Luncheon for Kermit Roosevelts, W. P. Blagdens and Alfred O. Hoyt. C. P. Stones Are Honored: Mr. and Mrs. Duer McLanahan Entertain for Them—Goodhue Livingstons Have Guests," *New York Times*, 6 August 1934, 12.

81. Vance and Lloyd, *Harold Lloyd*, 204–6.

7. FOR MOVIE STARS AND PRINCESSES

1. "Shirley Temple Black, Hollywood's Biggest Little Star, Dies at 85," *New York Times*, 11 February 2014.

2. "Princess Betty's Gift—S. Wales to Give Her a Miniature House on Sixth Birthday," *Sunday Mirror*, 14 May 1931, 10.

3. Farey's services as a draftsman were in great demand in the early twentieth century, with Sir Edwin Lutyens and other architects hiring him to produce perspectives for Royal Academy exhibitions. J. B. Lingard, "Cyril A. Farey: A Personal Tribute to St. Paul's Cathedral and the City of London, 1940–44," in *English Architecture Public and Private: Essays for Kerry Downes*, ed. John Bold and Edward Chaney (London: Hambledon Press, 1993), 311–13.

4. Marion Berry, "A Wee Cottage for a Small Princess," *New York Times*, 14 February 1932, SM10.

5. Kenneth G. Mensing and Rita Langdon, *Hillwood: The Long Island Estate of Marjorie Merriweather Post* (Brookville, N.Y.: C. W. Post Campus of Long Island University, 2008), 24–26.

6. "Duke of York's Message of Hope to Wales—Coming Harvest of Prosperity—'Splendid Courage of the People,'" *Western Mail & South Wales News*, 17 March 1932, 9. See also

"The Duke's Thanks to Wales—Birthday Gift to Princess—Y Bwthyn Bach," *Western Mail & South Wales News*, 17 March 1932, 11.

7. "Little Princess Will Get Her Model House—Fire Fails to Daunt Welsh Craftsmen," *Western Mail & South Wales News*, 22 March 1932, 7; "Princess Elizabeth's 'Wonder Cottage' Burns; Welsh People's Gift Was Being Sent to London," *New York Times*, 22 March 1932, 1.

8. *Princess Elizabeth's Miniature House: The Story of Y Bwthyn Bach* (London: published under the authority of the Committee of Control, 1932), 3.

9. Ted Rowlands, *"Something Must Be Done": South Wales v Whitehall, 1921–1951* (Merthyr Tydfil, Wales: TTC Books, 2000), 20 and 29.

10. "Industries of South Wales—Striking Array of Exhibits—Helping the Country and Charity," *Western Mail & South Wales News*, 23 October 1931, 5.

11. "Lord Mayor's Optimism—Guest of Cardiff Meat Traders," *Western Mail & South Wales News*, 9 February 1932, 8. In contrast, when Welsh MPs appealed to the Chancellor of the Exchequer for help in the early 1930s, "the word 'factory' never passed [their] lips," according to Ted Rowlands. Rowlands, *"Something Must Be Done,"* 29.

12. A. C. Benson and Lawrence Weaver, eds., *Everybody's Book of the Queen's Dolls' House* (London: Daily Telegraph and Methuen, 1924), 17 and 21.

13. "Other News in Brief," *Daily Mirror*, 16 October 1924, 2. "£80,000 from Queen's Dolls' House," *Dundee Courier*, 22 October 1924, 10. The conversion of 1924 pounds to 2024 pounds comes from the CPI Inflation Calculator: https://www.in2013dollars.com/uk/inflation/1924?amount=80000; accessed 4 June 2024. The conversion of pounds to dollars comes from the Xe Currency Converter: https://www.xe.com/currencyconverter/convert/?Amount=6095209&From=GBP&To=USD; accessed 4 June 2024.

14. "A Wonderful Birthday Present for Princess Elizabeth," *Western Mail & South Wales News*, 26 October 1931, 7.

15. Thomas Hajkowski, *The BBC and National Identity in Britain, 1922–53* (Manchester: Manchester University Press, 2010), 173–78.

16. *Princess Elizabeth's Miniature House*, 7.

17. "Margaret Lindsay Williams (1888–1960)," Wikitree, https://www.wikitree.com/wiki/Williams-97934, accessed 10 March 2022. The dual portrait was reproduced in *The Tatler*, 19 May 1937, 33.

18. The contents were so numerous that no one source listed them all. This paragraph draws primarily on "A Wonderful Birthday Present for Princess Elizabeth," *Princess Elizabeth's Miniature House*, and "Painting of Duchess of York. Welsh Artist's Portrait of Princess Elizabeth's House," *Western Mail & South Wales News*, 22 October 1931, 7. See also Benson and Weaver, eds., *Everybody's Book*, 160.

19. David Russell Davies, *Secret Sins: Sex, Violence, and Society in Carmarthenshire, 1870–1920* (Cardiff: University of Wales, 2021), 61–65.

20. The author of the music and original Welsh words was Thomas Lloyd, who went by the bardic name "Crych Elen" and worked in slate quarries before immigrating to the United States, where he died in poverty in 1909. E. Wyn James, "'Watching the White Wheat' and 'That Hole below the Nose': English Ballads of a Late-Nineteenth-Century Welsh Jobbing-Printer," in *Bridging the Cultural Divide: Our Common Ballad Heritage*, ed. Sigrid Rieuwerts and Helga Stein

(Hildesheim, Germany: Georg Olms Verlag, 2000), 182–84. The Welsh and English lyrics are available on the Internet Archive: https://ia801700.us.archive.org/12/items/wg35-2-6233/wg35-2-6233.pdf, accessed 28 February 2022.

21. A. G. Bradley, *Highways and Byways in South Wales* (1903), quoted in Richard Suggett and Greg Stevenson, *Introducing Houses of the Welsh Countryside* (Talybont, Wales: Y Lolfa, 2010), 174.

22. Roy Saunders, "Old West Cottage Architecture—West Wales Examples That Should Be Preserved," *Western Mail & South Wales News*, 22 February 1935, 11.

23. "Champion of a Dying Industry—Wants to Revive Art of Thatching in Glamorgan," *Western Mail & South Wales News*, 11 February 1937, 14.

24. The museum went on to establish a full-fledged Department of Folk Culture and Industries in 1936, but these collections were moved to the Welsh Folk Museum (later the Museum of Welsh Life) ten years later, leaving the National Museum of Wales to return to its original focus on high art in the European tradition. Rhiannon Mason, "National Building and the Museum of Welsh Life," *Museum & Society* 3:1 (March 2004), 19–20. See also Iorwerth C. Peate, "The Welsh Folk Museum," *Journal of the Folklore Institute* 2:3 (December 1965), 314–16.

25. "Champion of a Dying Industry," 14.

26. "Women of To-Day. Princess Elizabeth's Model House," *Western Mail & South Wales News*, 12 September 1931, 7.

27. *Princess Elizabeth's Miniature House*, 7.

28. "The Duke's Thanks to Wales," 11. For a photograph of Jean Blake in costume, see https://www.dailymail.co.uk/femail/article-2099859/amp/A-Wendy-house-fit-Queen-The-secrets-history-tiny-Welsh-cottage-grounds-Windsor-generations-royals-played.html, accessed 3 March 2022.

29. "Women of To-day. Welsh Terrier for Princess Elizabeth. 'Ianto Fullpelt' and the Model House Gift," *Western Mail & South Wales News*, 16 September 1931, 9. The thatched doghouse is visible in "The Queen's First House," a blogpost in *"Tweedland" the Gentlemen's Club*, 28 November 2018, http://tweedlandthegentlemansclub.blogspot.com/2018/11/the-queens-first-house-wendy-house-fit.html, accessed 11 March 2022.

30. Suggett and Stevenson, *Introducing Houses*, 166.

31. Suggett and Stevenson, *Introducing Houses*, 167. See also "Merthyr Mawr House," https://www.parksandgardens.org/places/merthyr-mawr-house, accessed 2 March 2022.

32. Eurwyn Williams, *The Welsh Cottage: Building Traditions of the Rural Poor, 1750–1900* (Aberystwyth: Royal Commission on the Ancient and Historical Monuments of Wales, 2010), 152.

33. Suggett and Stevenson, *Introducing Houses*, 166 and 173. Church Cottage at Merthyr Mawr does bear traces of limewash. "Church Cottage, a Grade II Listed Building in Merthyr Mawr, Bridgend," *British Listed Buildings*, https://britishlistedbuildings.co.uk/300011241-church-cottage-merthyr-mawr#.Yiu2Pi-B35Z, accessed 11 March 2022.

34. *Princess Elizabeth's Miniature House*, 7.

35. Richard Bebb, "The Theatre of the Welsh Farmer's Domestic Life," *Vernacular Architecture* 45 (2014), 29–53, especially 29–31.

36. The phrase was first written by Alfred Russell Wallace in 1843, but published in 1905 in his book *My Life*. Quoted in Bebb, "Welsh Farmer's Domestic Life," 31 and 52n4.

37. Bebb, "Welsh Farmer's Domestic Life," 42.

38. An image of the museum's newly installed Welsh farmhouse kitchen appeared in the *Western Mail & South Wales News* on the same page as a photograph of city officials standing in front of Y Bwthyn Bach just after the opening of the Ideal Homes Exhibition. "To-Day's Royal Wedding; Ideal Homes Exhibition; Welsh Museum New Wing," *Western Mail & South Wales News*, 24 October 1931, 12.

39. Bebb, "Welsh Farmer's Domestic Life," 32–33.

40. Details about the paint and appliances were gleaned from advertisements published in the *Western Mail & South Wales News*, 26 October 1931, 7.

41. *Princess Elizabeth's Miniature House*, 11.

42. "District News. The Princess's Model House," *Western Mail & South Wales News*, 13 April 1932, 4.

43. Michael Chance, *Our Princesses and Their Dogs* (London: John Murray, 1936), n.p.

44. Rodney Laredo, "One's Happiest Snaps! These Delightful Photos That Three Generations of Windsors Have Treasured Were All Taken by One Couple, Who Won the Family's Trust—Now, on the Eve of the Queen's Birthday, a New Book Tells the Story," https://www.dailymail.co.uk/femail/article-6927891/Delightful-photos-three-generations-Windsors-treasured.html, 19 April 2019, accessed 15 March 2023.

45. "A Royal Household Closely Concerned in the Constitutional Crisis," *Illustrated London News*, 12 December 1936, 1047.

46. It was widely reported that Edward VIII had said, more than once during his tour, "Something must be done." The king seems to have recognized the tour as an opportunity to burnish his own reputation, while also helping the Welsh. In October 1936, while the tour was in its planning stages, he let it be known through his secretary that "it would give His Majesty the greatest gratification if the Coronation Celebrations next year could be made to coincide with a real improvement in the lot of these unfortunate people." Rowlands, *"Something Must Be Done,"* 97–104; his secretary, Major Hardinge, is quoted on 98.

47. "Princess Elizabeth Is Little Mother in 'Toy' Gift House; Scrubs Floors and Washes Up," *Sunday Mirror*, 12 December 1937, 4.

48. "Princess Elizabeth's Little House for 6d," advertisement in *Games and Toys*, April 1939, 14.

49. Arthur Groom, "Her Majesty's Little House" ([London: Dean's, 1953]), n.p.

50. This information is drawn from the address, return address, and postmark of a copy of "Princess Elizabeth's Little House" in the author's collection.

51. Stephanie Gibson, curator, New Zealand Histories and Cultures, Te Papa, personal communication, 19 April 1921.

52. "Promotion Pieces," *Architectural Forum* 66:6 (June 1937), 98.

53. "Promotion Pieces," 98.

54. According to Gabrielle Esperdy, Insulux blocks "achieved a glowing luminosity when back-lit," which gave storefronts "24-hour selling power." Gabrielle Esperdy *Modernizing Main Street: Architecture and Consumer Culture in the New Deal* (Chicago: University of Chicago Press, 2008), 130.

55. As Elizabeth Fagan points out, the Owens-Illinois approach foregrounded the three-dimensional nature of glass block, while Modern architects, such as William Lescaze, tended

to use the blocks in plane, as infill for wall openings. Elizabeth Fagan, "Building Walls of Light: The Development of Glass Block and its Influence on American Architecture in the 1930s" (master's thesis, Columbia University, 2015), 43–44 and 53.

56. *Indianapolis Star,* 23 August 1936; *American Builder and Building Age* 58:11 (November 1936), 29; "A Little Glass House for Shirley," *Movie Mirror,* December 1936, 66.

57. Images of Shirley in a dark cardigan appeared in "Shirley's Eighth Birthday Spurs Race for Her Crown," *Times Herald,* 23 April 1937; Hubbard Keavy, "Shirley Temple Is Eight—But Still Unspoiled," *Bangor Daily News,* 24 April 1937; Hubbard Keavy, "Shirley Unchanged by Success," *Sioux City Journal,* 30 May 1937; and "Glass Houses for Work and Play," *My Weekly Reader—Edition Number Two* 6:18 (31 May–4 June 1937), 72. Images of Shirley in a pale dress trimmed in stripes appeared in *Charlotte Observer,* 24 April 1938; "'Happy Birthday, Shirley,'" *Leader, the Garland Times* (Tremonton, UT), 28 April 1938; and Lucie Neville, "Rubbernecking Through Movietown," *Asbury Park Press,* 28 May 1939. Thanks to Melissa Tonnessen and Rita Dubas for sharing their collections of newspaper clippings.

58. This was evidently not an endeavor sanctioned by the studio or the Temple family, as they had already rejected a proposal to link Shirley's name with an exhibition at the fair. According to Shirley's autobiography, Eleanor Butler Roosevelt (Theodore Roosevelt's daughter-in-law) had been refused permission to allow the Girl Scouts to give Shirley an exquisitely complete dollhouse that would first have been put on display at the fair. Shirley Temple Black, *Child Star: An Autobiography* (New York: McGraw-Hill, 1988), 222–23.

59. "Mrs. Vanderlip, Banker's Widow; President of the New York Infirmary Is Dead at 87," *New York Times,* 6 March 1966, 92.

60. "5th Ave. Prepares Windows for Fair," *New York Times,* 26 December 1938, 38.

61. "Replica of Shirley Temple Playhouse to Be Previewed Wednesday at Fair," press release issued 5 June 1939, New York World Fair Archives, New York Public Library.

62. George P. Smith, "Mrs. Vanderlip's Letter of November 22, 1939, Regarding Shirley Temple's Playhouse," 13 December 1939, New York World Fair Archives, New York Public Library.

63. "Animal Fair Is Repeated at Carnival and with Galapagan Tortoise an Entertainer," *New York Times,* 10 August 1939, 13.

64. The image and caption on the reverse are available in Digital Collections of the New York Public Library, https://digitalcollections.nypl.org/items/5e66b3e9-08bb-d471-e040-e0 0a180654d7#/?uuid=5e66b3e9-08bb-d471-e040-e00a180654d7, accessed 19 February 2022.

65. The image and caption on the reverse are available in Digital Collections of the New York Public Library, https://digitalcollections.nypl.org/items/5e66b3e8-e79f-d471-e040-e00 a180654d7, accessed 19 February 2022.

66. "Shirley Temple Glass Playhouse, Space: 1-C,D,F—1939," a typed report date-stamped 20 December 1939. New York World Fair Archives, New York Public Library.

67. National Advisory Committee on Women's Participation, meeting minutes, 29 April 1940. New York World Fair Archives, New York Public Library. The winner of the raffle was Louise Archul of Long Island City, New York. "Shirley's Glass House Raffled Off," *New York Daily News,* 31 October 1940.

68. For the racial ideology underpinning the planning and operation of Playland, see Kara Murphy Schlichting, *New York Recentered: Building the Metropolis from the Shore* (Chicago: University of Chicago Press, 2019), 134–42. For the role of families with children in securing the gentility of public places, especially in the late nineteenth century, see Galen Cranz, "Women in Urban Parks," *Signs* 5:3 suppl. (1 April 1980), 80–81.

69. It is not clear exactly when the Kiddyland playhouse was built, but a 1937 survey of summer play activities (conducted to inform plans for Children's World at the 1939 New York World's Fair) made no mention of a playhouse, commenting only on the site's "miniature replicas of several of the adult amusement devices, and some children's swings and slides." "Survey of Summer Play Activities," 1937, page 4, New York World's Fair Archives, New York Public Library.

70. Karen Morey Kennedy, "Playland Amusement Park," *National Register of History Places Inventory—Nomination Form* (1979), section 8, page 11. https://npgallery.nps.gov/NRHP/GetAsset/NHLS/80004529_text, accessed 16 March 2022.

Index

aesthetic reform: and elite identity, 14, 162–63, 191–200
Albert, Prince: and approach to education, 36–39, 95–96; and attention to children's spaces, 33–35, 39–40; and changes to Buckingham Palace, 39–40; and design of Osborne, 40–42; and Great Exhibition of 1851, 86, 96, 98; and housing for laborers, 66, 109–11; and interest in horticulture, 68, 84, 103–4; boyhood of, 75, 96, 330n22, 334n107. *See also Schweizerei*, at Rosenau; Victoria and Albert; Victoria and Albert, children of
Albro and Lindeberg, 194–95, 210
Albro House (Cedarhurst, New York), main house, 255–56, 360n12
Albro House (Cedarhurst, New York), playhouse, 257–59, 279
Alden and Harlow, 186, 189, 351n54
Alfred ("Affie"), Prince (Duke of Edinburgh), 37, 39, 68, 94, 99, 101, 107
Angelina Plantation (near Mount Airy, Louisiana), playhouse, 320n20
Arden Studios, 238–39, 357n72, 358n73, 358n74
Ariès, Philippe, 22, 322n13
Arts and Crafts movement, 14, 151, 194, 198, 229, 256, 322

Astor, Caroline, 339n22
Atkinson, William, 82–83
Awbury (Germantown, Pennsylvania), cottage, 345n4

baby books, 9, 166–67, 170–72
ballrooms, 123–24, 131, 136
Barry, Charles, 41–42, 327n92
bedrooms. *See* children's bedrooms; parents' quarters
billiard rooms, 43, 46, 124–25, 134
Biltmore (Asheville, North Carolina), 123
birthday celebrations: for children 49, 172, 349n42; in sentimental views of family life, 22, 207; recorded in baby books, 167, 171–72. *See also* Victoria and Albert, birthday celebrations of
birthday gifts: playhouses as, 203, 223, 228, 283, 355n45; Wharton's advice on, 192–93
Black Point (Southampton, New York), playhouse, 162, 184, 189, 191
Blore, Edward, 39–40
Borough House Plantation (Stateburg, South Carolina), playhouse, 320n20
Bossom, Alfred, 231, 233
boudoirs, 134, 151, 197, 199, 342n50
Bourdieu, Pierre, 2, 6, 121

Bowditch, Ernest, 139, 141
bowling alleys, 124, 184, 186, 190
Breakers, the (Newport, Rhode Island), after fire of 1892, 120–21, 141–42
Breakers, the (Newport, Rhode Island), before fire of 1892, 117–18, 135–36, 338n11, 344n73, 344n79; and renovations for Cornelius Vanderbilt II, 118, 149–51; children's spaces in, 138–39; landscape design at, 139–41, 342n57; rooms for formal entertaining, in 135, 138–9, 149–51, 153
Breakers, the (Newport, Rhode Island), children's cottage, 13–14, 116–17, 185, 339n18; as mechanism of parental control, 153; as priority for Vanderbilts, 118–19, 139, 149; as site of labor, 122–23, 153; as site of play, 122, 149, 152; as vestigial parlor, 146–48, 152; cooking and eating at, 149, 152; cost of, 117, 119, 143; iconography of ornamentation at, 144–46, 343n68; in contrast to Shirley Temple's "dollhouse," 278; kitchen in, 147–48, 151; modeled on almshouse, 123, 143–45, 343n67; servants at, 149, 151, 153–55; siting of, 140–41
Buckingham Palace, 20–21, 39–40, 329n4
Burke, Billie, 253–54, 259–61
Burkeley Crest (Hastings-on-Hudson, New York), main house, 259–60, 361n31; visitors to, 264–65; Ziegfeld's changes, to 261–62
Burkeley Crest (Hastings-on-Hudson, New York), play shed, 260–62
Burkeley Crest (Hastings-on-Hudson, New York), playhouse, 252–3, 262–5
Burton, Robert L., 15, 255, 279. *See also* Woodmere, New York

Carnegie, Andrew, 162, 193
Casa Cobina (Sands Point, New York), playhouse, 346n4
Charlotte, Queen, 24, 27, 29, 49. *See also* dairies, ornamental; Queen Charlotte's Cottage, Kew (Richmond, England)

child-rearing. *See* parenting
child-sized furniture, 5, 11–12, 165; in books of Helen Hayes Whitney, 169–71; in Shirley Temple's studio bungalow, 275–76; used by Fanny Glessner, 231–32; used by Helen Clay Frick, 184, 189; used by Queen Victoria's children, 22–23. *See also* plumbing fixtures
Child-Study movement, 3, 14, 160–61
childhood: and understandings of "the good childhood," 5, 22, 24, 142, 266, 274, 312; as recapitulation, 10, 151–52, 160–61
children's bedrooms: in elite houses, 173–4, 177, 178, 180–83; in middle-class houses, 165–66
children's clothing, 151, 344n81. *See also* sailor suits
children's cottages: as building type, 1–2; as tools of elite culture, 2, 16, 119; formal characteristics of, 5; nomenclature for, 9–10, 120, 143, 152. *See also* Breakers, the (Newport, Rhode Island), children's cottage; Elm Court (Lenox, Massachusetts), Cosy Cot; Idle Hour (Oakdale, New York), children's outbuildings
children's dining rooms, 14, 179–81
children's entrances, 14, 182–83, 224
Christmas: and gift-giving, 167, 171–72, 348n28
Claremont (Surrey, England): children's spaces in, 47–48
Clayton (Pittsburgh, Pennsylvania), main house, 196
Clayton (Pittsburgh, Pennsylvania), playhouse, 162, 184, 186, 189, 196, 351n54; siting of, 187, 190; use of, 186, 205
Coe, Mary (Mai) Huttleston Rogers, 162
Coe, W. R., 162
Colonial Revival, 143, 151; and conspicuous simplicity, 14, 198, 256–58; and white privilege, 159, 194; Henry Ford's interest in, 217, 219. *See also* Georgian Revival
conspicuous consumption, 122, 193, 251

conspicuous simplicity, 14, 15, 162, 191–200
cooking ranges. *See* stoves
Cornelius Vanderbilt II residence (New York, after expansion), 131–37, 342n50
Cornelius Vanderbilt II residence (New York, before expansion), 124, 126, 130–31, 341n47
cottages, 10, 144, 343n65; and royal life, 66, 77, 329n4; as term for Newport estates, 10, 117–18; as Arcadian retreats, 75, 331n24, 332n58; as peasants' dwellings, 90, 144. *See also* Queen Charlotte's Cottage, Kew Palace (Richmond, England)
Cubitt, Thomas, 19–21, 41–42, 48, 68
Currier and Ives: *Family Devotion*, 126–27

D'Hauteville and Cooper, 174–76
dairies, model, 83, 332n56
dairies, ornamental, 81–84
Darling, Frank W., 307–9
Delano and Aldrich, 158, 177, 180
Derrick, Robert O., 218–23, 355n39, 357n64
desks: *bureau plat* versus *secrétaire*, 91–92. *See also* Swiss desk
Dietz Doll House (Seguin, Texas), 320n20
dining rooms, 43, 46, 118, 123–25, 149
Disdéri, André Adolfe–Eugène, 104–107, 108, 336n142. *See also Osborne, Album, The*
Dodge Brothers Motor Car Company, 9, 203, 228, 248, 250
Dodge, Anna Margaret, 228, 239, 248–49
Dodge, Daniel, 236–37, 250, 350n97
Dodge, Frances, 203, 228, 237, 250, 312; and housework, 246, 249; birthday party of, 203, 243–45; news coverage of, 203, 247–48
Dodge, John, 7, 228
Dodge, John Duval, 248–49
Dodge, Matilda. *See* Wilson, Matilda Dodge
doll houses, 9, 299–300, 305. *See also* Nuremberg kitchens; Queen Mary's Dolls' House
Downing, Andrew Jackson, 41–42

Dows, Alice Olin, 162, 196, 210
Dows, Olin, 208–10
Dows, Tracy, 162, 196, 208, 210
drawing rooms, 43, 46, 124
Dutch colonial forms, 194–96, 351n68
Dyce, William, *Neptune Resigning the Empire of the Sea to Britannia*, 57–59, 328n123

E. F. Hodgson Company: and mass–produced play sheds, 165, 184, 260, 351n53
Edison Institute. *See* Greenfield Village (Dearborn, Michigan)
Edward Albert ("Bertie"), Prince of Wales (King Edward VII), 23, 32, 65, 68, 113, 329n8; at Swiss Cottage, 68, 100, 101, 107, 311; depicted as shepherd, 86–87; education of, 36–40, 55–56; in sailor suit, 27, 30–31; rooms at Buckingham Palace; 54–55, rooms at Osborne 54–57
Edward VIII, King, 1, 297–98, 367n46
elites, American: and aesthetic reform, 162–63, 191–94, 198; and attitudes toward domestic labor, 14–15, 151–52, 204, 216–19, 240–42; and children's marriages, 6, 122, 128, 134, 250, 310, 341n39; and conspicuous consumption, 122–23, 193–94; and European travel, 172, 237, 349n40; and higher education, 14, 204, 213–14, 353n3; and middle-class family life, 121–25, 129, 148, 162–63, 171–72; and new forms of domestic space, 122–25; and outdoor activities, 14, 204, 213–14, 237; and performances of elite identity, 121–23, 134–35, 150–53, 155, 160, 339n23; and sentiment, 122, 128, 148, 155; following British practices, 4, 8, 121–22, 128. *See also* parenting; wealth, relationship to
elites, British. *See* parenting; wealth, relationship to
Elizabeth, Princess (Queen Elizabeth II), 1, 4, 283–84, 297–99
Elm Court (Lenox, Massachusetts), Cosy Cot, 13, 119, 160

Elm Court (Lenox, Massachusetts), main house, 119, 338n11
engagement portraits, 85, 91
Ernest George and Peto, 144–45

Fallsburgh. *See* Foxhollow Farm (Rhinebeck, New York), playhouse
Field, Frederick, 212–14
Field, Lila Vanderbilt Sloane, 159, 161, 213–14
Field, Marjorie, 213
Field, Mary (May), 211, 213
Field, William B. Osgood, 159, 193, 211, 212–13
Field, William Osgood (Osgood), 160, 211–12
Flagg, Ernest, 255
footmen, 62, 111, 113
Ford Motor Company, 217–18, 223, 225–26, 249–50
Ford, Clara: gender politics of 8, 218–19
Ford, Edsel: and conflict with Henry Ford, 217–18, 225–26, 249–50; as parent, 224, 226–27, 250
Ford, Henry, 4, 216–18, 224, 225; Americanization efforts of, 217; and conflict with Edsel Ford, 217–18, 249–50; and relationship to wealth, 7, 249–51; anti–Semitism of, 8, 216, 354n27; gender politics of, 216–18; residences built for, 219, 355n39, 357n64. *See also* Greenfield Village (Dearborn, Michigan); Wayside Inn (Sudbury, Massachusetts)
Ford, Henry II, 226–27, 250
Ford, Josephine, 223, 250, 312
Fort Ticonderoga (Ticonderoga, New York), Y–D House, 231, 233
Four Hundred, The, 168, 200.
Foxhollow Farm (Rhinebeck, New York), playhouse, 162, 184, 194–96, 208–10
Frederick Wilhelm II ("Fritz"), Prince of Prussia (Crown Prince of Prussia, German Emperor): as marriage prospect for Princess Royal, 32–33, 90–91

Frederick, Christine, 215, 302
Frick, Adelaide, 162, 351n54
Frick, Childs, use of playhouse 205
Frick, Helen Clay, use of playhouse 186, 205, 351n54
Frick, Henry Clay, 162, 351n54
Froebel, Friedrich, 95, 160, 334n105

Gainsborough, Thomas, 77
Gaukler Pointe (Grosse Pointe, Michigan), main house, 219, 224–27, 356n51
Gaukler Pointe (Grosse Pointe, Michigan), playhouse, 185, 218–24, 227, 355n40, 355n45
gender: and children's spaces, 129–30, 132–35; and depictions of royal children, 31–33; and education, 36–39, 215–16; and industrial design, 217–18, 226–27; and spatial segregation in elite houses, 43, 124–25, 129–30, 132–35, 341n46. *See also* play and gender; playhouses and gender
George III, King, 22–23, 27, 29, 49, 57; and interest in farming, 68; as child; 38, as parent, 24, 68
George IV, King, 25, 84; as child, 38, 49, 55, 68
Georgian Revival: and white privilege, 8, 194; at Highlawn, 159, 345n1; at the Breakers, 143; at The Manor House, 181; at Westbury House 196
Gibson, Charles Dana, 320n20
Gibson, John, *Queen Victoria*, 51–53
Glessner, Frances ("Franny"), 230–31
Glessner, Frances Macbeth, 230–31
Glessner, John J., 230
governesses, 130, 149, 152, 153, 173, 181; at playhouses, 184, 186, 205, 207, 223; in Victoria's household, 36, 40, 108, 111, 326n66, 326n67
governors: in Victoria's household, 36–37, 38, 63
Great Exhibition of 1851: as source of Swiss Cottage Museum collections, 96; Crown Prince of Prussia at, 32–33, 90; images of royal children displayed at, 27, 86–87;

model housing displayed at, 66, 109–10; Princess Royal at, 90; royal cradle displayed at, 86–87; Swiss desk purchased at, 87–91

Greenacres (Beverly Hills, California), landscape features, 266–68

Greenacres (Beverly Hills, California), main house: children's use of, 273, 280

Greenacres (Beverly Hills, California), play yard, 266–73, 280

Greenaway, Kate, 146, 151, 344n81

Greenfield Village (Dearborn, Michigan), 217–19

Greenleaf, John C., 211–12

Greentree (Manhasset, New York), main house, 173–76, 194, 350n44

Greentree (Manhasset, New York), playhouse, 161, 184–85, 187–89, 194, 207–8

Grey Arches (Chestnut Hill, Pennsylvania), log cabin playhouse, 345n4

Grosse Pointe, Michigan, 218

Guy, Seymour: *Going to the Opera*, 124–25, 127–28

Hall, G. Stanley, 151–52, 160–61

Hamilton playhouse (Centerville, Massachusetts), 320n20

Handwerker playhouse (Memphis, Tennessee), 320n20

Hanson, A. E., 266–69, 271

Hart, Charles M., 286–87

Haskell playhouse (Alton, Illinois), 320n20

Highlawn (Lenox, Massachusetts), first playhouse, 158–60, 161, 184

Highlawn (Lenox, Massachusetts), main house, 158–60, 174, 177, 179–81, 345n1

Highlawn (Lenox, Massachusetts), second playhouse, 161, 185, 193, 209, family's use of, 186, 211–13

Hillwood (Brookville, New York), Deen-Wee, 286–87

Hollywood stars, 4, 15, 183–84, 260; and fan magazines, 265; and middle-class family life, 280; as leisure experts, 7, 254–55, 265, 311; children of, 266, 279

Homans, Margaret, 26

Homecroft (Chestnut Hill, Pennsylvania), playhouse, 346n4

Houseman playhouse (Austerlitz, New York), 320n20

housework: as play, 223, 228, 242–43, 250–51, 310–11; politics of, 214–16, 354n24; training children for, 215–16

Hunt, Richard Morris, 119, 120–21, 142, 340n26

Hutton, E. F., 286–87

Idle Hour (Oakdale, New York), 13, 119–20, 152, 338n12

industrial design: gender politics of, 217–18, 226–27

interior decorators, 239–40. *See also* Arden Studios; Jules Allard et Fils

Italianate villas, 19, 41–42, 327n92

Jekyll, Gertrude: advice on children's playhouses, 205–7

Jensen, Jens, 219, 354n37

Joyce playhouse (Grand Rapids, Minnesota), 320n20

Jules Allard et Fils, 131

Kahn, Albert, 224–25

Kapp, William, 228–29, 238–239, 358n73

Keen, Charles Barton, 255–58, 259

Kent, Duchess of, 47, 55, 56

Kerr, Robert: *The Gentleman's House*, 129–31, 341n42

Kiddyland. *See* Playland (Rye, New York)

kindergartens, 95, 160

kitchens in children's cottages and playhouses, 207–12; at Albro House, 256–58; at Burkeley Crest, 253; at Gaukler Pointe, 221; at Meadow Brook Hall, 243–44; at Osborne, 69, 71–73, 100, 105–7; at replica of Shirley Temple's glass block playhouse,

307; at Royal Lodge (Y Bwthyn Bach), 295; at the Breakers, 147–48, 151

La Farge, John, 131, 134
Ladies-in-waiting, 60, 62, 65, 111–13
Leitch, William Leighton, 38, 64–66
Letter-writing: advice on, 92–93
Lindeberg, Harrie T. *See* Albro and Lindeberg
living rooms: and children's play, 166, 173
Lloyd, Gloria, 271–72, 273
Lloyd, Harold, 7, 261, 266, 361n30; public persona of, 266–67, 271–72, 279–80
log cabin playhouses: and gender, 15, 23–31, 233–34; at Fort Ticonderoga, 231, 233; at Sears house, 229–30, 356n57; at the Rocks, 230–32. *See also* Meadow Brook Hall (Rochester, Michigan), log cabin
log cabins, 229
Lorillard, Pierre, 117–18, 139
Loudon, John Claudius, 41
Lowden, Florence Pullman, 162, 196–97
Lowden, Frank O., 162, 196–97, 199–200
Lutyens, Edwin, 289
Lyndhurst (Tarrytown, New York), Rose Cottage, 346n4

Manor House, The (Glen Cove, New York), main house, 181–83, 350n52
Manor House, The (Glen Cove, New York), playhouse 162, 184–85
Marlborough, Duke of: marriage to Consuelo Vanderbilt, 128, 341n36
Mass-produced play sheds, 163–64, 183–84, 260–61
McKim, Mead & White, 136, 168
Meadow Brook Hall (Rochester, Michigan), main house, 228–29
Meadow Brook Hall (Rochester, Michigan), Knole Cottage, 185, 202–3, 238, 241; and gender, 203–4, 228–29, 234–36, 245–46; and involvement of interior decorators, 239–40; as miniature middle-class house, 234–35, 237–39; as public relations tool, 246–49; cost of, 236, 240, 358n74; educational function of, 240, 242–45; kitchen in, 240, 243–44; scale of, 203, 234, 237–38, 240, 244; social events at, 203, 243–45, 246, 358n82
Meadow Brook Hall (Rochester, Michigan), log cabin, 185, 229–30, 236–37; and gender, 233–34, 245–46; cost of, 236, 357n68
Mershon and Morley: and mass-produced play sheds, 164, 260–61
miniature playhouses: at Albro House, 258; at Burkeley Crest, 264; at Gaukler Pointe, 221–23; at Greenacres, 268, 271; at Hillwood, 286; at Meadow Brook Hall, 237–38; at Royal Lodge (Y Bwthyn Bach), 289–90; at Shirley Temple's parents' house, 301
miniaturization, 11–12, 227, 251; and consistency in scale, 11–12, 221–23, 240; appeal of, 222, 243, 251, 301. *See also* miniature playhouses
Moderne aesthetics, 217, 226–27
monthly nurses, 33–34, 325n50
Mount Vernon (Mount Vernon, Virginia), 262–63, 362n41
Muttontown Meadows (Muttontown, New York), playhouse, 346n4

New York Infirmary for Women and Children, 16, 303, 305
New York World's Fair of 1939–40. *See* Shirley Temple's glass block playhouse, replica (New York World's Fair)
Newport, Rhode Island, 10, 117–18, 135–36 *See also* Breakers, the (Newport, Rhode Island)
Nuremberg kitchens, 105–7, 222, 242–43
nurseries, 11, 129–31, 173, 341n41; at Buckingham Palace, 39–40, 47; at Burkeley Crest, 260; at Claremont, 47–48; at Cornelius Vanderbilt II residence, 131–33; at Greentree, 173, 176; at Sinnissippi Farm, 174,

178–79; at the Breakers, 138–39; at Windsor Castle, 40; changing meaning of, 165–66, 173; furnishings and decorations for, 174, 184; in middle-class American houses, 165–66; in British country houses, 53, 130–31; in elite American houses, 14, 47; in Victoria's household, 12, 23, 33–36, 39–40, 49; locations of, 14, 47–49, 53, 139, 165, 174, 176. *See also* Osborne Pavilion, children's spaces in

nurses, 14, 108, 153, 173. *See also* monthly nurses; wet nurses

Olbrich, Joseph Maria, 114

Osborne Album, The (Disdéri), 18–19, 46, 54, 73, 104–6

Osborne estate, 6, 12–13, 18–21, 73; after Victoria's death, 21, 113–14; and conflicting versions of royal childhood, 24, 112; and impact on American trends, 21, 255; arrival of State visitors at, 50–51; compared to other country estates, 20–21, 43, 46–49; images of Victoria's children at, 21, 27–29; importance of Solent, at 56–58; in service of Victoria's public persona, 12, 19–21, 24, 43, 50, 62–63; landscape elements of, 50–51, 56–57, 67–68; model farm at, 20, 84; public perceptions of, 50, 113–14. *See also Osborne Album, The*; Swiss Cottage, Osborne

Osborne, children's precinct, 12, 40, 67–68; educational function of, 94–100, 103–4. *See also* Swiss Cottage, Osborne

Osborne, Durbar wing, 113, 321n2

Osborne, Grand Corridor, 19, 42, 44, 51–54

Osborne, household wing, 19, 44–45; after Victoria's death, 113–14; and differences from main wing, 60–61; as accommodation for royal household, 42–43, 47, 58

Osborne, main wing, 19, 44–45; after Victoria's death; 12, 113–14; and differences from household wing, 60–61, and gender, 53–54; as setting for court activities, 42, 50–53; children's spaces in, 13, 53–58; royal hierarchies within, 53–57, 58, 60; vestibules in, 56, 60, 329n125

Osborne, Pavilion, 44–45; after Victoria's death, 113; as expression of domesticity, 19, 20, 42–43, 50; as Italianate villa, 19, 41–42, 327n92; children's spaces in, 12, 47–49; entertaining spaces in, 43, 46–47, 49; family spaces in, 47–49; page's alcove in, 60

Owens–Illinois Glass Company, 16, 282–83, 301–3, 367n55

Parducci, Corrado, 220, 355n40

parenting, 2–3, 5–7; among American industrialists, 224, 226–27, 246–49, 249–51, 311; among Americans associated with leisure economy, 260–62, 266–72, 278, 311–12; among British elites, 36–38, 122, 130; among early twentieth-century American elites, 160–63, 167, 170–72, 201, 204, 310; among Gilded Age American elites, 120–23, 127–29, 155–56, 310–11; among middle-class Americans, 126–27, 160–61, 163–67, 340n33, 340n34, 347n11; expert advice on, 160–61, 165–66, 170–71, 215–16; scientific 160–61, 361n26. *See also* Victoria and Albert, as parents

parents' quarters: at Greentree, 173; at Osborne, 45, 47; at Sinnissippi Farm, 174, 176; at the Breakers, 138–39; at The Manor House, 182–83

Park-McCullough playhouse (North Bennington, Vermont), 320n20

parlors: children's use of, 166, 348n25; excluded from elite houses, 123, 124, 126, 128; in middle-class American houses, 126–27; in elite American houses, 124–125, 127–28

Peabody and Stearns, 116–19, 138, 141, 143–50, 338n9, 339n18

Peabody, Robert Swain. *See* Peabody and Stearns

Peleg Brown Ranch (near Reno, Nevada), playhouse, 320n20
Pell, Sarah, 231
Pell, Stephen, 231
Phipps, John "Jay" Shaffer, 162
Phipps, Margarita "Ditta" Grace, 162
Phipps, Peggie, 207
Planting Fields (Oyster Bay, New York), 162, 184
Platt, Charles A., 181–82
play: class differences in, 163–67, 167, 201, 349n31; gender and, 165–66, 228, 311–12; on organized playgrounds, 163, 201, 347n12; race and theories of, 10, 160–61, 345n2; visibility of, 160, 173, 250; with toys and games, 166, 184, 201. *See also* playhouses and gender
playhouses: aesthetics of, 194–201; and different modes of play, 10, 185, 245–46; and gender, 10, 15, 185, 223, 250; as birthday gifts, 203, 218, 223, 228, 355n45; as financial investments, 254, 279; as free-standing day nurseries, 183–91; as miniature middle-class houses, 15, 203–4, 221, 237–39, 295, 311–12; cooking and eating at, 14, 204–14, 231; governesses at, 184, 186, 205; in contrast to children's cottages, 10, 185, 200–201, 204; parental use, of 205, 207, 231; siting of, 187, 189–91. *See also* Albro House (Cedarhurst, New York), playhouse; Burkeley Crest (Hastings-on-Hudson, New York), playhouse; Greenacres (Beverly Hills, California), play yard; Jekyll, Gertrude; Meadow Brook Hall (Rochester, Michigan), Knole Cottage; Meadow Brook Hall (Rochester, Michigan), log cabin; Shirley Temple's glass block playhouse (Brentwood, California); Sinnissippi Farms (Oregon, Illinois), children's house; Y Bwthyn Bach to Gwellt (Royal Lodge, Windsor, England)
Playland (Rye, New York): playhouse at Kiddyland, 308–12

playrooms: in elite houses, 14, 182–83, 224, 260; in middle-class houses, 165–66
plumbing fixtures: and issues of scale, 222–23, 238, 244
Pond and Pond, 174, 177–79, 197–99, 209–10, 350n46
Post, George B., 124, 126, 132–33, 135–37
Post, Marjorie Merriweather, 286–87
Pratt, John Teele, 162, 181
Pratt, Ruth Sears Baker Pratt, 162, 181, 183
Pullman Palace Car Company, 162
Pullman, George, 196

Queen Charlotte's Cottage, Kew Palace (Richmond, England), 66, 75–77, 79
Queen Mary's Dolls' House, 289, 290, 305
queens and motherhood, 25–26, 63, 77, 284, 323n31

Red Scare of 1918–19: and attitudes toward housework, 14–15, 204, 214–16, 310–11
Repton, Humphrey, 78
Reynolds, Joshua, 85, 151
Roberts, Henry, 109–10
Robinson, Peter Frederick: and design of Swiss cottages, 69, 71, 79–81, 332n42
Rocks, the (Bethlehem, New Hampshire), estate, 356n59
Rocks, the (Bethlehem, New Hampshire), log cabin playhouse, 11, 230–32
Rogers, Henry H., Jr., 162
Rogers, Henry Huttleston, 162
Rogers, William Gibbs, 86–87
room names, 10–11
Rossiter and Wright, 255
Rousseau, Jean-Jacques: and encouragement of breast-feeding, 82–83; and popularity of Swiss cottages, 13, 78
royal children's cottages and playhouses, 114, 207. *See also* Swiss Cottage, Osborne (Isle of Wight)
Royal Pavilion (Brighton, England), 20–21, 84

Ruskin, John: and critique of Swiss cottages, 80–81

sailor suits: as children's clothing, 27, 29–31, 324n41
Saint–Gaudens, Augustus, 134, 137, 341n47
schoolrooms: at Buckingham Palace, 40; at Cornelius Vanderbilt II residence, 131–32; at Osborne, 47, 48, 49, 56–57; at Windsor Castle, 40; in elite houses, 53, 130–31
Schweizerei: at Rosenau (Coburg, Germany), 13, 75; at Villa Friesenberg (Baden-Baden, Germany), 86
Scott, Isaac, 230–32, 356n59
Sears playhouse (Chicago, Illinois), 229–30, 356n57
servants: at American children's cottages and playhouses, 149, 153–56, 208, 212; at Swiss Cottage, Osborne, 108, 111–12; at Y Bwthyn Bach, 295. *See also* footmen; governesses; governors; monthly nurses; nurses; tutors; wet nurses
Shirley Temple's glass block playhouse (Brentwood, California), 15–16, 282–84, 301–7, 312
Shirley Temple's glass block playhouse, replica (New York World's Fair), 8, 16, 284, 303–7, 368n58
Sinnissippi Farm (Oregon, Illinois), children's house, 162, 185, 197–200, 352n76, 352n77; kitchen facilities at, 207–10
Sinnissippi Farm (Oregon, Illinois), main house, 173–74, 177–79, 197
Sloane, Emily Thorne Vanderbilt, 13, 119, 124–25
Sloane, William Douglas, 119, 125
Smith, Hinchman & Grylls, 202, 228–30, 233–35, 237–39, 241, 357n68. *See also* Kapp, William
smoking rooms, 43, 124–25, 134, 327n92
Society for Improving the Condition of the Labouring Classes, 66, 109–10

Sousa, John Philip, 320n20
Stafford Plantation (Saint Marys, Georgia), playhouse, 320n20
Stockmar, Baron: advice to Victoria and Albert, 25
Stonehurst (Chestnut Hill, Pennsylvania), playhouse, 345n4
storybook imagery: at Gaukler Pointe playhouse, 219–20; at Greenacres play yard, 268–71; at Shirely Temple's studio bungalow, 273; at Shirley Temple's glass block playhouse, 301; at Sinnissippi Farm, 174, 179; in middle-class houses, 270–71
stoves: in children's cottages and playhouses, 207–10, 231, 253; at Breakers' children's cottage, 147–48; at Gaukler Pointe playhouse, 221–22; at Swiss Cottage, Osborne, 71, 73; at Y Bwthyn Bach, 295–95
streamlining: in automobile design, 217–18
Swiss Cottage Museum, Osborne (Isle of Wight, England), 2, 67, 96–97, 105; and preparation for royal life, 99–100, 113; arrangement of displays in, 96–97, 99; as educational site, 95–98; as site of Imperial power, 8, 98–99; source of displays in, 95–96, 98, 335n111
Swiss Cottage, Osborne (Isle of Wight), 2, 11, 13, 40, 72, 119, 311; and celebrations of family birthdays, 68, 100–102; and preparation for royal life, 13, 66, 68, 85, 111–12; and Princess Royal, 9, 85–86, 90–91, 94, 101, 104; as akin to ornamental dairies, 84–86, 333n62; as respite from royal life, 13, 66, 77, 112; as royal space, 111–12; boys' use, of 68, 100; caretakers' quarters at, 69, 72, 109–11, 336n159; construction of, 68–69, 330n12; cooking and eating at, 73, 84, 100, 311; German inscriptions on, 69–70; kitchen facilities in, 69, 71–73, 100, 105–7, 108; museum in, 72–73, 95–96; planting memorial trees at, 94, 102–3; published accounts of, 66, 103–8; Queen's Room in, 73–75; royal visitors to, 85; scale

at, 71, 107; Swiss design elements of, 68–70; Swiss desk at, 87–91, 114
Swiss cottages: as foreign invention, 69, 71; at Colosseum in Regent's Park, 80–81; at Virginia Water, 79, 81; critiqued by John Ruskin, 80–81; gifted to Charles Dickens, 81, 332n48; in pattern books, 69, 71, 79, 81; influenced by Jean–Jacques Rousseau, 13, 78; on British country estates, 78–81, 86, 331n32; popularity of, 66, 78–81; prefabrication of, 69, 81, 330n12. *See also Schweizerei*
Swiss desk, 9, 87–92
symbolic capital, 6; and adult sociability, 14, 131, 162, 172, 173; and leisure economy, 15; architecture and, 115, 121–22, 155–56, 254; children and, 115, 122–23, 153, 279; race and, 7–8

Tarnedge (Long Lake, New York), Doll House, 346n4
Teague, Walter Dorwin, 225–27
Temple, Shirley, 4, 282–84; "dollhouse" of, 278; and work as play, 274–75, 280; in fan magazines, 273, 275–77; parental control over, 278, 284; play shed, of 275, 277, 299; studio bungalow, of 273–76, 280, 364n71. *See also* Shirley Temple's glass block playhouse (Brentwood, California)
thatched roofs, 78–79, 207–8, 286, 290, 333n58; at Albro House playhouse, 256–58; at Greenacres play yard, 266–68, 270–71; at Queen Charlotte's cottage, 76–77; at Westbury House playhouse, 192, 196; at Y Bwthyn Bach, 292–93
Thornycroft, Mary: portraits of Victoria's children, 21, 27–29, 46, 86–87, 323n34
toys, 106–7, 151, 166, 201, 334n105, 348n26. *See also* Nuremberg kitchens
Trench & Snook, 124
Trygveson (Atlanta, Georgia), playhouse, 345n4
tutors, 130, 274, 364n72; in Victoria's household, 36–38, 54–55, 101

Vanderbilt houses: in New York City, 123–25, 127–28, 129–31, 132–35, 340n27
Vanderbilt, Alice, 123, 128, 142, 155, 341n38, 343n64; and changes to Breakers estate, 118, 120, 135, 139, 143, 148–49; and design of New York residence, 130; and use of Breakers' children's cottage, 152–53
Vanderbilt, Alva, 123, 128, 339n22, 342n59, 344n77
Vanderbilt, Consuelo: and use of cottages at Idle Hour, 119, 120, 152; marriage of, 128, 142, 341n36
Vanderbilt, Cornelius I (Commodore), 117, 124, 145–46, 343n69
Vanderbilt, Cornelius II, 123, 125, 128, 142, 155, 343n64; and changes to Breakers estate, 117–18, 119, 120, 135, 139, 148; and design of New York residence, 124, 130, 143, 149; children of, 14, 118–19, 338n8, 342n52
Vanderbilt, Cornelius III (Neily), 128, 134–37, 153
Vanderbilt, Gertrude, 134, 149, 151–53, 168
Vanderbilt, Gladys: marriage of 128
Vanderbilt, Gloria, 346n5
Vanderbilt, Maria Louisa, 127–28
Vanderbilt, William Henry, 6, 117, 124–25, 127–28, 338n11; children of, 125, 128, 340n35
Vanderbilt, William Kissam, 13, 117, 119, 123, 124; children, of 119–20
Vanderlip, Narcissa Cox, 303, 305–7
Veblen, Thorstein, 122, 193
Ver Beck, Frank, 168, 170–71
Victoria ("Vicky"), Princess Royal (Crown Princess of Prussia, German Empress), 23, 35, 36, 62, 84; and kindergartens, 95; associated with Swiss Cottage, 9, 90–91, 94, 101, 104, 107, 113; choice of marriage partner for, 9, 32–33, 90–91; depicted as "Summer," 27–29; depicted as gleaner, 86–87; education of, 36–37, 40; letter-writing of, 93–94; rooms at Osborne 56–58

Victoria and Albert, 6, 65–66; and concerns about Albert's status, 25, 31, 324n44; and dynastic concerns, 13, 23–24, 32–33, 112–13; and interest in photography, 19, 105; and sentimental view of childhood, 22, 29, 24, 107–8, 112; as parents, 22–25, 33–39, 49, 55–56, 62, 86–87, 113, 329n8; birthday celebrations of, 27, 49, 51, 68, 94, 100–101; Osborne's appeal for, 20–21, 24, 57–58

Victoria and Albert, children of: and mother's public persona, 26, 62–63, 107–8; and preparation for royal life, 62–63, 84–85, 112–13; birthday celebrations of, 49, 101–2, 328n107; education of, 36–39; gendered expectations of, 22; images of, 21–22, 27–33, 86–87

Victoria, Queen: and familiarity with Swiss cottages, 75, 81; and middle-class domesticity, 26, 47–48, 50, 310; and relationship to wealth, 6; and social distance from servants, 60, 62; and visit to dairy at Taymouth Castle, 80–81, 83–84; and visits to Swiss Cottage, Osborne, 68–69, 85, 94, 100–103, 108; as queen regnant, 21, 25–26, 50–53, 62; at Great Exhibition, 9, 86–87, 90; death of, 113, 207; depictions of, 29, 31–32, 51–53; public persona of, 3, 26, 62–63, 107, 114, 323n31. *See also* Victoria and Albert; Victoria and Albert, children of

Walker and Gillette, 191, 308
Warne, Louisa, 65, 72, 77, 108–9, 111–12
Warne, Thomas, 65, 108–9, 111
Wayside Inn (Sudbury, Massachusetts): "Old Kitchen dinners" at, 217
wealth, relationship to: among American industrialists, 4, 7, 204, 226, 249–51; among Americans associated with leisure economy, 4, 7, 253; among British elites, 21; among early twentieth-century American social elites, 3–4, 6–7, 14 162–63, 193–94, 196–201, 310; among Gilded Age American social elites, 3–4, 6–7, 21, 121–22, 124, 340n27; Queen Victoria's, 6, 26

Webber, Staunton, and Spaulding, 266
Welsh cottages, 290, 292–94, 365n20. *See also* Y Bwthyn Bach to Gwellt, (Royal Lodge, Windsor, England)
Welsh folklife: interest in, 289, 290, 292–94, 366n24, 367n38
Westbury House (Old Westbury, New York), playhouse (English Cottage), 162, 184–85, 189, 192, 196; cooking and eating at, 207–8.
Weston, Joseph, 267–68, 270
wet nurses, 34, 325n57; in Victoria's household, 33–34, 325n56
Wetli, Michel L., 87–89, 91
Wharton, Edith, and Ogden Codman, Jr., 191–94
White House Conference on Home Building and Home Ownership, 215, 216, 218
Whitney, Harry Payne, 168
Whitney, Helen Hay, 161, 167–72
Whitney, Payne, 161, 168
Willmott, Morgan, xiv, 285, 289–90, 293–94, 296–97
Wilson, Alfred G., 228, 238
Wilson, Matilda Dodge, 4, 203, 228, 250; and conflict with stepson, 248–49; and design of Knole Cottage, 238–40; publicity campaigns of, 246–49
window seats, 183, 184, 197, 209, 221
Windsor Castle (Windsor, England): children's spaces in, 20, 29, 40
Windy Gates (Baltimore, Maryland), treehouse, 345n4
Winterhalter, Franz Xaver: portrait of Bertie in sailor suit, 27, 29–31; *The Royal Family in 1846*, 21, 29, 31–33
Wollstonecraft, Mary, 25, 322n22
Woodmere, New York, 255–56, 259, 279, 360n9
Wyatt, Jeffry (later Wyatville), 78–80

Y Bwthyn Bach to Gwellt (Royal Lodge, Windsor, England), xiv–1, 15–16, 283–85, 296–97, 310–12; and Welsh folklife, 290, 292–95; as public relations tool, 284, 297–99, 301, 312; commercial character of, 283, 288, 295; completeness of, 289–90; damaged by fire, 287; media coverage of, 284–88; modern character of, 293–95; public display of, 284, 287–88; scale of, 284–85, 289–90; toy versions of, 299–301. *See also* Welsh cottages

York, Duchess of (Queen Elizabeth), 15–16, 284, 287, 290–91, 297–89

York, Duke of (King George VI), 15–16, 284, 287, 297–98

Ziegfeld, Florenz, Jr., 7, 253–4, 259, 361n29; and "the Ziegfeld touch," 254, 265–66; and anti-Semitism, 263, 362n44; and involvement with playhouse, 262, 263–64; and relationship to elite culture, 254–55, 264; and relationship to wealth, 260; as parent, 260–62

Ziegfeld, Patricia, 253, 260–62, 265, 279–80

Zoffany, Johann, 27, 29, 49, 151

ABIGAIL A. VAN SLYCK is Dayton Professor Emerita of Art History at Connecticut College. She is the author of *Free to All: Carnegie Libraries and American Culture, 1890–1920* and *A Manufactured Wilderness: Summer Camps and the Shaping of American Youth, 1890–1960* (Minnesota, 2006).